THE FALL OF THE
HOUSE OF ROOSEVELT

COLUMBIA STUDIES IN CONTEMPORARY AMERICAN HISTORY

COLUMBIA STUDIES IN CONTEMPORARY AMERICAN HISTORY

ALAN BRINKLEY, GENERAL EDITOR

THE FALL OF THE
HOUSE OF ROOSEVELT

———————— ❧ · ❧ ————————

BROKERS OF IDEAS AND POWER

FROM FDR TO LBJ

MICHAEL JANEWAY

COLUMBIA UNIVERSITY PRESS · NEW YORK

Columbia University Press
Publishers Since 1893

New York   Chichester, West Sussex
Copyright © 2004 Columbia University Press
All rights reserved

Library of Congress Cataloging-in-Publication Data
Janeway, Michael
    The fall of the house of Roosevelt : brokers of ideas and power from FDR to LBJ /
Michael Janeway.
        p.   cm.
    Includes bibliographical references and index.
    ISBN 0-231-13108-9 (acid-free paper)
    1. United States—Politics and government—1933–1945. 2. New Deal, 1933–1939. 3.
Roosevelt, Franklin D. (Franklin Delano), 1882–1945—Influence. 4. Rooselvelt, Franklin D.
(Franklin Delano), 1882–1945—Friends and associates. 5. United States—Politics and
government—1945–1989. 6. Political culture—United States—History—20th century. 7.
Johnson, Lyndon B. (Lyndon Baines), 1908–1973. 8. Janeway, Eliot. 9. Janeway,
Elizabeth. 10. Janeway, Michael, 1940– —Childhood and youth. I. Title.
E806.J27   2003
306.2′0973′09045—dc22
                                                                              203055414

Printed in the United States of America

c 10 9 8 7 6 5 4 3 2

CONTENTS

PREFACE: PUBLIC AND PRIVATE

I grew up inside the world this book describes. It is written at a junction of public and private memory of a time when reform ideas in the United States, and the power to act on them, were themselves joined. We are speaking of "the Roosevelt era"—the presidency of Franklin D. Roosevelt—and of the spirit engendered by it that was part of the history of the twenty years following Roosevelt's death in 1945. Then politics was confident and closely connected to people's daily lives, and modern government, freshly shaped, was widely revered. That confidence and respect had roots in a shared sense that the country's potential was unrealized, and that those in power were, however much in trial and error, striving to prime its engines and fulfill its promises. The politics of that time was not artificial.

To speak of the Roosevelt era is admittedly misleading, conflating as it does a presidency with the greatest challenges of the twentieth century. Its casual use, in turn, masks the signal fact that American leadership was equal to those challenges: the Great Depression, World War II, and its dangerous aftermath. Indeed, the Roosevelt era spanned the designs of effective progressive reform, coalition politics to achieve it, unprecedented mobilization of the country's resources in peace and then in war, and soaring expansion of our national and international vision. The initiatives of those years shaped the modern American state, and much of the world, for better and worse, for the rest of the century. And yet the political culture of those times has faded far back in our history.

"Politics" was in some ways closer to the nineteenth than the twenty-first century then. Television had barely been invented, media was not a term in use, political advertising techniques were primitive. Radical change was in the air, and so was radio, but candidates and officeholders, charismatic or plodding, were still connected to structured party coalitions as they used to function. Or, as reformers, they refashioned them—old pieces, new ones. To be successful from one election to the next, to govern effectively, those who presumed to lead those party coalitions had to present themselves effectively by means of traditional "retail politics" involving speeches, podiums, personal appearances, and close-in deals. The devastation of the Depression, the passionate social and economic movements it triggered, the success of the New Deal in positioning itself above them, all meant that politicians who aspired to be more than functionaries or one-termers had, as well, to engage with ideas that aroused public interest, concern, and aspiration. The gift, or trick, was to do all of this through a system much less manipulable by wholesale media image and media message than is afforded by today's television politics. Thus *leadership* and *governance*, along with *politics*, had different meanings then.

A combination of events in the 1960s terminated the political environment I describe in this book. One was the election of John F. Kennedy; a sharp break with the political culture that came together in the New Deal years. Another was that, as Lyndon Johnson was Franklin Roosevelt's heir—more so, I argue here, than is generally understood, so the collapse of his presidency punctuated the end of the Roosevelt era. Third, the nature of American government had changed; so had people's view of it. Fourth, in the 1960s and 1970s the spirit of our politics was lastingly unsettled by a sequence of international and economic stalemates, erosion, and defeats—alien experiences for Americans—simultaneous with waves of social change liberating to many, troubling to some. Fifth, coterminous with *all* this, the rise of television brought its own reconfiguration of the content and forms of politics as practiced before the 1960s.

This book is in part a meditation on the transit from the New Deal and wartime culture of ideas and power, a milieu now vanished, to the one we know today. For the key players who got their start in the Roosevelt years, the changes were shocking. A few of them wrote memoirs, but it was too late in the day for them to spend much time trying to make sense of how the old order had given way to the new. Those transformations have not been studied in direct relation to the careers of the idea and power brokers who bridge that era. I've attempted that task here as a child of those times, and the son of one of the company of brokers I describe.

So, with one part of my mind, I attempt to merge the purposes of family photo album and film or radio documentary, connecting the personal and the public. For me there's a blur; the idea is to bring them into register. With the other part of my mind I try to distance myself and consider the question whether that vanished era yields a legacy that has contemporary lessons.

. . .

It happened that my father and mother moved in the circles of those who had their hands on levers of national power in the years FDR was president, and some who continued to do so in the next two decades. If a child of theirs wanted it, and I did, a riveting, insider's view of what went on behind the political stage in Washington, at events like presidential nominating conventions, and out into the nation, was afforded.

Owing to the cast of principal characters in this story, and the ideas, events, and issues of governance that engaged them, the political arena to which I was given youthful access was rich in intrigue, passion, and sardonic insight, instruction in cause, maneuver, and effect—but also in consciousness of history. The reference points of American politics in the Depression and World War II were epic. Our national political leaders had an informed and tragic sense of the origins of those disasters in World War I and the decade that followed.

I took the bait. For many years the effect on me of behind-the-scenes exposure to the making of history, as for a child of the theater, was a mix of sophistication and enchantment; sometimes heartbreak. This book is in part an effort to overcome those spells and make sense of the experience.

My father and mother were self-made success stories; articulate, aspiring products of professional-class families, gentry laid low by the Depression. My father was an unusually wired-in journalist, economist, and eclectic meddler whose interests often took him inside politics and, indirectly, into government. My mother, a best-selling novelist, shared his interests. They became close to a tightly linked cohort of friends who came to public prominence in the late 1930s and 1940s; the young New Dealers who had influence at the Roosevelt White House.

In 1958, a week after I turned eighteen and graduated from high school, I went to work for the first of a succession of college-year summers in the employ of the mighty, brooding U.S. Senate majority leader who aspired to the White House. Lyndon Johnson would hint in those years, and his old New Dealer friends were certain, that he would complete the arc that began two decades earlier when he was elected to Congress from central Texas as a passionate supporter of Roosevelt and the New Deal. The equivalent of a spear-carrier in *Aida*, at once precocious and naive, it seemed to me then that out of this upbringing I was becoming, at the least, a first-hand witness to a heroic progression in our history. Roosevelt had saved the republic in the Depression; revived, reformed, and then guided it to victory in war against fascism, and on to free-world leadership. His protégé—my parents' friend—Lyndon Johnson would reclaim and advance this magnificent legacy.

. . .

Four, going on five decades after those summers in Lyndon Johnson's Senate office, when Franklin Roosevelt's leadership example was still the political gold standard, much of what FDR wrought appears, depending on how you look at it, either ancient history or to have come utterly unglued.

Roosevelt and the New Deal forced an arrogant, errant, shattered American capitalist system into regulation and reform, simultaneously empowering organized labor and establishing fundamental welfare-state services. They gave previously unknown borrowing power to millions of the underprivileged. They recruited the activist makers of modern legal, economic, and social thought—the "knowledge professions"—into a small, weak government that hitherto moved from systemic passivity to ad hoc activism only in emergencies and then went back to sleep. They upended the dominance of the undeveloped American South and West by the bankers and holding companies of New York and other capitals of finance. They co-opted the Republican progressivism that Franklin Roosevelt's cousin Theodore built and fashioned a modern Democratic Party that seemed to have a lock on the march of history, with the GOP allowed in only for periods of time-out while progressive gains were consolidated.

The pendulum swings. It swung hard against "the state" and toward "the market" from the 1970s forward. Yet, riding the swing, Richard Nixon and Ronald Reagan both acknowledged permanence in the contributions of Franklin Roosevelt and of the New Deal to American society and governance. Nixon publicly embraced Keynesian political economy in 1971 and thus one of the New Deal's most central and controversial tenets. Reagan, who voted for Roosevelt four times, often saluted his great predecessor's inspirational qualities of leadership, and cultivated comparisons with him. "The fact is that it was Franklin Delano Roosevelt who gave hope to a nation that was in despair and could have slid into dictatorship," remarked conservative Republican congressman Newt Gingrich upon becoming speaker of the House of Representatives in 1995.[1]

But, toward the end of the old century and in the first decade of the new one, the consolidation and permanence of relevant experience were eerily missing. Reactions against any revolution, together with the law of unintended consequences, are inevitable. But extending beyond them, it was as if the New Deal, its lessons, its net effects, revisions of it, expansions from its base in subsequent decades, had been ripped from the American history books. Our system of capitalism was in disarray. The theory and practice of government regulation of markets and industry had become a mockery. Shameless corporate and financial plunder was back, as if FDR's hard-driving Securities and Exchange Commission chairman had never sent a corrupt leader of the New York Stock Exchange, a member of the ruling-class Whitney family, to jail. Echoing the shattering effects of the Depression, young adults, their parents, and grandparents alike suffered damage to their career aspirations, their job and retirement security. The Social Security system was threatened. The medical one defied efforts by government and the market alike to bring it coherence.

The two national political parties had long since lost their relevance to vast portions of the public. But one, the Republican Party, had become adept in the void at managing a coalition of conservative and middle-class interests. The other, the Democratic Party that Roosevelt built, the instrument for the welding of progressive and reform ideas into effective action for so much of the past century, appeared to have fallen apart. Its genius and mechanisms for reform coalition building had vaporized. The linkage between its "brains trust" and the great mass of the nation's labor force and middle class had broken down many years back.

. . .

This was more than the inevitable swing of the pendulum through the years. It was the eclipse of a system and culture of governance that had begun to lose their anchors decades earlier. An obvious early sign was the success George Wallace and the pre-presidential Ronald Reagan enjoyed as they set about demonizing "pointy-headed bureaucrats" and the "welfare queen." They were reaping the harvest of the New Deal's success in moving millions of Americans from working-class to middle-class status and the mixed record of the New Deal's heirs in easing the conditions of racial minorities. Reform liberalism's partial victories in eliminating old bases of grievance revealed new ones. By the end of the century it was clear that our conservative party had figured out a way to manage the results and that our progressive one simply could not connect to the new lay of the land.

Thirty years earlier Lyndon Johnson openly and angrily brooded on another signal, harder to read—a signal he had been watching for a decade or more before that. The year was 1971. A CBS producer asked him what had changed since he started out in politics: "You guys," he responded angrily. "All you guys in the media. All of politics has changed because of you. You've broken all . . . the ties between us in Congress and the city machines. You've given us a new kind of [politician] . . . They're your creations. . . . Your product."[2]

Casualties of political warfare do not make judicious analysts. By then Johnson was a bitter loser, forced from the White House through a conjunction of policy, combat, communications, and personal failures. But he wasn't wrong in pinpointing so spontaneously, if in shorthand, the displacement of a political state based on classic definitions of leadership and policy making by the media state. In the state in which Johnson was reared and came to power, radio was an important instrument and opinion polling was useful. But the confluence of media and polling, and their determinative force in the selection of candidates, sorting out of winners among them, selection of salient issues, setting of policies, and exercise of leadership as it's now understood, lay decades ahead. So did the erosion of American political parties as rooted, meaningful forces in peoples' lives. By the millennium, political leadership, issue agendas, and governance derived more and more from what polling said they were, and by how they fared in televised form.

. . .

I was present at the transition, if you will, from the political state to the media state. Because of the circumstances of my upbringing, my view of *then*, and of *what happened*, is in part idiosyncratic. So this, in turn, is in part a family story, dating from that era when modern government was a novelty and those who created it were comrades in ideas and arms; my parents among their number. In part the story is as classically Greek as it is American, because so many of that remarkable company—the men who made their names on their brilliance and skill laying out new definitions of governance in Roosevelt's Washington—collectively became a study in hubris and fallibility.

Why tell it, given the shelves of books from the Roosevelt years, and subsequent history, biography, memoir, letters, diary, and reinterpretation? Because, in light of the contemporary disturbances of democratic politics, and the beginnings of the search for recovery from them, the time is right to reconsider the legacy of the Roosevelt era. And, for my own part, because the version of that legacy that I carry with me—a montage of public and private images—seems worth both deciphering and sharing.

THE
PARTNERS

❧ I ❧

Government by Brains Trust

"GOD BLESS YOU; KEEP SCHEMING"

In the 1930s a band of smart and able young men, some still in their twenties, gained extraordinary access to the power to shape an American nation in crisis. As "president's men" in a small, intimate system of government, then suddenly swelling into a vast administrative state, they gained an influence over the direction of the nation's economy, governance, and social fabric previously enjoyed only by presidents themselves, a few of their cabinet members, plus a congressional potentate or two. Together they formed the first modern, peacetime American effort to fuse expertise, including the scholarly variety, with political power on a grand scale, and in an institutionalized way. (A brief, piecemeal effort to do something like that in the area of American foreign policy at the end of World War I ended in rancor and disillusionment.) At times they faded offstage, but together they participated in decision making about the fate of the nation almost through the 1960s.

Except for periods of charismatic or crisis leadership at the presidential level, the executive branch of our government had until then been a compact, rather passive instrument run according to the initiatives of Congress and the courts. These "president's men" of the 1930s and forties executed a broad-based professionalization of policy making marked by strong departures in theory and practice—such as in governmental intervention in the economy.

Franklin Roosevelt, who empowered them, was politically accountable. Their prominence meant that they, or at least the policies they stood for, were too: the "New Deal" they collectively conceived and executed became, in effect, a new political party. They were the middlemen in the coalescence of reform thinking in the social sciences and in law with reform impulses in governance and in election campaigns. They helped weave the result into the permanent fabric of American life.

. . .

These men of whom we're speaking (the front rank in those days numbered very few women, though some shrewd ones stood a step behind the men) worked devotedly for Franklin Roosevelt and the New Deal. Those were not the same thing, for the New Deal came in contradictory flavors, and FDR himself was always balancing daring experimental and reform impulses with conservative restraints in Congress, in other established sectors, and in his own nature.

Contradictory scenarios for economic recovery and industrial reform were the instruments of a resourceful new president who, in Oliver Wendell Holmes's legendary benediction after his and Roosevelt's meeting in 1933, possessed "a second-class intellect. But a first-class temperament!" Those traits at work had already prompted Roosevelt's restless "use of other people's minds" through what a newspaper reporter in 1932 tagged his "brains trust," assembled as he prepared for his first presidential campaign. One of his early speechwriters observed four years later that "there will always be a Brain Trust as long as Mr. Roosevelt is President." These New Dealers, going and coming, were FDR's designated and enlisted "first-class intellects."[1]

Historians debate the issue of coherence in the New Deal's frankly experimental approach, and in particular "the conundrum the New Deal poses: how to square its energy, in a decade that dealt so cruelly with progressive governments elsewhere, with its monumental confusions." But for the most part they work with a distinction between the "First New Deal," roughly coinciding with FDR's first term and espousing partnership with industry in planning-based, centrally directed governance, and the more indirect managerial approaches that followed in the "Second New Deal." Roosevelt's dominant brains-trusters at the outset were Raymond Moley, Adolf Berle, and Rexford Tugwell, recruited together from Columbia University's faculties of political science, law, and economics as a tight, collegial team with a shared viewpoint. Reformers of banking, finance, law, and the agricultural system, they were also planners, advocates of top-down social engineering and a managed economy. Tugwell, the handsome romantic among them, penned gladiatorial words in his youth that came to light and gave New Deal critics a stick with which to beat the lot of them in the 1930s:

> I am strong,
> I am big and well-made,
> I am muscled and lean and nervous,
> I am frank and sure and incisive . . .

> My plans are fashioned and practical;
> I shall roll up my sleeves—make America over![2]

Franklin Roosevelt's first brains-trusters accepted industrial "bigness" as a fact of modernity. In this they assisted Governor Roosevelt in bridging the gap between the antistatist, Jeffersonian traditions of his party and the more nationalist, Progressive Republican position struck by his cousin Theodore, whose supporters FDR sought. The brains-trusters drew eclectically on principles of state capitalism, planning, and socialism in designing the National Recovery Administration (NRA) and Agricultural Adjustment Administration (AAA), the First New Deal's superagencies for directing the economy (as distinct from reviving it through public works spending and relief). By the time the Supreme Court declared the NRA and the AAA unconstitutional in 1935, Roosevelt had a number of reasons to reorganize his strategy, including problems with the top-heavy NRA and AAA in operation and feuding among his principal aides and advisers, as he prepared for his 1936 reelection campaign.[3]

Not the least influential figure in forcing his rethinking was Justice Louis Brandeis, latter-day Jeffersonian, apostle of civil liberties, rights of labor, social justice, and regulation of industry, but a fierce enemy of big government. Brandeis allied himself with the Court's reactionaries in finding the NRA and AAA statist abominations. When the NRA decision came down in May of 1935, Brandeis summoned Thomas Corcoran, just emerging as Roosevelt's chief aide, himself a former law clerk to Justice Oliver Wendell Holmes, to the Supreme Court robing room. There was Brandeis, "holding his arms aloft while a retainer removed his gown, and I thought he looked like an avenging angel," Corcoran remembered.

> Without a preamble, he said, "You go back and tell your President that this Court has told him it is not going to permit the centralization of power . . . [by] the federal government. . . . Furthermore, . . . I warn you to send back to the states all those bright young men you have brought to Washington. It is in the states where they are needed.

The theme of the New Deal became distinctly Brandeisian, often frankly stated as such (until World War II complicated the issue). But the young men stayed in Washington.[4]

The Second New Deal rejected "bigness" and the specter of cartelization on the NRA-AAA model. Moley, Berle, and Tugwell left town, or moved to the side. Led by Corcoran, the brains-trusters of the Second New Deal, less a faculty club meeting than a networked fraternity, stood for regulation of markets, aggressive antitrust measures, public investment in the economy, and its indirect guidance through fiscal policy. (Several of this Second New Deal team made their mark in Washington in 1933 at the AAA and retained an affinity for planning, but they came to front-rank government positions only after 1935.) They accepted the view that the government could reform market capitalism and "manage the economy without managing the institutions of the economy," as the First New Deal had attempted.[5]

These brains-trusters were no Socratic assembly. No less than in the emergency of 1933, recruitment to the Second New Deal's inner policy-making circle was keyed to a fast-paced drama. The sequences were the fight, in 1935–1937, to save the stumbling First New Deal from the collapse of the NRA and AAA, and seeming certainty of Supreme Court veto of other New Deal innovations, including the Tennessee Valley Authority (TVA) and Social Security. Next, in 1937–1938, the fight to save the Roosevelt administration from the "Roosevelt Recession," a largely self-induced replay of the downward economic spiral from the Crash of 1929 into the Depression. Next (to the dismay of those New Dealers who wanted to stay focused on reform at home), the challenge of responding to the fascist dictators' aggressions in Europe and Asia. And, as 1940 loomed, the connection of these struggles to the daring enterprise of reelecting FDR to an unprecedented third term as president.

Even before Roosevelt's death in 1945, a number of these New Dealers pulled away from important jobs in the administration, and even from lifetime appointments to the bench. Government salaries were meager; Depression-era financial insecurities ran deep. Roosevelt's cadre of second-level officials, with their unprecedented license literally to reform the nation, couldn't afford the privilege of continuing to do so: "This old curse of our crowd," was how Corcoran put it to my father in 1945.[6]

But for reasons that mixed youthful passion, combat together in the political trenches, continuing shared agenda and camaraderie with much colder interests, they found themselves again and again in configuration with each other in the years that followed. Along with Corcoran, the influential and memorable policy makers among them at the outset, closely linked (some fell out with each other over time), were Harold Ickes, Felix Frankfurter, Robert Jackson, William O. Douglas, Benjamin V. Cohen, Jerome Frank, Abe Fortas, James Landis, Thurman Arnold, James Rowe. Behind them came an army of smart young lawyers and economists recruited by the principal players among them, especially Frankfurter, Corcoran, and Frank.

From FDR's inauguration into the Truman administration Ickes was the highly combative secretary of the interior; the only true New Dealer who served for any length of time in the Roosevelt cabinet. Douglas and Frank, among other accomplishments, shaped a lasting New Deal innovation, the Securities and Exchange Commission. Roosevelt sent Frankfurter, Jackson, and Douglas to the Supreme Court; Frank and Arnold to the federal circuit courts of appeals, made Fortas undersecretary of the interior and Rowe de facto deputy attorney general when they were each thirty-two. Corcoran and Cohen, operating without formal designation as two of the most significant White House aides in history, held nominal positions in other government agencies down the line. They personified the fact that the intellectual and policy-making force of all these men was of greater note than their actual job titles.

Berle and Tugwell from the First New Deal remained loyal to FDR, and connected to the Second New Deal, though they were often at odds with it. An important ally of the younger New Dealers was Salt Lake City banker and businessman Marriner Eccles, the New Deal chairman of the Federal Reserve Board. Largely self-taught, he developed ideas that tracked closely, but independently, with the interventionist theses that become known as Keynesianism. Others, including Secretary of Agriculture (later Vice President) Henry Wallace, Secretary of the Treasury Henry Morgenthau, and WPA Administrator Harry Hopkins (later secretary of commerce, later still chief White House aide, replacing Corcoran) were important. But their relation to the fabric of New Deal policy making had less consistency or impact than that of the others; it was sometimes contrary; sometimes undependable or fleeting.

Most were Democrats, but important characters in the story like Ickes, Wallace, and Mayor Fiorello La Guardia of New York came from Progressive Republican ranks. As early as 1934, in the first phases of securities market regulation, James V. Forrestal of the firm of Dillon, Read came to Corcoran's and then Douglas's attention as that rara avis, a shrewd and able New Deal collaborator on Wall Street. They brought him to Washington on the eve of World War II, first to the president's staff, then to the Department of the Navy and the path that would make him the country's first secretary of defense. Across subsequent policy differences he remained these men's intimate friend and personal ally.[7]

In Congress, among the better remembered, were Hugo Black of Alabama (Roosevelt's first Supreme Court appointee), Robert La Follette of Wisconsin (a Progressive Republican), Claude Pepper of Florida, and three remarkable Texans, Sam Rayburn, Maury Maverick, and the young Lyndon Johnson. Dean Acheson was close to several of them, but only up to a point. Raymond Moley of the 1933 brains trust defected to the Republican opposition early. Joseph P. Kennedy held important appointments from Roosevelt but was not really a New Dealer; yet he maintained close alliances with several of the most passionately committed among them, notably Corcoran and Douglas. Senator (later Supreme Court Justice, later "Assistant President," later Secretary of State) James F. Byrnes, no New Dealer, was FDR's ablest wheeler-dealer with the unreconstructed potentates of Congress. Byrnes depended on New Dealers like Ben Cohen for his staff work. So did Sam Rayburn.

Journalism's rules were looser than those today. The best-known case is that of the mandarin Walter Lippmann, model for successors like James Reston in later decades, opining about issues in print; consulting and carrying messages about them among policy makers and legislators on the side. In the Roosevelt years Philip Graham, subsequently publisher of the *Washington Post*, was Felix Frankfurter's law clerk and a favored protégé and remained an influential force in these men's circle. The young Joseph Alsop chronicled the New Dealers for the *New York Herald Tribune* and the *Saturday Evening Post* as they made history, and became close to many of them. My father did the same at *Time*, *Life*, and *Fortune*. His nickname was "Henry Luce's ambassador to the New Deal," and he practiced a cross-boundaries participation in New Deal politics and policy making way beyond what Alsop, Graham, or Reston entertained then or later. Ernest Cuneo, a colorful lawyer, politico, and newsman, operated interchangeably as White House conduit to such diverse contact points as his former boss Mayor La Guardia, and to wartime British intelligence, and as ghostwriter and later attorney for Drew Pearson and Walter Winchell.[8]

Union labor leaders (it seems hard to imagine today) held formidable local, regional, and national power. The CIO's John L. Lewis, Philip Murray, and Sidney Hillman had enormous impact on the history of the Roosevelt administration, but it was a younger, much more cerebral man, Walter Reuther of the United Auto Workers, who became a member of the young New Dealers' circle. Clark Clifford started under Harry Truman, but became one of them; similarly Hubert Humphrey. Adlai Stevenson, who worked with Jerome Frank, Abe Fortas, and others at the AAA at the start of the New Deal, was one of them by association (Eleanor Roosevelt was always his strongest advocate), but not by interest or temperament. And there was a virtual battalion of others, a bit more in the shadows.

Some principals fell away, taking various members of the circle with them—Felix Frankfurter into feuding, machination, and a judicial form of neoconservatism; Joe Kennedy to the right, Henry Wallace to the left. A more obscure cluster of them, most notably Alger Hiss, Harry Dexter White, Lauchlin Currie, and Lee Pressman, lived out their lives under clouds of Communist Party associations extending all the way to espionage on behalf of the Soviet Union.

But the names of those who held to the main stage are forever identified with the legend of epic legislation and policy making that changed the way the country worked. They have been profiled (some only sketchily)—and judged. Some have recalled their great days and each other in memoirs, diaries, and oral histories. Well-worn themes have emerged: along with First New Deal planners versus Second New Deal regulators, "Dealers and Dreamers" (the title of one account of them). Of late, several scholars have considered the negative as well as positive meaning and value of their legacy.[9]

As a group, as a phenomenon, as a force beyond the years in which they held direct power under Franklin Roosevelt, they are largely unknown, except in sentences here and there that allude to credentialing, old association, or youthful and subsequent impact or controversy. That is not the way they knew each other, then or later.

. . .

Efforts since the 1930s to reinvent government by brains trust in the United States have been on a different order; or, when the New Deal model has been relevant, they have largely failed—in several cases, disastrously.

First, a group of advisers came on the scene to whom history has awarded iconic status: "The Wise Men" of the Truman administration, the closely knit, well-established, mostly patrician cluster of officials who, "working together in an atmosphere of trust, . . . shaped a new world order that committed a once-reticent nation" to alliances and initiatives including the Marshall Plan and NATO, designed to rebuild the postwar world along democratic lines, and contain Soviet Communism. Some of the ideas behind those policies, especially those tracing to John Maynard Keynes, connected to techniques of investment in economic development and management brought to bear in the New Deal. As for continuity, a number of the Wise Men lived on as senior advisers on the Vietnam War in the Johnson administration. But that model has less to do with innovative mobilization of brains and expertise in a reform setting than with the centuries-old European and early American tradition of the "privy council" or "government of all talents."[10]

Meanwhile, the reformed, vivified American government of the New Deal attained middle age; it began to sprawl and then to become dysfunctional. John F. Kennedy's cohort of "action intellectuals," as they were called, were supposed to cut through all that with newly minted, managerially crisp concepts like "systems analysis" and "counter-insurgency." *The Best and the Brightest*, David Halberstam's title for his account of the fruits of the Kennedy cohort's labors—the war in Vietnam—is tinged with dark irony. Before the Watergate scandal, government had begun to earn a bad name. A year before Ronald Reagan's ascendancy, a liberal political scientist, Theodore Lowi, asserted that the American republic had become "ungovernable." The sorry fate of the Clinton administration's healthcare task force in presuming to work in secretive removal from governmental "ungovernability" punctuated the problem.[11]

There were other factors. In the last quarter of the twentieth century American politics began to cease to function as a blend of broad coalition building and reform agenda setting, rooted in a consensus of belief in the efficacy of modern government. A tangle of adverse forces was at work in the 1970s: along with the disillusionment bred by the Vietnam War and Watergate, uncontrollable inflation, the rustbelt phenomenon, backlash against government regulation and against the reform and protest movements of the 1960s. All these were conterminous with the rise to social and cultural dominance of television; essentially an entertainment medium, relentlessly commercialized as such.[12]

Against that backdrop of political revisionism and public alienation, the one innovative presidential cohort that achieved its goals in the post–New Deal years is that which came to power with Ronald Reagan. As a brains trust, the neoconservatives and free-market libertarians who made the case for rolling back government and unleashing market forces were arguably as effective as the forerunners they set about reversing, the New Dealers.

. . .

By contrast to the Truman Administration's patrician Wise Men, the young, mostly unpedigreed, upwardly mobile New Dealers of whom we are speaking evolved a cooperative venture from the peak of Roosevelt's reform influence in the 1930s into the 1960s; a political version of the old Wall Street trusts in some respects—the House of Morgan and the rest. In a sardonic conversation in late 1945, Senator Lister Hill of Alabama, a New Dealer, asked Thomas Corcoran why the Chase Manhattan Bank's and Lehman Brothers' influence over some key Truman administration appointments was proving a tough match for "the House of Corcoran." Let's call the larger enterprise, of which Corcoran's operations were a subset, the "House of Roosevelt." Let's call the principals in it "the partners." Indeed, a cluster of them including Corcoran, Ben Cohen, William O. Douglas, and Jerome Frank had been, early in their careers, corporate or Wall Street lawyers. (Corcoran and Cohen lost enough money in the 1929 stock market crash to prompt a conspiracy theory that their careers as New Deal regulators were motivated by revenge.) Unlike prototypical ivory tower reformers, they knew first-hand the structures they set about reforming.[13]

Roosevelt's managerial style was oblique and vague, generally by design, sometimes by default. Until Pearl Harbor, he maneuvered in times of crisis among rivalrous factions for and against differing recipes for reform and government intervention at home, for and against neutrality in foreign affairs. Frequently his method, after Lincoln's but on a larger scale, was to bring representatives of warring camps into his official family, and attempt to manage the power struggles by managing the inevitable set-piece feuds.

His ablest agents learned to work through this maze, applying an unprecedented amalgam of analytic brainpower to legal and economic dilemmas, manipulating the president's ingenious but sometimes unhappy coalitions, confusing the enemy within as well as without. The history of the New Deal and of Roosevelt's management of World War II is, accordingly, an endlessly convoluted succession of doctrinal, factional, and personal struggles over policy and position; and of odd power vacuums and the sometimes odder filling of them. Lines of influence had little to do with chains of command or formal titles. "Roosevelt's rule" in running the war, my father wrote in 1951, was "that energy was more efficient than efficiency."[14]

If, under Roosevelt, policy and the control of it were fluid, the conveyance of information about them was crucial. As Arthur Schlesinger Jr. phrased the way Roosevelt operated,

> An executive relying on a single information system became inevitably the prisoner of that system. Roosevelt's persistent effort therefore was to check and balance information acquired through official channels by information acquired through a myriad of private, informal, and unorthodox channels and espionage networks.

Schlesinger's portrait is of a crippled man leading a crippled nation to recovery, unusually resourceful in creating ad hoc instruments for his task.[15]

Circles of affinity and influence came and went in the New Deal and World War II years. But these men who operated in unorthodox channels in FDR's service then, linked for a while under Corcoran's captaincy and also by cast of mind, interest, and friendship, became their own distinctive House of Roosevelt after 1945. Their use of "espionage networks" (in Schlesinger's phrase) and conspiratorial style in pursuit of great goals became ingrained. Francis Biddle, Roosevelt's last attorney general, to Corcoran in 1945: "God bless you. Keep scheming."[16]

Their bonds involved genuine political passion. Like Holmes, they distinguished between Roosevelt's unique mastery of the chemistry and theater of politics—his temperament—and their own mere intellects and skills. By the same token, as a function of their sophistication they tended to be well-informed about what one of them who loved FDR, William O. Douglas, called his "blind spots." From a May 1941 diary fragment in which, though working for Henry Luce, my father refers frequently to FDR as "the Boss":

> Train to Washington with Jerome [Frank.] He read at great length from Macauley's Essays. The old boy really went to town against the fuddy-duddies who doubted England's ability to absorb the debt created during the Napoleonic Wars. Way back then Macauley was able to cite much historical precedent to justify his casual attitude to the debt, which was quite modern. . . . This . . . emphasizes the most pathetic of the New Deal's failures. . . . [Deficit financing] finds eloquent expression, pungent advocacy, in one of the classics of the language. Nothing should have been easier than to have made the policy popular. Instead, the New Deal practically reduced the whole business to the level of a hotel conspiracy. . . . Dropped Jerome at [Abe] Fortas' [shortly to become undersecretary of the interior]. . . .
>
> Had a session with [Undersecretary of the Navy James Forrestal] at the Lynx Club. "Just like Churchill to gamble everything he has on Crete without stopping to think of the risk or importance of the objective" [says Forrestal]. "He plays at being the Duke of Marlborough,"

I agreed. "Roosevelt is the same way," he volunteered. I asked if he ever talked turkey to the Boss. "Oh, you can't," he replied. "He's always so good natured and tired. I always go in meaning to and then get disarmed."[17]

At times the question of Roosevelt's greatness, as against his flaws, divided them. My father would tell a story of young Congressman Lyndon Johnson late one night in 1943 or 1944 at Abe Fortas's house, Johnson's face in his: "The difference between you and me, El'yit, is, *you're for* Roosevelt, but *Ah believe* in Roosevelt."

The plebeian Truman and stolid Ike sat in Roosevelt's chair, but the memory of FDR and the influence of these custodians of his legacy, remarkable for their collective intellect and effectiveness, lived on. They labored mightily for William O. Douglas as Roosevelt's rightful successor in 1944 and 1948. They achieved a restoration of sorts with Lyndon Johnson, and to the extent that these Rooseveltians' influence (like that of the Jeffersonians and Jacksonians in the nineteenth century) depended upon guardianship of a heroic American legend, they were able to develop and employ a distinctive custodial mystique and style.[18]

🔊 2 🔈

Tommy Corcoran and the
New Dealers' Gospel

"YOU'RE BEGINNING TO BE AN OPERATOR —

HOW DO YOU LIKE THE WATER?"

T homas G. Corcoran ("Tommy" to friends, enemies, and the press alike) was the most celebrated New Dealer, and the quintessential one. He was "the leader of the group, and we all followed," one colleague reminisced fully four decades later. Following Felix Frankfurter's lead, he recruited young lawyers and economists into the new, expanding agencies of government all over Washington.[1]

"There was no bureaucracy, none at all," recalled Gerhard Gesell, who assisted Douglas at the SEC in sending the former head of the New York Stock Exchange to jail. "We were all people who knew one another. When there was a job vacancy, everyone of us would hear about it." Another young New Dealer: "We were moving mountains one shovelful at a time. . . . Tom [Corcoran] would see a job that needed to be done and he'd get one of us and say, 'How'd you like to try this?'" and the designated hitter would move into the government agency charged with the task. Then "if things didn't work out well, we'd be back with him again" and ready for reassignment.[2]

As young 1930s Washington bachelors, they shared houses together. Corcoran orchestrated evenings for the young New Dealers and friends from out of town, lending the musical talent that also on occasion charmed FDR at the White House. My mother remembered a vintage evening in Georgetown with Corcoran on his accordian, rendering "one of the great Confederate songs of the Civil War":

> Oh, I'm a dirty rebel, and that's just what I am,
> For this fair land of freedom, I do not give a damn,
> I'm glad I fought agin' it, I only wish we'd won,
> And I don't ask no pardon for anything we've done!

She added, "If you thought he meant it you would have fallen in a fit"; the point was the pleasure of the music—and of Corcoran's maverick spirit.[3]

A decade later, in the Truman administration, the view was split. Sam Rayburn remarked at a party at Congressman Lyndon Johnson's house late in 1945 that every administration "should have at least two Tom Corcorans." But Corcoran had become controversial as a go-for-broke lawyer-lobbyist and caught hell for it that season in an investigative profile in the *Saturday Evening Post*. When the *Post* piece appeared the suave public relations mogul Ben Sonnenberg told Corcoran to declare victory. Much of the article, he argued, gave voice to "people wanting to get even" for Corcoran's often brutal tackle-and-guard work for Roosevelt in his first two presidential terms. Meanwhile, why argue with publicity that said of its subject, "OK, he's Orson Welles, he's Shirley Temple, nothing has been so hot in this town for a hundred years. This guy is terrific, the smartest, the ablest, the most energetic"?[4]

Along the way, he had been the linchpin, the morale officer, "the unofficial party whip of the New Deal," the "leg man for a man who has no legs," "White House Tommy," proprietor of "Corcoran's OGPU" within the government, "the greatest wirepuller in history"; these were some vintage characterizations of Corcoran. Indispensable to Roosevelt before 1940, he had become by that year expendable. But out of government as in it, he spurred on confreres like Ickes, Forrestal, Douglas, Cohen, and Frank, accumulated protégés like the young LBJ, Fortas, Rowe and my father, and mentored them in his arts and crafts.[5]

Some intimate friends' taglines for Corcoran—"FDR's 'hatchet-man'" was one of William O. Douglas's—were interchangeable with those of his critics. My father in a letter to Douglas in 1945 about the man to whom they both owed so much: "After all, when everything that can be said about Tom has been said, he is a fixer—the best in America, as he blushingly admits." To his critics Corcoran was, after 1940, a manipulative fixer for hire with some grudges to settle, and merely that.[6]

An able corporate lawyer, legal draftsman, connoisseur of the classics, speechwriter, and strategist as well as political operator, Corcoran was a product of middle-class Irish gentility, born in Pawtucket, Rhode Island in 1901. From there to Brown University and Harvard Law School. At Harvard he won the patronage of Professor Frankfurter and the most coveted reward that "F. F." could arrange in the 1920s: dispatch to Washington as law clerk to Justice Oliver Wendell Holmes. For almost ten years, until Holmes's death at ninety-three in 1935, Corcoran came to him to read Montaigne, Dante, civil war history, and philosophy: "My first year with him was just an introduction to the wonder of him. . . . The old man would sit there half-prone and I'd be reading to him and the lights would be down. All of a sudden we'd be talking about the Norman knights in the melee. Ye gods! He was still in the Civil War."[7]

From 1927 to 1932 Corcoran learned the securities business and corporate law in New York working eighteen-hour days at the firm of Cotton Franklin. The firm's senior partner was an old Progressive. Nevertheless, taken together, Corcoran's intellect, education, and years on Wall Street made him the New Deal's foremost example of what Jerome Frank had in mind in writing FDR in 1933 about the categories of talent needed for effective economic reform and regulation. Frank, then general counsel of the AAA, told the president that his agency for managing the agricultural economy required lawyers capable of "dealing with industrial groups" that included "some of the largest and wealthiest corporations in the country, such as the packers, the millers and the tobacco companies. They retain as their counsel the ablest and highest-priced lawyers" from Wall Street. Consequently, "our lawyers must have considerable background of commercial and corporate law and a knowledge of industrial and corporate relations" and be "extremely ingenious and alert to detect subterfuges, evasions, and artful devices designed to frustrate the purposes of the Administration." In such agents' hands, as one of their chroniclers put it, "The New Deal became Progressivism without moralism."[8]

The various biographical sketches of Corcoran emphasize his gifts for entrepreneurship and for partnering; his intellect and charm. ("Quite noisy, quite adequate, and quite noisy" was Holmes's famous haikulike comment upon receipt of Corcoran as his clerk in 1926.) His can-do style, Irish good looks—wavy hair, ready smile—and his way with the piano and accordian added to the picture.[9]

Corcoran never held a formally designated top appointment from Roosevelt. At a time when Washington was so informal, he operated as a resourceful freelance across the three branches of the federal government from a base in a pre–New Deal agency, the Reconstruction Finance Corporation. He remarked once, "Holmes told me . . . never, never reach for a title," for there will always be others who want it. Instead, aspire to "command." Clerking for Holmes had yielded him, among other prizes, intimacy with the old man's junior partner, Justice Brandeis. And more than any of the other New Dealers, Corcoran prompted trust and clout (and later, because of his forcefulness, bitter resentment) on Capitol Hill. The proud congressman Sam Rayburn of Bonham, Texas, who with Democratic senator Burton Wheeler of Montana led the congressional part of the struggle to regulate Wall Street in 1934, said two decades later of the White House's legislative pointmen, Corcoran and Cohen, "Taken together, those two fellows made the most brilliant man I ever saw." Wheeler, even prouder, withdrew his own bill in favor of the Corcoran-Cohen version written for Rayburn because "their bill was more carefully drafted than mine."[10]

After the fight was won, Corcoran recalled, "the word went back to the White House that by God I could handle myself. . . . I became known in the White House as a guy who could go down and be a front-line fighter.

Roosevelt liked that kind of guy, and little by little, I was the guy who handled all the tough ones on the Hill."[11]

A few months later Corcoran's original mentor, Felix Frankfurter, Roosevelt's gadfly adviser at the Harvard Law School, wrote the president that he badly needed help in modernizing White House operations: "Fat reports are submitted to you without any precis, without any intellectual traffic directions. Equally intolerable is that you should not have at your disposal the kind of preliminary sifting of legislative proposals that you had when you were Governor of New York." Indeed, Corcoran in the indicated staff role would serve Frankfurter's purposes as well as the president's, connecting up the professor's own insistent transmission of counsel and job candidates, and diplomacy with Brandeis on the Supreme Court, where it counted.[12]

Corcoran's own recollection of the way he began to function on FDR's behalf is worth pausing on, for it illustrates literally the backdoor, direct-line, guerrillalike aspects of the style Roosevelt encouraged, which Corcoran came to personify. The president's able, trusted secretary and "other wife," Marguerite ("Missy") LeHand, is the featured player:

> [The] first thing I know, I am called in through Missy's office and she goes in and introduces me to [FDR] and says this is the fellow that Frankfurter thinks would be a good assistant to you. . . .
>
> Through Missy, I was given the privilege of using the White House telephone exchange for important calls . . . an incredible tool. . . . My position as a presidential lobbyist on the Hill was most unofficial (and depended on the continued good will of [RFC Director Jesse] Jones). I was only an RFC lawyer . . . but when I phoned someone, being able to say I was calling from the White House, or having a White House operator put me through—gave me a certain cachet. . . .
>
> I was also discretely warned by Missy to understand that I had to be very careful not to step on the toes of people who had come to Washington with Roosevelt after long years of service. Some had worked for him as long ago as the Wilson Administration. . . . And as in any administration, many of the entourage were very jealous. For that reason, it was arranged that each morning I would reach Missy's office through a lower passage in the West Wing which led to a private staircase. I'd tell her what I learned the day before, then wait to see if the President wanted to see me, or simply go about my business for the day. If Roosevelt needed to talk with me personally, Missy's office opened directly into his, and she showed me in. In that way, I avoided crossing paths with any of Roosevelt's old guard and kept the jealousies down to a manageable level.[13]

Others dispute Corcoran's aside in this account that "I was careful never to abuse [the presidential switchboard] privilege." Joseph Rauh once recalled, "Tom and I used to smile when he would grab the telephone in my lousy little office in the Interior Department, dial, and say 'Hello, Mr. Secretary? This is Tom Corcoran. I'm calling from the White House." Corcoran's ingenuity with instruments and props didn't stop with the telephone. Among his assignments in the 1930s was oversight of the Coast Guard. At moments when political time bombs were ticking and a party to it was on an ocean liner, Corcoran would order up a Coast Guard cutter, intercept the ship at sea, and seize the moment before the press waiting at the dock got into the act. One of those interventions helped put across Congressman Rayburn of Texas (Roosevelt's man—Corcoran at his side in the fight to regulate Wall Street) as House majority leader, on his way to his distinguished tenure as speaker.[14]

With his sidekick, Ben Cohen, who functioned similarly from no strong appointed status but from a second-level interagency position, Corcoran wrote some of the distinctive legislation of the New Deal (along with securities industry regulation and reform: breaking up the giant private utilities, establishing the minimum wage.) The cliché was that "Corcoran was a gregarious political dynamo . . . Cohen a thoughtful legal craftsman. They even looked their parts. Corcoran the Irishman had a jutting jaw and a ready smile; Cohen the Jew wore glasses and looked scholarly somber." In fact their qualities overlapped: Corcoran had a fine command of great literature; Cohen, in the thick of fights to see New Deal regulations across corporate America's defense lines in the courts, "his disheveled suit flaked with cigarette ash . . . dealing out wisdom in his quavery falsetto," outfoxing securities and utilities industries and their litigators, has been described as a virtual generalissimo.[15]

The enthusiasm, energy, and precision Corcoran and Cohen brought to their work for Roosevelt have received much attention. It was said that they ran "the only law firm . . . that stayed open around the clock." Less observed was the fact that this precision derived from their employment before 1933 in the field of corporate law and that, as followers of Justice Brandeis, they were cautious, even (in their own words) "conservative" regulators, not, in the first instance, radical planners. By contrast to the blunt administrative instrumentality of the NRA and AAA that aroused the Supreme Court against the First New Deal, the mark of Corcoran and Cohen's work was legislative subtlety. Their collaborator Sam Rayburn remarked sardonically that their first joint effort, the Securities Act of 1933, won such speedy congressional approval "because it was so damned good or so damned incomprehensible." Wisecracks aside, Rayburn would have been the first to observe retrospectively that its combination of savvy about markets and its constitutional soundness, as well as its efficacy and endurance, were the best claims for it.[16]

As noted, the Second New Deal focused not on planning but on regulation—of markets, of key manufacturing industries, of the utilities trusts.

Those trusts constituted a vast, monopolistic, politically entrenched empire that grew up around the new energy technologies of the first part of the century that powered industry and lit up offices and homes. (The utility trusts were in some respects the Microsofts of their day.) The utilities industry had one of its big feet on Wall Street and was well networked politically. Roosevelt, according to Corcoran, saw it early on as the key bankroller of conservative opposition to the New Deal in election campaigns.[17]

Additionally, the Second New Deal focused on wages and hours, credit systems, fiscal policy, the harnessing of natural resources for public purposes, and the construction of a national infrastructure of roads, bridges, and dams. Corcoran and Cohen were Roosevelt's primary agents ranging across those issues. Their work didn't stop at research, legal draftsmanship, strategy, thunderous speechwriting, or lobbying. At key moments each appeared as well in the highest courts in the land to argue successfully against tests of the new statutes they'd written, facing down pillars of the establishment bar including John W. Davis and John Foster Dulles.[18]

Then "what Corcoran and Cohen began, William O. Douglas and Jerome Frank completed," Jordan Schwarz has written: "the dismantling of Wall Street's monopoly of control over capital."[19]

. . .

It's time to consider the attributes necessary for admission by peers to the center of this Rooseveltian enterprise. First the core New Deal discipline, pushed to the fore by the Depression crisis: the ability to connect—as European education emphasizes but American education does not—politics to economics. In later years that translated out as renewable allegiance to certain principles of social, legal, and economic reform—especially dealing outsiders in, economic stimulus, and making over the backward regions of the nation.

Next the demonstration of an unusual gift for understanding power, a sangfroid about employing it, a knack for networking beyond the usual and predictable boundaries. A telephone exchange between Cohen and Corcoran about the name of one of the New Dealers' allies in the Roman Catholic hierarchy, Bishop Bernard Sheil of Chicago, being advertised as a supporter of the United Auto Workers' GM strike committee in 1946:

> CORCORAN: The Bishop had nothing to do with it. Eliot Janeway just assumed the right to do it.
> COHEN: Well, I don't see how he could do that.
> CORCORAN: Well, you don't know Eliot.[20]

Indeed Cohen, like Corcoran, did. The point was ironic. So, add a particular kind of brassy daring in pulling off plays against the odds; and no one had more bravado than Corcoran himself. "You know, Tom, you're the greatest goddamned blocking back the world has ever seen," my father remarked to Corcoran a few months earlier. Corcoran, for his part, distinguished between his own muscular entrepreneurship and the crude, arriviste style of newcomers to power. A henchman for one of Harry Truman's closest allies, he remarked in June 1945, "is one of these guys [who] thinks that to the victors belong the spoils, and he goes around bragging about it."[21]

Then too, these New Dealers didn't have to agree with a competing player to do business with him or even nurture cameraderie. The point was to develop connections, franchises, and constituencies formidable enough to command the respect of those in control of contending ones, as Corcoran did with conservative powerhouses in or near Roosevelt's Washington like Jesse Jones and Bernard Baruch. "Washington is peopled by men who in the very act of joining the political lists agree to act," Corcoran wrote years later. "I never learned to hate the men I disagreed with, nor those who opposed me when I had to act." Above all, politics to these men meant sophistication. Who was *smart* and who was *dumb* meant more than who was a loyal ally and who wasn't. Achievement of goals was at least as often threatened by the naïveté or ineffectiveness of saintly members of "our" team as by the diabolical might or wile of adversaries.[22]

Similarly, there were worldly, pragmatic businessmen who understood the regulation of business and markets was here to stay and who, as Douglas put it, "had decided to live under the law." There were even some Wall Street and corporate figures who drank outright from the cups of reform and social justice.[23]

On the other side of the business bargaining table, the quintessential New Deal labor leader, Walter Reuther, having displayed a capacity for strategic vision early in World War II, could have moved quickly into government, or into the auto industry in top executive roles. Sticking with his union labor base, he spread his wings instead as a formidable, independent industrial and social policy innovator (and sometimes as a troublemaker) beyond immediate labor goals and in the Democratic Party.[24]

. . .

A premise of the enterprise was that most wins and losses were really episodes in a complex dialectic of maneuver. A game with goals, of course, but ultimately a process without end. "Salute, boy," Justice Holmes commanded young Corcoran as they walked a path that followed a railroad spur as far as it went one day in 1928. Corcoran sprang to, then inquired, "'Sir, what have I saluted?' 'The true terminus of something,' Holmes replied. 'There are few of those in the world.'" My father would cite a remark by Lyndon Johnson: "Politics is the art of going to other men's funerals."[25]

The point of any play was thus also about future plays: how did the playmaker emerge, with what chits and markers for the next round? A play might turn on a middle-man and the occasional double agent, and on timing; laws of opposites, a transient coincidence of interest. The game itself turned on who knew whom and on the ways, accordingly, that off-the-record alliances, ambitions, and chance associations could get one to otherwise impossible destinations.

Some dramas in which these New Dealers came together to play influential roles were historic: the deployment of Keynesian fiscal polices in the face of the "Roosevelt Recession" of 1937–1938. FDR's improvisation of Lend-Lease in 1940–1941. The New Deal's elevation, long-term, of the American South and West out of underdeveloped status—in some ways, a dry run for the postwar Marshall Plan and the concept of foreign aid. The Supreme Court's *Brown vs. Board of Education* decision in 1954. Congressional passage of the first civil rights bill since Reconstruction in 1957. But behind any such achievement for the ages was a fluid, offstage process of maneuver, calculation, subversion, and charade, initiatives against conservative vetoes and inertia, manipulation of others' private agendas and public ambitions, and accident.

Several of the partners, like Corcoran, could bring off the most difficult of missions and damn the cost in controversy or other fallout. ("Corcoran was kind of a second-story man," my father observed years later. "If he set out to tear a wall down, there might be no building left.") Others, like Fortas and Johnson, excelled at the more sinuous, less visible design. Those who were known for sheer brains or ideals, like Douglas, or moral force in the public eye, like "Curmudgeon" Ickes, played less manipulative roles but were part of the game too, appreciative of the maneuvers their allies undertook. All were men of action.[26]

A special place of honor among the brilliant was reserved for Corcoran's New Deal "law partner," Ben Cohen. Ascetic, abstemious, a shrewd stock market investor; he never cashed in on his government career as Corcoran and Fortas did. Alone among the group, Cohen and Douglas developed genuine international expertise as the others did not (except as Washington "counsel" for American client states like Nationalist China—Corcoran and Puerto Rico—Fortas). He was always available to be "of counsel" himself to the enterprise; they called him their "saint," and they sometimes kidded him on that score. Cohen, reporting in to Corcoran early in his State Department tenure in 1945 that "I had [Secretary of State] Jimmy [Byrnes] write a little note to [Undersecretary] Dean [Acheson]" about a matter of mutual interest, earned this response, in jest. Corcoran: "Good! You're beginning to be an operator. . . . How do you like the water?"[27]

. . .

All this was gospel I was taught growing up; not so much articulated as understood and alluded to. It was by no means a gospel of mere opportunism or cynicism; indeed, some of it was sacred. For it was the gospel according to Franklin Roosevelt, or, one might say, his Common Law of Politics as these New Dealers took it from him.

This common law was informed by FDR's own shrewd conclusions about the fate of the great reformers of his youth who fell way short of their objectives: his uncontainable cousin Theodore, and the more austere president young Franklin served, Woodrow Wilson. Four years out of office, TR failed in his attempted return to the White House in 1912 as a crusader for progressive ideas of governance and against corruption. Wilson tried and failed to engage the United States in reforming the cynicism of world-power politics through a League of Nations. "During the war [FDR] talked to me many times . . . about Wilson's mistakes," William O. Douglas recalled. These Rooseveltians were allowed much closer in than any previous deputies and assistants on a president's grand designs for succeeding where others had failed. They knew well, too, that Roosevelt was a fatalist as well as a crusader. As he remarked in 1940 of his greatest predecessor: "Lincoln was . . . a politician who was practical enough to get a great many things for this country. He was a sad man because he couldn't get it all at once. And nobody can."[28]

At the same time, these New Dealers had no illusions about how coalition politics works, and about how hard they had to fight for their privileged place in Roosevelt's evolving sequence of coalitions, his scheme of things. In a private memo to Henry Luce, a year after Roosevelt's death, my father wrote,

> When all is said and done, the most vivid . . . index of the power the New Deal swings is not mystical or ideological or rhetorical. Like any other movement, its prestige and mystique are measured by the appointments it is able to buy or bludgeon from the Ins no matter who they may be. . . . The New Deal never expected more than a 50–50 split on appointments from Roosevelt, and rarely got that much. As a matter of fact, it never expected more than an option on a 50–50 split with him on the policy level.[29]

On FDR's 1936 campaign train Tommy Corcoran, then moving to the center of Roosevelt's inner circle, probed one of the president's modes of operation. He seemed that day to have promised the same job in Washington to a stream of aspirants. "May I ask sir, which one will you appoint" after the election?

Roosevelt laughed and replied, "The one who makes the most trouble if I don't."[30]

Four years later Corcoran had made enough trouble in his legendary operations on the president's behalf to have become the fellow without the job. He'd been warned in 1936 (in the period that Roosevelt began confiding in him so intimately) by a much more conventional-minded predecessor as chief White House aide-de-camp, Raymond Moley, to remember that in such a seemingly elevated role "you're a clerk, not a statesman." Moley added a short time later, "All promises of kings are presumptive . . . Tommy, and all of us are presumptively liquidable." Corcoran's name became closely associated with Roosevelt's two most bitterly fought and ill-fated second-term ventures, his 1937 effort to "pack" the Supreme Court and his "purge" of selected conservative enemies of the New Deal in the 1938 congressional primaries. (Roosevelt "lost" in attempts to dislodge conservative Democratic senators and "won" only one congressional race in New York, into which Corcoran poured himself.) Even some New Dealers told Roosevelt that Corcoran had become a problem.[31]

As Roosevelt began his unprecedented third term in 1941, he considered Corcoran, but failed to appoint him to one and then another key Justice, War, or Navy Department post. Harry Hopkins, suffering from a cancer that would him kill him five years later, punctuated his filling of the vacuum left by Corcoran by moving into the White House to live—conserving his energies while assuring that no one else would get close to FDR again.[32]

Corcoran picked himself up and invented the modern Washington lawyer-lobbyist practice. "I wish I had Tommy back," said Roosevelt to Henry Wallace late in 1942. "Why doesn't he call? I suppose Tommy is too busy making money. They say he is making it hand over fist"—as if his onetime intimate aide were in another country rather than across town.[33]

In a typical "Tommy operation," so my father's version went, from his soon-to-be golden exile in private practice and with FDR consumed by the war effort, Corcoran influenced an inordinate number of the Roosevelt administration's federal judicial appointments after 1940, as he had before. He worked through one of his "junior partners," Jim Rowe, well placed (by Corcoran) in the White House and then in the number two post in the Justice Department before joining Corcoran's law firm in 1946. My father liked to observe that, echoing the sturdy record of Corcoran's and Cohen's draftsmanship of New Deal statutes under the scrutiny of the Supreme Court, Corcoran's and Rowe's care in selection and attention to the congressional niceties assured that every one of those judicial appointments was confirmed by the Senate.[34]

Corcoran continued odd services to Roosevelt in spite of the president's apparent rejection of him. He earned some bad press for resisting a congressional inquiry into a New York radio station deal that, Corcoran told a confidant, threatened to expose financial manipulations involving several of the Roosevelts' hapless sons. "You realize why I was fighting those hearings so tough," he said a few month after FDR's death. "I wasn't fighting for me—I was fighting for the Lawd."[35]

After 1945, as in the 1930s when he lacked a formal White House title to match his extraordinary influence, Corcoran exemplified the proposition that these Rooseveltians didn't so much have "jobs" as they did bases from which they flew their extraordinary and irregular missions.

. . .

The gospel, then, was a mosaic of principle and maneuver, a mix of public and private interest woven into the sweep of events these men were striving to direct. No one but another partner could ever really know the balance in the New Deal Book of Ends and Means. In a December 1945 phone conversation, Corcoran and my father cover the Washington waterfront—who's coming and going in Truman's cabinet and on the Supreme Court, hostility between Truman and organized labor, a profile of Ben Cohen in the works at *Life* magazine. Then my father asks Corcoran if he's coming to New York anytime soon:

> CORCORAN: I've really got to get this year cleaned up. . . . The month of December is a serious month in the law business, my boy. It's the end of life for which the first is made.
>
> JANEWAY: I love you when you go commercial, my beautiful friend.[36]

Corcoran spinning tactical political maneuvers, quoting Browning, making money, cultivating protégés, was both his own man and managing partner of the House of Roosevelt. As attorneys, Corcoran, his subsequent law partner Jim Rowe, Clark Clifford, and Abe Fortas all managed pieces of William O. Douglas's and Lyndon Johnson's private as well as public lives, covering the ground from messy divorce, real estate, loans, and power of attorney (in Douglas's case) to disputed election results, personal finances, and business interests (in Johnson's). Corcoran's and the other partners' dependence upon one another came and went, yet was constant enough so that the network of relationships between them was something of an end in itself. All were astute enough to know that at times they were using each other.[37]

But who was to say that an odd or unseemly effort on behalf of a partner marked for political preferment (and Corcoran, Fortas, Rowe, Clifford, and my father expended many for Douglas and more for Johnson) was mere cronyism and self-interest? Who knew for sure which maneuver was at root a function of a larger design to advance the chosen Rooseveltian apostle to the top seat of power, which power would be mobilized to attempt a reinvention of the New Deal? (As indeed it was, by Johnson as president.) Sometimes they didn't know themselves. They were simply operating; it came naturally. What differentiated them from mere political cronies in their time was that they'd been in FDR's service as he brought the nation through unprecedented economic and war crises, helped him invent the modern American political economy and build a modern government.

And friendship? Through the New Deal and wartime years, the partners had lived (as my mother put it years later) in "each other's pockets." Then, as they consolidated their own power bases, the associations seemed to loosen. But the record conveys the echo of the friendships that had been distinctive and that from time to time snapped back into place. William O. Douglas's once intimate relationship with Lyndon Johnson broke down over the Vietnam War. But, as it did, with both men still healthy and in office, the president helped the justice find photographs for a book the latter, in his avenging environmentalist mode, wrote about the Texas terrain, and Douglas insisted that his publisher include "one of Lyndon's [own] photos . . . rich in color and warm in sentiment—a picture of the bluebonnets that he and Lady Bird and I loved so much." In the last years of his life my father said of Abe Fortas, "I loved him dearly when we were close," in the 1940s. A startling comment, because in the 1960s and seventies, I rarely heard him speak of Fortas except to harp on his flaws. The idea that he'd "loved" any associate "dearly" was itself out of character. Yet, because of what the Rooseveltian brotherhood had meant to, and done for, each of these men, and because of similarities in their intellects and natures, their words ring true.[38]

Many of these Rooseveltians married unusual women by the standards of the day. The casual attitudes toward extramarital sex of powerful men who make their own rules notwithstanding, most of them remained bonded to their wives. Hugo Black's wife Josephine was widely read; she wrote and she painted with some success. Abe Fortas's wife Carolyn Agger, an able tax lawyer, first built her own practice with Randolph Paul, a New Deal lawyer of note, and after Paul died merged it with her husband's firm. Tommy Corcoran's wife Peggy had been his secretary and remained his (and his friends') confidante.[39]

Tough-minded and an avid reader, Lady Bird Johnson (with Nellie Connally, wife of the young LBJ's dashing sidekick John Connally) ran her husband's congressional office while he was on U.S. Naval leave during the war. (There was serious talk of Lady Bird running formally for Johnson's seat in 1942 if his military interlude was prolonged.) She proved herself an able manager of their broadcast interests in Texas. Like Eleanor Roosevelt, these women defied the cliché that Washington is full of powerful men and the provincial women they married when they were very young.[40]

Of course, several of the marriages were disasters, variations on the theme set by Franklin and Eleanor Roosevelt. Forrestal's was particularly bad, and Douglas's series of divorces detracted from his reputation as one of the great Supreme Court justices of the century.

Johnson, Fortas, Forrestal, and Douglas had liaisons outside their marriages; here and there, ones that affected their relationships with each other. John Connally's biographer claims that Johnson once made a play for the attractive Nellie Connally but was rebuffed. My father claimed that Douglas and Carol Fortas had an affair; Corcoran told a confidant that the Fortases' "trouble" proved "it is not a good idea to marry a too intellectual woman." Douglas's first divorce profoundly upset the prudish Hugo Black, and Corcoran as well, who handled Douglas's wife Mildred's side of the matter. (See pp. 65, 241, note 69, for the effect of the divorce on the two men's relationship.) Some of the wives who stayed with philandering husbands went through painful times, yet seemed in the end to accept the truism about power as an aphrodisiac and to discount the husbandly behavior following from it. Infidelity, they evidently reasoned, was a function of the excess of personality and drive that brought such men to power—and their wives to second-stage prominence.[41]

My parents, I came to understand after some years, fit this pattern, with the twist that my mother wrote professionally—at first implicitly in novels, then explicitly in nonfiction form—about the politics of the sexes.

. . .

One harsh truth for this tough-minded cohort was that there was no assured protection against a lean season. These were not moneyed men who could walk blithely away from power to established law practices, inheritances, or family estates. That was a lesson learned in the Depression, but also in the inner circle of the New Deal, on occasions when the president's favor proved fickle. After all, as Corcoran remarked once to his protégé Jim Rowe, FDR never had to work for a living.[42]

A number of these Rooseveltians, even the crusading Douglas, demonstrated over time a certain . . . weakness in money matters; a reckless, or was it helpless, insistence on the need for protection in the form of unusual financial arrangements, in spite of how these might appear. Corcoran made his remark about "this old curse of our crowd"—the hangover of financial insecurity from the Depression, the low government salaries—in a conversation with my father in 1945 from the happy vantage point of his derring-do young law firm. There he maneuvered creatively in Congress, the executive branch, and the courts "in the same ways for his clients as he once did for the President . . . never able to make a distinction between them or to realize that what might be justified within the government cannot be from outside it," in one commentary.[43]

Corcoran's life became his buccaneering law practice. By late 1941 his energies freshly expended on behalf of clients had gotten him hauled before a congressional investigating committee. It was by no means his last such encounter. He seemed not to care what people said about his definition of entrepreneurship. But Lyndon Johnson, similarly determined to have a fortune, paid the price of journalistic exposés of his political interventions on behalf of his own broadcasting interests and his principal Texas backers, the powerful construction firm of Brown and Root. Fortas left the Supreme Court in disgrace after exposure of an off-the-books financial arrangement with a financier in trouble with the SEC. Douglas, always in debt, especially after he started paying alimony to former wives, faced a call for impeachment at the end of his Court service for a financial side deal. Two major figures of the twentieth-century American bench, both visionary reformers who left a mark on judicial history, one defrocked and the other tainted for appalling judgment. Whatever the balance between greed and financial insecurity in the actions of these two superb advocates, their dismissive rationales for their arrangements persuaded no one.[44]

. . .

So the Rooseveltian gospel, as I received it as a young man, was secular. Roosevelt was a great man, but had pronounced limitations and could not be relied upon; he was no god. On the other hand, insofar as the public (or what Thurman Arnold of the New Deal called, with respect, its "folklore") required a contemporary god, his name was Franklin Roosevelt. Nor was this mindless adoration, even at the level of vox populi. Everyone knew a great and shameless ham actor when they heard him delivering lines like "My friends: You are farmers. I am a farmer, myself!" But Schlesinger quotes a humble North Carolina millworker articulating the corresponding piece of the faith in the 1930s as I was taught it in the next decades: "Mr. Roosevelt is the only man we ever had in the White House who would understand that my boss is a son-of-a-bitch."[45]

In any event, there were true devils: the unbridled capitalist system that led to the Crash of 1929 and the Great Depression, the selfish industrial barons and plundering speculators, and Hitler and his Axis partners. The vanquishing of the devils required outsized abilities, and recognition of extraordinary work to be done, lest control of destiny fall to hacks or fools. "There ain't no point in having a leader if he's . . . just simply going where people take him," Corcoran remarked to Harold Ickes in the summer of 1946, despairing of Harry Truman's stumbling performance as president to date. "A democracy can't function except under leadership," Ickes replied, "and we haven't got any here."[46]

That such work was doable was fundamental to the gospel. These Rooseveltians flourished during years when the structure of authority in Washington was proliferating fast (the federal government doubled in size between 1933 and 1941.) As has been written, even more important than expansion in numbers was "the change during the New Deal in the *functions* of the federal government," with power flowing from Congress toward new administrative, regulatory, and redistributive agencies. Nevertheless the New Deal was a small-scale operation in and around an accessible government relative to today's scale; small enough for an able operator to know his way around, and manipulate. Then too, the New Deal enterprise came together in gear with the process of rendering government effective; a time when America's organizational willpower, know-how, and reforming energies seemed equal to its problems.[47]

. . .

These were some of the tenets, distinguishing characteristics, and flaws of the partnership into which my father was admitted in his twenties. The version of it described here became diffuse after 1945. At times it existed only as an amalgam of fraternal links or rivalries among onetime comrades in arms—a way of thinking and operating together with a good deal of nostalgia. That it did exist is evidenced in Harry Truman's successful 1948 campaign wargame. (Out of government, practicing law with Corcoran, Jim Rowe wrote what became Truman's election strategy paper. Truman hated Corcoran, and would have ignored a memorandum by the latter's law partner; White House counsel Clark Clifford took it over as his own.) And in Lyndon Johnson's presidency, which, as Corcoran wrote Johnson in 1965, "resurrects all the dreams we were dreaming when World War II came and we had to ditch Dr. New Deal for Dr. Win the War . . . all the Walt Whitman and . . . warmth and excitement about people and land and rivers . . ." (Shades of Rex Tugwell's "I shall make America over!") Scholars debate the mix in the Johnsonian version of the New Deal of continuity, completion, exhaustion, departure, success, failure. But they study it.[48]

By comparison the politics of the last decades of the twentieth century lacked connection to relevant antecedents. As a political genius who—harking back to Theodore Roosevelt's and Woodrow Wilson's unfulfilled reform agendas—changed the nation and the world, Roosevelt provided roots for the politics of the years that followed his presidency. His brains-trusters were the instruments of that legacy, helping to shape the environment of power for decades after his death. As an *idea*, a culture, a cadre who shared in a heroic exercise of power and custody of its legacy, these Rooseveltians' enterprise had a significant afterlife.

❧ 3 ❧

Making the New Deal Revolution

"THE SENSE OF BEING SPECIAL"

The art of political networking from the late 1930s to the 1960s assumed a landscape marked out by much firmer social, economic, and geographic boundaries and party affiliations than we know today. Some of them were already on their way to becoming fluid, but they were still clear-cut enough to be defining: Business, Labor, the Farm vote, the Negroes, the Catholics, the Jews, "the ethnics," the Democratic South, Republican Midwest, Progressive Northwest, and so forth.

Upon that landscape the two political parties organized themselves "from the courthouse to the White House," as Lyndon Johnson used to say. Big city bosses like Democrat Ed Kelly of Chicago and barons of party machinery like Republican Joe Pew of Pennsylvania were more powerful than the governors and senators they sent out to take the bows.

Some of the major provinces—Big Business, the Midwest, South, and West—were experiencing developmental ferment, their traditional order challenged by fresh forces like public power coalitions and labor unions. Women had been voting for only two decades; the suburbs were being invented. In some states Republican Progressivism was the force for reform; the conservatives were organization Democrats. The swelling black vote, blocs of immigrants, the growing ranks of small business, freshly organized consumer groups, veterans, Youth for This or That formed new lobbies and became targets of new election strategies. (Beginning with Nixon, the Republican Party's success in converting suburban dwellers from blue-collar and immigrant Democratic Party roots, and white southerners from their parental party loyalties, is the more recent chapter of the story.)

Organized labor, freshly protected by federal statute, building bargaining power and alliances (and voting in solidarity, no longer a weak and bloodied outsider), became a potent new political force all of a sudden in the late 1930s. Blacks were some steps behind labor, but increasingly to be reckoned with. New industries, elements of modern infrastructure, were taking off.

The arrangement of old givens and new forces was therefore subject to constant revision and major upset. World War II changed everything, industrially, politically, socially. Shortly after FDR's death Corcoran remarked of the Truman administration, "A gang of crooks has hijacked the funeral train of a great man." On such a landscape local barons and power brokers needed not only old friends, but new ones. This inchoate environment invited supple operators to cross the boundaries separating provinces; to arrange alliances, pressure, provocation, defection—deals. Roosevelt himself had helped set the pace for that style with his successful attachment of Republican Progressives to his cause.[1]

The New Deal opened up politics as part of the way it amended the old rules of socioeconomic order. Political networks became more textured. With previously disenfranchised blocs like labor gaining a place on the field, a smart player of the game had to be no more than one or two intermediaries away from another one. But much information was still exchanged at meetings, at clubs, in public speaking, over meals, at parties, by letter— as it had been a century earlier. Radio, long-distance telephoning, and air travel were speeding that communication up, though the war slowed down consumer access to many of the innovations. Still, it is unrecognizably old-fashioned by today's standards.

Franklin Roosevelt's ability to render his physical handicap irrelevant, finesse the problems of the disorderly evolution of the New Deal, and overwhelm his opponents involved oratorical gifts and inspired words on the air (many of which Corcoran, with an ear for the classics, crafted), as in:

> Governments can err, Presidents do make mistakes, but the immortal Dante tells us that divine justice weighs the sins of the cold-blooded and the sins of the warm-hearted on different scales. Better the occasional faults of a Government that lives in a spirit of charity than the consistent omissions of a Government frozen in the ice of its own indifference.

Roosevelt's muscular delivery, high dramatic pauses and all, could render combative lines like those, and the inspirational one that followed on it ("This generation of Americans has a *rendez-vous* with destiny"), as more than mere radio rhetoric. Movie theater newsreel versions punctuated his commanding visual presence, but by no means defined it. It was a time well before the telegenic factor, or the media event staged for the camera, began to change the rules of how politics was conducted, and how the news was understood.[2]

With their fingers on the intersection of government's regulatory and contracting powers in the new communications, transportation, construction, energy, and other emerging industries, and the labor forces for them, the New Dealers brokered this revolution of the political landscape across geographic, class, party, and interest group lines.

. . .

Advocates, craftsmen, or maneuverers, these men who did so much to shape the second New Deal were linked by ideas as well as their own nimble footwork and instincts for effective teamwork. Two new bodies of concept and practical analysis, both fiercely modern, both hostile to nineteenth-century dogmas, informed and motivated them.

The first, "legal realism," contested doctrinaire laissez-faire interpretations of the Constitution that had for decades constrained government and labor interference with the prerogatives of industry. The second, Keynesianism and associated thinking, challenged parallel laissez-faire economic theory.

Legal realism and Keynesianism were each iconoclastic—"radical" in the view of established thinking of the day. That thinking, enunciated by the Supreme Court in decisions like *Lochner v. New York* (1905), held that the corporation was protected under the Reconstruction civil rights–era Fourteenth Amendment as something like a person, entitled to "liberty of contract" and free from government interference or regulation. Legal realism and Keynesianism each embraced, at least implicitly, the counterentitlement of government to employ flexible powers and to intervene in markets.[3]

More precisely, if paradoxically, in the decades building to the constitutional crisis of 1937 a conservative Supreme Court *acted* to enforce laissez-faire and to stalemate New Deal–style activism. The legal realists, to the left, challenged that conservative activism. Still more simply put by Jerome Frank, legal realism made New Deal liberal reform possible.[4]

Legal realism argued that the *idea* of sacrosanct, established "truths" in jurisprudence, and for that matter of undisputed "facts" in legal cases, was a sterile, doctrinaire illusion. For judges were idiosyncratic, interpetive human beings; they "did not 'find' the law as oracles but 'made' it as mortals subject to the biases of their backgrounds." Further, demanding recognition of the proliferation of new knowledge in an ever more complex world, the realists sought to inform and integrate law with fresh social science. "In finance," recalled William O. Douglas years later, "we wanted to teach the anatomy of finance"—what, regardless of high-minded intent, were the perhaps disturbing facts on the ground, the data, the effects?—"as well as the rules of law. In criminal law, we wanted psychiatry as well as the criminal code."[5]

The New Dealers and the legal realists were linked in the ways that, as pragmatists and critics, they saw *process* as secondary to *results*. This of course opened them to charges of using ends to justify means. But they in turn were able to demonstrate that conservative judges, often holier-than-thou in their ritualistic self-presentation as custodians of the Constitution, in fact went about making definitive political, social, and economic choices. And so—the legal realists argued successfully—taking "an imaginative, modern, experimental approach to problem solving and to expanding the role of the welfare state," could Congress and the executive branch. At the height of Roosevelt's 1937 push to reform the Supreme Court, having sent legislation to Congress to expand (or "pack") it as had been done in previous eras (he opposed the more sedate approach of a constitutional amendment), outright legal realist rhetoric found its way into a presidential "fireside chat." The Court, vetoing New Deal measures to deal with the Depression crisis, "has been acting not as a judicial body, but as a policy-making body," charged the president. The prospect was for breakdown of the federal system, as happened under the Articles of Confederation before 1789, if the branches of government could not work more harmoniously. Given the residue of the Depression crisis, time was crucial, and

> we cannot rely on [a Constitutional] amendment as the immediate or only answer to our present difficulties. Even if an amendment were passed, and even if in the years to come it were to be ratified, its meaning would depend upon the kind of Justices who would be sitting on the Supreme Court bench. An amendment, like the rest of the Constitution, is what the Justices say it is rather than what its framers or you might hope it is.

Legal realism accepted change and embraced the concept of reform to manage change.[6]

Philosophically, legal realism held that modern society had to find its way experientially. In this it was informed, as has been written, by the destabilizing experiences of World War I and the Depression:

> Both were read as modernist "lessons." The War confirmed the illusion of permanency, as embodied by the breakdown of the "permanent" codes and alliances of "civilized" nations. . . . The Depression likewise revealed the impermanency of the economic institutions of unregulated capitalism, previously regarded as inevitable and inviolate.[7]

But legal realism looked back as well to Oliver Wendell Holmes, whose profound skepticism of abstractions and dogma was formed in combat one bloody engagement before World War I: in the Civil War. The new legal thinking flowed directly from Holmes's famous shot across the bow of laissez-faire doctrine, "The life of the law has not been logic: it has been experience." Selected at Harvard Law School by Holmes's disciple Frankfurter, several men who helped shape the New Deal along with Corcoran began their careers as law clerks to Holmes, late in his long life, or to his colleague

in dissent, Justice Louis Brandeis, or to Holmes's successor, Justice Benjamin
Cardozo.[8]

. . .

Among economic modernists, John Maynard Keynes (a Liberal rather than
a socialist or Labourite in Britain; a shrewd stock market investor) ap-
plauded Roosevelt's trial-and-error breaks with economic orthodoxy at the
launching of the New Deal. "You have made yourself the trustee for those
in every country who seek to mend the evils of our conditions by reasoned
experiment within the framework of the existing social system," he wrote
in an "Open Letter to the President" published in the *New York Times* at the
end of 1933. (Privately, he remarked at the time that FDR "had about as
much idea of where he would land as a pre-war pilot." That was all right,
in Keynes's view, as long as the president followed his healthy instinct for
soliciting advice from experts like himself.)[9]

Keynes led a rebellion against the idea that free societies had to be the
prisoners of boom-and-bust business cycles. His "countercyclical" argument
held that government spending would prime the engines of the stalled Depression economy, and that deficits brought on by government spending in
recessionary phases were in effect investments in economic revival and expansion. Then in the next swing up, alert, aggressive fiscal management
could deter overheating of the economy.

Roosevelt never bought Keynesianism in so many words. He always had
trouble with the sanctioning of deficits and found Keynes somewhat con-
descending in person. (It remained for Richard Nixon, in 1971, to call himself a Keynesian.) But the New Dealers to Roosevelt's left (by then, in their
enemies' words, the "Corcoran crowd") had no such trouble with Keynes's
ideas. In the "Roosevelt Recession" of 1937–1938, against FDR's conservative advisers' campaign to restore "business confidence" and his own
instinct for budget-balancing, Corcoran and Co. fought successfully for a
Brandeisian antimonopoly program and a Keynesian government spending
package. In the process they more or less won the Keynesian argument for
good.[10]

. . .

Jerome Frank, forty-eight in 1938, a leading legal realist, came to authority
in the New Deal from successful practice of corporate law in Chicago and
New York. There, as Thurman Arnold later wrote, Frank learned the "ways
of high finance," an astute sense of how to regulate it, and deep skepticism
of the "web of any economic doctrine" as well as of the "brooding omnipresence in the sky known as Jurisprudence." Widely read, gregarious, as
high-browed as Ben Cohen in personal appearance and intellect, Frank's
style in Roosevelt's Washington, where Jews for the first time could aspire
to more than an exception-to-the-rule presence, was out-front and take-

charge where Cohen's was behind-the-scenes. Frank's effective recruitment of youthful legal talent to Washington to the AAA in 1933, and then to the SEC after 1937, paralleled Frankfurter's and Corcoran's, drawing yet more former clerks to Holmes (Alger Hiss and his brother Donald) and other prodigies (Abe Fortas, Thurman Arnold, and Adlai Stevenson in their first New Deal assignments). Frank's *Law and the Modern Mind* (1930) set the modernist tone (with more than a nod to Holmes) three years before the Roosevelt administration took office.[11]

"Law, if it is to meet the needs of modern civilization," Frank argued, "must adapt itself to the modern mind. It must cease to embody a philosophy opposed to change. It must become avowedly pragmatic." Frank was deeply influenced by Freudian thinking (he and William O. Douglas both underwent psychoanalysis). He wrote, "Until we become thoroughly congnizant of, and cease to be controlled by, the image of the father hidden away in the authority of the law, we shall not reach that first step in the civilized administration of justice, the recognition that man is not made for the law, but that the law is made by and for men." (In similar terms Frank credited Holmes's powerful influence on the Court to "a vast knowledge of legal history divorced from slavish veneration for the past . . . He has himself abandoned . . . the phantasy of a perfect, consistent, legal uniformity. . . . He has attained an adult emotional status, a self-reliant, fearless approach to life, and . . . he invites others to do likewise.")[12]

Economic modernists among the New Dealers were also well represented in homegrown thinking and texts, well before John Maynard Keynes's influence crossed the Atlantic. Like the legal realists, as Laura Kalman has written, they saw economics "replete with meaningless abstractions." They revered Thorstein Veblen, a more sardonic iconoclast even than Holmes, who ridiculed classical economics' presumptions to have evolved itself as a science, as "a system of economic taxonomy." If they were arguably not original economic thinkers on the order of Keynes, they nevertheless were effective in making interpretive and applied connections between economics and law, and politics and government, that exceeded the powers of mere scholars.[13]

Thurman Arnold and William O. Douglas, who landed together by separate paths at Yale Law School with their good friend Jerome Frank, joined him there in bridging the distance between law and economics in their writing, on their way to putting their ideas to work in Washington. Like Frank, they were rooted far from East Coast elite circles. Both were sons of the West, Arnold boisterous and hard-drinking, Douglas a handsome, rugged outdoorsman and mischief maker. They were ribald, storytelling humorists and cut-ups; sardonic enemies of pretension and form.[14]

One night in New Haven in the early 1930s, Douglas and Arnold extended an "exciting" afternoon conversation about the law through a long cocktail hour in several venues, ambling home to Arnold's house an hour after he and his wife Frances had asked guests to dinner. "The moon was high and the evening air crisp," Douglas recalled. Arnold, powered by several hours of bourbon, paused near his front door and remarked, "'An ideal night to see the mortgage on my house.' Pointing to the sky, he outlined the mortgage—its size, its thickness, its durability." As he mounted his porch steps, Frances Arnold (Myrna Loy in "The Thin Man" to her husband's William Powell) appeared at the door; unamused, she threw Arnold bodily down the steps, crying, "And I'll do the same to you, Bill Douglas." "We must find more friendly people," said Douglas. "Friendly attitudes—that's the thing this city needs," Arnold replied; "Come with me." So Arnold drove his car down the sidewalk "from house to house, announcing as [each] host answered the door that he headed a good-will mission aimed at generating a more friendly attitude among the people of New Haven." This was all in the spirit of fun and seems not to have interfered with business or duty. "Thurman drunk," my father and Arnold's other friends liked to say, "was twice as effective in the court-room as any other lawyer sober."[15]

In *The Folklore of Capitalism* (1937) Arnold attributed "the complete failure of the language of law and economics" to its reflection of synthetic "creeds" based on abstractions and designed to paper over "current conflicting ideals and phobias." Institutional creeds and folklore of some sort, Arnold suggested, were inevitable and even necessary. Indeed, "every governmental creed must represent all the contradictory ideals of a people if it is to be accepted by them." But such a belief system had, at least, to be connected to reality.

Arnold drew vivid analogies: modern government called for distinguishing between pragmatic fact (considered against the backdrop of real social conditions) and doctrine, much as an understanding of modern language called for an understanding of "how it is spoken." (Arnold cited his good friend H. L. Mencken's *The American Language* as "a far greater contribution to the study of political institutions in America than Mencken himself realized when he wrote it.") Technocracy was no solution, he warned. "The difficulties of the engineer in government were illustrated by the career of [Herbert] Hoover. . . . It was his sincerity that wrecked his Administration. In the same way, a technical training in the psychology of sex is not particularly good preparation for a romantic lover."[16]

Arnold had been "a great teacher," Abe Fortas (another Yale Law School colleague in the years before they all moved to Washington) remembered long afterward, "in the sense in which a tornado, sweeping away shabbiness and decay, may be an instrument of urban renewal." He was a force to be reckoned with. As assistant attorney general for antitrust in the first phases of industrial mobilization for World War II, Arnold indicted defense contractors for antitrust violations "like a poker player putting down one ace after another," my father wrote in 1951. Arnold's point then, as in his Yale Law School faculty days, was pragmatic, not doctrinaire. Against business and military leaders' pleas for suspension of the antitrust laws "for the duration, Arnold argued that indictment and trial for such violations was the most efficient way to spur big business into speedier defense production."[17]

. . .

Arnold wrote with wry wit, Douglas with a prosecutor's measured intensity, and he was right for the part. "He looked like a Remington cowboy; a man of leather and rawhide tough," wrote Douglas's onetime law student Ernest Cuneo of his first classroom encounter with the professor:

> He was bursting with energy. He sat down, but he couldn't sit still . . . I noted that he was both quick and fast. There is a difference; in football [which Cuneo played for Columbia and then professionally] it is more important to be quick than to be fast. Quick means to get up momentum instantly, fast means to keep it going. The thing I remembered most were his eyes. His blue eyes, under the sandy-red thatch of the tassel which fell over his forehead were the distended, round eyes of a glaring eagle. . . .
>
> He was all over the room, cracking out his precedents and questions as fast as we could write, driving, driving, driving, driving us as he drove himself.

Fresh from law school, Cuneo became legal assistant to New York City's most notable politician and political street-fighter. "Of all the gunslingers I've ever seen, there are only two . . . who were dead shots and shot to kill," he recalled. "One was Douglas, the other was La Guardia."[18]

Douglas was never shy about getting on up the greasy pole, generating bidding wars for his inspired teaching and hard research into Depression-era corporate failure among Columbia, Yale, and the University of Chicago. He was similarly deft in advancing his career in Washington. When Roosevelt made him chairman of the SEC in 1937, Douglas, a youthful thirty-eight, switched gears and pulled a cagey Mark Twain act with reporters:

> As to . . . what kind of a bird I am, to tell you the truth, I think that I am really a pretty conservative sort of a fellow from the old school. . . . I think that from the point of view of investors the one safe, controlling . . . stand should be conservative standards of finance—no monkey business. I am the kind of conservative who can't get away from the idea that simple honesty ought to prevail in the financial world.

Douglas's alternative voice, that of the "driving" persona that Cuneo encountered in the classroom, is heard in his speeches and essays of the period. The unregulated barons of "predatory finance," he wrote, collectively divorced from social responsibility, are the chief agents through which our economic and financial blunders accumulate until the next blood-letting process. This is called a crisis. But it is nothing more than the rhythmic breaking out of the pent-up forces of abuse, mismanagement and maldistribution of economic effort and income.[19]

Douglas led the legal realists in focusing on the grit of *function* over the claim of principle, or *structure*. In the spirit of Holmes dissenting from the Supreme Court's enfranchisement of the corporation's "liberty of contract" in the 1905 *Lochner* decision, he charged in 1929 that the corporation was "not a thing. It is a method. It defies definition when removed from the background of the purpose attempted to be accomplished and the manner of accomplishing it." To his admirers his maintenance of such attitudes together with leadership of securities industry reform made Douglas the quintessential "fighting liberal." Douglas's "pragmatic idealism . . . fuses the great traditions of legal philosophy and old-fashioned populism with plain, tough know-how," my father wrote in the *Nation* in 1941.[20]

Douglas deployed his own barbed humor in real-world interactions as well as among intimates. His letters are laced with wicked anecdotes and deadpan wisecracks. A typical aside, in a note to my father, refers to his Court rival Felix Frankfurter as "our favorite author of dull literature." In the process of forcing a reorganization of the New York Stock Exchange in 1937, Douglas received a visit from a "smooth, suave and severe" official Wall Street emissary who told him,

> "Now that you are going to take over the Exchange, perhaps you'll need some technical advice. It's not self-operating. It needs manpower and brains. Perhaps I can help you."
> I remained silent for a while, pretending to be deep in thought. Finally I said, "There is one thing you can do for me. Tell me where you keep the paper and the pencils."
> "The message was clear. We meant business."[21]

Idealistic, theoretical, analytical, reform-minded (and ambitious), Douglas— iconoclastic law professor as "Remington cowboy"—was also practical and profane enough to fit in smoothly in Washington, and make a number of politicians comfortable. (In a handwritten note to Cuneo he recalled his late colleague Justice Frank Murphy, a devout Catholic who "never drank. Promised his mother." Douglas wrote: "One Sunday morning Frank and Joe Kennedy went to St. Patrick's in NYC for mass. They mounted the steps and were almost in the doorway when Joe said to Frank, "Frank, are you still sleeping with Mrs. Malone[?]" Frank was horrified. As he told me the story Frank said, "Can you imagine that? We were almost inside the holy place when Joe started talking about fucking!!") His sly wit and winning style in private caused FDR to single him out as a personal favorite.[22]

When sharp stock market declines signaled the onset of the Roosevelt Recession in the fall of 1937, an initial administration response was to focus for causes elsewhere than on its own budget-balancing moves that year, or on the impact of the new Social Security withholding taxes, pulling down consumer spending power. My father, coming into these men's circle at just that moment, described the time years later as "the resumption of the Hoover Depression under New Deal auspices. The economy stopped. . . . There was no investment. . . . We didn't know what we were doing." The president called his SEC chairman. Douglas's account:

"What about this market?" he asked.
"Markets are two-way streets, I replied.
"But this one is going down as a result of a conspiracy."
"Whose conspiracy?"
"Business and Wall Street against yours truly."
"Mr. President," I replied, "You are dead wrong. The market is going down because you cut spending."

The diagnosis was more complex, and the administration's Keynesian spending and Brandeisian trust-busting prescriptions for it had limited effect until war mobilization put the economy back into high gear. But for all his weaknesses as a coherent economic policy thinker, one of Roosevelt's greatest strengths was his ability to dramatize complex issues so that people could understand them. As in his dialogue with FDR, Douglas shared that gift. His unique blend of characteristics made him for a number of years the most influential figure in the lives of a number of New Dealers who sought a legitimate heir to Roosevelt, my father among the several of them most active on his behalf. (Chapter 4 is an account of how close Douglas himself came to achieving the presidency.)[23]

. . .

A third project linked these men. Wrote Thurman Arnold in 1941,

For the past twenty years the economy of the South and West has been developing along colonial lines. The industrial East has been the Mother Country. . . . The colonies have furnished the Mother Country with raw material. The Mother Country has been exploiting the colonies by selling them manufactured necessities at artificially controlled prices.[24]

Conversely, the barons of the old Democratic South (and industrialists of the New South) were Roosevelt's allies of convenience in Congress and in assuring national election victories. Convenience turned increasingly to tension and grievance as New Deal emergency relief brought a measure of recovery from the Depression and the Roosevelt administration began to advance its more systemic reform agenda. Increasingly New Deal relief agencies like the WPA, and landmark reform legislation like that establishing social security and the minimum wage, went up against the Southern establishment's control of cheap, racially segregated labor markets. "Georgia and the lower South may just as well face facts," Roosevelt protested in a speech at Gainesville in 1938: "The purchasing power of . . . millions . . . in this whole area is far too low." He lectured that the sooner the Southern standard of living rose, the sooner controversial New Deal pump-priming relief agencies could be closed down.

But again and again he paid the price of the South's veto power in his coalition. His administration accepted heavy compromises governing the reach of New Deal programs and laws in order for them to be operative at all, agreeing to the exclusion of vast categories of the workforce, especially farm and domestic labor, from their reach. Thus in 1938, at the moment of the last New Deal domestic legislative victory of note, the administration settled for the establishment of a minimum wage at twenty-five cents an hour instead of forty cents (in a forty-four-hour week instead of a forty-hour one), yielding as well to exclusions of the categories of the workforce the South wanted out. Even then, only twenty-two southerners voted to unlock the bill from the House Rules Committee and to pass it; Sam Rayburn and Lyndon Johnson were two of them.

On other fronts, where they had leverage, Roosevelt and the New Dealers of whom we're speaking challenged the South's power structure and its paternalistic economic rules. Thus, as with the TVA and other public power initiatives modeled on it, they engineered jump-start development of the backward portions of the nation through the breakup of private cartels, regulation of powerful industries, vast electrification and dam construction projects, investment in fresh entrepreneurship, and eased credit policies.[25]

FDR was "a New Yorker and an Easterner. But one of the first tasks which he set himself was the raising up of the South, economic problem number one," said Senator Lyndon Johnson of Texas in a speech at the Roosevelt Museum at Hyde Park in 1959. "He was an Easterner and a New Yorker but the second important task he set himself was to bring to the West the electric power, the rural electrification and the water which it needed to grow. And the West and the South will forever love him."[26]

This targeted concentration of the New Deal's public policy and political interests, and the fact that only heavy governmental artillery could advance them, was what bound many of the administration's leading policy makers, including Ickes, Eccles, Hopkins, Corcoran, Cohen, Douglas, Fortas, Arnold, and Frank, to freethinking, even radical politicians from regions far from the Northeast like George Norris of Nebraska, Hugo Black of Alabama, Rayburn and Johnson of Texas, Claude Pepper of Florida, Lister Hill of Alabama, Robert La Follette of Wisconsin, and Burton Wheeler of Montana. From collaboration between those two groups flowed more opportunistic ones with developers, especially Henry J. Kaiser in the

Pacific Northwest and Johnson's friends Herman and George Brown of Brown and Root in Texas. Those alliances triggered the construction projects that brought electricity and modernity to the South and West and freed them from the finance capitalists of New York, Philadelphia, and Chicago. Teaming up with wildcatters like Sid Richardson of Texas, they fed the new, independent oil industry, challenging the "majors": the established oil interests controlled by the Rockefellers and Pews of the Northeast. Working in tight knit with each other, armed with hard-edged, insider knowledge of what it was they were reforming, they were effective in action—they made the New Deal happen.

. . .

The New Dealers themselves, and scholars in later years, have commented on another defining dynamic within their ranks. Many, led and typified by Corcoran and Cohen, were born to Irish or Jewish immigrant families, invading the WASP halls of power in Washington for the first time in force, like a flying wedge. There were constraints and provisos, of course. For many of them, Ivy League or comparable credentials were crucial to their ability to make their way. Frankfurter spoke to his Harvard Law School protégé Corcoran early on about the flow of alcohol in Washington; Corcoran in turn warned fellow Irish American recruits to the New Deal against giving any rise to talk of the Irish and booze. There were concerns all around about how many Jews could be named to top jobs or clustered in one government agency before dangerous antisemitic reactions kicked in. Jews in top-ranking positions in the New Deal, especially Jerome Frank and Henry Morgenthau, themselves felt the need for caution on this score.[27]

Irish, Jewish, or simply from low rungs on the class ladder like Douglas and Harry Hopkins, many of the New Dealers stood out for their "relative social marginality." Indeed, "If non-WASP lawyers were professionally qualified and properly 'WASP' in their behavior," one scholar observed, they could—like Jerome Frank chairing the SEC and Abe Fortas as the youthful undersecretary of the interior—"achieve prominent positions hitherto reserved for WASPs."[28]

Fortas was deferential, careful, recognized for a precocious ability at the tactful brokering of disputes before he was twenty-five. He was, in one contemporary's description, also "elfin, . . . sly and cute," "puckish" and seductive. He played jazz and classical violin and performed in small and large musical groups. He comes across as something of a stylish Jewish prince despite a modest upbringing in Memphis. (Ironically, two leading New Dealers of white Anglo-Saxon Protestant descent, Douglas and Arnold, Ivy League law professors by pedigree, became known as unmannerly in their personal lives, though in Douglas's case not until his first divorce, in 1949.) But whatever their respective social ambitions, these New Dealers did in fact rewrite the rules for admission to American elite circles.[29]

Other scholars note the arrival in power of "the knowledge community," the professors of law and economics and other social sciences. In previous eras such professionally established intelligentsia figures rarely left the vicinity of academe—except, as Henry Adams did (to the more ambitious Oliver Wendell Holmes's disgust), to build a home facing the White House where he set up as a disaffected "critic" and intellectual gadfly to a ruling class and public that wouldn't particularly listen. Woodrow Wilson had his adviser Col. Edward House assemble such a group to plan for the post–World War I era, but it was shadowy and its members became deeply disillusioned at the Paris Peace Conference. The idea of harnessing reform-minded academic and policy expertise in the president's service faded away for more than a decade. These New Deal lawyers-as-experts and "knowledge professionals," in one characterization, "created, and by their systematic efforts, legitimated, various policy options from which the [Roosevelt] Administration could choose." To the point, they were pioneers in the art of doing so.[30]

The losers were the regular Democratic Party politicians interested in patronage. Their leader in Roosevelt's entourage, James Farley, remembered Corcoran, and what he and his team wrought, in his memoirs this way: "I was never certain whether the chubby White House confidant was working for the President or for himself; I was quite certain he was not too concerned about the Democratic Party."[31]

. . .

A final theme of scholarship about the New Dealers comes under the headings "moral relativism" or even "power corrupts . . ."

The moral relativism issue arose in part from the legal realists' disdain for abstraction: their insistence on the primacy of experience over moral absolutes, results over process. In the New Deal the legal realists won their argument that judges engaged in "manipulation of 'paper' rules of law to produce desired results," rather than interpreting a quasi-divine Constitution impartially, and that putative jurisprudential absolutes were merely relative. Sanctified but debatable "rules" could, the realists demonstrated, be revised and reformed.[32]

This view, amounting to a rejection of the concept of a higher law, drew heavy fire as fascism moved across Europe. The legal realists, after all, drew inspiration from Holmes, who with pragmatists like William James saw the world of their youth shattered by the Civil War. Seeking a livable compromise between the human animal and ideologies, their view, as Louis Menand has written, was that "beliefs . . . are just bets on the future." Holmes, James, and their friends "wished to bring ideas and principles and beliefs down to a human level because they wished to avoid the violence they saw hidden in abstractions." There was no such supple escape from Hitler's violence by the end of the 1930s. [33]

At that point the legal realists were under heavy attack for cynicism and relativism, from Catholic thinkers among others. A legal theologian wrote in 1942, "If man is only an animal, [legal] Realism is correct, Holmes was correct, Hitler is correct." Leaders among the realists, especially Jerome Frank and Thurman Arnold, reflected on the relation of ethics to jurisprudence from their new perspectives on the circuit courts of appeals in the 1940s. In his *Fate and Freedom* (1945) Frank called for (as Arnold, reviewing it, put it) "a social church" based on free will. Arnold's quarrel with that concept was that it was perhaps too accepting of economic concentration—insufficiently crusading. In retrospect, he wrote on the occasion of Frank's death in 1957, legal realism's "liberating values" in the pit of the economic and governmental paralysis of the early 1930s were considerable. But the doctrine was "not a sustaining food for a stable civilization" in good times. That is, legal realism was deficient in the "folklore," the mystique (specifically, the ideal of "rule of law above men") that, Arnold held, was "the cement which holds a free society together."[34]

Contemporary liberal scholars have updated this critique, connecting the theme of judicial agnosticism back to Holmes, and forward to the dull, impersonal machinery of the post–New Deal bureaucratic state. There, in what Theodore J. Lowi calls "a nightmare of administrative boredom," endless bargains are struck between regulatory agencies and interest groups. The "problem of power" has been delegated to these agencies; pluralism is served: but this is "policy without law"; a government of "no substance. Neither is there procedure. There is only process." Others, with Lowi, find a similarly alienating effect accumulating from the very adroitness of the New Deal's enactment of Keynesian economic thinking. "Where earlier reformers had sought economic arrangements that would cultivate citizens of a certain kind," wrote Michael Sandel, the Keynesian doctrine permitted vacating ideology and controversy in favor of a government by technocrats and experts equipped to "accept existing consumer preferences and to regulate the economy by manipulating aggregate demand." Leaping ahead, Sandel cites John F. Kennedy, setting the latter-day pragmatic tone in 1962:

> Most of us are conditioned for many years to have a political viewpoint, Republican or Democratic—liberal, conservative moderate. The fact of the matter is that most of the problems . . . that we now face are technical problems, are administrative problems. They are very sophisticated judgments which do not lend themselves to the great sort of "passionate movements" which have stirred this country so often in the past.[35]

Holmes, with whom the modern jurisprudential posture began, had of course been more than agnostic and skeptical in making the case for judicial neutrality. Again and again he expressed himself with mordant cynicism as well. "I always say . . . that if my fellow citizens want to go to Hell I will help them," he wrote Harold Laski in 1920. "It's my job." Then, as noted in the previous chapter, in the decades that followed the New Deal a significant number of the men whose pragmatism looked back to Holmes, and who rewrote the laws and the rules in the 1930s, were seen to have a tendency themselves to operate as if they were above them in private financial dealings that blurred with their public roles, and in other respects. Among them were Corcoran, James Landis, Edward Prichard, Abe Fortas, William O. Douglas, Clark Clifford, and Lyndon Johnson. My father had a touch of this strain. The scholarship looks for explanations to the scars of economic insecurity instilled by what the Depression did to their families and to them, and also to "the sense of being 'special' . . . a 'chosen' group." The young New Dealers, especially the lawyers, were "the 'best and brightest' of their era," notes G. Edward White,

> chosen by their age, their education, their talent, and their participation in a transformative experience. . . . For accomplished persons of the New Deal legal generation, power came so rapidly, policies changed so fast, and the old guidelines of the moribund market capitalist order collapsed so suddenly, that law, politics, ambition, and self-esteem all became blurred together, *and the only restraints on one of the chosen group were seen to be the limits of his intelligence and his acumen.* From the insight that the nation was ripe to be directed along different paths, and that a new class of persons was eligible to be the directors, it was perhaps a small step to the perception that this class of persons was not subject to the same rules as less specially favored mortals (emphasis added).[36]

This comes very close, especially the nuance about the singular limit they *did* feel. But it omits, I think, one elusive element, which I sensed first as a boy in absorbing New Deal lore from my father and his friends. That is what we might call the shared culture of highly sophisticated, inside operations; the mystique of comrades' closely held, inner-group power, exercised in concert with each other.

These princes of the New Deal came of age in a charged, combative environment where, for the initiated, conscience takes a back seat to the sheer *skill* with which power is understood and managed and action undertaken, now indirectly, now directly. Some of them, later in life, went over the top. Corcoran in his "I am a Pirate King" mode wrote in the twilight of his life, "As an operator with the friendly CIA, I've rented an aircraft carrier from the U.S. Navy, purchased an embassy for one foreign state, taken away one from a rival, and watched revolutions begin." But, in their own minds and, in fact, in Roosevelt's service, they fought fire as no one since Lincoln and his generals had. This was an environment that opened to a select few the inner workings of power, and not simply contact with its effects. It bred in them a hands-on, rough-and-ready confidence about *the way the world works*. In this these men operated as a mutually supportive cadre, allowing for each other's bothersome quirks, leaping to each other's cause at various moments, turning the wheels.[37]

⇶ 4 ⇷

The Fight for the
Rooseveltian Succession

"DOUGLAS'S ARMY"

Who was to be Franklin Roosevelt's designated political legatee? Before 1940 Vice President John Nance Garner and cabinet members Harry Hopkins, James Farley, Cordell Hull, and Henry Wallace all coveted the honor. Succeeding to the vice presidency in 1941, it was Wallace's to lose, which he did.

There is little evidence that Roosevelt accepted and understood in the late spring of 1944 how fast his death was approaching, but White House visitors and those close to him were alarmed by his deterioration. And so the fight for the 1944 Democratic vice presidential nomination became a ferocious struggle for the Roosevelt inheritance, and for the question whether the New Deal would survive FDR or whether the Democratic Party would settle back to its old organizational roots.

Roosevelt's own preferred choice was a wild card. He had sent William Orville Douglas to the Supreme Court in 1939 at the age of forty, thought of him as his friend, and, in 1944, as the most attractive candidate to be his fourth running mate and deputy. In pressing Douglas on an inner circle of Democratic Party leaders in 1944, Roosevelt remarked suggestively that his protégé "had practical experience from the backwoods of the Northwest as a logger; . . . looked and acted on occasions like a Boy Scout, and . . . played an interesting game of poker."[1]

Douglas was the man of power for whose advancement these House of Roosevelt partners, my father prominent among them in this set piece, worked most singularly and hardest. (On balance their efforts on behalf of Lyndon Johnson come in second.) Incisive, difficult, and elusive, Douglas is one of the most mysterious figures in recent American history. The tale of

how close he came to the presidency of the United States affords a backstage
view of this Rooseveltian enterprise as it prepared for Roosevelt's disappearance from the scene—of history up for grabs, and daring bids for it.
The might-have-beens that attach to the episode include the possibility of
an entirely other history of the nuclear age, and of the course of postwar
American Asian policy.

My father's involvement at the center of this episode is the most documented of his political operations. For me it became a side study of him in
action. And of the world as it was when he operated full-throttle in it. So I
pause on the story, a conjunction of archival record and family lore, for
what it's worth. Because Douglas himself spent most of the key weeks in
seclusion, without a telephone, and because, in any event, political communication relied so much more on mail than it did after long-distance
phoning became commonplace, letters will tell a good part of the tale.

. . .

Born in rural Minnesota of rugged Scots stock, Douglas grew up in Yakima,
Washington. He was all his life a passionate outdoorsman of the Northwest
(he kept getaway retreats in later life in Oregon and then in Washington
State), an environmentalist and explorer of the "Third World" before such
phrasing came into vogue. Thus he loomed in the years when he was
deemed presidential timber not only as a cerebral New Dealer and favorite
of FDR's but as a vigorous son of the frontier who annually renewed his
connection to its natural beauty and rough-hewn common folk.

Douglas's later fame was as one of the century's preeminent Supreme
Court civil libertarians. He made his name first at the SEC in the 1930s in
the hard-boiled task of regulating Wall Street once and for all. He turned
his cold anger not only on exploitation of boom-bust cycles by "predatory
interests," but on the mandarins of academic economics who, by "en-
dow[ing] cycles and crises thus created with natural attributes," had in effect
"cleverly washed the hands of high finance and excused it from social
responsibility."[2]

Douglas knew whereof he spoke. He had a promising start at the Wall
Street firm known today as Cravath, Swaine and Moore in the 1920s
(John J. McCloy occupied the cubicle next to his) before joining the Columbia Law School faculty, and then Yale's. He left for Washington, D.C.,
never to return, in 1934 and became chairman of the SEC in 1937.[3]

When Franklin Roosevelt's enemies denounced him as "a traitor to his
class," Douglas was perhaps more than any other presidential agent the one
who perpetrated the treason: it was his initiative that sent Richard Whitney,
the influential former president of the New York Stock Exchange—like
FDR, an alumnus of Groton and Harvard—to jail for embezzlement. ("Dick
Whitney," Roosevelt said over and over when Douglas first brought him
news of the matter, "I can't believe it.") In a farewell to some of his staff
after Roosevelt appointed him to the Supreme Court, Douglas remarked,

"I shot those fellows down, but there's going to be a war. You guys hold the fort."[4]

At the SEC, and later on the Court, Douglas become one of a small circle of friends with whom the president relaxed over cards and cocktails. Roosevelt "maintained that I made the best dry martinis of anyone in town," Douglas recalled. "He liked them dry—six to one—and very cold, with lemon peel." His sardonic turn of mind and taste for earthy stories helped him to achieve a relaxed rapport with Roosevelt, which among the important New Dealers rivaled, after 1941, only that of Harry Hopkins, resident in the White House. "I suppose you've got another of your untellable stories tonight," the president would say to Douglas, who would reply, "I don't want to pollute your ears with it, Mr. President." "Oh, come on, pollute me," FDR would counter. Douglas was one hard-edged liberal reformer who could make the president laugh.[5]

Having gone to the Court at forty, restlessness was inevitable. Roosevelt talked to Douglas in 1941 and subsequently about taking special wartime assignments (such executive-branch assignments for sitting justices had precedent), or leaving the Court to coordinate war mobilization. (FDR later induced Justice James F. Byrnes to do just that, whereupon Byrnes's all-but-official title, upstaging the wobbly Vice President Wallace, became "Assistant President.")[6]

Along with his intellectual acuity, effectiveness, and wit, Douglas had another side: he could be cold and punishing, withdrawn and seemingly cavalier about others and about fate. His father, a Presbyterian minister of modest means, died when he was five and his mother, who nursed him through a severe childhood illness, became an enormous figure in his life, from whom he then felt compelled to distance himself. These experiences left him conflicted about dependency and human relations and haunted by psychosomatic illnesses and overpowering fears. In his thirties, while teaching at Yale, these sources of distress led him to psychoanalysis. (A coincidence: his analyst, George Draper, was also an epidemiologist with a special interest in polio who helped attend Roosevelt medically during his bout with that disease in the 1920s.)[7]

Like Theodore Roosevelt, Douglas's willpower in overcoming adversity was enormous, but it did not help him out of loneliness. He married four women and divorced three. "He is a great man," the second of those wives told one of Douglas's biographers, "but an unhappy one."[8]

. . .

But that was later. In 1940 Franklin Roosevelt tested the idea of taking Douglas as his vice presidential running mate, and in 1944 made a direct move for him. There was talk of Douglas as the 1944 Democratic presidential nominee if Roosevelt decided not to run. In 1948, when Harry Truman in his unpopularity appeared likely to be dumped by his party, Douglas was one of two most-mentioned alternative Democratic presidential candidates. (The other, who had not yet decided his party affiliation, was General Dwight Eisenhower, and there was much talk as well of a "dream ticket" of Ike and Douglas.) Then he became Truman's own first choice as his running mate.[9]

Douglas's supporters through those eight years of flirtation with fate were a diverse mix. They numbered among them some of the more radical New Dealers, some party regulars looking for continuity of the New Deal coalition, influential current or former Wall Street figures, beginning with James Forrestal, with whom Douglas had collaborated on securities industry reform, and Joseph P. Kennedy, for whom Douglas initially worked at the SEC. (Increasingly reactionary in his own views, Kennedy persisted in viewing Douglas as an able, deserving protégé, someone the old pirate could do business with as he'd once done business with Roosevelt.)[10]

Corcoran was, as usual, the hub of the Douglas group (despite some rivalry between the two before 1940), whose members enjoyed each other socially as well as politically. Mutual appreciation within it might be ironic (Forrestal on Douglas to my father: "The Great Voice and Jurist of the Northwest is back in town and looks fine") or deeply in earnest. Douglas, claimed my father in the *Nation* in 1941, was "a new kind of reformer, . . . for reform because he is so practical"; because only "drastic reforms [will] revitalize" the American system.[11]

Douglas himself brought his wry humor to his friendships. On the road in Texas for a speech in 1941 he found Lyndon Johnson's campaign for a special election to the Senate whirling by and presented himself deadpan as just another constituent summoned to the platform to meet the candidate. "Where in hell did you come from?" asked Johnson, on double take and only after the ritual howdy and shake. "Step aside and wait for me— you're the man I want to see." Talking with Forrestal about wartime proliferation of memos and paperwork, Douglas suggested one day at lunch, "Why don't you write a two-page memo and put in between the two sheets a half-dozen pages of the same size containing excerpts from the *Odyssey* or *Iliad*?" Forrestal did so and told Douglas later that "the whole thing came back initialed by everyone, including George Marshall."[12]

In May 1943 my parents named my brother Bill after Douglas, who wrote, "Three cheers and hurrah for the young Marine! . . . Tell him that before he arrives at the age of eighteen, I have a good barroom song I would like to teach him." That fall, on assignment for *Life* and *Fortune*, my father toured the West and with my mother visited Douglas in the Oregon mountains. My mother remembered that their rented car ran off the road as they neared Douglas's cabin, "and Bill sort of showed up through the trees, and whistled." Three men, probably "old woodsmen pals," appeared from the forest "and picked the car up and put it back on the road." My father wrote Forrestal,

Babs and I have just returned from God's self-confessed country. We
. . . [slept] in our underwear for five days at Douglas' mountain sa-
loon—where they have a caste system: if you need water in your liquor
you're the kind of guy [gentleman liberal publisher] Marshall Field is
for.[13]

The two Douglas supporters who worked hardest to replace Vice President
Wallace with their man as Roosevelt's running mate in 1944 were Corcoran
and my father, functioning as a team. As early as January 1943 Wallace
himself recorded in his diary "the steady build-up going on for Bill Douglas.
Janeway of *TIME, LIFE, Fortune* is very active. Also Tommy Corcoran." Later
in the drama a weekly dispatch to London from the British Embassy in
Washington, probably drafted by Isaiah Berlin, reported that Douglas's key
supporters were Ickes, Corcoran, and "Eliot Janeway, a malicious and effective writer in [*sic*] *Fortune*," working to persuade Henry Luce to put his magazines behind the drive to make Douglas vice president.[14]

Douglas had several strong supporters among hard-bitten Democratic
Party regulars as well as in the New Deal ranks, but the most surprising, if
unwitting, agent of support for his political advancement in the 1940s became Henry Wallace. As secretary of agriculture before 1941, Wallace revealed the inconstancy and naïveté that would, down the road in 1948, lead
him into the hands of the communists and fellow travelers who controlled
his third-party candidacy for president. Wallace's undependable nature was
an issue of limited import while he served in the cabinet. But elected vice
president in 1940, as the onset of war raised the leadership stakes, and later
as anxiety about Roosevelt's health began to climb, the specter of Wallace
in the White House became ever more alarming to those who knew the
score. Douglas, by contrast, was a proven manager and strategist at the
SEC, a New Deal leader and native radical, but his own man, free of
Wallace's dreaminess and susceptibility.[15]

History is littered with what-ifs, but had Douglas become Roosevelt's
running mate at the Democratic National Convention in Chicago in July
1944, succeeding him upon his death the following April with almost four
years to govern, the course of history would almost certainly have been
different. In particular Douglas was a fierce critic of the decision to drop
the atomic bomb on Hiroshima and Nagasaki in 1945. (He said afterward
that he would have favored the "demonstration" option, dropping an
atomic bomb on an uninhabited island under Japanese control prior to
bombing a military or civilian target.) Additionally he favored prompt recognition of the Chinese Communist regime in the late 1940s. He argued
that Roosevelt (who ended a decade and a half of American nonrecognition
of the Soviet Union in 1933) would have so acted—and in the acting
avoided the march of history that led the United States into Vietnam.[16]

As a firm anti-Communist liberal, Douglas would probably have wound up with foreign policies similar to other Truman administration initiatives (especially the Marshall Plan and subsequent foreign aid policies), possibly with less military emphasis than they came to have. But his alliances to the center of the political spectrum (such as with Forrestal, Ferdinand Eberstadt, and others of prestige from the business world), his economic sophistication, and his executive branch experience would have enabled him to proceed more assuredly in domestic policy than did Harry Truman, and to avoid some of the mishaps that shaped the opening of the Cold War and nuclear eras abroad. For while a postwar pendulum swing against the Democrats was inevitable, Truman's poor performance in his first years as president fed the Republican congressional sweep of 1946 and the right-wing hysteria that would become infamous as McCarthyism.[17]

. . .

It was only because the war was still raging in mid-1944 (but, with the invasion of Normandy on June 6, going well) that the question of Roosevelt running for a fourth term was easily answered. But because his physical decline was the talk of the political circuit, because it was assumed that the war might drag on for several years, because tensions in the wartime alliance with the Soviet Union were on the rise, because Wallace (chosen as a mid-westerner in 1940 largely for geographical reasons) had demonstrated his weaknesses to key New Dealers as well as to party regulars and conservatives, the matter of the vice presidency was crucial.

Maneuvers over the 1944 Democratic vice presidential nomination were that much more out of the ordinary because of Roosevelt's blend of direction and indirection in dumping Wallace and in indicating his preference for a replacement. Behind his shadow play, which featured letters to key players that did not mean what they seemed to say, FDR was managing rising tension among important forces in his coalition. These included labor, its muscle strengthened by the rapid spread of industrial unionization and its role in the war effort; the ever more important northern urban black vote; and, in growing reaction to these two new forces, the old-line Democratic South.

A measure of the stakes was that before the episode played out Roosevelt had double-crossed two of his most abiding supporters and allies, Wallace (labor's candidate and that of many New Dealers) and "Assistant President" Jimmy Byrnes of South Carolina (the conservatives' candidate). But this was nothing personal ("After all, Jimmy, you are close to me personally, and Henry is close to me," Roosevelt told Byrnes sweetly on the eve of the convention; "I hardly know Truman. Douglas is a poker partner.") And the ranks that Byrnes and Wallace represented came away from the convention feeling they'd each won a major victory: conservatives in the dumping of Wallace, liberals in the humiliation of Byrnes.[18]

Adding to the shadow play atmosphere was Douglas's extreme caution about appearing to seek the nomination as a sitting Supreme Court justice. The "Roosevelt Court" itself had begun to divide along ideological and personal lines, with Douglas (to the left) and his onetime mentor, Justice Felix Frankfurter (to the right) each bitterly accusing the other of political machinations. This made Douglas twice shy about an open move for the vice presidency. Against that inhibition, a stronger presidential signal, or a deadlocked convention breaking toward Douglas, would probably have made him the choice, and the next president.[19]

Roosevelt was not only aware of the rising concern about Henry Wallace as his running mate, he fed it, dispatching his vice president on a long trip to the Far East in the spring of 1944 that was sure to advance talk of his dispensability. (Wallace questioned the value of the trip, prompting the president to reply, "Oh, you must go. I think you ought to see a lot of Siberia.") When Roosevelt's chief labor ally, Phil Murray of the CIO, called at the White House to talk up Wallace, the president "puffed at a cigarette and looked at the ceiling." Then, in a reference to Wallace's embarrassment in the 1940 campaign over involvement with a guru mystic, Roosevelt remarked, "Oh, you are talking about the Yogi Man."[20]

But Roosevelt was aware of Wallace's symbolic and even passionate following among liberals and the more important fact that he was labor's bargaining chip in the game. So the president gave his vice president lip service in the form of a letter ("I personally would vote for his renomination if I were a delegate to the convention")—but made plain he would not "dictate" that the convention do so.[21]

To Interior Secretary Ickes Roosevelt conveyed his concerns about Wallace and interest in Douglas. (Ickes disliked Wallace; wickedly, FDR said he planned to make his vice president ambassador to China, "where he would fit in well.") Roosevelt encouraged the active aspirations of others, especially the able Jimmy Byrnes. Thus Byrnes on the right and Wallace on the left stood to cancel each other out. That gave Roosevelt room to maneuver.[22]

Primaries were not a factor; all of this unfolded in the two weeks before the 1944 Democratic National Convention in Chicago in mid-July. But the labors on Douglas's behalf had been evident for months. In September 1943 Henry Wallace entered another diary note on the subject:

Justice [Robert] Jackson said that the Chief Justice [Harlan Stone] was deeply concerned about the way in which Bill Douglas was running for President or Vice President. [Justice Frank] Murphy told Bob Jackson that Tommy Corcoran was in Douglas' office very frequently. Eliot Janeway of the *TIME, Fortune* crowd is working with Corcoran in managing Douglas' campaign. Bob says that Joe Kennedy is also very active.[23]

On July 11, 1944, six days before the Democratic National Convention opened, Roosevelt gathered the managers of the Democratic Party machinery together with a cluster of big-city bosses for dinner at the White House to review the vice presidential bidding. They discussed the obvious candidates: Jimmy Byrnes, Senate Majority Leader Alben Barkley of Kentucky and Speaker Sam Rayburn. The big-city party leaders considered the first two too Southern. Rayburn, a true New Dealer (he was Corcoran's alternative candidate, after Douglas), was occupied in a messy battle with the right wing of the Texas Democratic Party that had that state's delegation tied up in knots. Roosevelt then "spent some time extolling Douglas," according to one of the party regulars present. But with Democratic national chairman Robert Hannegan in the lead, most of these party regulars had begun to settle on one of their own as a compromise: Hannegan's fellow Missourian, Senator Harry Truman. Roosevelt said that "Douglas would have the greater public appeal," but supposedly acknowledged that Truman would make "you boys happy, and you are the ones I am counting on to win this election."[24]

As his own compromise the president wrote out in longhand a letter to Chairman Hannegan for the latter's use at the convention saying he'd be happy to run with one of two men.

For decades insider argument has raged over the riddle of the order of the two names the president put forth: Truman and Douglas or Douglas and Truman. Roosevelt's able secretary Grace Tully's version is that Douglas's name originally came first. But days later, she wrote in a memoir, Roosevelt traveled by train to the West Coast and paused in Chicago. Apparently calculating that Roosevelt was too weary and distracted to care what happened next, Hannegan came aboard, spoke with the president, and emerged insisting that the command was for a typed version of the letter with the order of the names reversed: Truman first, Douglas second. This is what Douglas and all his supporters went to their graves believing, and the matter became politically explosive at the convention. A new investigative biography of Douglas by Bruce Allen Murphy makes the case that Roosevelt wrote out Truman's name first, and reprints the (or a) handwritten note. But it is unpersuasive in arguing that Tommy Corcoran made the whole "Douglas first" version up and leaves the full and final truth of the affair still in question. In any event, the typed letter to Hannegan, postdated by a week to the Wednesday of convention week, went forth reading

July 19

Dear Bob,

You have written me about Harry Truman and Bill Douglas. I should of course be happy to run with either one of them and believe that either one of them would bring real strength to the ticket.

Always sincerely,
Franklin D. Roosevelt.

At the convention, Hannegan had his wife Irma carry the presidential letter in her purse by day and sleep with it under their hotel room mattress, until the moment he felt it would do Truman the most good.[25]

. . .

In such a chaotic situation, anything could happen, including a convention revolt one way or another. Byrnes's and Wallace's supporters were organized, but as Ed Pauley, a kingpin of the bosses' cabal for Truman recorded later, "the only organization that Douglas had at the convention was Eliot Janeway, who was then with *TIME* Magazine; George Killion, . . . who was working for [Interior Secretary Harold] Ickes . . . and Bob Kenny [attorney general of California]."[26]

Harold Ickes records in his diary that my father called him in Washington on July 15, the Saturday before the convention opened, to urge him to go to Chicago on Douglas's behalf, noting that "Tom Corcoran came in while I was talking to Janeway." Corcoran had become too controversial to operate openly in Chicago, so he worked by phone through his on-site collaborators, principally Ickes, my father, and Ernest Cuneo. Other overt and covert members of the Douglas camp at the convention included Attorney General Biddle, Senator Francis Maloney of Connecticut (a popular Senate insider and good friend of Douglas's since the latter's Yale Law School days), liberals in the West Coast delegations, and Lyndon Johnson's and my father's well-connected New York lawyer friend, Edwin Weisl. (Anxious and preoccupied with the slugfest between the Texas New Dealers and conservatives for control of the state Democratic Party, Johnson stayed in Texas but supported the choice of either Rayburn or Douglas.)[27]

Half the Douglas camp's strategy was to protect a sitting Supreme Court justice from charges of unseemly politicking by making plain that he was a draftee in an emergency and not an active candidate. As he was still young—forty-five in 1944—his supporters were also at pains to keep him a viable prospect for 1948. Douglas's personal strategy was to disappear to his remote cabin in Oregon, unreachable by phone.

Senator Maloney wrote the justice at his mountain retreat the day before the party regulars met at the White House to hear the president's case for Douglas. "The Janeways visited us over the week-end," he reported, and said my father persuaded him that Douglas's defensive strategy ought not to go so far as a statement that he would not run. "It is my feeling," wrote Maloney, "that if you are called upon to be a candidate"—drafted—"you can not . . . decline."[28]

"The situation created by Roosevelt having to drop Wallace," my father wrote Douglas the next day, means "he has to find a way to show that he is not going to play machine politics and that he stands 100 per cent for idealism." Attempting, like Senator Maloney, to ease Douglas toward acceptance of the effort on his behalf, he added, "I think it will be clear that, if this [a draft] happens to you, it is a sacrifice on your part."[29]

But three days later Douglas wrote the senator an extraordinary, if somewhat coy, disclaimer of interest in longhand. "My dear Frank," it began, "Yesterday I came down out of the mountains to discover that my name was being prominently and seriously mentioned as a candidate for Vice-President." Proclaiming his devotion to the Supreme Court and need for the Court to be above politics, Douglas deputized Maloney to represent his position at the convention:

If by any chance the nomination were tendered me, I would not accept it.

I do not know very much about the political situation. For some days I have enjoyed the solitude of my cabin in the Oregon mountains, occupying myself there with my family and with an accumulation of court work . . .

I am returning now to my cabin and will start tomorrow on a ten day pack trip into the high mountains relieved of the burden of the problem which confronted me when I came down. For your kindness in taking care of this somewhat delicate problem for me I will be deeply grateful.

Yours faithfully,
Wm. O. Douglas[30]

For all the order at his command, Roosevelt had created chaos. In Chicago personal contact and messages sent and delivered privately were everything.

Coordinating with Corcoran in Washington, Cuneo, my father, Senator Maloney, and the others maneuvered among bosses, brokers, delegates, and (great message senders) reporters, conveying word that Wallace was out, Byrnes a nonstarter, and Douglas the president's real choice—unless the bosses blocked him and put Truman across. One problem was that Democratic national chairman Hannegan was suppressing Roosevelt's letter to him about his running mate choices. He feared that the surfacing of Douglas's name on the document with FDR's signature under it would trigger a boom that would eclipse the bosses' man Truman. Corcoran and the others sought in vain a way to smoke out Hannegan about the presidential letter and its riddle of name order. "I don't know why none of us asked to see [Roosevelt's] original note," my father told Douglas biographer Bruce Allen Murphy in 1990. "We just didn't. You have to understand it wouldn't look good for us to be challenging the Democratic Party Chairman at the Convention on behalf of a Supreme Court Justice."[31]

In the next scene of the drama, Senator Maloney reached my father by phone from Jimmy Byrnes' hotel suite and reported the second hot piece of paper, Douglas's "would not accept" letter, just delivered by hand. "What do I do with it?" Maloney asked.

"Lose it," my father replied.

Maloney did show the letter to Jimmy Byrnes—who was bitter because Roosevelt first blessed his candidacy and then promiscuously scattered his blessings—to assure him that Douglas was being honestly represented as reluctant. But otherwise he kept Douglas's letter private.[32]

"[W]ith Eliot Janeway in my rooms on frequent occasions," Harold Ickes was witness to the wonders of Tommy Corcoran at work. "Tom got word to me that Bernie Baruch had lined up for Douglas" and that Baruch "had reached Jimmy Byrnes to try to persuade Jimmy to go in for Douglas."[33]

. . .

One of the bosses was operating on his own. According to Abe Fortas and my father, Mayor Ed Kelly of Chicago (a principal among the party regulars who met with Roosevelt at the White House on July 11) was in fact worried about "bossism" as a campaign issue for the Republicans. Previously sympathetic to Byrnes, practical before he was ideological, Kelly began to lean to Douglas. In this account New York lawyer Ed Weisl, who knew Kelly from his own days as a federal prosecutor in Chicago, persuaded the mayor to put the name of the undistinguished Senator Scott Lucas of Illinois in as a favorite son in order to encourage other states to play the same game, thereby tying up the convention. (Kelly first cleared the move with Roosevelt, who—still trying to outfox the other bosses by indirection—encouraged him.)[34]

My father liked to recall standing near Senator Lucas behind the convention podium while Mayor Kelly praised Illinois's "favorite son" with improvised words meant to damn the ethereal Henry Wallace. "Prairie statesman" Lucas, Kelly intoned, "belongs to no *thinking group!*" (Angry jeers from Wallace delegates.) My father claimed Lucas turned to him and whispered, "Jeez, the Boss is going all out for me!"[35]

. . .

A recurrent dilemma for Franklin Roosevelt's biographers and historians of the Roosevelt years is the question just how far to take the strain of ruthlessness so visible in one of history's great liberal reformers and humanitarians. It is the wise historian's mission, after all, to be judicious rather than accusatory or didactic. Thus, most of those who have written about the 1944 Democratic National Convention have held back from the conclusion that Roosevelt was doing his cold-blooded best to manipulate the players and the fateful game—even as they contribute evidence that this is precisely what he was up to.

Moreover, even some of the most sophisticated published accounts of the fateful Democratic National Convention of 1944 are influenced by the outcome, written as if Harry Truman's nomination was inevitable. Their premise is that Roosevelt decided on Truman before the convention and then set about getting the others out of the way.[36]

Firsthand accounts, including that by conservative California oilman Ed Pauley of Truman's camp, aren't so certain. Senator Maloney and my father wrote Douglas their versions, focusing on how close they came to achieving a stalemate as the basis for introducing Douglas's name; a stalemate they had evidence that Roosevelt wanted too.[37]

"It was a strange Convention, Bill, and one that would take a half day to explain," Maloney wrote Douglas a week after its conclusion. "I think that had the Convention passed a second ballot they would have attempted to draft you."[38]

"You were 20 minutes away from being nominated," my father wrote Douglas, nothing if not dramatic:

> As the session opened, the Wallace people were sure that they were only 23 votes short. As Ed Weisl kept repeating, they had no idea of how many votes they had (except for [Senator Claude] Pepper [of Florida] who knew the score throughout—he's our kind of guy!) Their estimates fluctuated erratically, like the [stock market] ticker during a panic. . . . The southern group, however, never saw the Wallace strength as realistically as we did.

"We," in this account, means the New Dealers who knew Wallace was dead meat, but combined with his delegates to show New Deal–bloc strength on the first ballot in order to play their next card—Douglas—from maximum strength. The southerners, my father continued,

> did not understand that Wallace would have been out altogether two days before the balloting if our friends—I mean your supporters— had not done a magnificent job of keeping him in and showing his zanies how to fight. . . . [The southerners] just sat, sweated and had visions of Wallace handing out free milk to the sharecroppers.[39]

With 589 votes needed to win, the first ballot gave Wallace 429 1/2 votes, Truman 319 1/2, and 393 1/2 to thirteen favorite sons from states hither and yon. As matters stood, Wallace was the New Deal choice; Truman the candidate of the bosses and of the southerners, Byrnes having withdrawn his name in anger. The favorite sons had the balance of power. At that point the name of the game, as in other Democratic conventions, was ever more clearly Chicago and its boss Mayor Kelly. From my father's postmortem to Douglas:

> At the end of the first ballot, it was plain to all but the left-and-right wing crackpots . . . that Wallace had run his race on the first ballot and that Truman would have his chance on the second. Between bal-

lots, Frank Maloney saw Ed Kelly . . . As Frank knew, [Kelly] was all
primed—first by Tommy [Corcoran], then by Ed Weisl . . . They
[agreed] to recess directly after the second ballot and work the thing
out for a landslide compromise for you on the third ballot.[40]

My father told Douglas that Mayor Kelly, "ordinarily soft-spoken," was
by this point

cursing [Bob] Hannegan [and his fellow bosses Ed Flynn of the Bronx,
Frank Hague of Jersey City, plus Ed Pauley of California], calling them
. . . sons-of-bitching lunatics, . . . swearing that they would never
steam-roller Truman through or everybody would go to jail. He made
it plain that Illinois would stick with Lucas on the second ballot and
as long as it was necessary to dead-lock the convention. Just then
[Senator] Bob Wagner came up, and agreed, saying that he was going
back to the New York crowd to talk [the stalemate plan] up [with] the
fellows who had been fighting Flynn in your behalf.[41]

In the big delegations, my father continued, "Wallace was never more
than an opening option against the [bosses'] syndicate and you were the
real choice of the real people." (He did not include in this account his
recollection years later that Joe Kennedy told Senator Maloney he'd send
$1 million in cash to keep the convention going indefinitely if that would
put Douglas across.)[42]

Finally, my father's narrative to Douglas reports, Senator John Bankhead
of Alabama, knowing Mayor Kelly was contriving to keep the balloting
open,

decided to stay in [as a favorite son] and play for a Southern bloc.
[This and other maneuvers] made it clear that the second ballot would
not be decisive for Truman—until the . . . Wallace zanies misinter-
preted the action of Alabama and Illinois as the end of Truman—and
the Southerners heard and believed them. When [Senator Millard]
Tydings pulled Maryland for Truman it was all over. That's the way
it happened.[43]

My father's version of the denouement closely parallels Ed Pauley's, who
wrote his for the Truman White House archives. Just how inevitable which
conclusion was, or when, is lost in the historical wash, as if Pirandello rather
than Machiavelli had been in attendance. Even Harry Hopkins, who was
jealous of the Roosevelt-Douglas relationship, observed that Roosevelt
"would have preferred Bill Douglas, because he knew him better and he always liked Bill's toughness." But—the consiglieri's kiss of death—"nobody
really influential was pushing for Douglas."[44]

You give the job to "the one who makes the most trouble" if he doesn't get it, Roosevelt had confided to Corcoran in 1936 about how to reconcile conflicting promises. But this time, also according to Corcoran, Roosevelt told Jim Rowe, "Truman will make the *least* trouble for me." With Truman the choice and the Democratic machine bosses on top, inertia was in the saddle. My mother's image of this drama in later years was that Roosevelt was the great tree in the shade from which no strong and fresh roots could grow.[45]

. . .

In the wake of the convention Douglas's close friends wrote him long letters at his Oregon retreat reporting on the byplay in detail, citing each other's roles and offering him reassurance that, in the absence of a deadlock and genuine draft, his position as a Supreme Court justice had been protected.

Interior Undersecretary Abe Fortas:
The pressure to arrange that you be drafted for the Vice-Presidential nomination came originally from [Secretary] Ickes, to the best of my knowledge. Subsequently, . . . Tom Corcoran became extremely active. . . .

Eliot Janeway kept in constant touch with the situation and had many discussions with Frank Maloney. Through Eliot, Ed Weisl was interested. Weisl attended the Convention in Chicago, and talked particularly with Mayor Kelly . . .

I think I can say with assurance that nothing occurred which was in any respect prejudicial to you or your position on the Bench. . . . If anything, your stature has been increased as a result of the genuine and widespread sentiment evidenced on your behalf.[46]

Senator Frank Maloney:
I saw . . . [a number] of your friends and admirers from California and Washington and Oregon and elsewhere throughout the country. I fought like hell to keep some of them from nominating you [that is, putting Douglas's name forward after it was clear the party bosses had the votes for Truman]—as did Messrs. Janeway and Weisl. Mr. Weisl is a wonder. You know Eliot.[47]

My father:
I am sure that you were both protected, and built up: those whose judgment I respect agree. You will never know under what pressure we were to let your name go to the floor.

His letter included a roster of the first fifty names that came to mind ("There were so many more") of those who helped the Douglas cabal in Chicago, including such new faces on the scene as Walter Reuther, Adlai Stevenson, and Stuart Symington, annotated with notes on the role of each.[48]

. . .

The effort to make Douglas vice president in 1944 signaled passionate enthusiasm and the emergence of a Rooseveltian enterprise that would be
around when Roosevelt himself was gone. That Roosevelt would not be
around for long was, of course, what triggered the extraordinary drama of
the 1944 vice presidential nomination to begin with.

Then too, conservative resurgence in Congress in 1938 and the war had
put the New Deal into eclipse. The weary Roosevelt himself acknowledged
that, absent a tide of reform behind him, he needed the Democratic bosses'
engaged enthusiasm to win. The question my father put to Douglas in his
long postmortem letter was, who would be heir to Roosevelt and the New
Deal when the pendulum swung back; when the backroom politics of the
1944 Democratic National Convention were dry history? Roosevelt may, as
some reasoned, have been able to deny to himself that he was fading fast,
may have rationalized that he was picking "just another vice president" to
help him through the election to a term he would serve out, and that there
was plenty of time for the issue of a true successor. But his own "Truman
or Douglas" (or Douglas and Truman) juxtaposition could not have dramatized more boldly the question whether that successor would represent
the New Deal and take it forward, or represent the natural inclination of
old-line Democrats back to business as usual.[49]

But these House of Roosevelt men's belief that Douglas was FDR's legitimate heir was at odds with their candidate's complicated and cryptic nature.
A shrewd man, Douglas was right in his implicit message to his supporters
that, in addition to the inhibitions on any overt political move posed by his
Court role, you don't *run* for the role of deputy and presumptive successor
to one of the greatest figures in the history of the country as his health fails.
(Implying a previous conversation to this effect, my father noted in his
postconvention recapitulation to Douglas, "You also felt that a Justice cannot be promoted to the Vice-Presidency and should not want to be.")
Douglas told Ickes in the fall of 1944 that if Roosevelt had asked him to run
with him he would have done so, but that the direct signals to him were
too oblique. But what began as observance of rules of the game became
tangled in psychological quirks. With his trips up and down the mountains,
between communion with nature and sphinxlike utterances, Douglas presented himself as a sage but teasing prophet in the wilderness.[50]

Wallace was a foggy "mystic." Douglas's quirks frustrated his most influential supporters yet permitted them to present him (no less than Wallace's
advocates presented their hero) as a man of principle first. That added a
piquant touch to the fervor with which the more secular among them
worked, for secondary agendas were apparent. For example Corcoran, having lost favor and direct clout at Roosevelt's White House, had obvious
interest in building it anew. I. F. Stone, who had been a friend of Corcoran's
and was in 1944 a diehard Wallaceite, wrote in the *Nation* that

Douglas has been [Corcoran's] pet candidate for President or Vice-President ever since the 1940 campaign. Tom loves politics and he loves power. The manipulation of men and events satisfies his deepest instincts. He is charming, shrewd, energetic and ruthless. He feels that he has made several Supreme Court justices, at least two Cabinet members, a brace of Representatives and Senators, and many lesser officials, and he would like to make a President.

Stone claimed that it was as a function of "Tom's plot" that Navy secretary Forrestal was lobbying on Capitol Hill for Douglas, and he saw the fine hand of corporate and moneyed power in league against Wallace: "The private interests [Corcoran] serves today run counter to the public causes that once had the benefit of his great abilities."[51]

Corcoran's best friends knew there was some truth to Stone's overall thesis. Yet, flowing from the source of New Deal ingenuity in reforming and regulating business, these were bonds that had their own touch of the mystical. For a figure like Forrestal, commitment to Douglas appears unlikely, in light of what happened next. After 1945 Forrestal became an aggressive Cold Warrior. Douglas began a path of liberal foreign policy dissent. Yet the two men remained close, and Douglas tried repeatedly to help Forrestal with the dilemmas and fierce attacks on his policies that were tearing him apart, walking alone with him around Washington on a succession of evenings. On the night in May 1949 that Forrestal, in the grip of mental breakdown, jumped out of a sixteenth story window at Bethesda Naval Hospital, Douglas, according to his account, "wept, for I had been on my way to the hospital and might have saved my friend's life. . . . I felt I had let him down." (Douglas believed the odd wrinkle in their intimate friendship was that for Forrestal it represented a way of acting out ambivalence about the establishment of which he was a pillar.)[52]

. . .

What explained my father's devotion to Douglas? He was, after all, still a working journalist and in theory responsible to Henry Luce, even if licensed by his editor and publisher to roam freely. (Indeed, he published a detached report on both the Democratic and Republican national conventions for *Fortune* that season.) But his counsel to Douglas after the 1944 convention was at first glance an oration out of a Frank Capra movie.[53]

Moving from reassurances that Douglas's judicial role had not been compromised, my father wrote,

To your role as a Justice has been added that of a leader. You have an organization. You did not build it. You did not ask for it. You have implored those of its leaders and members who have come to you to go elsewhere . . . Those who believe in you would not continue to do so if you had not tried to convince everybody—and above all yourself—that you are merely a Justice.

Here, departing from his customary style of tough-guy commentary, he delivered the kind of peroration reserved for intimates who seek to provoke or persuade another to a higher calling:

[But] just as you have succeeded as a man, as a symbol and as a leader by your sincere and passionate failure to convince your followers that you are merely a Justice, so from here out you will fail as a man if you try to deny . . . that *an army of people* in whom you believe both as people and as believers in the people has welded itself to you as a leader. This has been a long time happening. The momentum of this army will accelerate at an increasing rate in the next few years. Nothing you do can stop it (emphasis added).[54]

With this theory of Douglas's "army," my father's case for his man went further than did that of the other Rooseveltian insiders. They all saw Douglas as immensely able and marked by destiny. At the SEC he'd been the point-man in the fusion of the old Progressive Party and New Deal designs of breaking the private power trusts; opening the South and West up to both public power-fueled development and fresh liberal political leadership. Then on the Court he'd been handed the chance to assume a statesman's mantle.[55]

But Corcoran and the others tended to see Douglas as Washingtonians of standing see one of their own. Roosevelt had been an inspirational leader on a scale and for a duration unrivaled in American history, but he was sick and tired. So were many of those closest to him at the end, like Harry Hopkins. Ironically, Henry Wallace cited my father as author of the cynical view that by late 1943, left to themselves, "Roosevelt and the gang around him" constituted de facto, "the Tories"; the forces of inertia in the saddle.[56]

My father's point, beyond the Washington byplay, was that if the idealism of the New Deal and of this epic war gave way to the disillusionment and drift that followed the much smaller American commitment in the First World War, if the "army" he wrote to Douglas about (which, he added, "has its fellows on aircraft carriers too") had nowhere to go, "It will cost the America in which you believe a terrible price." The day after the Labour Party's defeat of the Churchill government in July 1945, my father pressed the point on Corcoran, noting the votes of men in uniform who, he observed, are key among those who "want the New Deal in England." Corcoran agreed: "That is what I am interested in, that it is the first real soldier vote."[57]

. . .

The intriguing might-have-beens of 1944 rolled over, in pace with Harry Truman's lackluster performance in the first years of his presidency.

In the summer of 1945 there was talk of Douglas becoming Truman's secretary of war. "I think that Bill has to make up his mind to take his chances," Corcoran told a confidant over his wiretapped phone in August

1945, early in the bidding, "and he is never going to do it sitting up there waiting . . . the days for that to happen are gone." That is, they ended with Roosevelt's death. (The circumstances of the taps on Corcoran's phone lines are explained in the next chapter.)[58]

"Bill should not be a candidate" for Truman's cabinet, my father argued with Corcoran three weeks later, and "nothing is more important than that none of his friends should be lifting a finger for him"—that is, asking the unfortunate Truman for anything. Corcoran agreed with him for the moment but remained ambivalent.[59]

Then, early on February 15, 1946, Douglas called Corcoran to say that "I had about three or four hours last night with Sam Rayburn and Lyndon [Johnson] and the heat is really on." The purpose of the heat: to persuade Douglas to take over the Interior Department from the disgruntled, departing Harold Ickes. (Proposing to replace Ickes with an equally committed Rooseveltian was a significant gesture on Truman's part: Ickes had just sabotaged the Senate confirmation hearings of the president's crony and 1944 Democratic convention agent, California oilman Ed Pauley, for the post of undersecretary of the navy.)[60]

That evening, a garrulous Johnson acknowledged that he and Rayburn were operating from a presentiment that Truman's incompetence was going to cost the Democrats control of Congress in the elections that fall. ("Sam says we've got to have some brains in there. . . . You know how bad off we are, don't you?") Indeed, the plan called for Douglas to be formally assigned, beyond the Interior Department, the task of rebuilding the New Deal political coalition in the Truman administration—"calling the signals," as Johnson put it to Corcoran; "somebody's got to do it." This was an unorthodox scenario, not generally found in political science texts. A variation on it would, with dark irony, resurface in a design of Robert Kennedy's toward the end of Johnson's own presidency.

Johnson boasted, however, that he was appealing to Douglas's own high ideals and political prospects as well as to the good of all. Douglas, Johnson told Corcoran, is "an awfully cautious fellow"—possessed of the kinds of insecurities that, ironically in history's eyes, Johnson himself wallowed in decades later as president: Douglas, reported Johnson, was lamenting that he "had lived on the other side of the tracks. He didn't have any magic. So I asked him what folks on the other side of the tracks would think of him if [the country] went right straight to hell and he had a chance to save it and didn't do anything." Johnson told Corcoran he'd argued that Douglas "had his chance now to get the goddamn ball and run with it and we'd all run with him, and [that] he couldn't do much for the three-fourths of the people of the world that couldn't read the Atlantic Charter with his ass up there on that [Supreme] Court."

Corcoran debated the case with Johnson: "I think it's a terrific sacrifice to ask of this guy, to get aboard a sinking ship and think he's going to pump it out, and if it sinks he goes down with it, while on the other hand, he's got the safest job in the world for the rest of his life." But in a youthful rendition of what would come to be called the "Johnson treatment," the congressman warmed to his theme with apocalyptic allusions to the atomic bomb: "Well, he hasn't [got security], goddamn it. In this age none of us may be livin' by January if it keeps goin' like it is. . . . This security thing is out, by God, with Hiroshima." Corcoran turned around: "Well, I'm for you boy. I'm going to step in and try to get this guy to say yes." (In fact, Corcoran remarked the next afternoon that Douglas would be "an awful chump to do this.")[61]

In New York Douglas met all that day with my father, who opposed Douglas taking the job, and in the evening with another intimate of all concerned, Ernest Cuneo, who liked the larger strategic role it promised for their man. But, canny and perverse, Douglas elected to continue to fly solo. To Truman Douglas said that Chief Justice Harlan Stone emphatically opposed the departure from the Court of so strong a member (Stone told Truman that as well). But in a poker-playing mood, referring to Rayburn's and others' grander design for a political leadership role for him with Truman, Douglas asked the president (in Corcoran's replay of that meeting to Forrestal), "what more will there be for me to do other than just sit here and watch the sea lion pelts and the seal fisheries." Truman, reported Corcoran, failed to rise "very well to that kind of challenge, but merely in a kind of an honorable, helpless way said, 'I don't know, I just want you to help.' Which didn't give 'our hero' much to go back and tell the Chief [Justice] why he was being drafted."[62]

In his memoirs Douglas added a coda on yet another, contemptuous, note:

> Having been active in the conservation field, I felt I knew more about Interior, its drawbacks, its heavy-handed bureaucracy, its tie-in with the Establishment, than [Truman] did. I also knew about the two great polluters among the [Interior] agencies—the Bureau of Reclamation, which tainted our rivers with salt, and the Bureau of Mines, which allowed coal operators to fill our streams with sulfuric acid. I trusted Truman on most domestic issues, but not those of Interior, so, convinced that I would be cast to the dogs

if he accepted, he said no. If Truman really wanted him, Douglas wrote, "I went on to say that there was one way to get me: . . . Secretary of State." That was not to be.[63]

. . .

In November 1946 came the Democrats' devastating loss of Congress. Roosevelt had endured close races and congressional election setbacks, but the return of control of Congress to the Republicans for the first time since FDR's election as president advertised stark vulnerability. "I don't know if there'll be enough left of Truman to put on a [1948] ticket," Ickes had remarked to Corcoran weeks earlier as the Democrats' 1946 campaign prospects went from bad to worse.[64]

As 1947 began, the Democrats were in disarray. The singular hero of World War II, Eisenhower, agonized over his next moves, courted by Democrats and Republicans alike. Douglas's supporters remained enthusiastic; he remained elusive. Yet the one step he never took from 1940 on, gestures of protestation aside, was personally to order his closest friends to cease and desist all political activity on his behalf once and for all.

They understood that, as Fortas put it delicately to Douglas in the summer of 1947, "if you were asked, you would say no" to the idea of his name going onto presidential primary ballots or into state conventions to select delegates, but that his wish was not intended to forbid his intimates from encouraging rank-and-file supporters. ("I know of nothing I can do to stop" such action in Oregon, Douglas replied with his Zen face on.) Early in 1948 Douglas gave a thunderous civil liberties speech in Chicago in honor of Illinois's fighting liberal governor of the 1890s, John Peter Altgeld, who, he orated, "as a politician . . . did not follow the safe course of indecision or of ambiguous pronouncement when his instinct for justice told him to meet an evil head on." The press reaction emphasized Douglas's national political prospects.[65]

With Wallace mounting a 1948 presidential run from the far left and the Dixiecrats preparing secession from the Democratic Party, Truman faced a third challenge: New Dealers critical of him organized themselves as "Americans for Democratic Action." The president's view of his situation had the virtue of clarity if not soaring eloquence: "Tell those amateurs at the ADA," he is said to have remarked, "that any shithead behind this desk can get renominated." Nevertheless the Democratic Party factionalization meant Truman needed all the help he could get. This time the bosses as well as New Dealers leapt to the idea of Douglas for vice president. Truman's stock was so low, however, that Douglas's confidants could see no good reason why their man should take the offer, as against waiting for Truman's impending political demise.[66]

At the 1948 Democratic National Convention in Philadelphia Truman's friend Bob Hannegan, retired as Democratic national chairman but acting as Truman's agent, asked my father, an alternate delegate from Connecticut, to try to reach Douglas in what was by now his ritual political season escape to his incommunicado cabin. In this round, by prearrangement with the Forest Service, an "ancient and rickety" phone line, as Douglas described it, had been "strung through many miles of forests and suspended from trees." Douglas added, "all along the line there were probably a dozen people listening in" on his calls. My father recalled his conversation with Douglas this way:

We did it as burlesque [expecting the call to be reported to the White House], you see? . . . It was obviously an open line: "Hey, Bill, I'm sitting in the Warwick Hotel in Philadelphia and I'm a pretty important fellow." He said, "Well I know that. Why are you bothering with me?" I said, "Bob Hannegan instructed me to. That's what proves I'm so important." He said, "What did he instruct you to do?" "To call you and tell you to go on the ticket and say if you did . . . you'd have the [presidential] nomination in 1952. He said, "Call Bob back and say he got there late. Stu Symington [then secretary of the air force and close to both Truman and Douglas] and Abe Fortas have called and given me the same message. I said, "Well you've got the message now from me. So that means the message is confirmed from them. I'll call Bob back and tell him I gave you the message." He said, "Well, you're a good reporter. I'm sure you'll get it straight."[67]

And that was that—despite calls to Douglas in the hours that followed from Eleanor Roosevelt and finally from Truman himself. Colloquially, Corcoran wrote Douglas in the mountains, "Dear Willum, From left to right there's nothing more need be said. You know I think you done right." Truman recorded acidly, "I'm inclined to give some credence to Tommy Corcoran's crack to [former senator] Burt Wheeler that Douglas had said he could not be a No. 2 man to a No. 2 man."[68]

I remember watching television for the first or second time with a school friend on her parents' brand-new set in rural Connecticut in January 1949. Flickering through the electronic snow was live footage of Harry Truman's inauguration. The pageantry, so vivid when my father spoke of such events in our house, was minuscule and clouded. My friend's mother, who worked with my parents in the local Democratic Party and knew their passion, said solicitously, "Well maybe it'll be Justice Douglas next time."

Jim Rowe wrote Douglas a scenario for getting nominated in 1952. But as Jordan Schwarz has written, "After 1948 liberals seemed to tire of Douglas's game and he settled down on the Court for the longest run in its history." He became, with Hugo Black, one of the foremost civil libertarians in American judicial history. At first Douglas and Black seemed to be loners in the wilderness, but those instincts as operators that distinguished them in Roosevelt's eyes prevailed. Together, coalescing shrewdly with two of Eisenhower's Supreme Court appointees, Earl Warren and William Brennan, they drove, as insiders, the Court's emergence as an engine of reform in what was otherwise a period of relative conservatism. And, unhappy and restless at home, Douglas commenced his series of divorces and remarriages, wandering the world and producing books about travel and the environment.[69]*

The potential for an "army" of motivated liberal activists in search of a leader that my father wrote about in the summer of 1944 manifested itself in real if fragmented ways. It was the stuff of postwar liberal veterans' organizations, of reform movements that sprang up against old-line party organizations in cities like Minneapolis and produced fresh leaders like Hubert Humphrey, of grassroots support for Adlai Stevenson in 1952, and thereafter, and for Eisenhower too among supporters who saw him as a high-minded, nonpartisan force for good government and internationalism.

If my mother's trope of Roosevelt as the great tree whose shade blocked the growth of anyone comparable was on the mark, then perhaps it was fortunate that Truman came in not as FDR's protege, but as the choice of

---

*An odd family note: Corcoran's decision to represent Mildred Douglas in late 1953 put a chill on an increasingly complex Corcoran–Bill Douglas relationship. But Douglas's latest biographer, Bruce Allen Murphy, exaggerates in writing that the divorce "cost [Douglas] his friendship with Tommy Corcoran." His source is my father, whom he quotes as saying of Douglas and Corcoran, "They broke completely . . . and they did not speak again after the divorce for decades thereafter"— until (according to that account) my father brought them together for lunch in 1979 (see page 207).

Alas, my father had suffered a stroke before the set of interviews Murphy conducted with him in 1990, and his command of detail about the past became unreliable. In fact, the record of letters, visits, and gifts exchanged between Douglas and Corcoran resumed in April 1954 and continued through the years, marked for long stretches by warmth and empathy. Corcoran had a kidney operation in the spring of 1957; Douglas visited him afterward and they apparently bared their souls to each other, prompting Corcoran to write suggestively to Douglas's second wife, Mercedes: "I was much pleased by Bill's talk about himself the other day. I think he has really found the root of his trouble. Whether I have found the worm that is inside of me I don't know."

On the other side of the ledger, the relationship did suffer another rupture, after Corcoran was exposed as having lobbied Douglas's Supreme Court colleagues Hugo Black and William Brennan on a pending case in 1970. Douglas wrote coldly about Corcoran in the second volume of his memoirs.

Corcoran like my father and Douglas's other friends (and enemies) did feel he lost interest in the Court and in Corcoran's words, "was not as great a justice as he could have been." The cause had to do not only with disappointed political ambitions. Dating from years of debt, and punctuated by Corcoran's "hell of a deal" for Douglas's first wife in his first divorce settlement, followed by subsequent ones, "Bill was always in financial trouble," in Corcoran's words. After 1948 Douglas expended energy on becoming a popular writer ("those nature books"). "As a result he was too diverted from his work on the Court."

the machine bosses, apparently mediocre. (And perhaps Roosevelt, being shrewd above all others in such matters, knew this in permitting his selection over Douglas.) That is, arguably a true Rooseveltian would have failed until fresh ground could be plowed. According to that premise, it was better that any reform "army" break down into smaller efforts around the country, on the model Justice Brandeis commended to Corcoran in 1935.

Douglas—vivid, aloof, and mischievous, charismatic and self-defeating—remained a subject of my father's passion and regret, as of others. (In a tense moment over another matter a year later, Abe Fortas told Corcoran that Douglas was fishing in Oregon. Said Corcoran, "Those fish of his. They've cost us more per pound. . . . They are the most expensive fish in human history.")[70]

Douglas's was not, it emerged, a first-class temperament. It began to be time for these talented men of the House of Roosevelt, their enterprise and energy primed, to identify another among their company as the designated legatee.

Figure 1. "The young Lyndon Johnson operated on fuel that laced breathy aspiration with high-test anxiety." The newly elected Congressman Johnson and Governor James Allred welcome FDR to Texas in 1937. *LBJ Library*

Figure 2. "I got the circuit moving . . . " Thomas Corcoran testifies before a Senate committee. *AP/Wide World Photos*

Figure 3. In FDR's service Benjamin Cohen and Tommy Corcoran ran "the only law firm . . . that stayed open around the clock." *Paul Dorsey/TimePix*

Figure 4. Abe Fortas was "elfin . . . sly and cute," 'puckish' and seductive." FDR's first Supreme Court appointee, Hugo Black, Interior secretary Harold L. Ickes standing behind him, swears Fortas in as his undersecretary in 1942. *Collection of the Supreme Court of the United States*

Figure 5. James Rowe: one of FDR's wartime presidential assistants "with a passion for anonymity," number two man at the Justice Department, Tommy Corcoran's protégé, and an LBJ friend who would tell Johnson what he didn't want to hear. *Maurice Constant/Courtesy FDR Library*

Figure 6. William O. Douglas as chairman of the SEC: A law student remembered, "He looked like a Remington cowboy; a man of leather and rawhide tough." *Bettmann/Corbis*

Figure 7. Douglas *(center)* with two fishing companions in Oregon in 1943. Corcoran to Fortas of their friend's retreats to the Northwest at key moments: "Those fish of his. They've cost us more per pound. . . . They are the most expensive fish in human history." *Author's collection*

Figure 8. Jerome Frank succeeded Douglas as chairman of the SEC. As a leading legal realist and, later, a judge, he was skeptical of the "brooding omnipresence in the sky known as Jurisprudence." *George Karger/TimePix*

Figure 9. James V. Forrestal: Bill Douglas prompted him to slip two sheets of excerpts from Homer's epic tales into a wartime memo; "the whole thing came back initialed by everyone" including General Marshall. *AP/ Wide World Photos*

Figure 10. Elizabeth and Eliot Janeway in 1943. My mother recalled, "He knew a lot. He knew things I wanted to know and I guess I knew things he wanted to know." *Serge Balkin/ TimePix*

Figure 11. FDR at Hyde Park, September 1941. My mother, recovered from falling "flat on my face" over Roosevelt's steel leg braces, is seated square in the middle of the photo, face turned toward the camera, wearing a white flowered headband. *Courtesy FDR Library*

Figure 12. LBJ to Eliot Janeway in the early 1940s: "The difference between you and me, El'yit, is, *you're for* Roosevelt, but *Ah believe* in Roosevelt." *Author's collection*

Figure 13. Thurman Arnold (*right*) leaving court with his client Owen Lattimore: as assistant attorney general, he indicted defense contractors for antitrust violations "like a poker player putting down one ace after another." *AP/Wide World Photos*

Three Who Dallied with the Soviets

Figure 14. (*top left*): Harry Dexter White: his chief Henry Morgenthau said White became "increasingly brash and overconfident. . . . He could be disagreeable, quick-tempered, overly ambitious, and power went to his head." *Tony Linck/TimePix*

Figure 15. (*top right*): Lee Pressman, aide to Jerome Frank at the start of the New Deal and powerful labor official, was "embittered. Burning, searing grievance against the system. Endless ability. Disciplined Communist." *AP/Wide World Photos*

Figure 16. (*left*): Lauchlin Currie, influential in the wartime White House: my father told Henry Luce that Currie was "the least arrogant heavyweight brain I know." *Tony Linck/TimePix*

Figure 17. John Connally, with LBJ in 1957: Texas, once a New Deal stronghold, became "concerned about money and how to make it." Connally anchored Johnson's base back home. *Thomas D. McAvoy / TimePix*

✿ 5 ✿

1945—The New Dealers'
Government-in-Exile

"I GOT THE CIRCUIT MOVING"

The New Dealers involved in regulating the relationship between government and business had run a risk foreseen by two of their political forbears, Woodrow Wilson and his adviser and friend Louis Brandeis. Disputing Teddy Roosevelt's "New Nationalism" in the 1912 presidential campaign, before he himself became a regulator as president, candidate Wilson articulated a tenet of his "New Freedom":

> If the government is to tell big business men how to run their business, then don't you see that big business men have to get closer to the government even than they are now? Don't you see that they must capture the government, in order not to be restrained too much by it?[1]

Brandeis, Wilson's chief collaborator in framing the New Freedom, was a regulator, but with provisos. He saw states and cities as the appropriate venues for regulation, and feared the effects of its imposition at the federal level. Echoing the pre-presidential Woodrow Wilson, Brandeis warned early on that government regulation to break up industrial power carried inherent risks: "Do not pin too much faith in legislation. Remedial institutions are apt to fall under the control of the enemy and to become instruments of oppression." Indeed, Alan Brinkley has written, the Brandeisian view held that "large corporations were not only dangers in themselves. They were also dangerous because controlling them would require the state to become a Leviathan."[2]

Several business reformers and pragmatists were White House confidants in the recovery phase of the New Deal and recruits to Roosevelt administration service. While in FDR's employ, Corcoran pioneered in drawing corporate figures like Lincoln Filene of the Boston department stores, and less high-minded others, to help finance the sometimes bitter election campaigns of New Deal candidates. Some of these businessmen were first in line at Corcoran's and the others' new law firms as corporate clients.[3]

Corcoran, developing the Washington lawyer-lobbyist role in the early 1940s, paved the path for junior colleagues like Fortas, as he had in government. They were making a career in the management of the risk Wilson and Brandeis warned about: the specter of big business capturing the new regulatory state. By nature, by style, by habit they did so with confidence that they could master that risk. Such mastery involved style, *panache*. In 1944 House Speaker Sam Rayburn had a tough fight for renomination in the Democratic primary in his East Texas congressional district. Thereafter, as Corcoran put it to my father, "Rayburn, as he says, always runs scared" whether he was secure in his seat or not. As a matter of habit, he would call Corcoran for help. Whether Rayburn really used infusions of funds for campaigns, or just needed to know they were there for the asking, he could, my father claimed, always prevail on Corcoran (though the latter sometimes became cranky about the chronic requests) to go to business clients in campaign season on behalf of the speaker.[4]

In 1938 WPA administrator Harry Hopkins allegedly stated the New Deal creed with cynical candor (at a New York racetrack, for added spice): "We shall tax and tax, and spend and spend, and elect and elect." Had Corcoran spoken in such bald, universal terms after leaving government, he might have said something like this: "We shall advance our business clients' interests through our New Deal friends in government, we shall advance our New Deal friends' political careers with our clients' campaign donations, we shall master the political alchemy of doing well while doing good."[5]

After Roosevelt's death Abe Fortas and Thurman Arnold, once "legal realist" Yale Law faculty colleagues and prominent New Deal administrators and regulators, built their own Washington corporate law firm, riding the waves of Corcoran's dreadnought success. A third New Dealer, former FCC chairman Paul Porter, soon joined them. Individual and firm clients, some of whom they'd dealt with in government, included the Chesapeake and Ohio Railroad, Lever Brothers, Coca-Cola, Federated Department Stores, ABC, and Pan American Airways.[6]

Harry Truman's ablest White House lieutenant, Clark Clifford, had not earned his stripes in New Deal service; he arrived in Washington just after the fact. But he became the Rooseveltians' man in the Truman scheme of things: architect of Truman's Fair Deal, updating the New Deal agenda. Pleading financial insecurity, he left Truman in 1950 to start his own law firm, which after a while rivaled Corcoran's and Fortas's as a Washington powerhouse. Soon he represented Howard Hughes, Phillips Petroleum, Standard Oil, Kerr-McGee Oil, Allied Chemical and Dye, RCA, RKO,

AT&T, the Pennsylvania Railroad, and the government of Indonesia, among others.[7]

Were they all opportunists, acting out Wilson's and Brandeis's sorry forecast? Had they all "sold out"? Said Fortas, who called the shots at Arnold, Fortas and Porter, a "corporate malefactor or a presumably saintly civil libertarian" each deserves legal representation. He guided the firm in standing against what years later he called "the hysteria [that] reached its apogee in the mad behavior of Senator Joseph McCarthy." Arnold, Fortas and Porter represented, along with its corporate clients, a series of individuals targeted by the postwar red-baiters, beginning with former State Department China specialist Owen Lattimore. Following Fortas's inner sense of rhythm, the firm's approach was cautious and controlled. They refused to take acknowledged Communists and passed "iffy" potential clients—Lillian Hellman was one—off to less circumspect counsel.[8]

Nevertheless, the going got rough. Thurman Arnold wrote a friend during Senate Internal Security subcommittee hearings on Lattimore, "Never in my life have I seen anything more vicious or contemptible than the way the committee is trying to break Lattimore." The demagogic chairman, Senator Pat McCarren of Nevada, "threatened to throw Abe out of the hearing room. He also threatened to throw me out for attempting to protect [Lattimore] against . . . unfair questioning." They showed courage when others hid.[9]

. . .

Personal styles varied. Fortas's political approach was restrained where Corcoran's was brash. As the mercurial Harold Ickes's wartime deputy, Fortas often helped calm the waters, pursuing his instinct for arrangement with those affected by administration policy. His fledgling law practice reflected a fabric finely woven from those years. Thus, at the Interior Department, Fortas dealt closely with the government of Puerto Rico, in complex transition from American territorial to commonwealth status. Puerto Rico became an early Arnold, Fortas and Porter client, its government relied on Fortas's judgment in making policy, and he was the island's de facto ambassador in Washington *and* promoter of investment in Puerto Rico by his corporate clients.[10]

By the 1960s Fortas was representing clients experiencing problems with the federal government, and later, sitting on the Supreme Court, while simultaneously serving as first counselor and crisis manager for his friend— and longtime legal client—Lyndon Johnson, across town. Wheels within wheels, his nuanced mode of operation fell quietly into place.[11]

As Lyndon Johnson rose to power in the Senate, then at the White House, his dependence on Fortas increased, and so, in pace, did criticism of Fortas. Growing up, I heard my father's sardonic references to "the Fortas firm" become increasingly edged. The "edge" reflected views of Fortas shared by others, beginning with Ickes, who in 1946 wrote in his diary that his undersecretary had been "evasive and weak" in an epic fight over California tidelands oil, at the close of their work together at Interior.[12]

The word on Fortas in his role as Johnson's intimate also picked up on his instinct for monopolizing the king's ear, and that of a piece with the way he guaranteed the flow of business to his firm. Another theme, following from the first, was that unlike others of the New Deal band, especially Jim Rowe, Douglas, and my father, Fortas was loath to presume on his friendship with Lyndon Johnson to challenge him, especially when, in fear of Texas conservatism after 1948, Johnson played it safe or veered to the right.[13]

By contrast, Rowe told Johnson in the early 1950s that he was running too scared of Texas on civil rights ("Your old friends, who remember the high-stepping, idealistic, intelligent young man who came here as a bright young congressman . . . expect more of you"). In 1960 he told Johnson that his mistrustful, abusive treatment of staff was making it impossible for able people to work for him.[14]

Douglas told Johnson in the early 1950s and in 1961 that he "would not listen" to the facts about anti-Communist dictators like Ayub Khan of Pakistan. "My test of an overseas regime," Justice Douglas wrote Vice-President Johnson, "is highly personal. I ask 'if Lyndon Johnson were a citizen of that country, where would he be?' . . . Under Ayub you would be in prison; and you would be in prison if you were a Taiwanese under Chiang Kai-Shek." During Johnson's presidency Douglas was a persistent thorn in the side of his old friend on environmental issues ("The sonic boom is doing us in at Goose Prairie," Douglas's Washington State retreat), and concluded, as he wrote the director of the Sierra Club in the fall of 1968, that, environmentally, Johnson "is a complete phoney." Douglas transmitted peace-feeler messages from the North Vietnamese to Johnson through Indian intermediaries as late as the Tet Offensive in 1968, but he had all but broken with Johnson over Vietnam by 1964, and stoutly supported challenges to the war that found their way before the Supreme Court.[15]

My father fought with Johnson over the latter's reluctance to oppose President Eisenhower's conservative economic policies. Later, marking the end of their friendship, he attacked him for his failure to finance, and thus acknowledge, American escalation in Vietnam. Most notably among Johnson's advisers from the Roosevelt and early Truman days, Clark Clifford sacrificed the hitherto total trust Johnson had in him in the fight he led to stop military escalation in Vietnam in 1968 and turn to negotiations. (These episodes are dealt with in later chapters.)[16]

Fortas rationalized his approach in classic "enabler" terms: psychologically, he felt, Johnson "*was*, indeed, 'insecure'"; the political leader needed his counselors to bolster his confidence if he was to perform at his best. "If Lyndon Johnson wanted something, Abe was usually all for it," said Clark Clifford; "I might not be supportive at all." But that does not fully explain the levels of mutual dependency at which Fortas and Johnson operated. Fortas's biographer, Laura Kalman, wrote of the relationship of these two insiders who never got over feeling like outsiders, "Something in their backgrounds had led both men to deviousness and dissembling" beyond the norm. To Johnson's other friends, he and Fortas seemed to be intent on a virtual cult of the secrecy of their arrangement.[17]

Johnson, said Douglas, was "crippled" when Fortas's counsel was unavailable to him. Another Court colleague, probably William Brennan, told Fortas's biographer that on the Supreme Court "Abe was sitting in Lyndon Johnson's lap." My father at his harshest focused on the courtier mentality: Fortas "was a great lawyer," but he "wrote no [judicial] opinions of distinction comparable to his professional talents." Instead, "a shrewd politician in personal relationships, [he operated] essentially as a stooge—Douglas's stooge, Ickes' stooge, Lyndon's stooge."[18]

Clark Clifford's style after he left the Truman White House in 1950 to start a law practice flowed from his sonorous, disarming, utterly disingenuous protestations about his firm not having "any influence of any kind here in Washington," simply "an extensive knowledge of how to deal with the government on your problems." Clifford was influential under Truman across a broader range of issues than Corcoran covered for Roosevelt, for Clifford's role extended to foreign and national security areas that were dormant in the 1930s. But Clifford was more a staff-man in government, and less an entrepreneurial force than Corcoran was in the days that Justice Brandeis controlled the balance of power on the Supreme Court and Corcoran was middleman between him and FDR, as he was with barons of Congress. Like Corcoran, Clifford held no more than a secondary post (White House counsel) when he founded his law firm. But he extended his private sector reach beyond Corcoran's, developing a studied, convincing impersonation of an august statesman. (Dean Acheson was one of Clifford's early models on that score.) And after a while, he became one.[19]

Like all these men, my father was also an afficionado of wheels within wheels, the inside shot. Apart from Washington, to the side of the direct power game there, by the early 1950s he was applying the Corcoran-Fortas-Clifford lesson, converting contacts with business figures—men he'd covered for *Time, Life,* and *Fortune* or come to know through New Deal friends—into clients for his economic consulting and newsletters and as business coventurers. Like the others, he played a free agent's game, but the alliances persisted. (Fortas, for example, offered him a start-up investment stake in his newsletter in the early 1950s—"wanted a piece of it.") Like Corcoran, Douglas, and Clifford, he also liked to maintain side deals with the political rivals of his principal allies.[20]

. . .

The case of Tommy Corcoran in later life, measured by such criteria, looks easy at first. One reason was that he openly enjoyed the stand-up, tough guy, can-do aspects of his "fixer" reputation, and talked the talk, high and low.

To a New Jersey congressman in July 1945 in search of a favor for Jersey City Democratic boss Frank ("I am the law") Hague requiring "machinery in motion of the very highest kind" (that is, Truman White House support): "You can report to Frank that every goddamned thing in the world has been pulled on this thing, and I think it will come off."[21]

To a powerful senator, explaining Franklin and Eleanor Roosevelt's children's corruptibility: "One of the difficulties I was constantly in" as FDR's lieutenant was that "I was supposed to take care of these 'chillun' and I couldn't take care of them without saying things about them to papa and mama that weren't very well received."[22]

In the same 1945 season the New Dealers were pressing President Truman to name Abe Fortas to the circuit court of appeals where, as Corcoran put it, he could "protect the interests" of the SEC and other regulatory agencies against industry challenges, which "all go through this court." Corcoran to Fortas: "I really put your name in the pot hard . . . today. . . . I put it in with Prich [White House assistant Edward Prichard], with Lyndon [Johnson], with Thurman [Arnold], with Harold [Ickes], with [Hugo] Black, and with [secretary of the Senate and Truman intimate] Leslie Biffle, and I got the circuit moving."[23]

I got the circuit moving. In the 1940s Corcoran did not labor to advertise himself in a statesmanlike light. He was candid, even brazen, where others in the Washington influence business, especially Clifford, grew sanctimonious. The saga reached epic proportions when it became known that Corcoran, representing the United Fruit Company, was smack in the middle of the CIA coup against the leftist but legal government of Guatemala in 1954.[24]

In the spring of 1960 Corcoran was again in front of a congressional investigating committee, accused of backdoor contacts with federal power commissioners on behalf of a private utility client. Covert intervention? Improper tactics? "I walked down the corridors of that commission as I always have," Corcoran testified, "in broad daylight, with a brass band behind me." A wink to the friendly committee chairman and back to work.[25]

. . .

But the story was more complicated than that in the first years after Roosevelt's death. The failure of the attempt to put Douglas across as FDR's 1944 running mate left the Rooseveltians without a safe harbor. The words and tones in which they tried to find one were recorded.

The background to the Truman administration's wiretap on Corcoran was this: the roots of his and Truman's enmity were deep, but resentment is a cheap commodity in Washington. The real issue was Corcoran's independent power and penchant for using it, as he had for Douglas, against Truman, at the Democratic National Convention in 1944. J. Edgar Hoover, who had his own history of trouble with Corcoran arising from the latter's sway at the Justice Department, appears to have found common cause with the new president in the spring of 1945 on the wisdom of a tap on Corcoran's phones. The justification for the record was pursuit of evidence of influence peddling on Corcoran's part that could be prosecuted.[26]

Senator Harry Truman chaired the watchdog legislative committee on national defense which, beginning in 1941, called Corcoran several times to testify about arrangements with clients for whom he was pursuing government defense contracts. One of these was the "New Deal's favorite businessman," developer Henry J. Kaiser, who had built the Bonneville Dam and other great Roosevelt administration projects, contracting in the 1930s with Washington through the offices of Ickes, Corcoran, and their allies. (In the 1940s Corcoran and Kaiser fell out over the size of the fees the former New Deal official charged for facilitating government contracts in his new role as a lawyer-lobbyist. "I thought Tommy was an idealist," Kaiser complained, according to my father.)[27]

Another two of Corcoran's clients, growing out of a designated administration role for him after 1940 coordinating lend-lease supplies to China, were General Claire Chennault's Flying Tigers and Chiang Kai-shek's powerful brother-in-law, the financier and politician T. V. Soong. Corcoran's version of the record, not inaccurate, was that "eight months before Pearl Harbor," even as the fissure between them was opening, "Roosevelt gave me China"—that is, "ordered me [in effect to direct] China Lend Lease" as a private citizen. Over the years Corcoran's footwork was nimble indeed in juggling his New Deal–rooted alliances with these prime pieces of his practice, on their way to becoming the core of the right-wing "China Lobby."[28]

Truman's relations with other New Dealers were also sour. To the point, Corcoran's much publicized influence in various branches of government after he left Roosevelt's employ was especially extraordinary in the Justice and Interior Departments. His friends Attorney General Biddle and Interior Secretary Ickes were prominently allied with him at the 1944 Democratic National Convention. Neither had a future in a Truman administration. Corcoran's maneuvers at such levels, however, extended beyond the realm of "fixing." With his network of executive, congressional, and judicial-branch contacts, and his private sector ones from business to law firms to the Roman Catholic hierarchy to the press, with his ability to affect traffic among them, he ran a power-center out of government almost as remarkable as the one he directed in FDR's service before 1941.[29]

So it seemed to others even then. The wiretap transcripts record Corcoran in a conversation with the shrewd Senator Lister Hill of Alabama (a New Dealer who succeeded to Hugo Black's seat when Black went to the Supreme Court and assistant majority leader and chairman of the Senate Military Affairs Committee in June 1945) about Corcoran's inside line on the Truman White House through his "spy system," and use of it: "Well, Tommy," marvels Hill (who spoke a mellifluous Southern patois) over a valuable piece of inside skinny, "you interest me. You fascinate me always. . . . Damn it you astound me." (In a subsequent conversation that touches on a business venture Corcoran is about to execute, Hill echoes such tribute: "Good gracious alive. You make me dizzy. You make me dizzy.")[30]

Corcoran's stock in trade was his ability to play private and public corners at once, and to find hidden angles (as well as angels). As noted, his background as a Wall Street lawyer before he went to Washington enabled him to identify covert or overt New Deal allies in the business world. Fifteen years before the CIA's coup in Guatemala that implicated the United Fruit Company and private attorney Corcoran, White House agent Corcoran began converting his New Deal connection to United Fruit's president, Samuel Zemurray, into significant financial support for liberal politicians including Claude Pepper of Florida, Robert La Follette of Wisconsin, and the young Lyndon Johnson. (Zemurray, Corcoran recalled in a sentimental note to Vice President Johnson in 1961, "many years ago mightily helped FDR and helped me to help you.")[31]

On a much murkier note, Corcoran was well ahead of Fortas in coming to the aid of an early target of what was to become McCarthyism. The time was June 1945. The target of investigation was a young State Department China hand, John Stewart Service. Service was chief political officer on the wartime staff of Chiang Kai-shek's bitter critic, General "Vinegar Joe" Stilwell. Service became one of several U.S. China experts whose darkening view of Nationalist Chinese failure, and of American policy in China, left him vulnerable to the red-hunters' charges that he was a fellow traveler or a spy.

Service made the charges easier by leaking secret State Department documents and information to the publisher of a left-leaning magazine, *Amerasia*. He did so with an unseemly gusto, oblivious to the fact that, seeking to influence policy, he'd stumbled into an outright espionage ring closely monitored by the FBI.

Corcoran's concern with the case, of course, was a function of his own web of interests in China policy, which included plans for lucrative postwar business with Nationalist friends and clients. But the case had potential for fueling dangerous feuds. For Service was a protégé not only of the uncontrollable maverick, General Stilwell, angry enough at his superiors to want to air dirty laundry about the corrupt Chiang Kai-shek regime and American support for it. The young China hand was also close to Corcoran's

New Deal friends at the center of China policy making, John Carter Vincent at the State Department and Lauchlin Currie at the White House, who'd been at bitter odds with administration conservatives about the shape of American policy in postwar Asia.[32]

Here was a pot of poison in need of discrete disposal. Corcoran leapt in. Meanwhile, his closest friend and New Deal partner Ben Cohen, adroit in his own political relationships, had wound up at the side of war mobilization administrator James Byrnes in the Roosevelt White House. When Truman named Byrnes secretary of state at the end of June 1945, Cohen accompanied Byrnes to his new post, with the rank of counselor of the department.[33]

"I don't want to be out front" in the Service case, said Corcoran to Lauchlin Currie about John Stewart Service three weeks before the Byrnes appointment, "because of the interest of other clients that I have got at the State Department"—principally, the Chinese Nationalists. Nevertheless in talking to Cohen about the case the night before, Corcoran tells Currie, "I said, 'If it has to be, I am not going to let them push this kid around. If we have to get to the ulcer in the stomach stage, I will be very much tempted to step in [and defend Service] myself without charging for it.'" Then, a characteristic statement of steely purpose and midnight method: "I would rather work around on the edges of this thing for a day or so to see if I can liquidate the whole goddamned thing."[34]

If Corcoran-style work around the edges doesn't suffice, he reassures Ben Cohen three days later, he has a lawyer of record in mind for Service who "is the ablest customer [in] the civil liberties business in the country" and who "will leave the Department of Justice tomorrow to take this case" if need be.[35]

By August Corcoran's plan succeeded, up to a point. Working through Truman's new attorney general Tom Clark and his deputies, Corcoran got Service separated from the espionage prosecution that sent several participants to jail. (Service's culpability was limited, Corcoran tells Cohen, compared to those he was helping, who had been "pretty stinkin.'") He tells Service he has the case "double riveted from top to bottom." In fact, the FBI, having bugged Service's interactions with the *Amerasia* network of operatives as well as Corcoran's phones, knew that Service never became fully candid about how far he'd gone from time-honored leaking to the press toward something much more culpable. The case refused to die completely. Currie, Vincent, and Service were caught up in the "Who Lost China?" inquisition, Joe McCarthy gave new life to the wilder charges about Service, and the latter never got back on his once-promising career path.[36]

. . .

Whatever the blur of Corcoran's interests, for some time after April 1945 New Deal–based common cause still filled much of his time. On the same summer days in 1945 that he was arranging for the Service case to be "double riveted from top to bottom," Corcoran was helping Ickes manage the fight against exploitation of California tidelands oil, pressing Douglas's political prospects, helping strategize the campaign of the New Dealers' candidate to succeed New York's Mayor La Guardia, sharing with liberal senators his own espionage on Truman's plans to displace Roosevelt's last cabinet appointees with party functionaries, working to get Fortas named a federal judge, and more. He was no less tireless in acquiring needy business clients.[37]

"If we could find one financier who thought as [developer] Henry Kaiser does, we could show the world that our ideas will work," said Corcoran in 1941. As with Kaiser and Zemurray of United Fruit, as with the Chinese Nationalists, Corcoran had a gift for the seamless weaving of business with higher political and policy interests.[38]

Harry Truman was the first to complain about Corcoran and Co. as "professional liberals" in league against him. Douglas, Truman wrote, "belongs to that crowd of Tommy Corcoran, Harold Ickes, Claude Pepper crackpots whose word is worth less than [FDR's undependable son] Jimmy Roosevelt's."[39]

By contrast, Corcoran could be philosophical as well as tart in his assessment of Roosevelt's successor. Fourteen months into the Truman presidency, he observed to Drew Pearson:

> Looking at what the difficulties are of staying in power and being reelected, and keeping your party in [Truman] doesn't choose to face them. . . . [People] come to him and say, "Well, we've got to think this one through," [and he replies,] "No, I'm going to do what I want to do and let the chips fall where they may, I don't care." . . . Now that may . . . suggest an unwillingness to face perplexities, [or] it may be very deeply and emotionally sincere, but it's . . . very puzzling. . . . I think he's going to wake up and decide he does want power.[40]

The Corcoran wiretap transcripts tell a complicated story. They tell it, too, in language that radiates personalities and reveals character, much more vividly than do letters and memoirs. And this is so even though the always well-informed Corcoran alerts those at the other end of the line that his phones are probably tapped, and though he and his interlocutors make spasmodic attempts to speak in code. (In one conversation newly named Secretary of State Byrnes is "St. James," his soon to be recruited undersecretary Dean Acheson is "the bishop's son, the man with the sartorial perfection," and a somewhat neurotic Ben Cohen is "our pet poodle.")[41]

Here are the confreres on parade: Douglas, the laconic cat who walks by himself; the crafty but insecure Fortas, the operatic Lyndon Johnson, the righteous Harold Ickes, a gossipy Archbishop (not yet Cardinal) Spellman, and a pompous Bernard Baruch. My father is the journalist as Jacobin.

Conducting the symphony, Corcoran dances among political ploys and espionage, deals, moneymaking and literary allusion, coach in the locker room and philosopher in his chair. Together their language blends inner sanctum, scrimmage line, and bar car; they speak of each other, maneuvers, and the fate of the nation. And their talk is never idle. "Well, it doesn't look too hot, Tommy," says Archbishop Spellman of a presidential appointment the Church is interested in; "Can you think of anything I should do now?" "I said when you ski, fellow, they teach you to lean forward and not fall on your face," Corcoran boasts of telling Truman's cautious attorney general. Get word to a prominent senator "not to take any position on this atomic bomb until he talks to me," intones Baruch. Cutting into a briefing about intrigues involving the disposition of the wartime intelligence services, Corcoran says, "I get it, I get it all. . . . I know how to do it." These are men with their hands on pieces of the action.[42]

Conversation by conversation, the transcripts lay out ever richer, more subterranean maneuvers. But, cumulatively, they also suggest a larger project woven through the machinations: the issue of the New Deal legacy, and of the future of the Democratic Party.

Commencing in June 1945, the transcripts focus on the early moves of the Truman administration to force out the last Roosevelt appointees, including Ickes, Biddle, and Forrestal, and staff the government with their own men—Democratic Party regulars, many of them hacks. Corcoran and his interlocutors speak of Truman's instinctive reliance on these party operatives; the ranks from which he rose in Kansas City and which Roosevelt pushed to the side. Truman's line is, "Let me have men about me not too smart," remarks Corcoran in June 1945.[43]

To New Dealer Lister Hill, Corcoran recounts the early stages of the Truman administration's first domestic political crisis: the mounting confrontation between Interior Secretary Ickes and Truman's West Coast ally, oilman Ed Pauley, concerning control of California tidelands oil. He warns that the fight has the potential to become a scandal rivaling Teapot Dome, which disgraced the Harding administration. Ickes has asserted federal title to the tidelands, reports Corcoran, prompting Pauley to say "he's going to have Ickes' head."

Senator Hill asks, "Is there something we can do to save" Ickes?

"Yeah, there's a lot you can do," replies Corcoran, in his best blocking-back style, and outlines a course of pressure on the White House "through Hugo [Black]" to a mutual Senate friend of Black's and Truman's. Corcoran continues,

> It was funny last night. I was out at Bill Douglas' with Hugo [Black], and Ickes . . . and some others and I couldn't help saying to myself, "Well, here's a bunch of guys . . . that had the world in their hands last year, and now they're just a bunch of political refugees . . . a helpless bunch of sheep."

Hill agrees with Corcoran's urging that they sit down with others who think as they do, like Senators Robert La Follette of Wisconsin and Claude Pepper of Florida, and "begin to play the ball a little" instead of "sitting around letting the ball play us." Corcoran offers "my house and my ration book" for a dinner.[44]

. . .

Roosevelt brought Progressive Republicans like La Follette and Ickes to his side, but he never managed to ease the New Deal's dependence on conservative Southern Democrats and old-guard Democratic machine bosses, like Truman's Missouri mentors, to pass its legislation in Congress and turn out the vote at election time. Even before his failed "purge" campaign against such Democrats in the 1938 primary elections, Roosevelt talked covertly about forcing these contradictions to a clear-cut conclusion by other means. In 1936 Corcoran was a principal White House agent in a scheme for reshaping the parties; not the least reason party regulars like James Farley and Ed Flynn complained about Corcoran and "his ilk."[45]

In his third term Roosevelt pursued such a scenario with his defeated 1940 opponent, Wendell Willkie, among other Republicans. The idea was that, led by Roosevelt and Willkie, the New Deal wing of the Democratic Party would fuse formally and for good with liberal-minded Republicans (TR's and FDR's reform impulses united at last), leaving Democratic and Republican conservatives to their joint devices.[46]

Corcoran suggests an almost Darwinian process along these lines in play in conversations in 1945 and 1946, posing the New Deal and Truman circles' resentments of each other in dramatic terms, as more than mere factionalism. "Two new parties are in the process of formation" he says to Senator Hill in July 1945; a "crossroads" is at hand. In the midst of Truman's effort to recruit Douglas to the Interior Department in 1946, Corcoran tells an old Roosevelt ally and appointee, Fred Vinson, Truman's treasury secretary, that Douglas, "has the sense of alliance, which is the great thing that is lacking" at the White House.[47]

With Ben Cohen also on the line, visiting from the State Department, Corcoran waxes philosophic as he recalls the old days to Vinson, once a New Deal congressman: "I was saying to Ben this afternoon the honest truth is that you don't get anything as . . . cohesive as a party that can run a country of 130 million people." American governance requires strategic coalition building on a grander scale than simply the mechanical assembly of "natural, sentimental" factions—"little parties," as in France. Roosevelt's political success flowed from the proposition that "this is an alliance and you gotta run it as a conscious alliance—in peace as well as in war." Corcoran, after all, "had to learn" this rule because Roosevelt "picked me out" to run around Jim Farley's end and manage New Deal coalition outreach to Republican Progressives and independents in his second and third term reelection bids.[48]

But as the months pass he and the others consider the game along several strategic lines. They hold some cards, which appear to grow stronger as Truman, in his bumbling first years in the White House, falls deeper and deeper into trouble.

Several conversations point to a strategic theme: control of crucial positions of power in time for the next presidential election. My father and Ernest Cuneo report in to Corcoran regularly during 1945 on the campaign to put across William O'Dwyer, the Rooseveltians' candidate to succeed La Guardia as mayor of New York in a complicated field, keeping New York organization Democrats off balance. "What have you been doing there, playing cut and counter-cut?" Corcoran asks my father about the mayoral race. (The game plan involves splitting up the field with a profusion of lesser candidates around whom theirs can maneuver. They prevailed up to a point; William O'Dwyer won but, in office, was swamped in scandal.)[49]

In early 1946 James Forrestal, like FDR a product of New York's Dutchess County, contemplates a run for the Senate or for the governorship but has against him the fact that he's a lapsed Catholic. A state Democratic official writes him (Forrestal tells Corcoran) "that he's ready to launch the campaign [for Forrestal] for governor but he's got to get this straight . . . 'Am I Catholic or am I not?'"

Why not "write him back, 'Both,'" jokes Corcoran. But he and my father have a serious plan for Forrestal to clear a campaign with the New York Catholic archdiocese.[50]

Lyndon Johnson prefers to wait for a second try for the Senate two years hence rather than run for governor in 1946, Corcoran tells Ernest Cuneo, because "the governorship is a dead-end in Texas. . . . Well, that might be true. . . . But it would control the delegates, boy, in 1948."[51]

The point behind these and similar cockpit interactions recorded in the Corcoran transcripts is the larger stratagem of securing distinct Rooseveltian power bases around the country. These would then be deployed, perhaps imminently, on behalf of a national candidate—Douglas or possibly Forrestal— in the event that Harry Truman were to self-destruct, or even to challenge him.

With just a slight adjustment of the dial, Corcoran shifts from an oppositional sense of his role as proconsul of the New Deal government-in-exile to that of "wise man" trying to save the Truman White House from the consequences of its own provincialism. With the independent-minded treasurer of the Democratic National Committee, George Killion, a Douglas-for-vice-president man in 1944 who was also close to the Truman circle, Corcoran muses on Charles Beard's recently published *Basic History of the United States,* and on what future historians will write about the 1940s. "That depends on you and me," purrs Corcoran; that is, on an ability to build bridges. "Yeah," Killion agrees, "we are sort of joint trustees of the future of the country."[52]

In December 1945, ironically, the Truman wiretaps pick up Corcoran claiming to have persuaded Roosevelt men Ickes and Forrestal to stay in the cabinet. The reasons are a lack of a better option (and because the perquisites of office are a consideration) in Ickes's case, and in the cause of nothing less than "the institutional vitality of democracy" in Forrestal's. Says Corcoran to Lister Hill,

> I said, Jim . . . "If you can't pull this system off, except with an FDR in office, there's something wrong, and if we haven't got the strength to rally around and see that even if we had a blind man in the White House that we could make the damned thing work, there isn't much to us."[53]

Early in 1946 Truman gave a set piece radio address calling on "the most powerful pressure group in the world," by which "I mean the American people," to move a stalled Congress to action on domestic economic and labor legislation. Corcoran concedes to Senator Hill that Truman's words are "courageous," but "radio speeches don't help this fellow. . . . You're beginning to find how peculiar to the predecessor [FDR] was the personal technique by which he put things across."

Lacking his successor's eloquence and command of media, Truman's only hope is therefore "a strong group of Senators and a working nucleus in the House" of the kind Corcoran helped keep in line for Roosevelt. More, "what we got to do is get a gang of people together who more or less caucus regularly and stick together and [turn such a cohort into] an operating mechanism." He meant, move formally to organize a New Deal Party.[54]

. . .

Douglas's decision to stay away from the Truman cabinet in 1946, and against running with Truman two years later, meant the Rooseveltians would go their own way, and Truman his. One other 1946 event narrowed their ranks and, as in a Greek play, set the stage for a bloodbath that played out for years to come.

Well after midnight on August 13 a distraught Corcoran monitors the returns in the Wisconsin Republican primary race for the Senate between the distinguished liberal incumbent, Robert La Follete Jr., and an upstart named Joseph R. McCarthy. "This thing isn't running right," he says, and by mid-morning the next day, La Follette has lost by some five thousand votes. A true New Dealer on all domestic issues, La Follette had benefited in previous elections from crossover Democratic and labor support in Wisconsin's open primaries and November elections, aided as well by his family's patented Wisconsin Progressive Party. Nevertheless he'd made enemies at home, having moved from prewar isolationism, to support for FDR's third term (though opposition to a fourth one), to early criticism of the Soviet Union's postwar expansion in Europe. Meanwhile, in 1944 the La Follettes' Wisconsin Progressive Party closed up shop; the senator no longer had his own secure base. The full extent of the irony that Joe McCarthy beat Bob La Follette in the open Republican primary with the crossover help of then-Communist-controlled ranks of some Wisconsin labor unions would be appreciated only in years to come.[55]

On the phone La Follette thanks Corcoran for his heavy efforts in the campaign. Corcoran says, "You're the greatest guy in the world, and . . . I hope it it doesn't hurt you too much—I mean, hurt you inside. . . . Don't let it break your heart, Bob." Corcoran tells Douglas at his mountain retreat, "Labor let him down," and urges Douglas to call La Follette and console him.[56]

To another confidant Corcoran laments, "We've lost a lot more than you know—[we've lost] position."[57]

. . .

"Tom, did you ever realize . . . that you put Felix" Frankfurter on the Supreme Court? columnist Drew Pearson asked Corcoran in June 1946.

"I've always had one answer to that," replied Corcoran, citing the jaunty Fiorella La Guardia's famous apologia: "'When I make a mistake it's a beaut.'"[58]

There are many lofty accounts of how one of the central alliances of the New Deal fell into bitter acrimony, with repercussions on much more than friendships. The split between Justice Frankfurter and his allies, and Corcoran, Douglas, Black and theirs, was the back story for bitter doctrinal battle on the Supreme Court from the 1940s into the 1960s. It was also the context of fights over top executive and judicial branch appointments under Roosevelt and Truman. It further crystalized the Corcoran-Douglas group's sense of themselves as Roosevelt's true political legatees.

Frankfurter had been friendly with FDR since the Wilson administration. (Frankfurter kept his Harvard appointment and only visited Washington until Roosevelt sent him to the Supreme Court in 1939. Corcoran, as noted, became Frankfurter's "inside man" in Washington; on his frequent trips down from Cambridge "he would see Roosevelt and then he would see Tom and Ben," recalled one of his and their acolytes.) In the 1930s Frankfurter had been supportive of Jerome Frank and Douglas as well. But by the mid-1940s Douglas, Hugo Black, Corcoran and Co. could not speak of Frankfurter without venom, nor he of them, and most of them spoke to Frankfurter directly not at all. (Jerome Frank kept the connection up, barely, but is also probably the author of a witty send-up of Frankfurter's turgid style, rendering the Gettysburg address as "F.F." would have, beginning, "A semi-centennial, three decades and seven solstices preceding the present, our

paternal progenitors gestated and regurgitated upon the western hemi-
sphere [49 longitude, 38 latitude] a pristine commonwealth.")[59]

The fight at the level of issues was judicial, and sprang from an important
civil liberties case. Its polite face became the division, for the duration,
between the new "judicial activists" led by Black and Douglas, and advocates of Holmesian "judicial restraint," led by Frankfurter. At the next level
down—the personal one—the question was whether "Professor" Frankfurter, senior in age and prideful personal custodian of "the Holmes-
Brandeis tradition" (two traditions, in fact) would continue to lead—in effect, to dominate—"Professor" Douglas and the others. "The son of a bitch
thinks I'm still in knee pants," my father claimed Douglas said to him of
Frankfurter.[60]

Corcoran had in fact had a good deal to do with Roosevelt's appointment
of Frankfurter to the Court in 1939. But in 1941, when FDR's other Court
appointees—Black, Douglas, Stanley Reed, and James Byrnes—wrote the
president supporting Corcoran's candidacy for the post of solicitor general
(the Justice Department's representative before the Court), Frankfurter ac-
tively campaigned against him on grounds of unsuitable "temperament".
Disingenuously, he wrote FDR that "Tom lacks mental health just now"
because of the president's removal of his White House quarterback from
the field, and should be taken care of with a War or Navy Department
appointment. By the mid-1940s bad feeling was the source of wisecracks
like one attributed by my father to Douglas: "Know why Frankfurter never
had any children? Because Holmes didn't." Frankfurter's enemies saw him
as alternately pompous or obsequious, depending on whom he was dealing
with.[61]

. . .

The unfolding politics of the matter were more than personal; they were
operational. Frankfurter was interested in controlling turf as well as directing
policy, and he was effective in doing so. He condemned Douglas, and also
Black, for being "political" justices, but was ever pious about his own maneuvers. (One difference was that Frankfurter, unlike Black and Douglas,
had no potential as an elected official; that arguably called for clothing his
extrajudicial maneuvers at a higher level of piety than they did theirs.)

Corcoran enjoyed his sway in the Justice, Interior, and Navy Departments and the regulatory agencies. Across town Frankfurter relished coun-
tervailing influence at the War and State Departments, at the White House,
and of course on the Court. Frankfurter's energy as job placement agent as
well as manipulative policy maker was as boundless as Corcoran's, but because of his need to cover his game, given his Supreme Court status, more
sly. (Corcoran on his former mentor's gift for subtlety: "Felix works in other
ways his wonders to perform.")[62]

Frankfurter's most extraordinary avenue of influence in the war years was through the aged Secretary of War Henry Stimson, who had been the young Frankfurter's own mentor in the *Theodore* Roosevelt and Taft administrations. Stimson's words on the subject in 1945, in the odd third-person format he and his coauthor (the young McGeorge Bundy) settled on for his memoirs, include these:

> Without the least deviation from his fastidious devotion to the high traditions of the Supreme Court, Felix Frankfurter made himself a continual source of comfort and help to Stimson. . . . He found Frankfurter always the most devoted of friends *and the most zealous of private helpers* (emphasis added).[63]

When, with the onset of the war, Roosevelt began to see the New Deal as a distraction, Harry Hopkins at his side abruptly followed his lead. Frankfurter had done the same, Corcoran, Douglas, and their allies believed, especially thanks to the Stimson appointment and the opportunity it gave "F.F." to manipulate diplomatic and military policy through the elderly war secretary. To Frankfurter's certain delight, Hopkins helped knock down the president's interest in drafting a strong man — specifically Douglas; Wendell Willkie was another candidate — to run war mobilization on grounds that neither one "knew anything about production." (Hopkins, wrote Douglas later, "was adept at 'throwing sand in the gears'" of any potential competitor for influence over FDR.) Stimson, no doubt prompted by Frankfurter, told Roosevelt the idea of Douglas for the role was "hideous."[64]

Whatever the higher calling of public service, the elements of intrigue soon became the talk of the town. Douglas wrote of a 1943 dinner conversation with Roosevelt on the subject of a Supreme Court replacement for Justice Byrnes, whom FDR called to the White House as war mobilization administrator following his flirtation with Douglas about just that scenario. The president was chatty: "I am not going to appoint [court of appeals judge] Learned Hand." Why not? "This time Felix has overplayed his hand . . . You have never seen the kind of campaign that he has put on. Why, today I saw a dozen people with the same burning message — that I should appoint Hand. I saw so many that my Dutch is up, and I just ain't going to do it."[65]

Junior and senior Frankfurter protégés alike, from Stimson and Hand to associate Supreme Court Justice Robert Jackson, ascendant State Department official Dean Acheson, and White House assistant Ed Prichard, considered him their bosom friend as well as sponsor. "The Justice is probably the closest friend I have," Acheson recorded years later; "I cannot write about him at arms length." A devoted comrade to such men, Frankfurter could also deploy his protégés as virtual chess pieces on the table in a match of high stakes.[66]

Young Edward Prichard did business with both sides of the feud, and his prominence (like Corcoran's) as a source for Drew Pearson and other reporters led the FBI to tap him as well as Corcoran in the mid-1940s. But his loyalty to Frankfurter took precedence, and the tenor of his talks with the justice falls somewhere between the dramatic dialogue of Shakespeare rendering conspiracy and David Mamet rendering speech patterns.[67]

A brief sample, from lengthy conversations in 1945, about Frankfurter's intervention to help persuade Undersecretary of War Robert Patterson to succeed Henry Stimson as secretary:

PRICHARD: Well, the question was put [officially, by a top Truman aide] this afternoon . . .

FRANKFURTER: What did the Judge [Patterson had been a federal judge] think?

P: Well, he thinks he wants to take it.

F: Wants to?

P: Well, he thinks he sort of . . .

F: I don't think he wants to . . . I don't think he's coquetting about it. . . . I'll have more, better judgment on it when he talks to me [again] Monday morning . . .

P: Was he surprised when you talked to him?

F: Absolutely. Oh, absolutely! Flabbergasted. . . . I really did a swell job. I don't know when I did such a good piece of . . .

(*Later*)

F: Well, did [the Truman aide and Patterson] have a good talk? Did he . . .

P: Oh, yes.

F: When was this, Prich?

P: This afternoon, three-thirty.

F: Uh-huh, and [the Truman aide] said he spoke for the all-high, did he?

P: Sure he said so, because he did.

The fastidious jurist had time for many more such conversations.[68]

A confidant of Secretary of State Byrnes tells Corcoran in November 1945 that a plan is underway to merge the wartime intelligence services, into what would eventually become the CIA, and place them in the State Department. There, the two men speculate, they would fall under what Corcoran calls the "Frankfurter axis" (principally Undersecretary of State Dean Acheson.)[69]

Corcoran and Acheson worked closely together at the Treasury Department in 1933, when Acheson was undersecretary—"I was once his valet," Corcoran remarks wryly to another friend. (He was his deputy.) In the 1930s Acheson tried to recruit Corcoran to his prestigious law firm, Covington and Burling. In a 1946 conversation he tells Ernest Cuneo, at issue is the question who will control the flow of intelligence operations: Acheson?

"Well, he's Felix . . . The guy that's keeping him coked up is F.F. . . . I don't believe all the dirty things that are said about Dean. I do believe them about Felix."[70]

My father wrote Henry Luce at this time that "Frankfurter's tortuous intrigues can be summarized in this simple fashion. He wants to run the Chief Justice. He wants to continue running the State Department. . . . He wants to get Douglas off the Court, but not into the State Department," the one appointment that appealed to Douglas. And "he wants to control the [next Court] appointee." (The young Arthur Schlesinger Jr., a recent Luce recruit to Time, Inc., strove to make sense of all this for *Fortune* magazine late in 1946. He recorded encounters with "Eliot Janeway, a brilliant busybody," acting both as an influential player at Time, Inc. and as a "one-man protection gang for Douglas"—Schlesinger's article was critical of the Douglas-Black position. Fires cooled, friendships were formed.)[71]

Inherent in these exchanges is that by 1946, at the heart of a fair share of Washington politics and policy making, was the explosion of the New Deal's formidable intellectual energy into a savage feud. To Corcoran and his friends, Frankfurter's chess game had less and less to do with the New Deal, or with principles of policy, and more and more to do with personal influence. Hopkins and Frankfurter, said Corcoran, were responsible for "busting up" the once closely knit New Deal circle "into three" factions. The first two belonged to Hopkins and Frankfurter, in this rendering. The third, the only one that kept the New Deal in focus, was the one organized around core New Deal senators and congressman, Corcoran's alliances in all three branches, Harold Ickes for the ten months he stayed in Truman's cabinet, Black and Douglas on the Court, and Douglas's political prospects.[72]

. . .

In the spring of 1946 the feud tearing the New Dealers apart became poisonous. Frankfurter was pushing Robert Jackson to replace Harlan Stone as chief justice, a step up that Jackson and others swore Roosevelt had promised him years earlier. Meanwhile Jackson's role as Nuremberg war crimes trial prosecutor troubled people of all sorts of political stripe, who reacted against the notion of ex post facto "victors' justice." (Douglas later wrote, with emphasis, that Chief Justice Stone, Associate Justices Hugo Black, Frank Murphy, "and I thought that the Nuremberg trials were unconstitutional *by American standards.*")[73]

Corcoran and other New Dealers, meanwhile, were pushing a somewhat reluctant Hugo Black for chief justice. Black and Jackson had fallen into a bitter, personal acrimony, behind which, according to Black's biographer, "was Frankfurter," who "had run out of justices to convert" to his thrall. Goaded by Frankfurter, Jackson saw Black as the leader of the enemy Court faction.

Prosecuting the Court feud rather than the Nuremberg cases, Jackson unleashed a bitter personal attack on Black for not recusing himself from a case in which a former law partner appeared before the Court and cabled Truman insultingly about his intentions for the chief justiceship. To Bess Truman the president wrote that Jackson had "surely gone haywire." To his former Senate colleague, Truman said of Jackson, "Hugo, let him sink in his own piss mire."[74]

"Remember the time when we were all friends?" Corcoran asks Drew Pearson wanly after Jackson's blast at Black. Compounding the trouble, says Corcoran, are the president's apparent naïveté about designs by manipulators (specifically, Frankfurter), and by those of the conservative opposition laying in wait to profit from Truman's sloppy performance and weakness for hacks.

"They've been waiting a long time," says Pearson of the conservatives. "They had a smart guy" to contend with "in the White House before, but now they've got a dumb cookie."

"Money never sleeps," Corcoran replies. "Fools always do. [The presidency] is a twenty-four hour a day job."[75]

. . .

A general, a duke, as well as a lieutenant; a strategist as well as a co-conspirator, Corcoran was endlessly creative, could recruit allies, build coalitions, manage fights, move mountains. He played more versatile roles for Franklin Roosevelt, and for the upwardly mobile Lyndon Johnson in the first decades of his career, than lay within the powers of the others.

Yet, after years of intimate trust between them, Roosevelt concluded that Corcoran was a force whose assaults on current problems tended to create new ones. With deep ambivalence and words claiming opposite intent, he parted with him.

"This is the most critical year in our country's history and you simply cannot leave me now," FDR wrote his aide on January 20, 1941, the day of his third inauguration.

> You must know that I understand fully how much your front-line fighting has put you "on the spot" and that you can no longer contribute effectively without portfolio. As our plans unfold, National Defense will have positions of rank and responsibility where your great talents and powers will be desperately needed. All this, as you will be the first to appreciate, takes time.[76]

Post after post for Corcoran—beginning with those of solicitor general and assistant secretary of the navy for air—came up for White House consideration between 1941 and 1945. At such moments those heavily promoting his appointment included Ickes, Douglas, Hugo Black, Forrestal, Rayburn, Johnson, and others whose own interests Corcoran had been the prime mover in advancing. One question was whether senators Corcoran had offended in fighting Roosevelt's battles were numerous enough to block his confirmation for a cabinet or subcabinet appointment. Another, raised by friends as well as rivals, was whether Corcoran could ever play a singular, disciplined, second-string role, or whether, by learned behavior, he had to be in charge, at the center of action, unmanageable. Roosevelt's delivery on his statement of intent in January 1941 never came.[77]

Johnson's precocious prominence in Washington, like Douglas's special relationship with Roosevelt and potential for national office, was greatly owing to exercise of influence by Corcoran beyond repayment. The points of connection, whether they involved the New Deal's mastery of Wall Street, the New Deal's fight for public power, Roosevelt's election campaigns, the use of White House power to elect New Dealers (and purge enemies) in state elections, and presidential appointments at all levels, all flowed through Corcoran. Yet Corcoran's history with Roosevelt repeated itself. Both Douglas and Johnson came to prefer dealing with the sinuous Abe Fortas and the shrewd, elegant, slightly bogus but always discrete Clark Clifford to counseling with the ever ingenious, bare-knuckled, high-risk Corcoran.[78]

. . .

Corcoran's image of his Rooseveltian partners in disarray in 1945 ("a bunch of political refugees . . . a helpless bunch of sheep") begged the question of his own role as the center of gravity for the enterprise. Joseph Alsop, who knew Corcoran well in the 1930s and forties, had a tart view of him as a "spinning top" who had been "purged of basic ideals" in the 1920s by that "corrosive skeptic," Oliver Wendell Holmes. That view misrepresents Corcoran's genuine reform interests, but nevertheless the two metaphors together—center of gravity and spinning top—suggest the unstable elements of the House of Roosevelt. As the partners headed off on their own, their joint resolves became more contingent, less concerted.[79]

On the other hand, what was left was not just loose association. Scholarly analyses of the New Deal's legacy tend to focus on shortcomings in policy agenda going forward and to neglect its long-term impact on the organization of power nationally. Until Roosevelt, progressive reform and populism had not been able to fuse effectively, and the South and West were on the outside looking in. By 1945, spurred by New Deal development of the resources of those regions, and by mobilization in World War II, Texas and California were beginning to rival states like New York and the industrial midwest in the national scheme of things.[80]

That was part of the thinking behind a message Corcoran sent Douglas at his Oregon cabin in the summer of 1948, at the climax of an extraordinary race for the U.S. Senate in Texas, that "Lyndon . . . is very important from many points of view."[81]

IN MY FATHER'S HOUSE

❧ 6 ❧

Rise of an Insider

"WE'RE GOING TO GET HUBERT

SOME DOUGH"

T he New Deal elite was a natural group for my father to align himself with as a young man. Like them, he had lofty aspirations and
a scrappy personal makeup that linked passion for theory and dissent, instinct for original information—and for political maneuver.

His story in a thumbnail, as I first learned it, was a blend of early prominence and shrouded mystery. He was the "baby" of three children (his sister
and brother were twelve and eight years old when he was born in 1913).
Their father, a hard-working doctor, died suddenly in 1937, and their mother
was a very old woman when I first knew her as a boy in the 1940s. I was
at first told not more about these grandparents than that they were hard-
working European emigrants who thought for themselves, and who succeeded in America.

As my father told his story, he'd gone up from the old Townsend Harris
School in New York to Cornell in 1928 as a fast-track freshman at the age
of fifteen, passionate about baseball and reading but with a smart-aleck
contempt for conventional teachers. He drifted at Cornell (he liked to boast
later that he flunked economics) until rescued by an erudite teacher who
inspired a lifelong taste for writers gifted at subversion: Voltaire, Moliere,
Proust. From there to philosophy, his major, and then to Marx and Veblen,
John Reed and Lenin, Keynes and Schumpeter. In 1931 he was a "brash
visitor" to New York from Ithaca with an introduction from another Cornell
faculty patron seeking assignments from John Chamberlain, an editor and
critic for the books pages of the *New York Times.* "Eliot wanted to take on
books about Hegel and William James," Chamberlain recalled, "but had
to be satisfied with a Western story."[1]

Then in 1932, his senior year, age nineteen, he left. Next stop: the London School of Economics. His fleeting allusions to this and the subsequent period of his life suggested "youthful escapade," even romantic outlawry, but no narrative line attached to them.

He would convey this much, in oblique asides more than any other way: Under the lead of LSE teachers like R. H. Tawney and Harold Laski ("a phony"), he studied Marx, moved left, went to Sunday evenings for students at the home of John Hobson, scholar of imperialism and influence upon Lenin and Keynes. Through friendships with the poet John Cornford, the journalist Claud Cockburn, and others, he found his way into Communist Party circles in London. Then he took off for Moscow to see the revolution, returning to New York in 1934. Of Marxism he said in his seventies, "I was intrigued. . . . It was the only theory around." Candid, unbuttoned, in the family, he would remark, "As a kid, I was too radical for the Communist Party."[2]

The one startling aspect of his résumé he did not work overtime to hide in later life was that he failed to take degrees from either Cornell or LSE. His version was that he'd been an implacably precocious young man, "no discipline, no purpose," in too much of a hurry for institutional education. "The class bastards who had never been in trouble with their mothers," he remarked in an interview in the 1980s, "all passed Civil Service examinations. They were the only jobs around. Those of us who couldn't or wouldn't" follow such a course, the "perpetual rebels, became graduate students."[3]

In London my father encountered Keynes's theories of public investment, alternatives to systematized ideologies on the right or left, before they became well-known in the United States. Like many young radicals who flirted with Marxism and contemporary Communism in the first few years of the Great Depression, he was drawn over to Franklin Roosevelt's course of pragmatic experimentation, and encouragement of radical thinkers like those who would become the American Keynesians. But he did so from the left, and skeptically, seeing the Roosevelt administration as confused about how and when to act on the new doctrine of government intervention in the economy. He saw that, politically and intellectually, the New Deal was up for grabs.

Back in New York in 1934, another spur to his appetites came from John Chamberlain, who began paying the young man to read proofs and help him select books for review in the *New York Times*. Still involved with Communism, my father "found it boring to distribute Marxist pamphlets in Harlem," Chamberlain remembered years later, "but it was the boring quality of the pamphlets . . . that turned him away from orthodox radicalism." He published some freelance pieces in magazines on the left and, with Chamberlain's help, in the business and weekend sections of the *New York*

Times. In 1935 he found work on weekday mornings with a business economist who ran a small research bureau monitoring commodities markets.
Salary: $21 a week.[4]

As an economist his specialty became the interplay of markets and political forces. In 1937 he began publishing pieces in the *Nation*. In several of
these he attacked European establishment support for fascism in the 1930s.
A residue of a Marxist overview in his writing is evident. Driving British,
French, and American acquiescence in support of Franco's rebellion in
Spain, he wrote in September 1937, and even more significant than Hitler's
and Mussolini's backing of the Spanish fascists, was "the most powerful and
respected group of men in the world today—the international of world
capitalism," bankers and business consortiums with an interest in regimes
with which they could do business comfortably. Rhetoric aside, he was also
an alert reporter, poking into disturbing topics like German and Japanese
appetite for American export of strategic materials, and of the mix of com-
placency, inertia, and fascist sympathy in elite circles in the democracies
that was nurturing the traffic. Another set of pieces anticipated and dissected
the "Roosevelt recession" of 1937–1938.[5]

With these articles my father brought himself to the attention of influential New Dealers. Yet it was only after he published the first several that
he was, by his own account, "no longer a Communist." No longer a Communist, but a skeptic of the order of things for whom the Marxist critique
of capitalism continued to be suggestive. In the wake of the Cold War, of
espionage, betrayal, scandal, hysteria, and bitter reckoning with all of these,
it is difficult to imagine a time so long-gone that, as he put it in his seventies,
"the cross-pollination of one or another kind of self-styled Communists and
New Dealers" was part of the political environment. An example was the
charge in 1938 by New Dealers led by Harold Ickes (echoed privately by
the president himself in conversation with Douglas) that the Roosevelt recession that year had in fact been brought on by "a capital strike"—literally,
a capitalist conspiracy.[6]

. . .

"Too radical for the Communist Party," my father was just right for New
Deal brains-trusters like Corcoran, Cohen, Douglas, Arnold, and Frank,
radical thinkers and men of action who looked more to the home-grown
radicalism of Thorstein Veblen than to Marx.

Jerome Frank, an SEC commissioner in 1938, read the *Nation* and knew
its publisher, Freda Kirchwey. My father petitioned Frank for help that
spring for an article about New Deal economic stimulus. They met and
took to each other. Within weeks Frank was offering him part-time consulting work, making confidential documents available, and writing solicitously about a premier issue of the day, "When you are in Washington next

I shall surely want to get you together with some of the [New Deal] economists with reference to the immediate difficulties you see ahead of us with
respect to [spurring economic] consumption."[7]

Sometime later Frank recalled my father as someone he'd found "unusually brilliant" and "introduced and commended to many top-flight
Washington officials . . . and to whom I gave much information about official doings when I was on the SEC." Frank also secured him an SEC
consultancy and office in its New York branch for some months. He ad-
vanced the eager young man at once to Douglas and Corcoran and urged
Henry Wallace's deputy to recruit him, "with [his] quick grasp of any situation and a capacity for vigorous action," as head of the Agriculture Department's Commodity Exchange Administration. (A civil service job, it
carried overly strict requirements and the idea died.) From there it was a
short step to Ickes, Fortas, Arnold, and many others.[8]

A budding economist who was wired the way these New Dealers were,
had a knack for calling the next turn, and could as a journalist prod the
administration and especially the slow-witted and conservative forces in it
was an appealing ally and confidant. "Very confidentially," Frank wrote him
in August 1939, "I wish you would reflect on the possibility of doing a piece
. . . along the lines of the following idea, which the President has in mind,"
which involved demonstrating that the economy was less productive than
existing measurements of it claimed. One by one these men and their extended network added my father to their brotherhood.[9]

. . .

A year earlier, according to my father's account, Henry Luce's trusted business manager Charles Stillman, who thought *Time* magazine's business coverage was worthless,

> told a fellow called Ralph D. Paine—I used to call him Crewman
> Paine (he rowed . . . on the Yale Crew and was that kind of journal-
> ist)—that he was either going to get fired as business editor of *TIME*,
> or he was going to find one and get promoted. Stillman said, "How
> can we be charging these outrageous advertising rates when we have
> nothing to sell in the middle of a depression?"

Resorting to old school tie, Paine went to see chairman of the SEC William O.
Douglas, former bright light of his alma mater's law school. Paine said (so
my father claimed), "I'm about to be fired unless I can find someone who
can satisfy *Time*'s advertisers without catering to them." Douglas sent Paine
to his new friend Janeway. My father started at *Time* in early 1939. Thus
did the young Cornell dropout, just turned twenty-six, owe his job as business editor of *Time* to Eli Yale.[10]

Henry Luce had an eye for writers of unusual and unorthodox talent.
Among his employees in the late 1930s and early 1940s were James Agee,

Dwight Macdonald, John Hersey, Theodore White, Robert Fitzgerald, John Kenneth Galbraith, Irving Kristol, and Daniel Bell. But Luce cultivated a relationship of mutual interest with my father that went far beyond his taste for restless, iconoclastic young writers.

A Republican but an inquiring freethinker, thoughtful but inarticulate, Luce disliked the New Deal and the sometimes glib New Dealers. Nevertheless he and Roosevelt occasionally dealt with each other as potentates, finding common cause against isolationism on the eve of World War II, for example. But Luce, a moralist, was, as a biographer puts it, "always anxious to expose Roosevelt as a devious opportunist." A shrewd newsman, he also recognized his magazines' need to report on Roosevelt and his administration authoritatively.[11]

In my father Luce had a combination of inside track to Washington and against-the-grain nature. The idea of holding Roosevelt to account, and pouncing on the administration's fumbled balls and failures of imagination, suited both Luce and his new employee fine. My father provided inside stories for *Time, Life,* and *Fortune,* and arranged and mediated off-the-record sessions for Luce with suspect but influential New Dealers. On occasion he caused Luce heartburn, and induced so much of it regularly in the Time, Inc. bureaucracy that Luce sometimes reined him in. (The writers apparently liked him; he claimed to have run the office dart game with James Agee.) But most of the time Luce enabled his exuberant young reporter-editor to operate in Washington, in effect, as a combative New Dealer. He consulted him as well on corporate matters.[12]

Together with Luce he also met several times in 1940 with the Republican publisher's favorite presidential prospect, utility executive Wendell Willkie, to debate privately the latter's contentions about New Deal agencies and policy and to contest my father's coverage of him in *Time* and *Fortune.* (Characteristically, my father reported back to one of his administration intimates, Jerome Frank, who'd succeeded Douglas as chairman of the SEC, on such Willkie charges as that Frank was "quite cynical" in a move against Willkie's corporate empire, and was "one of the most brilliant lawyers in the country and all that, but just a tool in the hands of the [New Deal] sharpshooters who have perverted the merits of cases in their determination to get" Willkie.)[13]

Then a flip of the use of influence, for with the coming of the draft my father's view of his situation was as the essential inside reporter on Roosevelt's management of the war effort, not as a soldier in battle. He pulled strings in Washington to stay out of uniform but needed his employer's backing. Time, Inc. appealed for his exemption from the draft on grounds of indispensability, in these terms:

> The launching of the national preparedness effort made it imperative
> that someone with a skilled grasp of the workings of the economy be

associated with the Editor-in-Chief [Luce]. . . . Supplementing TIME
Inc.'s News Bureau . . . [Janeway] must contact for the Editor-in-Chief
. . . at both the policy and news-gathering and editing levels . . . editors, publishers, writers, Congressmen, Senators, National, State and
local Government officials, businessmen, labor leaders, farm officials,
religious and minority group spokesmen and foreign visitors. . . . This
job calls for unique and unusual editorial capabilities.

It worked.[14]

. . .

Playing both sides of the street, my father's expansion of connections thereafter was swift. He wrote economic analyses for Corcoran, Douglas, and
Frank, and for their protégés at the SEC, Treasury Department, the Federal
Reserve Board, the Justice Department, the White House, and an unusual
arm of its response to the 1937–1938 recession, the Temporary National
Economic Committee (TNEC). These New Dealers in turn became unusually candid sources for his reporting and writing. Rexford Tugwell of FDR's
first brains trust recorded in his diary in the spring of 1941 that he, Corcoran,
Douglas, and Ickes were feeding my father material for a *Life* article that
spring designed to "converge on the President from numerous sources" with
the proposition that "if what we have got is worth surviving in competition
with what Hitler has got, we must . . . [use] its revolutionary possibilities"
against totalitarianism rather than simply mounting a military response.[15]

Development of these relationships brought my father into contact too
with the New Dealers in Congress and in the war mobilization effort. Mobilization was a story that *Time, Life,* and *Fortune* needed to cover. But the
war limited casual travel. In contrast to the more Washington-bound New
Dealers, he began to broaden his horizons on Henry Luce's ticket. He
learned how to move through Chicago, St. Louis, Denver, Seattle, and find
his way into a reportorial command of local and regional politics (Republican as well as Democratic) and economic and social trends. The smart
entrepreneurs, power brokers, and newspaper publishers in those cities became new sources, points of contact on his network.

Mobilization also meant recruitment to Washington of more businessmen, some relatively liberal, like Corcoran's and Douglas's friend James
Forrestal, some more conservative. Forrestal and my father became fast
friends, and the connection led the younger man to many other business-
world sources.[16]

Another new and special friend of the second New Dealers was the garrulous, ambitious, and able young congressman from central Texas whom
they called on each other to assist. My father's version of part of the story
was this: at lunch one day in 1939 Secretary of the Interior Ickes told him
that Roosevelt and Corcoran were enthused about this remarkable young
man Lyndon Johnson, recently arrived in Congress. Indeed, my father

would recall, Ickes told him that FDR had confided in *him* "that if he hadn't gone to Harvard, that's the kind of uninhibited young pro he'd like to be; and that in the next generation the balance of power would shift south and west, and that this boy could well be the first [modern] Southern president."

After lunch my father took the train back to New York. There he had a message from his lifelong co-conspirator, Wall Street lawyer Edwin Weisl, personal attorney for Harry Hopkins among other points of political connection. Weisl said he'd had "a funny kind of call" from Hopkins urging him to get to know "some kid in Congress named Lydie Johnson." And so the young LBJ, passionate advocate of TVA-like public utility projects for impoverished central Texas, strung his first private power lines north of Washington.[17]

As a journalist who traveled, my father became astute at picking up on raw talent, and helping new players like Johnson make the right connections themselves. He was in on the emergence of Walter Reuther, then rising in the United Auto Workers and developing a plan for war production, and helped bring him to Douglas's and his other Washington friends' attention and to Time, Inc.'s. One night in the first year of World War II, when Washington hotel rooms were suddenly scarce, Reuther was stranded there with no bed for the night. He called my father, who opted to call Lyndon Johnson for help. Reuther spent the first of some nights in those years on Lyndon and Lady Bird Johnson's living room couch.[18]

. . .

For years I'd noted my father's tracks in the published diaries, memoirs, and biographies of politicians and other public figures from the 1930s through the 1960s. After his death in 1993, in an effort to see him whole and to try to reconstruct the world as it seemed to him and his friends, I put them together, with the help of unpublished letters and other materials in library archives and a pungent set of oral history transcripts he made in the 1980s. A chronological sampling:

In 1940 he was part of a dialogue Supreme Court Justice Hugo Black entertained about putting his name in the ring as the liberal Democratic candidate for president if Roosevelt opted not to go for a third term. Later that year, without leaving Henry Luce's payroll, he became part of Corcoran's team, coordinating with Mayor La Guardia, managing the Roosevelt third-term election campaign outside of organization Democratic channels. Typical among his messages to campaign headquarters were one on how to exploit the record of New Deal agencies' rescue of local businesses in key cities, another on how to counter the Willkie campaign's inroads into the black vote.[19]

This was a leap for a still somewhat raw and newly rooted policy gadfly and journalist into the national political arena, though not unusual in the culture of New Deal talent recruitment. Luce—writing his own journalistic

rules, putting Time, Inc. squarely behind Willkie's presidential campaign—
indulged the arrangement, in the manner of a corporate magnate who
contributes heavily to both political parties. At that and other moments
Luce rose above the outrage of his more conventional-minded lieutenants.
(Frustrated about my father's "fit" at Time, Inc., one of them wrote Luce
of a suggestion to give him more autonomy early in his tenure there:
"Janeway floating through interstellar space would send off a shower of
meteors that would put some terrible craters in our well tended fields.")[20]

Harold Ickes's diaries for the spring of 1941 record lunch with "Elliot [*sic*]
Janeway, one of the editors of *Life* and *Time*, . . . a great friend of Bill Douglas, and . . . very well informed as to what is going on in Washington." The
topic, inevitably with the solipsistic Ickes, was the interior secretary's feuds
with his rivals within the administration. That same season, working with
Corcoran and Jim Rowe, my father raised substantial money in New York
for their friend Congressman Johnson's run for the Senate in a special Texas
election.[21]

In the spring of 1942 Rex Tugwell, then Roosevelt's governor of Puerto
Rico, stopped in New York for dinner with old friends, including Jerome
Frank and "Eliot Janeway, who always regarded discouraging events as
disasters rather than as difficulties." My father, wrote Tugwell, "says the
reactionaries are incapable of becoming good soldiers. They have to stop
their war work every time someone says 'New Deal' and make a speech.
And they would rather prevent public ownership of something than win a
battle any time."[22]

In 1942–1943 he was a regular at Interior undersecretary Abe Fortas and
his wife Carol's "New Deal salon parties." He counseled with Fortas, who
feared his career would be inhibited by Washington's small-town antisemitism, about leaving the capital and building a law practice in booming Los
Angeles. He went to ball games with former postmaster general James
Farley, on the outs with Roosevelt but still in the political swing, and with
Mayor Ed Kelly of Chicago. In April of 1943 Ickes came to New York and
had dinner with my parents at "21"; the next day my father brought Luce
to Ickes's hotel and the three handicapped the 1944 election.[23]

There are many references to his role, at Corcoran's side, in trying to
engineer the 1944 vice presidential nomination for Bill Douglas. But, as
recounted in the last chapter, Harry Truman, having won the ring, proceeded as president to authorize wiretaps on the phones of the irrepressible
power broker at the center of the effort to edge him out of the vice presidential designation the previous year. My father turns up on a number of
the Corcoran wiretap transcripts, trading inside signals with Corcoran about
Truman's new atomic diplomacy, his cabinet selections, prospects for political advancement for Douglas and James Forrestal, Walter Reuther's rise
as a national labor leader, Corcoran's view that Truman's conservative ju-

dicial appointments "will kill" the New Deal's regulatory agencies by reversing their decisions on appeal, and much else.[24]

In 1946 my father corresponded with Alvin Wirtz, then Lyndon Johnson's most influential backer in Texas, as to whether the congressman should run for governor of Texas that year or stay in the House and run again for the Senate in 1948. With his friends Corcoran, Fortas, and Forrestal he explored possible newspaper purchases, toward a New Deal–oriented newspaper chain. He played intermediary between Luce and Forrestal about a possible sale of Time, Inc. to the latter. When that failed to materialize, he urged Forrestal to square away the issue of his lapsed Catholicism with the powerful, newly minted Francis Cardinal Spellman as a prelude to becoming a candidate for governor of New York, and then for president.[25]

And so on, through the decades that followed.

. . .

Over the years my father's personal style—writing and conversational—hardened into a lordly, insistent certitude about life, and most particularly about the inner workings of politics and economics. This certitude he based on a unique access to information about what was *really* going on, together with a command of that information that left scant room for disagreement.

Much of that persona had its roots in his nature. But it seems to me that much of it traces too from the sequence of didactic influences on him in his youth. For he'd moved swiftly, before he was thirty, from the determinism of Marxist theory in the face of capitalist collapse, into the power elite of the liberal New Deal and Roosevelt's administration of the war, and at the same time into the inner sanctum of Henry Luce, the conservative who set the haughty tone of *Time* magazine in the years of its greatest influence.

Many who were drawn to Communism in the early 1930s retained its conspiratorial as well as intellectual style long after their politics moved on, or moved right. Scholars have commented on Marx's rhetorical armory of "slogan, climax, anaphora, parallelis, antithesis and chiasmus," the last especially in phrasings like "The weapon of criticism cannot, of course, supplant the criticism of weapons." Such didactic, epigrammatic style was one of my father's signature touches from his twenties to the end of his life (typically, in 1968, "Because America still refused to recognize that Dulles had died, England found herself forced to pretend that Keynes had never lived").[26]

His secret of youthful Communist involvements perhaps foreclosed appointment in a Douglas administration in 1945, or, in the wake of anti-Communist hysteria over the next decade, to high public office later on. But few independent operators of his generation managed their access to mainstream political power, once achieved, with a more seasoned talent for the dialectics of Higher Intrigue.

. . .

My mother and father met in 1935 at a party in New York, ran into each other again at a subway stop, and began seeing each other. "He knew a lot. He knew things I wanted to know and I guess I knew things he wanted to know," she would say in later years, and, at other times, "He was simply the most intelligent man I had ever met." She was born Elizabeth Ames Hall (nicknamed "Babs" by a Scottish nurse) to Brooklyn gentility, granddaughter of an Episcopal minister and daughter of a naval architect. They were a professional family whose savings were wiped out by the Depression.[27]

My mother started college at Swarthmore in the fall of 1930; then, as the Depression took its toll on her family, transferred as a history major to Barnard so she could live cheaply at home and commute to college by subway across the boroughs of New York. She supported herself with part-time work writing advertising copy at Abraham and Strauss and handling orders at the Book of the Month Club. My mother's student radicalism, she recalled in an oral history interview fifty years later, extended not much further than friendships and group events that featured inspired renditions of the Communist anthem. In a Barnard tap dance class, "one of my friends and I worked out a routine that we could do to 'The Internationale.'" She joined a boycott of her graduation ceremonies in 1935 in protest against Columbia president Nicholas Murray Butler's firing of some radical instructors. Shortly afterward she published her first fiction in *Story* magazine and began to work on a novel about two sisters, caught up in the dislocations of middle-class life in the Depression years, called *The Walsh Girls*.[28]

Photographs of her from those years convey a stylish, smiling, intelligent face just short of beautiful; rich dark hair, sometimes piled high, dark eyebrows, often a cigarette in hand. My father lost most of his hair in his forties, but in those early photos it's curly and dark. Posed together they are a handsome, sophisticated pair, his frame towering over hers, warmly engaged with each other. From an early age I was struck by how smoothly of an evening, to a record or out where a band played, they moved out of their roles as thinkers, writers, authorities and into a graceful foxtrot. Women (a high school friend's mother told me in the 1950s) often found my mother "frighteningly smart." The reason, I think, was a shyness at her core that left her short on small talk. The photos don't show either side of such a coin; they portray a warm and relaxed presence.

The Walsh Girls was published by Doubleday in 1943. The *New York Times Book Review* ran a front page piece heralding "a novelist who can be as penetrating (and delightful) as Jane Austen—and modern enough to treat Freud as a next-door neighbor." John Dos Passos among other established writers praised it; it became an immediate best-seller. Two years later a sophisticated novel of the war years, *Daisy Kenyon*, added to her success.

Twentieth Century Fox bought it for what seemed like a lot of money then ($150,000) and made it into a vehicle for Joan Crawford.[29]

Sometime in 1935 my parents moved into an apartment together on LaFayette Street below 14th Street. In 1938, just before my father went to work for *Time*, they married and headed uptown to West End Avenue, then to the East 70s, and then to the spacious apartment I remember as a child, a twelfth story penthouse at 444 East 52d, with a terrace overlooking the East River.

I'd been born in 1940, my brother Bill in 1943. But from the start my father's gift to our mother, what she came to call their "bargain," was that she had "help"—a cook, and a nurse for my brother and me. She was a writer, not a housewife. They were cosmopolitan New Yorkers who enjoyed good restaurants, theater, night clubs, their times; they'd been among the hundreds dancing in the aisles at Benny Goodman's 1938 Carnegie Hall Jazz Concert. (Into her sixties, when the right tune was on the record-player, my "frighteningly smart," no-small-talk mother would step out in a deft, solo swing dance step in the living room, poised forefingers wagging in thirties style.) Together they'd clawed their way out of what the Depression had done to their families and millions of families like them, and they were never going back.

. . .

In 1946 we moved to Redding, Connecticut, seventy miles into lush Fairfield County. My father had left Time, Inc. with a consulting arrangement with Henry Luce and a contract to write a book about Roosevelt's administration of the war. My mother was deep into a new novel. I entered first grade at Redding Public School in the fall.[30]

My father took train trips to New York and plane trips to Washington; sometimes we came along. In Connecticut guests came to stay, and some of them had names you heard on the radio news of the day, like Walter Reuther or Justice Douglas or Secretary of Defense Forrestal. The time Reuther came to stay he organized the after-dinner cleanup into an assembly line.

My father was on the phone a lot; first, a warm-up chat with the local operator who placed the long-distance calls, a gossipy Democrat helping my parents and their friends move in on the local party organization. He allied himself with the ascendant Democratic boss of Connecticut, John Bailey (later John F. Kennedy's national campaign manager and postmaster general), maneuvered with Bailey among rivals for office who became national as well as state political figures: Brien McMahon, Chester Bowles, Thomas Dodd, and later Abe Ribicoff. According to Joseph Lieberman's biography of Bailey, the latter "needed a horse" in the 1946 governor's race. He picked the lieutenant governor, a former Wesleyan professor and poet called Wilbert Snow, and commissioned my father to organize a "vigorous" issues campaign around soaring prices and other economic issues, especially those concerning returning veterans, in order to hold the line in a landslide Republican year. He got Snow to dramatize the sky-high price of meat by calling a Montana rancher who "pledged to ship steers to Connecticut at a fair price if the state would pay the freight charges." But the candidate had a fatal penchant for missing appearances, and, my father claimed, "wanting to give speeches in verse."[31]

In 1948 my father's picture was on posters on telephone poles around Redding and street-corners in Bethel and Danbury, the nearest metropolises. He was running for the Connecticut legislature—in a deal, he said, to help the Democratic ticket, headed that year in the state by Chester Bowles, running for governor. He liked to add that he ran several hundred votes ahead of both Harry Truman and Bowles, "but God forbid I should have won and had to go to Hartford!"[32]

This immersion in local and state politics added to the authenticity of his claims as an insider, often expressed in sardonic commentary on the typology of the players. John Bailey, whom he would agree to disagree with about Jack Kennedy in the next two decades, and continue to do business with, was "a pro. Nobody like him. He's my friend." Bowles was the liberal idealist as ambitious amateur who didn't know how to operate; he "can't keep his word." Ribicoff was, able, "good government," no superstar; a Jewish Democrat whom Catholics, Protestants, and Republicans could take to, so mainstream he made "highway safety" a top issue as governor in the late 1950s. At the close of one of Ribicoff's races my father called the candidate to see how the contest was going and signal the imminent arrival of a brokered campaign donation. How especially was he doing in Fairfield County, adjacent to New York state, swelling with postwar suburban development?

"Fairfield County's *on fire for me,*" Ribicoff pronounced. In fact, the flames were low and Ribicoff had a close call that year. The point of my father's rendition was that a slightly pedestrian, safe, "sleeper" candidate was, endearingly, as susceptible to self-inflated pronouncements as a flaming demagogue.

. . .

The family colloquy to the background sound of *Pal Joey* or Schubert on the record player stopped on command for evening radio news and commentary. ("Listen to Murrow—tomorrow," Drew Pearson, or "Pierce Gruesome" as he was known at our house, Walter Winchell's rank puns and malicious insinuation.)

My father's orchestration of conversations at the table led from the news, folding in as well the daily phone take from his throbbing information network. This he varied with dazzling bits of insider history laced with arch wit, often a vignette from a sort of Forbidden New Deal. Tales of secret deals and alleged affairs, Lyndon Johnson's with fellow members of Congress Helen Gahagan Douglas and Clare Boothe Luce. On the latter liaison: "I told Lyndon if he thought that was the way to get publicity in *TIME* he'd better lay off." Johnson, he would note, complained that Clare "wasn't so hot and you had to listen to her."[33]

Or, "Joe Kennedy and Missy LeHand, who was Roosevelt's smart and tough secretary and his girl," I remember him saying one night, "stole the Massachusetts delegation from Al Smith in 1932 and delivered it to Roosevelt. Missy was wired into the Church, you see. They did it through Spellman, who was still a Bishop in Boston. When Missy had her stroke in '41, Roosevelt just dumped her. He couldn't deal with it. Kennedy and he weren't speaking by then, but Joe got into the act and paid Missy's bills until she died in 1944. It was his way of saying 'fuck you' to Roosevelt."[34]

The theater of this sort of talk was multidimensional. My father loved telling such tales. From a young age I couldn't hear enough of them. It was the form our father-son bonding took. I was his captive audience, but a willing and eager one. My mother took part in this storytelling, sometimes contesting the details or lessons. Their tales were for me the stuff of glowing legends from the great world brought home; initiation into that world by hearing, again and again, stories of their intimacy with it.

Physicality marked a number of the anecdotes, making them that much more vivid. There was one about my parents sitting with Forrestal in the secretary of the navy's box at a freezing cold Army-Navy football game during the war. Custom dictated that the secretaries of war and of the navy take salutes from their respective marching bands at halftime. The undersecretary, which Forrestal was then, substituted if the secretary was away. He was, and Forrestal was called back to the office with his official entourage during the second quarter, leaving my parents alone in the secretarial box. At halftime the Navy band marched inexorably toward the box to give the salute. A Walter Mitty situation for real; my father took and returned the salute as he imagined it should be done.

Another involved my mother hurriedly taking a seat at an outdoors occasion at the president's home in Hyde Park in 1941. Remarks were being delivered; the Roosevelts were seated in a front row.

> Mrs. Roosevelt wanted to greet us, and she turned and said, "Do come down." And so I started down to shake her hand, and I fell over FDR's feet [with their heavy steel braces], *flat* on my face. And he leaned down, and he just picked me up like that, you know, very powerful arms, because he had to use the crutches. And he sort of [set] me on my feet.

She remembered that the president seemed serene, she the one with the disability.[35]

But she was hardly unassertive, then or afterward. Once "Eliot, Abe [Fortas], and Ben Cohen were writing a speech" for the New Deal's premier polemicist, Harold Ickes, she recalled in the 1980s. Owing to technical incapacity on the part of those three,

> I was typing it. I thought of this often after the women's movement [laughter] became active. . . . There I sat at the typewriter with . . . three men dictating to me [but] I didn't feel at all put upon. . . . My attitude at that time went back to my radical past, and I said, "I control the instruments of production! There is nothing that goes through this typewriter that I don't approve of! I won't type it, and they can't!"[36]

. . .

A number of the tales involved the tightly fought 1940 presidential election campaign. "I [was] working for Tommy," my father explained in a 1980s interview—that is, as noted, moonlighting from *Time* by helping Corcoran with the independent campaign for Roosevelt's reelection, working outside the realm of the old-line Democratic Party machine organizations.[37]

A favorite theme in his narratives was that the higher the stakes, the lower the comedy. Roosevelt's 1940 running mate Henry Wallace, it will be recalled, had unusual side interests: he was involved with a White Russian cult leader, one Nicholas Roerich, to whom as secretary of agriculture he'd written bizarre, coded letters addressed, "Dear Guru." A Republican newspaper publisher had copies of the letters, and the word was out that he was preparing to print them, rich in "mystical occult language." According to Douglas, newly arrived on the Supreme Court, Roosevelt sought the justice's legal advice on dumping Wallace and designating a new running mate. In New York my father and Rex Tugwell, in 1940 working for Fiorello La Guardia, met with the mayor to discuss damage control.[38]

La Guardia was just off to Detroit to make a speech for Roosevelt; Tugwell and my father drove with him in his limousine to the airport. The mercurial La Guardia kept pounding his fist into his hand as he counseled the need for a move that would consume reporters' attention should the "Guru Letters" break in print. "We've got to keep this story off page one of the *Daily News*," he said. The three agreed to think hard about how to stage such a distraction. La Guardia would call them from Detroit. The afternoon and evening wore on; no call. Finally my father turned on the radio for the evening news and heard the lead item, to this effect: "New York's Mayor Fiorello La Guardia, speaking at a Roosevelt campaign rally in Detroit, today physically assaulted a heckler."[39]

The New York tabloids had a good day with La Guardia's hands-on demonstration of how you make news with the intent of changing the subject. The payoff was that the Wallace-Roerich story was buried in a mutual deterrence trade, whereby the Democrats stepped back from putting out word about Wendell Willkie's long-running affair with Irita Van Doren, book review editor of the *New York Herald Tribune*.[40]

My father would tell of watching Roosevelt give one of his classic, crowd-pleasing speeches at Madison Square Garden a week later, pouring ridicule on isolationist opposition to war preparedness led by three Republicans the alliterative rhythm of whose names in his rendition brought the audience along in unison: "MAH-tin, . . . BAH-tin . . . and FISH!" (Congressmen Joseph Martin, Bruce Barton, and Hamilton Fish.) He recalled that, in a choice position near the official entourage, he felt embarrassed by Roosevelt's stagy histrionics. Gradually he realized two keys to Roosevelt's performance. He used his head, shoulders, arms, and voice with such dramatic excess in order to shroud the immobility of the rest of his body. And that the point was to project that mobility where it counted: not to the VIPs near the platform, but to the rank and file, far out in the Garden's balconies.[41]

My mother remembered Roosevelt's 1941 inauguration as "open house at the White House." An invitation sufficed; "You just walked over and went in." My father's few audiences with the president himself were group events, occasioned by a senior official sponsor like Forrestal or Ickes. At one of these, he told Doris Kearns Goodwin, he was riveted by Roosevelt's command of his physical situation: "He was smiling as he talked. His face and hand muscles were totally relaxed. But then, when he had to stand up, his jaws went absolutely rigid. The effort of getting what was left of his body up was so great his face changed dramatically. It was as if he braced his body for a bullet."[42]

A favorite tale involved the actress Miriam Hopkins, a dazzling blonde from Georgia favored by Ernst Lubitsch in his 1930s romantic comedies, and an established actress on Broadway. In private life a fervent New Deal Democrat, Miriam was an active Roosevelt supporter in the 1940 campaign. Eager for the company of people with ideas, she took to my parents and they to her, and she became a kind of aunt figure in my life.

Miriam took over Tallulah Bankhead's Broadway role in Thornton Wilder's *The Skin of Our Teeth* in 1943. Thanks in great part to Henry Luce's press empire, Wendell Willkie was widely thought to be the presumptive Republican presidential nominee in 1944, having given Roosevelt the run of his life in 1940. One night he took in Wilder's play. A partying fellow, Willkie sent a note backstage inviting the alluring Miss Hopkins to join him for a late supper.

As Miriam and my father would tell the story in duet in later decades, the next thing she knew she was back at her Sutton Place apartment, the more than dutiful Willkie insisting on seeing her in. Then, blurting something about "fires burning deep inside," Willkie lunged heavily for her. Miriam reached for an instrument of defense and found it in a lamp, knocking Willkie senseless. (She would mime this scene with dramatic flair.) Seeing the potential for disastrous publicity, needing help, she called my father and woke him with these words, in her Georgia drawl: "El'yit, ah think ah've just killed the next Pres'dent of the United States."

My parents lived then around the corner from Miriam. My father rushed over to her apartment and helped her revive Willkie with cold water and coffee. Henry Luce's designated candidate and his journalistic bad-boy knew each other well enough by then. Gossip about Willkie's affair with Irita Van Doren having damaged him in 1940, Willkie saw that a quick end to this evening was indicated. Tempted by the possibilities, my father nevertheless had to protect his friend Miriam Hopkins. Meekly, the once and perhaps future Republican nominee for president suffered the employe of his friend Henry Luce and part-time operative of the 1940 National Committee of Independent Voters for the reelection of Roosevelt to usher him discreetly out to elegant Sutton Place and a taxi.[43]

. . .

The folding of my brother and me into our parents' circle of accomplished friends had felt to us, growing up, seamless. Hanging in the hallways in the series of our country homes and rented New York townhouses and apartments in the 1940s and fifties were framed cartoons of Bill and me as dashing World War II fighter pilots by Milton Caniff, creator of the "Terry and the Pirates" and "Steve Canyon" comic strips. Ethel Barrymore Colt, daughter of the grand dame and a lovely singer and actress on Broadway in her own right, made a special recording of bouncy numbers for the two of us ("Gonna dance with a dolly with the hole in her stocking, / Gonna dance by the light of the moon.")

In my father's study were signed photographs of the Washington eminences—Hugo Black, Jimmy Byrnes, and Douglas in judicial robes, and the rest. There was one from Lyndon Johnson, cigarette dangling from his fingers in his wavy-haired 1940s matinee idol pose, addressed to Bill and me "with my best wishes always."(And there, staring at me in the 1990s from the midst of momentous letters about historic events in William O. Douglas's papers at the Library of Congress, typed by my mother or father or a secretary on *Fortune* stationery in the years when they were as family with Douglas, is this note:

> Dear Uncle Bill: I didn't see you for a very long time. Will you come over in the daytime and see me because I might be asleep in the night time when you come. I think Bill would like to see you too. Give my love to Aunt Mildred. When do you think you will be here. . . .
> Love and kisses—from Bill too.

The signature is added—"Mike"—in a four-year-old child's awkward scrawl. An official Supreme Court stamp notes the date of receipt: April 12, 1945, the day Franklin Roosevelt died.)[44]

In 1952 my parents declared the Connecticut years over, and back we went to New York. My father's arrangement with Time, Inc. after he left its daily employ in 1946 had involved writing a weekly memorandum of insider news and analysis for Luce derived from the network of sources around the country he'd developed working for his magazines and moonlighting in Washington. But Luce's needs as well as his tastes were changing as he moved from the role of "founder" and news-hungry editor in chief to CEO and then chairman of his proliferating corporation. My father decided to try the principle of the weekly memo for Luce as a newsletter for sale to people—mostly business executives—who wanted to be in the know. It took hold; business clients followed.

Every six of eight weeks my parents gave a large party, which we were allowed, even encouraged, to join. The organizing principle for these events was to blend my mother's place in the literary world and my father's across the intelligentsia to politics and business. They were friendly with a community of established writers, some of whom my mother had begun working with on issues like copyright at the Author's Guild, of which she became president in the mid-1960s. These included John Cheever, John Hersey, Ralph Ellison, Dwight Macdonald and their wives, writing couples like Robert Penn Warren and Eleanor Clark, Francis Steegmuller and Shirley Hazzard, Katherine Ann Porter, and the publishing first circle of the day: Blanche and Alfred Knopf, Mary and Cass Canfield, Dorothea and Roger Straus. Odd links popped up in conversation. Cheever and Ellison were alumni of the New Deal's Federal Writer's Project. Hersey, MacDonald, and Eleanor Clark had worked with my father at *Time, Life,* and *Fortune*; with my parents they shared recollections of less decorous, more alcoholic evenings in the 1940s involving stars who flamed out too soon: Jim Agee doing his imitation of Leopold Stokowski, with all the orchestra sounds to boot, and Wilder Hobson, stripped to his drawers, doing a flawless FDR: "Students of the ah-Case School of ah-Dentistry: Youuuu . . . ah DEN-tists! I-ee . . . am a DENT-tist . . . ah-too!"[45]

Then there were theater friends, along with Miriam Hopkins, including Elmer Rice and Abe Burrows. Once to a small gathering, Ethel Barrymore, full of delicious gossip from the 1920s (one was invited to wonder just how friendly she'd been with Winston Churchill then). I recall Burrows, writer-director of *Guys and Dolls* and *How to Succeed in Business Without Really Trying,* telling a tale of his youthful days as a Wall Street runner during the Crash of 1929. And there were journalists, scholars, businessmen, and lawyers; bookish visitors from England like Denis Brogan, suave figures from international finance and their elegant, erudite wives.[46]

On one of those crisp, cool nights that signals the start of a New York season, Jean Stafford, chic in a "little black dress" and a dazzling pearl necklace, plumped herself down on a sofa, accepted a stiff first drink, and set the tone for the evening: "I love this dizzy burg."

At intermissions of Broadway musicals, at "21," Sardi's, or Toots Shor's, at the Oak Room of the Plaza to hear Lisa Kirk or Ella Logan sing cabaret, at Ed Weisl's box at Yankee Stadium, my brother and I were trained in patience with the flow of our parents' progress and small talk across the burg's dizzy spectra: Why, here were Mayor O'Dwyer, Mayor Wagner, Lillian Hellman, John Lardner, Marietta Tree, Irving Kristol, Irving Howe, Senator Javits, Governor Ribicoff, Mary Lasker, Chief Justice Warren, Helen Gahagan Douglas, Walter Winchell, Ken Galbraith, Jim Farley, Zero Mostel . . .

Once in 1957 or 1958, with snow flying outside, I came in late from a teenager's night out. My father, hearing the key and the door, called down, "Mike, come up and meet a great man." This was Alf Landon, governor of Kansas and Republican candidate for president against FDR in 1936, an enlightened, old-fashioned progressive in his own way. That could have been, but wasn't, an evening when Miriam Hopkins, who brained Wendell Willkie that night in 1943, was stopping by.

. . .

To be around my father, to be—as a boy of twelve or fifteen—invited to listen in on a phone extension as he traded in information or engaged in maneuver with men like Corcoran, Johnson, Douglas, Reuther, John Connally; mayors, governors, senators, candidates, power brokers of all stripes, Republicans for purposes of arrangement, trading, and espionage, was to be witness to the hum of the discrete machinery of influence.

In action, my father's words and manner conveyed an authority that was part intellectual, part tonal, part *physical*. As he aged, posture firm and baronial, balding in a caesarlike way, his face conveyed pulsing intellect, weight of presence, an ancient resourcefulness. Eyes, impassive between sharp, almost Asiatic cheekbones, would narrow and widen for emphasis. Beneath them half-glasses, auxiliary armor, sat midway down an aquiline nose. He signaled shifts in tone: assertive, ironic, confidential. The voice was high-middle New York—articulate, mordant, nasal: directive. It said (whatever the subject or words), *This is the inside story, product of an extraordinary experience and intelligence network, presented now with a command of context, an appreciation of intrigue and shading, more sophisticated than you ever imagined—or could. . . . It's my pleasure to share this unpublished piece of it with you.*

His demonstration of sophistication always took into account received wisdom, as a means of mooting it. It included distinctions between those players who were "smart," "terrific," from those who were "idiots," "Boy Scouts," "phonies." His acid asides left you eager not to be associated with the latter. On Thomas E. Dewey, from a recorded interview: "By the time Dewey ascended to his reward, he was . . . more interested in being able to call David Rockefeller 'David' [than anything else]. As if David Rockefeller knew anything about the banking business." Of Dewey's running mate in the 1944 presidential election, John Bricker of Ohio: "Then a very popular governor. . . . Didn't have a clue as to what was going on in the world, but neither did Ohio."[47]

. . .

My father used body language like an actor or a politician. One mode was ever so relaxed, as if to say, "I'm *always* working, but this is the kind of side conversation I've got time for." He seemed taller than his six foot-one, comfortable standing together with men of imposing bearing—Lyndon Johnson, Stuart Symington, Clark Clifford.

Another mode—sitting or standing—escalated fast from certitude to intimidation. Thus his signature facial expressions—a favorite was to raise his left upper lip and eyebrow as he narrowed his right eye—conveyed editorial asides like, "This is beyond confidentiality" or "I'm telling you this dead-pan to underscore its absurdity" or "X is beneath contempt—and so are you by association if you buy into him."

In those years Washington's parochialism and separateness from New York, and Main Street's separation from them both, gave the individual who could bridge those distances leverage. Persuaded or not by my father's authoritativeness about those far-flung domains, his interlocutors were at least intrigued by his presentation and style; wired, different, provocative. For this thousands of them over time—consulting and newsletter clients, audiences for his lectures, syndicaters of his newspaper columns and publishers of his books—paid good money, beginning with the base-rates of $100 a year for his retailed newsletter, $500 for a more confidential one.

In the early 1950s, his newsletter selling well and pulling in consulting work, he incorporated himself and took on an office staff. My weekly allowance became a salary for reading the *Congressional Record* and clipping it for items of interest to him; my car in college leased and written off as a company car. He got into investment ventures, mostly real estate; through these merged his office and family residence arrangements, with tax advantages. There were more servants than ever. He took on a limousine and driver.

At the end of the 1960s, after thirty years of renting New York apartments, my parents finally bought a home in the city. They set up residence and offices in a six-story town house on 80th Street east of Fifth Avenue (previously Elizabeth Arden's home), in blithe defiance of their own past delight in Veblen's theory of conspicuous consumption. With it their transmutation of their commanding intellects into a design for living and for material reward seemed complete.

. . .

He would begin with an offbeat idea for remedying a problem, then look for a place for it to go. Some were unlikely.

A typical overheard phone conversation one weekend morning in 1958: "I haven't been near Lyndon with it," my father says to the Senate Republican leader, the stolid but friendly Bill Knowland of California. Twenty years after Roosevelt's team got smart about deficit spending, anticipating the Kennedy tax-cuts of the 1960s, my father is frustrated with Johnson's reluctance to risk his "moderate" stance in Texas by confronting Eisenhower over the issue of economic stimulus in the face of recession, and they've exchanged cranky letters on the subject. ("Dear Lyndon: It was with a heavy heart and a deep sense of shock that I read . . ." and "Dear Eliot: Frankly, I never object to accepting responsibility for my actions. . . .")[48]

So my father has come up with an idea for backdoor executive-branch spending that would stimulate the markets, force Johnson's hand, and be opportune for Knowland and his colleagues, worried about the economy hurting Republicans in the fall elections. One of his side shots.

In the exchange of information his topics were usually the interior machinery of the government's relation to the economy, but sometimes they were straight politics, or its ugly sibling, political dirt. (He had, for example, an accurate handle on what became known as the Joe Kennedy–Jack Kennedy–Frank Sinatra–Sam Giancana–Judith Exner linkage, and on its implication—J. Edgar Hoover's blackmail of the Kennedy family—as it was happening, years before informed opinion was exposed to it.)

But he was more analytic and entrepreneurial about information than most of his Class A network. They would trade intelligence in single components. He would put two and two and two together and broker the results, whether as a mainstream exercise through channels or (more fun) as a guerrilla maneuver.

Sometimes he made a play for the sake of impact, to stick a foot in the door—or, as he put it once in his *épater le bourgeois* voice, "to keep the chaos organized."[49]

. . .

Another family moment; about eleven on the morning of an election day: "We're going to get Hubert some dough."

On the days leading up to a primary or November election, he would be on the phone with candidates for office around the country: with their managers, with the journalists covering them, with businessmen, lawyers, labor leaders, others with an investment in the incumbent or challenger.

From 1940 on those candidates included an odd lot defying clear order, Johnson and Ribicoff, Helen Gahagan Douglas and Wilbur Mills, Hubert Humphrey and Jimmy Carter, Stuart Symington, Estes Kefauver, Eugene McCarthy, Fritz Hollings, Hugh Carey, George McGovern, Gary Hart, Sam Nunn, Jim Wright . . . Many, many now forgotten others. Republicans, usually at odds with their party's old guard, including La Guardia and La Follette in the old days, Jacob Javits, John Lindsay, and Lowell Weicker later. Or someone he'd been known to scorn but with whom—spin of the dial—he was now in tactical conjunction. Always, the long-lived men in the middle: Corcoran, Clifford, Jim Farley, John Bailey, Robert Strauss.

Explicitly the subject would be the contest, the angles, the issues, the odds, money. Implicitly it was the question of influence and leverage next week, next month, next year.

We're going to get Hubert some dough . . . —who was "we" in my father's formulation? That could be interpreted in a number of ways, depending on circumstances. It could mean just him and a co-conspirator of convenience, or a cluster of them, with links back to the Rooseveltian brotherhood, plus an interested business client or two. There were many possibilities. "We" was for my father a house of a term in which there were many mansions.

But this was election day. What did he mean, "going to get"? When?

That was the point. Sometimes, as important as the amount and the source was the timing. If it was money from heaven that helped put the dark horse or the embattled incumbent across at the eleventh hour, or if it was Republican money hedging bets on a Democrat slated to win, then the elegance of the gesture was in its last-minute arrangement. No matter the source of the money, the influence of the co-conspiracy in channeling it could as a rule be leveraged more effectively if it arrived at the climax of the campaign. Most politicians of consequence were, after all (my father would frequently observe) "ungrateful sons of bitches." It followed that one needed to emphasize one's advantages in dealing with them.

I asked if the deal was done.

"Not yet," he said. His sardonic smile conveyed the spirit of the game. "It's too early."

7

Ends and Means

From his youthful radicalism my father retained profound skepticism of the establishment and a taste for carefully targeted subversion in the service of his goals. Less as a matter of doctrine than contrarian judgment call he would now and again wind up in a radical position on an issue of the moment. The day after the dropping of the atomic bomb on Hiroshima in 1945, for example, he remarked to Corcoran, "We will never live this down." He held to that view.[1]

Toward the end of his life he recalled an odd encounter with Wendell Willkie, in the wake of the latter's defeat in the 1940 presidential election (but before the midnight encounter with Miriam Hopkins). Willkie, former Democrat and liberal by Republican standards, was toying with the idea of running for governor of New York, his friends in the Luce and Cowles press empires urging him on. Through intermediaries among them, my father recalled, Willkie approached him in a spirit of friendly co-option. In response, he says he gave this only slightly disingenuous account of himself:

> I told him politics was always an extension of my own center of gravity, which was trying to figure out how things worked; that I was not in politics in any professional way. That I'd be a poor aficionado for him to have. But more than that, that the only times I ever did anything [political] was out of desperation, when I thought ideas had to have legs attached to them. And that my affiliations were Democratic . . . that I was too much of an anarchist, an individualist, an eccentric at heart to be able to line up and salute inside the Republican organi-

zation and that Will Rogers' definition . . . was the best one I knew:
"I belong to no organized party. I am a Democrat."

In fact, the purely cerebral satisfactions of attaching legs to ideas notwithstanding, he loved to mess about in politics—according to his definitions
of goods and evils, opportunities and threats, order and anarchy.[2]

Operationally, as a man of the Second New Deal he believed that government—appropriately directed, manipulated and, when necessary, sub-
verted—was the crucial factor in a sophisticated industrial economy. Business and industry were the engines of the machine but decidedly not the
brain.

The brain could not be institutionalized either in government or business. It depended on people like him who could travel between the two;
who had command of relevant information, inside information, about each.
In one of his public tributes to Douglas, my father characterized him as "a
Jeffersonian phenomenon—a man of ideas who symbolizes the power of
those ideas." Add Douglas's less well-known political operator attributes to
the mix. There was a model.[3]

. . .

As something of (in his words) an anarchist, my father was a connoisseur of
the chance convergence of ideas and power, of markets and the fears of
people in the street. As a "New Deal hortatorian" (as his friend at *Time*,
Theodore White, wrote of him once), he took his lead from those who, with
Roosevelt, believed in the power of improvisation in managing American
resources against fascism.[4]

In the summer of 1941, amid talk of Bill Douglas as the indispensable
man to administer the war effort, as Bernard Baruch had for Woodrow
Wilson in World War I, Douglas wrote Jerome Frank (one of those strongly
urging Roosevelt to make the appointment) by hand,

> To me it is absurd that I am the only one who can swing the defense
> job. The country is full of talent—untapped and unused . . .
> Furthermore, the success of the effort would seem to turn less on
> any one man than on the coordination of a whole army of men . . .
> Furthermore, the problem goes deeper than organization.[5]

From Douglas's antiheroic note to Frank in 1941 about himself, to my
father's 1944 words to the inward-looking justice about Douglas's "army" in
search of its commander, to reflections, to a theory: "The militaristic totalitarianism of Roosevelt's period seemed at the time to be an omnipotent
masterpiece of organization," my father wrote a decade later at the end of
The Struggle for Survival, his history of Roosevelt's administration of the war
effort. "To organize its defeat, [Roosevelt] put his faith in the unorganized
momentum of American democracy." He argued that without that mass

mobilization, leadership was by definition hollow and that the real cynics—those who believed democracy was bankrupt—would prevail.[6]

This cohort of Rooseveltians prided itself in being tough and hardheaded, and faulted Henry Wallace in the 1940s and Adlai Stevenson in the 1950s for ineffectuality. To an extent the coherence of their own faith depended on Roosevelt. To an extent it was their energetic powers of interpretation and application that established the bona fides of Roosevelt's often vague and compromised claims to high ideals. Work to be done.

Six months before Pearl Harbor, *Life* published a long, detailed report of my father's on Roosevelt's diplomacy called "Roosevelt vs. Hitler"; this was the piece Tugwell, Corcoran, and Douglas fed him material for as an occasion to influence FDR's thinking. Its theme was that a mighty arsenal and ringing patriotism were not enough to defeat totalitarianism. He concluded with an evocation of the president's great "Four Freedoms" speech a few months earlier: "Not very exciting to us, perhaps even too commonplace to be taken seriously. But what does freedom of speech mean in Warsaw, freedom of religion in Vienna, freedom from want in Paris, freedom from fear in Rotterdam?" The hold of Hitler (a "mystic illiterate") on Europe, he added, may seem mysterious, but

> to the discouraged, to the despairing, it is not only the glamorous way of parades and sacrifice, it is the easy way in which your thinking is done for you. It has an appeal. We should recognize it . . . [and] with new hope, see the weapons we have against it and, backed by our technical might of farm and machine, of food and armaments . . . say to Europe and the East: You need not submit. Here in this country we are free in body and in mind. Listen to our President. Freedom is your birthright too.

(Reflecting Luce's unusual arrangement with my father was a boxed editorial statement that accompanied the prominently displayed report, which stated in part,

> Mr. Janeway, an associate editor of *TIME*, has long been close to the group known as "the President's men." Much of what he says could not, for obvious reasons, be said for quotation by Government officials. Regardless of what many Americans may think of the war and the New Deal, *LIFE* believes they should know what the U.S.'s grand strategy is.)[7]

On the occasion of Roosevelt's death four years later, he wrote what served as the Luce magazines' eulogy for him, also in *Life*. In it he celebrated the president's "almost magical skill" in responding to America's greatest crises since the Civil War, in these terms:

> History will of course remember Roosevelt as a great war leader, as a reformer, and as an architect of international policy. But the other

figures of Roosevelt could never have existed if the politician had been maladroit, stupid, doctrinaire or conceited. On the politician's success hinged any opportunity for statesmanship.

From the New Deal to the war years, he argued, Roosevelt succeeded in directing American versions of the "explosive forces of racial, religious, ideological and class intolerance which have reduced so much of the world to rubble" into "political terms," thus avoiding bloodshed on these shores. If, he argued, FDR's "opportunism" was the essence of his political skill, "Let us remember for once the simple things for which that skill was used: for unity, for tolerance, for the chance that the future may be better than the present."[8]

. . .

Beyond such showcase pieces of journalistic pronouncement, my father occasionally took on a cause that, whatever the self-interest quotient, partook of outright idealism.

In a 1949 novel my mother wrote of the United Automobile Workers' strike against General Motors in the winter of 1945–1946:

After the last war . . . the big pattern-making strike had been in steel. That had been for money, too, ostensibly, but it had not *really* been, any more than this strike was. Both of them were tests, tests of whether the power labor had gained during the war could be kept, of the amount of control the men who ran the machines could exercise over the economy.[9]

The UAW's General Motors strike featured one of Walter Reuther's innovative concepts for labor-management relations extending to broad social and economic policy. (The idea was not only to solidify labor's wartime gains but to advance the New Deal policy of increasing workers' purchasing power by getting GM to agree to raise wages but not prices—and to open its books to prove it didn't have to raise prices. The strike succeeded only up to a point, but it propelled Reuther into the UAW presidency.) At Reuther's behest my parents helped run the National Committee to Aid Families of GM Strikers, which (my mother as secretary of the committee, reported to Reuther at the end of the strike) raised over $200,000. Gracing the committee's roster were names like Eleanor Roosevelt, Harold Ickes, Reinhold Niebuhr, and Rabbi Stephen Wise; my parents enlisted such unexpected additions as Henry Luce and Harold Stassen. Reuther's biographer credits my father's influence for Luce's endorsement of UAW strike principles through the pages of the Time, Inc. publications. "More than any one else your efforts are responsible" for the success of the committee, Reuther wrote them after the strike; "a most important factor in bringing our struggle against the General Motors Corporation to a successful conclusion."[10]

My father's narrative style, in a report to Reuther on his efforts with the committee to support the workers' families through the months without wages, smacked more of the trenches than did my mother's:

> Yesterday I fought on the phone for an hour with Governor [Frank] Lausche [of Ohio] who told me that I was being used as a front by the Communists and that no [auto-worker family] distress existed in Cleveland because Cleveland social conscience would not tolerate it. The Governor is an old friend of mine, but he . . . sees red everywhere. . . . Lausche has promised to call me back.[11]

He was capable of drawing the cheers of others. Working to ignite a "draft Douglas" movement in 1948 from rural Connecticut, handicapped by primitive phone service and no formal power base, he was in feverish touch with politicians and Douglas enthusiasts all over the country, exploiting what looked like Truman's potential to drag down other Democratic candidates. One of his collaborators was James Allen, a Douglas aide at the SEC turned influential California business executive and dabbler in politics. Allen wrote him in the midst of the effort, "Baby, you're superb! I can't believe that in the whole country there can be another imagination capable of self-generating a political campaign! I'm not kidding."[12]

. . .

At times of loss he always had an epitaph, polished with spin. One of my first recollections as a child is of being in our wartime apartment on East 52d Street when the news came of Franklin Roosevelt's death. My mother and our Irish nurse and cook, Anne and Mary McManus, wept. My father was in charge: "It had to happen. He was failing badly." Then, quick to the phone to dissect the fall-out with his Washington network.

I remember his and my mother's shock in Connecticut four years later when word came that James Forrestal had leapt to his death at Bethesda Naval Hospital, having copied out lines from Sophocles' "The Chorus of Ajax" ("Thy son is in a foreign clime . . . / Worn by the waste of time / Comfortless, nameless, hopeless save / In the dark prospect of the yawning grave"). Like Douglas and others, he had first-hand anecdotes about Forrestal's collapse into paranoia and depression. He'd visited him in Washington during his decline and waited while the butler persuaded the disintegrating secretary of defense to come out from behind heavy drapes at his home. But his preferred rationale when I was growing up was not mental illness per se, but rather that struggling with the dilemma of use of the atomic bomb as the Cold War deepened "is what killed Jim."[13]

In February 1953 former senator Robert La Follette committed suicide with a shotgun. Two versions of the reason why circulated. One, in the newspapers, was that he was worried about a serious heart condition. My father's and Corcoran's, based on phone conversations with La Follette that season, was that he'd been profoundly depressed by Wisconsin voters' return of Joe McCarthy to La Follette's old Senate seat the previous November. In the 1946 round, McCarthy had been an unknown, a former Democrat, and La Follette had been vulnerable. Six years later McCarthy's demagogic opportunism was toxic in the land, and Wisconsin, the state the La Follettes had built into a laboratory for progressivism, had acquiesced in it.[14]

This explanation passed over the fact that Corcoran had been directing work to La Follette from the United Fruit Company (which in earlier years, as noted, had contributed to the senator's campaigns at Corcoran's behest). The work included lobbying officials in the newly elected Eisenhower administration to take action against the leftist government of Guatemala; the campaign that led the next year to the CIA-United Fruit overthrow of that government. The question what net effect that work might have had on La Follette's mental state is not known.[15]

When Peggy Corcoran died suddenly in 1957, Corcoran was devastated. But what he said to my father over the phone was, "I've still got my boys. I've still got my Margaret" (his talented daughter, who was to become Hugo Black's law clerk and herself die suddenly at age twenty-eight). "That's Tommy," said my father, coming off the call. "Always, always defiant."[16]

. . .

In viewing the tableaux of the present and immediate past, the passing of moral judgment was, most of the time for my father, a relative thing. No illusions: thus Lenin was as murderous as he was brilliant, and Stalin, in taking over Marxism-Leninism and destroying (along with the lives of millions of people) the remotest semblance of anything democratic or idealistic in it, further rendered the Communists monsters, the worst that anyone said of them. Only a naïf could imagine that Stalin and his collaborators would have stopped short of executing their colleague Nikolai Bukharin at the height of the purges, cutting a deal with Hitler in 1939, murdering Trotsky in exile in Mexico in 1940, institutionalizing the police state. Their evil was a given. But what mattered in reckoning their impact on the world (and, therefore, how to act in clear-eyed awareness of them) was that they'd solved immediate problems of power, at least long enough to moot challenges to their shot at making history.

That was arguably an amoral, even cynical view, but not to be confused with the view of totalitarian power held by Hitler's appeasers, prone to romanticize their monster and invest in his lies and promises. To recognize Stalin as "a killer," as my father would refer to him, to speak similarly of Joe Kennedy, or ruthless barons of the Senate of the 1950s like Robert Kerr of Oklahoma (a Democrat) or Styles Bridges of New Hampshire (a Republican), or Nixon's accomplice John Mitchell a decade later, was to see them for what they were—the better to deal with them or fight them, depending on what you were trying to get done. It was never to imagine that such creatures of brute force were driven by anything but greed for more of what they had.

. . .

At my father's side, sometimes ahead of him, my mother intuited the interior lives of people in or near power. The protagonist of her 1949 novel *The Question of Gregory* (for whom, beneath the surface, she drew on the conflicted inner nature of Bill Douglas) absorbs news of the death of FDR with this imagined interior dialogue:

> The President is dead. I knew him very well.
> Really! What kind of a fellow is he? What kind—what kind—what kind—
> Oh yes, I knew him very well.
> Oh yes, Mr. Gregory's an old inhabitant. You came to Washington in 1935, didn't you?
> Nineteen thirty-four.
> Really! What kind of a fellow—
> Why—it's a little hard to describe—You have to know—Charming, yes. Magnetic, yes.
> Does he know—does he mean—
> Sincere? My dear fellow—. . . [17]

She dealt with politics in her fiction only for context. Indeed, she disliked "political" literature. Commenting on the culture of the 1930s in which she came of age, she wrote once,

> My taste for seeing people in a landscape, responsive to pressures of social givens and temporal shifts, doesn't mean that I admire novels (and the thirties were full of them) that turn individuals into allegorical figures. The "socialist realism" of that period descended too easily into the cartoon plot, familiar from Soviet films, which we summed up as "Boy meets girl meets tractor."[18]

Her dislike of clichés paired with my father's, and they enjoyed being smart about current events together. He admired her mind and might defer to her political responses and judgment. He loved the fact that among their prominent friends husbands—including Douglas, Forrestal, Jerome Frank, Henry Luce, and Lyndon Johnson—as well as wives, read her novels and wrote letters about them. "You may remember that I was the original Babs Janeway fan," wrote Douglas. Forrestal would restrain himself, he remarked, referring to the *New York Times*'s praise for her first novel, from "address[ing] you as the Jane Austen of the Roosevelt era." The legend of his lack of interest in books notwithstanding, Johnson insisted to my father early in 1946, "Tell Babs somebody gave [Lady] Bird 'Daisy Kenyon' for Christmas, and I read the whole book Christmas Day. I couldn't put it down until I finished it." He wrote her directly, similarly, when her next novel appeared.[19]

My mother appreciated my father, having gained, thanks to him, entry into an infinitely more exciting world than she could have hoped for as a girl with a desire to write, out of Barnard by way of genteel Brooklyn Heights. If they hadn't found each other, she told my brother once, she might well have fallen into marriage to a sweet, suitable, and dull accountant or lawyer.

Of the two, she was sometimes the one who fielded others' critique of my father—and sometimes responded. Jerome Frank wrote her in 1944, having read some of her novel *Daisy Kenyon* in draft manuscript,

> You might bring out the fact that mingled with [ambition in figures like Corcoran and Forrestal, on whom one of the characters is loosely based] was a component of valid "idealism," "romanticism," if you please, about the country's (and the world's) future. Don't let Eliot's (journalistic) cynicism overwhelm you; it hasn't overwhelmed him for all his hard-boiled talk.

Some months later, in a note thanking Henry Luce for his compliments to her on the novel, she responded to a striking comment by the most powerful publishing baron of the day about his young associate:

> Why do you think Eliot knows too much? He knows a lot. Why "too much"? I don't think he misuses what he knows. Seems to me "too much" comes only when the individual can't handle the knowledge any more, and loses control of his material;—in such case to the material itself, which tends to become autonomous and compelling. I can think of people to whom this has happened, but it ain't happened to Eliot.[20]

Growing up, I grasped that my mother—resourceful in her insights— had an astute sense of my father's acquisition of his power, and her own artillery as well. And yet the chronically inarticulate but shrewd Luce had a point that went beyond reason, which eluded her.

. . .

I became aware that for my mother dealing with my father meant "handling" him; something between sophisticated, passive appreciativeness and a crafted, measured participatory role that might, deftly managed, influence him. The success of her performance of these roles, plus the force of her own intellect, earned her the standing to confront him outright, now and then, and tell him that this time the engine of his mind had turned out a product that was fundamentally, to the core, wrong. These confrontations stand out in memory because they were so rare.

More routine was a physical dance between them, not to be confused with her own light swing step, or theirs together, on a dance floor. My father's way of dispensing lavish, open affection with women he liked and presumed upon, especially my mother, involved big, squeezed hugs and heavy pats, more like whacks, on the head or derriere, also pinches; a kind of rumpusy love play as if to say, "You release the outrageous in me!" My mother and other women tended to take it in that spirit while also telling him to *stop it* (an early childhood bit of mimicry on my part was supposed to have been the appeal "Pleeze Oiliot!") My mother would whack him back and kick him in the shins, and when he would commence this conquest of a woman guest, urge her to do the same.

Outside the house he could be counted on to complain and become royally imperious in restaurants if the table, the service, the mix of the martini, or cut of the beef were not to his liking, to rail at his chauffeur and at cabdrivers for lack of aggressive driving technique ("Make that light! . . . Get your bumper in there ahead of the bastard! . . . *Hit 'em!*). Generally, short of crunching metal, he got his way.

My father's words for those for whom he had no use could be brutal. I recall only a few incidents in which he became more physically overt than in his antics with my mother and their women friends. One stands out: in the fall of 1952, in the furnished apartment on East 64th Street my parents took when we returned to New York that summer from our six years in Connecticut. On a Saturday morning my father returned from a meeting at the Biltmore Hotel with Adlai Stevenson's campaign managers, some of whom he'd been allied with in pushing Douglas in 1944 and 1948.

A strong ray of sunshine fell through tall French windows into the formal library, a still room full of deep chairs, thick drapes, and floor-to-ceiling bookcases. My mother and I were talking or reading. In strode my father, tight-lipped with anger. He *hurled* his fedora at the floor as if it were an axe. *"GODDAMNED FOOLS!"* he roared. *"GODDAMNED IDIOTS! There's no helping them!"* And so forth. I remember focusing on the play of the dust driven by his hat, lit up in the ray of sun.

. . .

As I grew a bit older I was folded into some of my father's operations. In these I was witness, student, and licensed apprentice to his stage management.

It was not that he wanted to be celebrated at home so much as to engage his son as protégé and afficionado, to telescope in time his own precocious influence, the passion and swagger that flowed from it, and to have his lead followed. There were flashes of recognition for me in the scene in *The Godfather* in which Marlon Brando and Al Pacino reflect together on generational destinies of the Corleones: the fascination of father for son, the total immersion in the insider game, trumps questions of ends and means.

One day in the spring of 1964 he took me to lunch in New York with two men he thought could help each other, Senator Eugene McCarthy of Minnesota and Donald C. Cook. McCarthy had a serious shot at becoming Lyndon Johnson's running mate that summer. My father was trying to help him build unexpected, influential support.

Don Cook ran a major private utility, had chaired the SEC under Truman, and was an intimate of Lyndon Johnson's, Bill Douglas's, and my father's dating back to the early 1940s. Cook had declined Johnson's invitation to become secretary of the treasury but was interested in the play of economic policy in Washington. McCarthy was knowledgeable about that. So, lunch in Cook's private dining room.[21]

Cook was in fact ready to help. A subtle and sophisticated man in manner, experienced in the political arena, he launched into what was for him, if you were reading him closely, an almost crude account of what he and his company, American Electric Power, could do for McCarthy. He did not ask McCarthy much about himself or about his rapport with LBJ—then very good—or why he was interested in being vice president. He knew about these, which is why he'd agreed to lunch.

"We don't look so big, but we're interestingly placed, geographically," said Cook, more or less for hello. "We're in West Virginia, Kentucky, Ohio." He meant, states with Democratic Party organizations and delegate selection processes susceptible to influence. McCarthy, himself unusually sophisticated and subtle (another reason for lunch), missed the cue, either ingenuously or perversely, and started on a sardonic, off-point response. I could see my father kick McCarthy under the table. The senator got serious.

❧ 8 ❧

Forbidden Version

"CONTINUE JANEWAY INQUIRY"

Along with the secret history and glimpses of power in play to which I was exposed, there were also sensitive family matters, hidden away. On the one hand my father reveled in the display of his inside information. On the other hand there were aspects of his own story he'd long ago buried deep.

I was fifteen when I found out that he was Jewish, born Eliot Jacobstein, and had changed his name—at fifteen.

At the same moment I learned that my father had had a first wife. Cleaning out some closets for extra allowance, I came upon a set of legal documents, starkly official in blue State of New York folders, certifying the name change in 1928 and his divorce from Carol Rindsfoofs Janeway a decade later.

The difference in meaning between the two sets of documents was vast. One was about destiny, heritage, centuries of history, the other evidently a detour. But stumbling on them simultaneously in their matching official jackets at such an impressionable age compounded their power; their taboo as Secrets.

My father and I never talked about either fact. The politics of the family, which put a premium on studied self-presentation, made them unmentionable.

. . .

Of the two secrets, his first marriage became accessible—just. One evening a year or so later I answered the phone and when the caller asked for my father I responded, as I'd been trained to, "Who's calling?"

"Carol Janeway."

I reported this to my father. He moved around a corner to the phone and in a low growl chilled with anger, reflecting a threat to his control of his environment, said, "I told you never to call here."

The facts were that Carol had been a Cornell undergraduate in the early 1930s, transferring from Ohio State. She evacuated Ithaca with my father in his senior year and they married; he was nineteen, she was eighteen. In 1932, with no jobs in New York, they'd sailed together for England, where Carol entered the University of London while he studied at the London School of Economics. Blonde and alluring, she, and perhaps he, was not faithful. The marriage foundered during the Moscow leg of the European adventure.

By the 1950s Carol was a ceramicist and artist who lived somewhat flamboyantly in Greenwich Village, occasionally had money problems, and called my father for help. Now and then she would turn up in the gossip columns or tabloids. Shortly after my discovery of the divorce records in the closet in 1955, a *New York Post* news story reported that the ". . . blonde, beautiful ceramicist of some reknown, . . . divorced from economist-author Eliot Janeway . . ." was involved in a romantic spat with legal fallout.[1]

There appeared to be no deep ill-will between her and my father; indeed, she came to call at my parents' apartment shortly after I was born. Much of this my mother told me in a conversation after the incident of the phone call.

Why then, I asked, beyond the obvious fact that turning up occasionally in the gossip columns embarrassed my father, did he react to her call with such savagery, and why was her existence, so far as I was concerned, a Secret?

Pause.

"Your father," said my mother more or less conversationally, "is someone who doesn't like to admit that he made a mistake."

Thinking back on that moment years later I realized that the lightness of her tone was deceptive. She'd given one of his signal inner drives a lot of thought.

Filling in the blanks after my father's death, I learned that his grades at Cornell had been uniformly terrible at first, leading to warnings and probationary periods. After he found his mentor, a waspish, witty professor of romance languages and literature called James Mason, they moved from Ds and Cs to Bs. But in the spring term of senior year, before he took off with Carol, an entry appeared in his transcript: "Dropped permanently by Committee on Student Conduct. . . . May not be reinstated in the Univ."[2]

What was that about? I don't know. I ran into a rumor about that time that he and a friend (so the friend's daughter told me) had been caught reselling filched Cornell Library books. Outlaw times, of course, but clearly another "mistake."

. . .

The Jewish secret was infinitely more highly charged for my father, and for me, than his marital misfire or undergraduate mishaps. He never—ever—discussed his Jewishness to my knowledge and signaled his unapproachability about it by means of clear deterrent signals. Close friendships with Jews like Abe Fortas, Jerome Frank, and Ed Weisl allowed for their ethnicity, and for problems involving their ability to maneuver politically that occasionally arose from it, but never for any question of his. Americans of elite German Jewish descent like Walter Lippmann distanced themselves from the unwashed masses of eastern European Jewish immigrants and were comfortable as assimilated members of a broad elite of meritocracy and wealth. Without the German Jewish credentials, my father assumed a similar elite, authoritative persona, presenting himself as a non-Jew in almost every way (a rare exception was an occasional sardonic use, with intimates only and generally concerning a Jew, of a choice Yiddish epithet such as *macher* or *yenta*).

How much was this calculated, or reinforced, by his rise in Henry Luce's domain, with its decidedly WASP, Ivy League coloration? How much by concern about being stereotyped in the eyes of mainstream elites beyond Time, Inc. in those times if his Jewishness were coupled with his early Communism? Hard to say; the personal makeup had long been in place; he'd made the name-change choice in adolescence. Israel's self-image—shrewd, resourceful, tough, sardonic—fitted in with his own. Occasionally with Luce and others, not often, he raised a word or hand on that nation's behalf, from the point of view of a power broker toward an ally. But this was never personal, and he never acknowledged even in a vague way Jewish religion, culture, or heritage.[3]

He honored his father's memory, and his mother in life, complete with their old-world eccentricities. He loved his older brother Bob, had a more complicated relationship with his sister Ruth, and took a warm, avuncular role with Ruth's talented sons. Whether because Ruth felt natural in a "West Side" Jewish persona or because her husband, a fine musician, died young and she needed my father's help unexpectedly, his support for her, which included setting her up in late midlife as a stockbroker to whom he steered clients, came with the price of impatience and small humiliations. Fortunately she could laugh. That was as close as my brother and I could get to what a real Jewish family was like. My father had no contact with his large and far-flung extended family. The single time I saw him with his openly Jewish cousins—at Ruth's funeral in 1976—his discomfort was palpable.

He was prone to refer to an individual who exhibited stereotypical Jewish traits as "a low-grade Jew," and would let my brother or me know if he thought this or that friend of ours, boy or girl, was, in effect, too Jewish for his comfort. With WASP or parochial midwestern businessmen he was even capable of an offhand crack about this or that Jewish public figure in his bombsight that his listeners were invited to take as mildly antisemitic.

At high school and around New York in the 1950s, most of my friends were sons and daughters of the Jewish intelligentsia and professional classes or, like me, half-Jewish. It was the time of (the half-Jewish) J. D. Salinger, who set the tone for our generation of sophisticated New York youth, up against "phonies" and "preppies," shallow and one-dimensional. Jewish wit, antic or doomsday, Jewish neurosis, fatalism, and awareness, were our wit and awareness. When at fifteen I found out about my father's suppression of his Jewish roots—in that world at that time—I felt suspended in ambiguity, masked.

Exceptionalism was the flag my father flew. When the topic of World War II and his avoidance of military service came up, he would say, "I figured this was no war to get killed in." *If not that war, then what war?* What he meant was that he was too remarkable a youthful intellectual specimen and player to be cannon fodder or away from his natural callings (which of course included pushing policy in the right direction—a guerrilla warrior in his own conception). For him, intervention by Luce and the Roosevelt inner circle to keep him out of uniform followed naturally from that fact.

Having set such standards for cool calculation and action on the basis of it in his own teens and twenties, and in the face of world war, he signaled that there was no place in his scheme in the decades that followed (and by extension, should be none in mine) for the mundanities of adolescent development, for conflicted questions about identity or heritage. By example he seemed to say:

Inconvenient circumstances of birth, and such mistakes as are made by others in your view (or by you in theirs), are correctable by power of mind and action. Like me, you are free to be anybody you want to be, decide to be. Jacobstein is not my name or yours. Sentiment, let alone vulgar emotion in such matters, is not for serious people like us.

. . .

I wanted to know about my paternal grandparents' journey and got this storybook outline of it:

My father's father, Meyer Jacobstein, and mother, Fanny Siff, came to this country in the 1880s, my grandfather from Germany, my grandmother from Poland or Russia—the territory passed back and forth, but Fanny could remember as a young woman (my mother told me) having to kneel and bow her head to the passing czarina. Fanny and Meyer met at a settlement house on the Lower East Side of Manhattan, but my grandfather failed to catch my grandmother's name and knocked on the neighborhood's doors until he found her.

They labored—Fanny as a garment worker—to make enough to help bring over a sequence of brothers and sisters; four on Fanny's side (Jenny, Esther, Samuel and Irving Siff).

Meyer's parents stayed behind, but his brother Benjamin and sister Sarah came, and several uncles. Uncle Joseph became a cigar maker in Rochester, New York and fathered nine children. One of these, another Meyer Jacobstein, went to Congress from Rochester, New York as a Republican in the 1930s.

My grandparents ran a small stationery shop. Meyer worked his way through one of the city's medical schools (no B.A. degree was required) and in 1908 became a doctor, developing some community standing. Fanny helped in the office. Meyer moved the family to an apartment with a view of Central Park on 110th Street in Harlem, then a fashionable address for Jews, and they took on a live-in maid; then to the Grand Concourse in the Bronx. My grandfather embraced reason, science, Western culture. He and Fanny were socialist or social democratic in their politics, antireligious, not particularly drawn to Zionism; a representative assimilationist outlook. For them as for many other first- and second-generation Jewish immigrants in the early decades of this century, official Judaism was the instrument of the reactionary rabbinical tyranny they had fled. They were Americans.[4]

A photograph of Meyer around 1916 shows a strong, smiling man in a moustache and frock coat, one arm across his chest, the other cocked up and holding a cigar. His smile conveys confidence, humor, success. He was a paterfamilias. He read Conrad, Dickens, and Dreiser and in his spare time he tried to write: socially aware fiction on the order of those he liked to read. One of Meyer's cousins recorded his affectionate account of his wife Fanny's week in these flush years: "On Sundays she sees the ads in *The Times*, Monday and Tuesday she shops, Wednesday the packages arrive, Thursday she decides what to keep, Friday she sends things back, Sunday it starts all over."[5]

A staple of first-generation immigrant Jews was that professional licensing for themselves if possible, without fail for their children, was the ticket onward and upward, as well as a piece of protection should anything like the pogroms come to the land of the free. Meyer and Fanny enabled Ruth, born in 1899, to take a law degree at NYU. Robert, born in 1902, went to Cornell and became a successful automotive engineer. The baby, Eliot, born New Year's Day 1913, followed Bob, to Cornell. But majoring in philosophy, he signaled intellectual rather than professional inclinations.

In a fleeting moment of reminiscence about his youth (and of attempted parental direction to me) my father told me once that Meyer worried in the early 1930s that his younger son's explorations amounted to dilettantism. (No doubt Meyer worried about more than that when my father was banished from Cornell, but the anecdote didn't extend that far.) He described Meyer standing at his mirror, shaving with a straight razor, and arguing that if young Eliot failed to follow the family track toward professional credentialing he would wind up "driving a taxi."

127

My father always spoke about Meyer with respect and affection. Yet such an account, however edited in memory or presentation, suggests Irving Howe's moving description of the distance between first- and second-generation immigrant Jews:

> During the early years of the century, it was a common feeling among Jewish garment workers and bakers and storekeepers that, while they might succeed in working themselves up a little . . . they were still caught in the grip of the old world, the old ways . . .
>
> But the sons—*they* would achieve both collective Jewish fulfillment and individual Jewish success. . . . The sons could find a path such as Jews had never been able to discover.[6]

I suspect my father's fundamental drive in youth, subsuming his Communist years, was toward cosmopolitanism—to move out of his parents' version of the Jewish immigrant success story and toward something better still. Meyer, worldly but fundamentally *sensible*, would naturally worry that—"mistakes" forgiven and peccadillos aside—young Eliot was too smart for his own good, in too big a hurry, too unwilling to pay professional dues.

Meyer died at sixty in 1937 of a heart attack. He'd worked through the Depression with reduced income, diligently serving a loyal clientele, many of whom could not pay their bills. He left some real estate holdings in Manhattan. With help from my father and his brother Bob, these supported Fanny in a comfortable widowhood until her death in 1961; a roomy apartment in the West 80s, some weeks in St. Petersburg, Florida in the winter.

By the time I knew Fanny, as a child growing up in the forties, she was an old woman of sharp wit, strong and still finely-shaped face, an independent-minded but affectionate nature, and certain quirks. She and my father, and she and my mother, had a high appreciation of each other, so her vernacular idiosyncracies echoed in our house in my parents' whimsical use of them: "rich with money," "positive, so" for "yes, indeed," "make a light" for "turn on the light." Certain traits signaled constancy. She had a taste, dating to her days helping with my grandfather's medical practice, for free sample medications from doctors' offices. When my father trafficked with Walter Reuther, who, Fanny knew, embodied the genuine social democratic tradition, he would make a point of reporting this to her, referring to the labor leader, as she did, as "daht Royter."

What was never mentioned was her Jewishness. My father had managed some fundamental sundering of the role of son from that of race and heritage. Her accent so far as I was given to understand was simply central European. At some point I learned that Fanny had two nameplates for the buzzer panel in the lobby of her apartment house, Jacobstein and Janeway, and changed them depending on whom she was expecting.

. . .

At some point after I'd come upon the closeted legal documents at fifteen, I found an opening for a question to my mother about the name change as well as the first marriage.

Product of WASP gentry, granddaughter of an Episcopal divine, she answered in matter-of-fact tones that antisemitism was much more pronounced in the 1920s than now, and that when in 1928 my Uncle Bob went to work in an industry and city (automobiles, Detroit) where Jews were particularly suspect among the elite, he decided to change his name. My father had simply followed suit.

Once, and only once, someone not in the immediate family, and uninhibited by its internalized code but with a standing to press a few direct questions—my first wife, Penny—got my father to talk for a moment, reluctantly, about the world from which Meyer and Fanny came. What, she asked, had happened to the relatives who had stayed behind in eastern Europe?

His answer signaled distance: "We always assumed," he said, "that they were wiped out in one of the massacres at the end of the First World War"—anarchic troop movements, pogroms. End of conversation.

After my father died I heard from relatives who thought of him as the Sun King of the family but guessed I might be interested in details of Meyer's and Fanny's story and that of the larger family. On some scores the mystery deepened.

Meyer's name when he emigrated, it emerged, wasn't Jacobstein at all. His mother was Rousah, the only daughter of Jacob Jacobstein; his father was Elias Jankelevitz (there are other possible spellings; one is Jankelevic). Meyer took his mother's and her brothers' last name in about 1889, after arriving in New York, in solidarity with the growing Jacobstein clan in America. (In fact, they don't seem to have been Jacobsteins to begin with, for that is a name not found in Lithuania. Probably the name was Jakobsohn, which is common there, and probably the emigrant Jakobsohns adopted Jacobstein upon arrival in New York.)[7]

Gradually I connected dots from Shaki and Shavli, the two shtetls west of Vilnius (whence in fact Fanny and Meyer came), to the ethnically neutral household in which I grew up, the grand townhouse off Fifth Avenue where my parents lived at the peak of my father's success, and the chauffeured Cadillac in which they moved about New York.[8]

. . .

My father's message was this: more important than the fact of his heritage was his power to erase it. Information was power, and so of course information might be power used against one.

That was the case with one other secret: my father's fling with Communism in London, Moscow, and back in New York in the early 1930s. But with a difference: whereas his Jewishness was unspeakable, he would, as noted, allude to his radical youth in throwaway remarks. He could be similarly cavalier about his connection to American officials whose careers were tainted or ended by suspicion of Communist association.

His references came as fragmentary verbal snapshots. With John Cornford, dashing young British Communist and son of Bloomsbury who died fighting for the Loyalists in Spain, he shared an apartment in London for a time: "Cornford's girl had a miscarriage in our bathroom," he would say. In Moscow Walter Duranty, the flamboyant, avowedly Stalinist correspondent for the *New York Times*, "took me to a rehearsal for what became the purge trials, in the period when Stalin was turning the heat on Bukharin."[9]

The point of his flashing of these vignettes of youthful radicalism seemed to be severalfold: to underscore his own maverick intellectual and personal style, always skeptical and independent, against the grain even when attracted to a mass movement. To savor once again his own daring as a young man. To advertise his trademark flair for knowing people all over the political map.

In the late 1980s he recorded a set of oral history interviews and made some passing comments about those years. His death came in pace with the opening of archives in the former Soviet Union, so I sent for what references to him could be found and also for what turned out to be a voluminous, frequently updated FBI file on him. In the absence of better documentation, these fragments are full of holes and, in part, contradictory. The FBI report includes much hearsay and speculation (through the years it never gets the family name right, making it variously "Jacobson" or "Jacolstein"). But they suggest a trail to which he himself would refer cryptically.[10]

In London in the winter of 1932–1933 the Communist Party itself wasn't "having me," he said in one of the interviews,

> because I was flowing over with ways of updating, amending, aligning into reality the crudities of Marxism. . . . And they'd say, "Who the hell are you? We want leaflets handed out. We want pickets. We don't want ideas."
>
> [I was] rejected as a deviationist before signing on . . .

In March 1933 Roosevelt was inaugurated, and my father got his first sense of the New Deal as a radical far from home. At a party of American and British students the night Roosevelt closed the banks, "we sang . . . 'Ca-pi-tal-ism's falling down' to the tune of 'London Bridges.'" He remembered "loitering around" the London World Economic Conference that spring— "a phony" presided over by "a senile Dutchman [who] used to turn up every day in a frock coat with white gloves on." In July, to the consternation of conventional wisdom and applause of its critics, Roosevelt sabotaged the conference in favor of restoring American stability with his New Deal recovery program. (Keynes was one of those on the sidelines who cheered Roosevelt on.) Here was, my father thought, a leader from the otherwise bankrupt establishment who could think for himself.[11]

From London he and Carol went to Moscow in August 1933. A 1941 FBI report quotes "a foreign source" as stating they were "influenced" in making the journey to Moscow by Serge Dinamov, a figure in official Soviet cultural circles who was friendly with various American writers on the left. The FBI claimed my father told the Soviets that while he was not a Communist Party member he intended to become one after he returned to the United States.[12]

In Moscow in 1933 he worked for the *Moscow Daily News*, an English-language paper funded by the Soviet government. According to the FBI, he claimed to be writing "a history of the United States from a Marxian viewpoint." He returned to England late in the year without Carol. In a sequence of Groucho Marxian twists, Carol stayed on in Moscow with a new amour, obtaining a Soviet divorce decree in 1934. (That proved worthless in the U.S., requiring a second round of divorce proceedings in New York in 1938—the documentary residue of which I found in the closet seventeen years later—before my parents could marry.)[13]

Back in England in late 1933, the FBI says my father joined the Communist Party of Great Britain. His oral history account is murky, claiming that, as when he first arrived in England in 1932, "The Communists wouldn't let me in. Lord knows I tried." Nevertheless he seems to have held British Communist Party membership for a short while.[14]

In a communication in the Soviet Communist Party archives dated late 1933, a London-based agent of the Communist International's executive committee reports to a Party colleague, "About Jameway [sic], I am not easy." My father, the agent writes, "was mixed up here with a bunch of Soho Communists," and though he'd done "quite good" work for the British CP against a Labor candidate in an important parliamentary by-election, he was unreliable, an "agent provocateur" who had foolishly been in touch with a leftist the Party suspected of spying for the British police.[15]

According to my father's own account,

> The Communists [tried] to get me involved (which they did up to a point though I checked out) in a scheme to shanghai a Yugoslav Communist off a ship in Liverpool. . . . That was a youthful escapade that we managed to wriggle our way out of. . . . I guess they were looking for a young American intellectual to get implicated.

A late entry into his FBI file (the bureau was picking up hearsay on the case right into the 1960s) cites an allegation that he "embezzled" British Communist Party funds and "spent the money on an Austrian woman."[16]

He left London for good for New York in February of 1934, and simultaneously the British *Daily Worker* announced his expulsion from the Party. In New York, he recalled,

> Before finding employment, I spent some months . . . trying to get [back] into the Communist Party. . . . I was a hanger on, not a fellow traveler. But I'd sort of try to squirm my way into manipulations, into operations, while also updating Marx and critiquing him.

(This was the period when John Chamberlain recalled him choosing between handing out Communist leaflets and making his name as a writer.) The FBI's version states that he acknowledged to the Communist Party of the U.S.A. that the British Party had "disciplined" him. In April, two months after his return to New York, according to the KGB documents, officials of the CPUSA queried their British comrades for information and guidance on my father's case. They wrote, "At the present moment, Janeway is working in the American League Against War and Fascism [an important U.S. Communist front], and is very anxious to redeem himself, with the purpose of . . . readmittance into the Party here."[17]

That season, he claimed, "I pulled off my first political coup": working with the American League to deliver Father Divine and his Harlem followers to the New York Communists' May Day Parade of 1934. In February 1935 the CPUSA sent another request to their British counterparts, stating that "Janeway has been and still is considered as a 'close sympathiser' for [*sic*] the American League Against War and Fascism" and asking for word on my father's suitability for membership in the American party from "the CP of GB for which we have been writing so many times."[18]

There the Soviet document trail runs out.

In 1935 my father also found his first job, analyzing commodities market trends, and met my mother. Moving into the New York intelligentsia of the late 1930s, my parents were friendly with writers on the left like Joseph Freeman, Robert Cantwell, James Agee, and Lillian Hellman, and with those in transition from the left like John Dos Passos and Sidney Hook. My father also trafficked with intense Communists or conduits to them like Lee Pressman, of Jerome Frank's staff at the AAA at the start of the New Deal, later principal aide to John L. Lewis and then Philip Murray at the CIO. Involvements of all sorts on the shifting landscape of the left were the norm then. Only later did it become important to mark who, what, when, and where they amounted to.[19]

My father rarely took time out for films in later life but was aware of their impact. He knew who Warren Beatty was because of Beatty's association with the McGovern campaign of 1972. When Beatty's film *Reds* came out in 1981, I mentioned it to him, thinking I might get back a spark. I'd picked my moment well: *"Warren Beatty's made a movie about Jack Reed?"* he exclaimed in stunned wonder, as if I'd stopped the presses. The radical

American journalist John Reed died in Moscow in the fall of 1920. It was only thirteen years later that my father adventured there as a romantic, activist intellectual on the Reed model. One's politics evolved, of course, but the heroes and icons of youth remained.

. . .

In the decades that followed my father took pleasure in letting one know of his conservative relationships: Henry Luce, Bill Knowland, the industrial and banking titans of the Midwest. Against these, he would mention, provocatively, friendships with controversial figures on the left who posed serious problems for New Deal Democrats.

For example, *"I got Lauchlin Currie his White House job."* This was, to begin with, an exaggeration of the sort my father was given to; several among the New Dealers got Currie his White House job in 1939. Currie was a Harvard and LSE-trained economist at the Federal Reserve Board who moved to the White House in the first major modern expansion of the office of the president just before the war. There he became one of six new presidential assistants (Jim Rowe was one; James Forrestal, on his way to the Navy Department, was another) who were to function "with a passion for anonymity." Currie served in that post, with important additional wartime assignments, through the Roosevelt administration.[20]

My father and Currie had been close since Jerome Frank brought them together in 1938. Currie, "the least arrogant heavyweight brain I know," as my father described him to Luce, was a subject of and major source for his reporting for Time, Inc. Early in 1940, at Luce's behest, he arranged a dinner in New York for his boss to meet Frank, Currie, and several other New Dealers with influence on economic policy.[21]

Currie left the White House in June 1945. Harvey Klehr and Ronald Radosh, authorities on the *Amerasia* case (in which Corcoran came to the defense of John Stewart Service and spoke a number of times to Currie about him), speculate that Currie was feeling the heat of the FBI's interest in the matter and, potentially, in him. Currie was one of a handful of Roosevelt administration officials whom Elizabeth Bentley, in appearances before the House Un-American Activities Committee in the summer of 1948, named as espionage agents for the Soviet Union. (She and Whitaker Chambers named Alger Hiss in the same sequence of testimony. Chambers had previously mentioned Currie.)[22]

Currie, by then having set up as an international economic consultant in New York, denied the charges. But when in 1954 he gave up U.S. citizenship (he'd been born a Canadian) in the face of passport renewal difficulties and settled in Colombia, he assured a permanent cloud over his name. The widespread impression was that he'd fled the country. In the mid-1990s publication of the decoded Soviet cable traffic to and from wartime Washington, code-named "Venona," together with the opening of Soviet archives in Moscow, confirmed and compounded Chambers' and Bentley's charges against Currie as well as the others.[23]

Another typical aside: *"Harry White's last phone call before he died was to me; he was petrified and looking for a place to hide out."* Harry Dexter White, another son of Lithuanian Jewish emigrants, was like Lauchlin Currie a product of the Harvard Economics Department. He became a highly influential aide to Secretary of the Treasury Henry Morgenthau, later assistant secretary of the treasury, and in 1946 a top official of the newborn International Monetary Fund. My father's relationship with White was also thanks to Jerome Frank's assistance in 1938. White's strong interest in his work, my father reported back to Frank in the weeks the latter had him working as a consultant to the SEC, meant that a decision should be made whether he became "Treasury or SEC property."[24]

Chambers and Bentley accused White of Soviet espionage along with Hiss before the House Un-American Activities Committee in 1948. Ten days after Chambers's HUAC testimony White appeared before the committee to attempt to clear his name. Three days later he died of a heart attack at his retreat in New Hampshire. In White's case, too, the opening of the Venona documents and Russian archives deepened the evidence of complicity in espionage for the Soviets throughout his government career.[25]

White and Currie were fascinating, difficult cases. Each had reputations in Washington for brilliance and acerbic style (in White's case, as "one of the pushiest, least agreeable men in town" as well), and for influence far beyond their job descriptions. Publicly they were Keynesians, in that much of their energy went into advancing American fiscal and monetary policies patterned on those of the great Englishman. They helped to popularize Keynes's innovative thinking in this country and worked with him closely on wartime economic policy matters. For White, however, collaboration with Keynes, which included designing the Bretton Woods postwar monetary structure, was a sometimes tense wartime necessity; a function of service to policy set at the White House. In the words of Keynes's biographer, White's longterm interest was in "a social democratic United States, a planned international economy and a US-Soviet condominium to guarantee the peace."[26]

Each was skilled at "managing" a less sophisticated boss: in White's case the somewhat slow-witted Henry Morgenthau, in Currie's the shrewd but unschooled chairman of the Federal Reserve Board, Marriner Eccles. Influential in policy areas that intersected with my father's own primary expertise in economic markets, White and Currie were sources and allies for him, less publicly prominent than Corcoran and Forrestal but no less essential to his early success as a journalist and operator. Better informed, more manipulative, and less discreet than their highly visible superiors, Currie's and White's abilities to maneuver paralleled my father's in his relations with Henry Luce and other elders. One of them, Harold Ickes, offers this revealing dual portrait in a diary entry about a meeting with Luce in 1943 arranged by my father: Luce

> gave me the impression of having a high regard for Janeway's opinion about national political affairs and Janeway has no hesitation about making his views known. At that, I think Janeway does keep in very close touch with the situation and there is no doubt that he is an intelligent person. Jane [Ickes's young second wife] does not like him. She thinks that he plays up to prominent figures and doubtless does not conceal the fact that he travels among the great and prominent. Be that as it may, he has been friendly to me, not only in what he has said, but in what he has written.

Indeed, my father liked to show off the traits the sharp-eyed Jane Ickes spotted. To one of Luce's biographers he remarked that "the best way to manipulate [Luce] was to look around, lean forward, then whisper these words to him: 'Harry, keep this to yourself, but . . . ' "27

Quite apart from charges of Communist fellow-traveling or espionage, White and Currie maneuvered in Washington "subversively," outside the rules. They traded in information and deployed their bureaucracies and their bosses against competitors and adversaries. In this they could be said to have been compleat New Dealers, for they were thriving in the byzantine bureaucratic environment FDR shaped and nurtured. It was Roosevelt who set up Treasury secretary Morgenthau as his point man in easing munitions procurement for Britain and France in 1938 and 1939, around the ends of his secretary of war (an isolationist) and secretary of state (a possible candidate for president in 1940). White was Morgenthau's agent in the matter. With Currie at the White House, subsequently in league with Corcoran on the outside, White performed the same role in finding shortcuts for aid to our Asian ally, China.28

Backdoor channels, off-the-books agendas, manipulation of the system, sponsorship by powerful patrons; these were crafts my father was versed in; the ways he too was learning to move around in Washington and beyond it.

. . .

Moving closer to subversive inclination in an ideological sense, White, Currie, and my father shared a strong early interest in Marxist theory and the Soviet experiment, followed by attraction to the Keynesian approach; an instinct for the international and strategic implications of trade, monetary and economic policy. Relied upon as they were by superiors for the shrewdness and originality of their thinking, all three were also susceptible to the temptation of being too drawn to intrigue, too ambitious, too clever.

The consensus verdict of students of the Harry Dexter White case is that White was a fellow-traveler of a particular kind: less an *apparatchik* than a man with an ego big enough, and status and influence unusual enough, to believe he could, and should, undertake a task no less grand than to remake the world along anti-imperialist, progressive lines. After White's death, more in sorrow than in anger, his longtime chief Henry Morgenthau lamented that his trusted aide could be "increasingly brash and overconfident. . . . He could be disagreeable, quick-tempered, overly ambitious, and power went to his head." White had reason for that sense of power in the form of Morgenthau's long-time reliance on him and in Vice President Henry Wallace's high regard for him during the war years and afterward. (Early in 1948 Wallace said that if elected president he would make White his Treasury secretary.)[29]

With the Soviets White played a calculating game. He was less an agent than a source. He never joined the Communist Party. Instead, he found and protected government jobs for a small, hard-core ring of American agents for the Soviets, themselves Party members. Even before the Venona documents became public White's scrupulously fair biographer, David Rees, concluded on balance that he probably did, as charged by Chambers and Bentley, pass documents to Soviet agents, at least in the Popular Front years of the 1930s. Now it is clear that he did so through World War II. Yet White's relationship to the Soviet intelligence apparatus appears to have been one of long-term flirtation and dance, at times a very nervous one, rather than programmed zealotry.[30]

The Currie case is murkier, and before the Venona revelations Currie's complicity in serious espionage was more in question. He was defended, and defended himself, as having been guilty of nothing worse than indulgence in unorthodox contacts on the left. "In view of the current atmosphere," Currie wrote a friend in 1951, "I was probably too accessible [to Communists in and around the government] and not sufficiently circumspect." But Venona cable traffic and KGB files make plain that, though Currie "gave assistance to Soviet intelligence cautiously and on a limited basis," that assistance included handing over sensitive, secret documents late in the war on such crucial issues as Roosevelt's policy designs for postwar France and Poland.[31]

There is in these cases the puzzle of reconstructing the world as it was at the peak of the wartime alliance against Hitler. After all, Roosevelt himself set the standard for challenging imperialism at the source, sometimes harassing Churchill for his unreconstructed reverence for the British Empire, calculatedly and personally, in front of White House guests and in meetings with Stalin. There are hordes of refugees from oppressive regimes, he would say for maximum effect with Churchill in the room, and "as for us old-line Americans, why most of us were born anti-British." Keynes's biographer Robert Skidelsky notes,

White's beliefs were not much different from those of Harry Hopkins or Vice President Henry Wallace, who "saw in the march of history a coming together of the Soviet experiment in Russia with the New Deal programs of the United States" for the greater good of mankind. . . . Left-wingers in the New Deal much preferred the idea of an American partnership with "progressive" Soviet Russia to one with reactionary, imperialistic Britain.[32]

For most top American policy makers, as for most citizens, the trouble didn't start until the end of the imperative to maintain the alliance against Hitler in 1945. Penetrating the subtleties of motivation on the part of those who dallied with Communism in the 1930s, or with versions of espionage on behalf of our Soviet ally during the war, before the march of Stalinism across eastern Europe and the Hiss and atomic spy trials, became the stuff of inconclusive detective work for more than four decades. This was especially so when, like White, Hiss, and Currie, those charged denied such involvement sweepingly, offering no help in the deciphering of context to allow for shades of gray—and red. It took the release of the Venona documents in the 1990s to confirm the worst allegations.

My father's references to his Communism were in the context of his student days in the early thirties, when the Communist "Third Period" line was narrowly doctrinal and confrontational toward bourgeois democracy. The FBI and Soviet and Comintern documents take his interest as late as 1935. His remark about his breakthrough articles in the *Nation* ("At this point I was no longer a Communist") implicitly takes it to 1937. It seems likely that White's and Currie's interest in Marxism-Leninism was theoretical in the early 1930s, and that recruitment of them into more compromising activity came after they left Harvard for Washington in the Popular Front period, by which time my father, on the available evidence, was moving on from Communism.[33]

. . .

In the spring of 1941, shuttling at full gear between his high-level contacts in Washington and his increasingly influential place in Henry Luce's scheme of things, my father's past caught up with him, and the shock was severe. Prominence came at a price.

The May 5 issue of *Life* featured his article "Roosevelt vs. Hitler," orchestrated in collaboration with Tugwell, Douglas, Ickes, and Corcoran. On May 23, citing the piece, a report to FBI headquarters by the special agent in charge of the New York office identified its author, according to an informant, as "a known Communist" who, "while in Russia . . . wrote a number of articles that were highly favorable to the Soviet regime, and was complimented on a number of occasions by the Russian government." He asked for an investigation "for the purpose of determining whether . . . Eliot Janeway might be considered for Custodial Detention pending investigation."[34]

The request was granted, and agents unleashed for research and interviews with former employers and editors at journalistic outlets, and with those at Time, Inc. An interim report went to J. Edgar Hoover on July 21; a stew of entries rehearsing my father's Jewish origins, adventures in Communism in London, Moscow, and New York, his first marriage and divorce, past associations with left-wing organizations and journals, and word that "Janeway had been present 'officially'" as a member of "the Communist Party Undercover General Staff [*sic*]" at a 1936 meeting of radicals discussing a plan for "digging up as much 'dirt' as possible concerning John Edgar Hoover." It also cited his relationships with Roosevelt administration officials, and conflicting comment from denunciatory confidential sources and supportive interviewees, about the evolution of his views.[35]

Word of the investigation got to my father. He called for help from his friends. One of them, Ernest Cuneo, then operating out of the White House as American liaison with British intelligence, called Hoover two days after the first findings went to him and tried to stop the investigation. Cuneo, peculiarly among members of the New Deal circle, maintained a good relationship with Hoover, bolstered by his connections to Drew Pearson and Walter Winchell, the latter a prime FBI mouthpiece. The FBI recorded that

Cuneo advised the Director that Janeway was a very close friend of . . . Secretary of the Interior Harold Ickes and Undersecretary of the Navy James Forrestal. Mr. Cuneo also stated that Presidential Advisor Harry Hopkins also knew Janeway very well and that Janeway was known intimately to the White House where he was relied on for information on situations in Japan and Asia. Cuneo related that [White House aide] David K. Niles felt that the allegations of Communist leanings . . . were "phoney Communist steers" caused by the fact that Janeway had fought the Communist Party so often.[36]

According to Hoover, Cuneo described my father as "a very well-bred young man from Cornell," but the director wasn't buying. Corcoran's name, anathema to Hoover, had been mentioned by agents' interviewees as one of my father's patrons, which didn't help. The name of another patron, Jerome Frank, seems to have become confused with that of Felix Frankfurter, leading (an outraged Hoover wrote Clyde Tolson and other deputies, after another talk with Cuneo) to rumors "around New York that I was investigating Justice Frankfurter." He was furious that the investigation's cover had been blown: "Censure NY for mishandling this," he scrawled in a note to his deputies; "Continue Janeway inquiry but have it done in right manner."[37]

The bureau kept itself busy on the case through the summer of 1941, but the accumulation of reports on my father's loyalty and standing from his important friends in Washington and colleagues at Time, Inc. seemed to quiet it down. (A source, name blanked out, told an FBI agent that "Janeway was well-regarded . . . was a strong supporter of the present Administration and . . . acquainted with some of the Administration leaders. . . . He is considered an outstanding economist.") Nevertheless the case had caught Hoover's attention. Over the years the file grew—and occasionally twitched. The lines blacked out in the copy furnished to me often leave the specific stimuli for the FBI's later appetite a mystery, but a safe bet is that, as with Corcoran, a past target who advertised eclectic, unpredictable connections kept the bureau's primal instincts charged up.[38]

In 1942, in light of Janeway's "alleged Communistic tendencies" and "alleged connection with Government officials," the bureau forwarded "the derogatory information concerning Janeway" to the State Department in the context of an unnamed other case. The details of his time in London and Moscow grew richer; allegedly he used the pseudonym "Max Lehman" for some of that time; personal details piled up. ("He was said to possess an excellent personality, to always be the center of the attention, is clean cut and clear spoken.")

Would Hoover have blocked my father's taking a top position in a Douglas administration, or, as was his wont, would he have saved his dirt for bargaining or blackmail purposes? Hoover did have his eye closely on him in 1945, for reasons blacked out on my copy of the file, and in 1947, because former Minnesota governor Harold Stassen (whom my father had recruited in support of the United Auto Workers effort the previous winter) asked Hoover about him, and again in 1952, because of his contacts with officials of the Truman administration's Defense Production Agency. And so on, into the 1970s. Some of this is serendipitous (a connection of his name to others), some the result of direct inquiry, here and there the occasional delayed-reaction denunciation by someone who knew him way back when. Always—because whatever the bureau's intelligence or ignorance, it never forgets—the reports flow forward but rehearse my father's Communist associations in the 1930s.[39]

. . .

After the war, drawing on sources in the Corcoran and Cuneo networks, my father gained a second, inside perspective on the issue of Communists in Washington. In January 1947, a year and a half before the Chambers and Bentley testimony that ruined Hiss's, White's, and Currie's public careers, he reported in one of his weekly memos for Henry Luce about conflict within the Truman administration over how to handle the FBI's thickening dossiers on high level government officials suspected of spying for the Soviets.[40]

His reporting focused both on Alger Hiss, for whom he had a low regard (following the lead of Jerome Frank, who'd employed Hiss at the AAA at the start of the New Deal, and found him untrustworthy), and on Harry Dexter White. (In his own mind he was reporting emerging facts, not switching colors to suit postwar tastes or Luce's predilections. Along with many others at Time, Inc. who'd worked with Whitaker Chambers, he also thought of that scourge of Hiss and other Soviet accomplices as half-mad and personally loathsome.) He advised his former employer, Luce, that his former highly placed source, White, was involved in a "money scandal," having taken thousands of dollars from the Soviets. White did take gifts, and the Venona documents discuss payments for his daughter's education.[41]

Studying the White and Currie cases prompts disparate shocks of recognition, one that goes to character traits. A covert note my father was sending when he spoke of his own early Communist involvement and his later friendship with White and Currie, beyond his self-advertisement of radical intellect and far-flung network, was this: he liked to signal a kind of reckless daring about playing, on occasion, close to the cliff. Whether or not he knew these officials as men who had compromised themselves through Communist associations, he knew them as insiders, not very differently from the way he dealt with a more frankly Communist figure like Lee Pressman, on the one hand, or Washington insiders like Abe Fortas and Clark Clifford, on the other. Knowing each of them was part of how he did business.

Late in life he described Pressman as

> embittered. Burning, searing grievance against the system. Endless ability. Endless capacity to work. Disciplined Communist. . . . Pressman [de facto] ran the CIO and that include[d] the Maritime Union— which means that Stalin had access to all the dope on who was going where with what [cargo]. . . . I tried to have communication with him in 1944. He knew me very well. It was like talking to a telephone answering mechanism. You got back Communist slogans: "Let's open the Second Front."[42]

To know Pressman as easily as Alf Landon or Mayor Kelly of Chicago or Tommy Corcoran was not to be the instrument of any one of them; it was rather an emblem of remarkable range. Like Corcoran, he seemed to be saying, if you play for high stakes as one who can reach anybody, and manipulate the action so as to accomplish the impossible, then suggesting the possibility of recklessness—going where others dare not—is part of your cachet.

. . .

One more cryptic note on the subject: Michael Straight, son of the founders of the *New Republic* and later its editor and publisher, includes a short sequence in his memoir, *After Long Silence*, involving my father. Straight knew the Burgess-MacLean-Philby-Blunt circle as a graduate student at Cambridge before the war and became entangled in the beginnings at least of their Communist espionage activity. Subsequently he had trouble breaking the ties (though he was socially connected to the Roosevelts through his parents and worked in 1940 as a White House speechwriter, reporting to Corcoran). In his memoir Straight recalls toying in 1945 with the idea of running for Congress from Manhattan the next year, then hearing from a top Democratic Party official that word was around that he'd been a Communist before the war. Straight learned the source for this information was "my friend the financial columnist Eliot Janeway." He writes that he called my father and

> asked him if it was true that he had spread the story about me.
> "The question," said Eliot, "is not who spread the story but how you respond to it."
> "How should I respond to it?" I asked.
> "That," he said, "is for you to decide."

Straight decided not to make the run.[43]

There is much unsaid in this anecdote, including any indication of how the deeply ambivalent Straight felt about this revelation about him by "my friend." But there's a suggestion anyway, if you knew my father's story (and I believe Straight did), of a message from one product of youthful Communist involvement in England to another: *Ambiguity about the Communists, a pastime of our youth, is no longer possible. You must choose to stay with them or leave them forever. Anything less marks you as self-indulgent, an indecisive dabbler.*

. . .

In the end it remains a mystery whether my father left something else concealed about his connection to the subcultures of Communism, as to chronology or duration of association, or as to substance. He had a natural bent for conspiracy and for daring. As he clothed himself in subtlety, so he liked to operate with his foot on the gas pedal. The Soviet documents and his own account suggest that he had not been an extraordinarily significant recruit in the eyes of the British or American Communist Party, or in Moscow's view, but neither had he been a passive face in the crowd. It's possible that in seeking favor in those quarters he tried to prove his bona fides in some way that went beyond generational radicalism and "youthful escapade."

That he acknowledged his involvement in teasing ways, in contrast to the thicker stories of Jewishness and first marriage he buried alive, argues for the inconsequentiality of his Communist turn. And yet. While many former Communists from the 1930s who became the backbone of the New York anti-Communist intelligentsia were his friends, including Sidney Hook, James Wechsler, Dwight Macdonald, Arnold Beichman, and the ex-Trotskyites of *Partisan Review*, he never presented himself as being "one of them"—though in fact he was. (Instead, it could be his pleasure to use his influence in Washington on their behalf. A lush example: in the 1950s he had Senate Majority Leader Lyndon Johnson's office intervening with the Treasury Department on behalf of *Partisan Review*'s tax status.)[44]

But he hated to appear sectarian, predictable, typed. Also, as my mother said of his first marriage, he hated to admit mistakes. Dealing with his Communist youth would have required the ritual recantation and stereotyped him to a degree. He lived for defiance of such categories.

In a 1945 letter Jerome Frank scolds my father for being a distracted, inattentive friend of late. Frank refers cryptically to a season in the early 1940s—this is very likely the hour of the FBI's investigation—when the younger man feared losing his job at *Time* "if an unfair article about him were to appear in a certain column"; and so "at his urgent request, I spent many hours phoning Washington and seeing divers persons in a successful effort to suppress that article." Here again is a hint of friends and enemies chewing over my father's secrets. (Also in 1945, for example, Felix Frankfurter tells White House aide Edward Prichard over the latter's tapped phone line that "Eliot Janeway was born Eli Jacobstein.")[45]

If my father worked to neutralize danger to himself in the 1950s when Joe McCarthy and his allies seized on the "Communists in government" issue to discredit the Roosevelt and Truman administrations, he undoubtedly worked again through the resourceful Ernest Cuneo (who remained close to Hoover) and also through one of the odder back channels of his network.[46]

His closest co-conspirator in New York was Edwin Weisl, rainmaking counsel for, among others, the Hearst and Paramount corporations and, as noted, personal attorney to Harry Hopkins and (along with Abe Fortas) to Lyndon Johnson. A tutor to my father since the 1930s in the art of networking at the top, Weisl was intensely private, never ostentatious about his powerful connections, extremely able, friendly. A lush apartment on Central Park South, a chauffeured limousine, and a good cigar at the ready were his only apparent indulgences.

Early in his career, in the 1920s, Weisl was a federal prosecutor in Chicago. He knew J. Edgar Hoover well. One of his sidelines was to be "of counsel" about issues large and small to a collection of New York judges, mostly Tammany Hall Democrats with whom he generally met for lunch on Sundays.

One of them, a pillar of the New York City Democratic Party organization, was Judge Albert Cohn. Cohn's aspiring son Roy was the brains behind Joe McCarthy, and McCarthy's conduit to and from J. Edgar Hoover. Though several of the judges had served in Congress, they didn't "travel" politically; Tammany Hall, not Washington, was their capital. Weisl did travel. His law practice and his political influence were national, and he had his own way of talking to brash young Roy Cohn, and often did. Cohn in turn fancied his own influence in both political parties and listened to

Weisl. I would guess that at some point, as McCarthy and Cohn raised the heat under Democrats vulnerable to charges of Communist connections, my father had a talk with his friend Eddie Weisl and that, through young Roy, whatever needed to be worked out was worked out.[47]

. . .

Coda: with my parents, as a child of thirteen, I watched Edward R. Murrow's historic broadcast in March 1954 attacking Joe McCarthy, a broadcast that helped turn the tide against the senator's reign of terror. My mother wanted to send Murrow a telegram of support. My father thought this rash. They quarreled. She was being a "crusader." He was failing to stand up for reason and decency. I watched, said nothing, went off to bed.

At the time the argument appeared to be about idealism versus prudence; a mere disagreement on tactics. When I was older and knew the outline of my father's story, the incident rang another bell. In early 1954 McCarthy and Co. were still on the rampage and destroying careers of people who flirted with radicalism in the 1930s. As a journalist my father was skilled at getting Republicans to talk to him, not just his New Deal friends. With that base he'd begun to build a thriving career as a well-established business economist and consultant. Of course his political connections flowed from his New Deal base, but he'd become deft at presenting himself as a wide-ranging skeptic rather than as a partisan or an ideologue. If he'd had a chat with Ernie Cuneo or Eddie Weisl or selected some other channel for deterring red-hunters' scrutiny of the FBI reports on the youthful Communist intrigues of Eliot Janeway, also known as Jacolstein [*sic*] and Max Lehman, he didn't need to go looking for new provocations. The more so if, instead of a chat with his strategically situated pals, he was just sitting tight.

The tension between my parents that night of the Murrow broadcast, and my father's suggestive remarks to me about his Marxist fling (which came only in the 1960s, as if to say, "I was a radical then, and I'm a radical— or at least an iconoclast—now"), stand in memory as virtual freak occurrences. True, they related to his studied presentation of himself as a provocateur, but they were dangerous; bad for business. His candid recollections about his Communist years in his mid-seventies, with the end of his life on the horizon, were for an oral history interviewer, to be sealed. For the most part, until then, he conducted his life in the present as if the facts about this part of his past, like the others he kept secret, simply didn't exist.

In this way what might have been a streak of vulnerability in his defenses became part of his posture of command, because he controlled these secrets, or seemed to. No one, other than the New York tabloids in throwaway items about Carol Janeway, raised any of them. It was many years before I realized what his FBI file must look like, and more before I saw it. However much he feared his secrets in bad hours, the message he sent was that they were inadmissible.

RECEIVERSHIP

Enter LBJ, Stage Center

"AVERAGE IN HONESTY,

ABOVE AVERAGE IN ABILITY"

Even in the glow of youth, his career prospects charmed by Franklin Roosevelt's personal favor, he was a handful for his friends; temperamental as a racehorse. The young Lyndon Johnson operated on fuel that laced breathy aspiration with high-test anxiety.

A note to my father in 1942, covering a copy of a commencement speech on winning the war while keeping faith with the New Deal:

Dear Eliot,

Here is a copy for you and one I want you to get Mr. Luce to read. After that terrible picture in *TIME*, I want to try to break into *LIFE* with a better impression.[1]

A 1946 exchange between my father and Secretary of the Navy Forrestal,

Dear Jim:

Your boss [President Truman] is still hazing poor Lyndon. . . . I appeal to you to get him to begin talking to Lyndon again. Please deliver.

Would the South be more livable if it boasted more psychoanalysts?

(Forrestal replied, "Wilco—Navy code for effort.")[2]

An occupation of the Rooseveltians was frequent communication about each other. In August of 1945 my father wrote Douglas that "Lyndon tells me he has received a good many queries" about running for governor of Texas but was "scared of what it might be to cope with a hostile Legislature." After a talk with Douglas about the race, my father urged Johnson to run, adding that he'd seen samples of the Fascist literature [far right-wing attacks on Johnson and other New Dealers] being circulated in Texas. It is vicious and it is transparent and it will boomerang. . . . [Winning the governorship] will make you a symbol in the eyes of the entire nation of the Roosevelt heritage in Texas.[3]

A letter to my father early in 1946 from Alvin Wirtz, wily state capital lawyer and lobbyist, a leader of the Roosevelt forces in Texas and Johnson's most influential political supporter there, subscribed to the Johnson-for-governor plan. It gives the flavor of the time, of Wirtz's baronial style, and of his clear eye on the young LBJ:

> My dear Eliot:
>   . . . . First, I think [Lyndon] could win, and, second, I think that he should run and take his chances, win, lose, or draw. Politics in Texas are in a Hell of a mess. The people are as honest, liberal, progressive and wide-awake as the people of any state in the Union. But we have had a minority group in this State which has been enriched by oil or other fortuitous circumstances entirely apart from the merit of the individual. These men have used their money to obtain influence out of all proportion to their deserts. The [state] capitol is much worse than the Temple when Jesus had to scourge the money changers. I do not think we will find anyone comparable to our Savior, and certainly I do not rate Lyndon this high. However, I think that while he is of the average in honesty he is above the average in ability.[4]

. . .

The outline of Johnson's swift rise to power has been repeatedly drawn, but the picture is blurred. That is in large part because Johnson in all his subtlety and guile attracts biographers with contradictory interpretive instincts; some simplistic.

The basic facts again, as they relate to this story: Johnson went to the House of Representatives in a special election in the spring of 1937, under Wirtz's sponsorship. A remarkable Texas friend of the New Deal, Wirtz served in the Texas legislature in the 1920s with Johnson's father. By the 1930s he was a leading lawyer for entrepreneurial new businessmen who built the dams, bridges, and later the military infrastructure whereby the New Deal transformed the face of Texas. "His handling of the Lower Colorado River project has been masterly," wrote Harold Ickes, an ally in making that development a New Deal showcase, in a 1939 diary entry. Wirtz was in some ways as interesting to the New Dealers in Washington as Johnson just then. Early in 1940 Wirtz became Harold Ickes's undersecretary at Interior—positioning him as well, Ickes frankly acknowledged, as a forceful lieutenant in the push for a third term for the president. Six months later, angling to become secretary of war, Ickes told Roosevelt that "just in case

I should fall dead at any time, you could safely make Wirtz Secretary of the Interior. He is strong and able and he has our point of view."[5]

As a young Roosevelt supporter (he'd been the dynamic Texas director of the New Deal's National Youth Administration), Johnson's winning platform in the 1937 special election in a crowded field of eight was all-out support for FDR's most quixotic but doomed crusade: to "pack" the reactionary Supreme Court by adding to its numbers. By winning that race while Roosevelt was losing his court plan, Johnson secured a favored place in Roosevelt's eyes. And in Corcoran's network, for Johnson's second Texas patron was Congressman Sam Rayburn. Rayburn, it will be recalled, was Roosevelt's principal congressional ally in passing much of the great regulatory legislation of the New Deal, with Corcoran as draftsman and point man.[6]

Tight small world.

A striking photo of FDR and LBJ together in Galveston in 1937, clasping hands in warm celebration of the former's election to Congress on the court-packing issue—FDR was on a fishing trip in the Gulf of Mexico that week—became an iconic political poster for the young congressman. Roosevelt in turn personally guided him to a committee assignment, the House Naval Affairs Committee, that made little sense for a young member from a land-locked district in central Texas, except—destiny knocks—for its place in the heart of the president who'd made his name as assistant secretary of the Navy in World War I, and its potential for winning Johnson statewide recognition. For, with the approach of war, that post enabled him to secure lucrative defense contracts for the state and thus protective cover from conservative attacks. Roosevelt told Johnson to call Corcoran as soon as he got to Washington.[7]

In the spring of 1940, in league with Wirtz and Corcoran and Co., young Congressman Johnson dared to sabotage anti-Third Term maneuvers by FDR's discontented, conservative vice president, fellow Texan John Nance Garner. Driving that drama was a struggle for control of federal spending in the state between the New Dealers and Texas conservatives. The latter were led in Washington as well as locally not by Garner but by the formidable banker Jesse Jones of Houston, who in 1940 became Roosevelt's secretary of commerce, consolidating his authority through the 1930s over New Deal loan agencies. The stakes were high and the moment tense; "If you move fast you can crystalize a new leadership in Texas around your man, Lyndon Johnson," the president was advised by one of his aides; "if you wait, the old crowd will get together again." Johnson's brazenness in leading the challenge irritated even Sam Rayburn, but the young interloper was now playing in a bigger league than Texas.[8]

Johnson's performance in that fight, "when all the [other] Texas leaders were frightened rabbits, is proof of what he can do," wrote Jim Rowe, then an assistant to the president, to his boss the next spring, counseling him on how to put Johnson across in a special election for a suddenly vacant U.S. Senate seat. Wirtz left his Interior Department post to go home and manage the campaign. (Roosevelt wanted him to run the campaign and keep his post at Interior, accepting his resignation only when Wirtz explained that as Johnson's manager "he would have to handle money.") In phone and telegraphic liaison with the White House, Johnson ran a strong candidacy as an all-out New Dealer. First he was deemed the victor by over 5,000 votes. Then the vote-stealing began, at the end of which conservative forces counted him out by 1,311 dubious votes, setting the stage for his famous second try in 1948.[9]

Sharing the same New Deal sponsors and friends—Corcoran and Ickes at first, Hugo Black, Douglas, Fortas, and Rowe as well—Johnson and my father quickly became close. Both self-made, they shared certain traits, especially a taste for nuance, intrigue, and satiric humor, and outsized personalities. My parents' circle of close friendship extended to the rest of the early Johnson circle: Alvin Wirtz, Lady Bird Johnson, and Johnson's able assistants John Connally and Mary Rather.[10]

Then as my father's journalistic focus turned to mobilization for World War II, and Johnson developed expertise and clout on the House Naval Affairs Committee, they drew closer. He always claimed to have been the agent of Johnson's first financial backing outside of Texas, "creat[ing] a balance of payments crisis in New York" by directing substantial northern money south for Johnson's 1941 special election. He helped legitimate Johnson (whom Corcoran described in those years as "one of the wild boys") with the cautious Ed Weisl, counsel to Hearst, Paramount, and Lehman Brothers, and with other influential New York business-world contacts. He did it again at his new friend's behest for another New Deal ally, former Texas governor James Allred, running for the Senate in 1942.[11]

By 1944 a rising tide of conservatism in Texas targeted Johnson as "Roosevelt's pin-up boy," a label he and the White House invited with heavy promotion of his favored status for New Deal patronage. But Roosevelt's instinct on meeting Johnson in 1937—to buy him political insurance with conservatives in the form of association with national defense—saved the ambitious young politico after other New Dealers in the region, like Congressman Maury Maverick of San Antonio, bit the dust. As Johnson's and my father's friend Donald Cook (who, on Douglas's recommendation, took leaves from top posts at the SEC to staff Johnson's House Naval Affairs Committee investigations) put it, Johnson could have been "a New Dealer first and an FDR man second." But Roosevelt himself was moving beyond the New Deal.[12]

Thanks to the Naval Affairs Committee, Johnson could present himself as a lieutenant in Roosevelt's "Dr. Win the War" efforts, on two political battlefields. On the home front he was instrumental in steering naval base and shipbuilding projects to Texas's coastal cities, and inland naval air base construction as well, with his close friends and backers, the Brown brothers of Brown and Root, often the contractors.[13]

Meanwhile, in Washington, he developed skill at holding the managers of the military establishment and of industry to account as they built the war machine. Sometimes he acted with the backdoor help of top officials, frustrated with their own bureaucracies. Secretary of the Navy Forrestal actually solicited such congressional pressure, writing the powerful House Naval Affairs chairman, Carl Vinson, in 1945,

> The task of the Armed Forces in this war was so vast that it would be absurd for anyone connected with its administration to assert complete infallibility and freedom from error. For this reason the Navy regards the work of the Naval Affairs Committee of the House as an adjunct and asset to its own activities, and the report of Mr. Johnson's sub-committee . . . bears out that relationship.[14]

The last scene of the first act of Johnson's career was a *New York Times* story the day after Roosevelt's death in April 1945 featuring a grief-stricken, cigarette-holdered Johnson as a prototypical son of the New Deal, recalling that FDR had been "just like a daddy to me." Thereafter, the Texas political landscape was remade by the surge of its new oil industry, by new money, by the inability of organized labor to gain ground in the state, and by the eclipse of the New Deal. Johnson moved right, took out a business stake in an Austin radio station with the help of Lady Bird's inheritance; survived.[15]

. . .

It's tempting, retrospectively, to view Johnson's progression from fiery New Dealer to chastened, opportunistic "moderate" as a tale of raw ambition, tacking with the wind. Such a view leaves out the enormity of the forces transforming the country and its politics in the 1940s.

If Washington was a small, sleepy town before the New Deal, Texas was raw frontier country. The Democratic Party's heroes going back in time, Jefferson and Jackson, had achieved greatness not only as exponents of liberty but as daring organizers of power and men of action. Jefferson, for his part, flouted "Jeffersonian" principles to execute the Louisiana Purchase, the nation's first great leap westward. Jackson, general of war as much as president, laid the ground for the United States to annex Texas by force. Jacksonian politico Francis Preston Blair and his sons, one a Civil War general and congressman, the other Lincoln's postmaster general, were crucial to the Union's retention of Maryland and (by arms) Missouri as the Civil War began; a near thing. At age seventy Governor Sam Houston of Texas took a Union stand in 1861, in vain; he swore he would have fought secession if he had been ten years younger. These were men who, like the first-generation settlers in William Faulkner's novels, literally carved the country out of the wilderness. In Texas, home of the Alamo, the history of such national development (to appropriate Faulkner's words) was "never dead. It's not even past."[16]

Roosevelt organized his national power base in alliance with illiberal forces to his right. Their strongest leaders in his official circle were Texans John Nance Garner and Jesse Jones. The swing of the pendulum and his own second-term mistakes cost him his overwhelming congressional margins in the 1938 elections (they were not recovered until Johnson's own presidential election triumph in 1964). In the 1940s, as war came, the country's domestic policy direction was unclear. Roosevelt and Harry Truman could win presidential elections but could legislate virtually no domestic social or economic measures against the will of the conservative Southern Democratic–Republican bloc in Congress. Picking up there as Garner and Jones faded from the scene, Robert Taft of Ohio, Harry Byrd of Virginia, and Richard Russell of Georgia personified its leadership, representing what has been well described as "a class coalition uniting regional business elites with small-town and rural economic interests in the North and South against a welfare state."[17]

"The Lone Star State is concerned about money and how to make it, about oil and sulfur and gas, about cattle and dust storms and irrigation, about cotton and banking and Mexicans" (and has "little cause to be obsessed about the Negro"), wrote V. O. Key in 1950. Texas's turn away from the New Deal is commonly attributed, in more singular fashion, to the rising force of the oil industry in the state, controlled after the opening of vast new Texas oil fields in 1930 not by corporate moguls in the Northeast but by ambitious Texas wildcatters, self-made and selfish. But there was more to the story than that. Half a million Texans moved from farms to cities between 1941 and 1947. The state's population shifted from a slight rural predominance to a ratio of 62 percent urban and 37 percent rural in 1950. Oil production rose, but the big push came in manufacturing and heavy industry. Texas counted only 127,000 industrial workers in 1939; that tripled by 1944 and their total wages quadrupled. But labor's effort to organize those workers lagged far behind, handicapped by a wave of anti-union laws championed by Johnson's nemesis in the 1941 Senate race, Governor W. Lee ("Pappy") O'Daniel, and extended by O'Daniel's successors. Texas's union labor force was never more than 15 percent of the state's 2 1/2 million nonagricultural workers, into the 1950s—less than half the comparable number in states including California, Illinois, Michigan, Missouri, and Pennsylvania, and about half the national average.[18]

Those suddenly made solvent by wartime prosperity, let alone made rich by boom times in Texas, began to react hysterically to organized labor and its "inflationary" wage demands because of the insecurity they felt about their new holdings. But in Texas as across the South they were part of a network of hysteria that included Southern farmers of substance (increasingly mechanized) and white-collar workers. They saw a vast force on the left composed collectively of the AFL, the CIO and its Political Action Committee, the National Association for the Advancement of Colored People, Roosevelt's Fair Employment Practices Committee, Franklin and Eleanor Roosevelt personally, controversial Roosevelt allies like Henry Wallace and the CIO's Sidney Hillman, and the Supreme Court in decisions like that of 1944 that invalidated the Southern "white primary" elections. (That decision took up a Texas case.)[19]

Johnson stood with Roosevelt and Truman on a number of key votes through the war and into 1946, including support for price controls on oil and against tax breaks for the wealthy. He could still sound like a radical on the floor of Congress; thus, in the summer of 1946, in a hitherto unnoted talk:

> I was a kid, some 13 or 14 years old when cotton dropped from 40 cents to 6 cents, and we lost our homestead. The experts on children tell us that one of the necessities . . . is the feeling of security in the formative years. I know that as a farm boy I did not feel secure, and when I was 14 I decided I was not going to be the victim of a system which would allow the price of a commodity like cotton to drop from 40 cents to 6 cents and destroy the homes of people like my family. Because it was the same cotton. We fought the same boll weevils to grow it. We sweat the same amount of sweat to hoe it and pick it. It cost the same amount to gin it. The freight rates were unchanged.[20]

Johnson could instinctively challenge the law of markets—"*Because it was the same cotton . . .* "—but he had no personal orientation toward the situation of organized labor (despite my father's linkup of him with Walter Reuther in search of a bed for the night in wartime Washington, and Reuther's subsequent visits). On the management side of the fence anyway with his and Lady Bird's soon-to-be lucrative Austin radio station, and running scared of Texans' anti-union sentiments, he began to turn on organized labor, supporting votes to override Roosevelt's veto of a curb on wartime strikes, and Truman's of the Taft-Hartley Act in 1947, conservatives' revenge against labor's New Deal gains. After the war the tidelands oil and emerging civil rights issues found him an unequivocal Texas congressman and then senator, opposing the White House on them down the line.[21]

Some biographers look at Johnson as his sponsor Roosevelt faded from the scene, as he shifted to the right and accommodated himself to the backing of Texas's new entrepreneurs, and conclude that the point is essentially personal. Johnson, Robert Caro states many times over, was both compassionate and ambitious, but "whenever those two forces collided, it was the ambition that won." That is accurate in part, but it is far from faithful to the interplay between nature—and Johnson's was guileful, selfish, and often alternated between ruthlessness and trepidation—and historical context. It magnifies the role of the individual, and pulls it away from the world as it was.[22]

The issue for Johnson and his allies was about the building of a power base in increasingly hostile circumstances. As for nineteenth-century frontier politicians, concerns with social justice and reform remained part of the equation. But the seizing of opportunities given the facts on the ground in the state, and the ferocious struggle for power there, took precedence. The missing piece in Texas as they made their calculations was an organized labor force of any significance demanding a place at the table, as labor could in states where it was better positioned, right alongside the new-money entrepreneurs.

Johnson's backers George and Herman Brown won one government contract after another with Johnson's help, often with Tommy Corcoran as their Washington lawyer, moving from dams to military projects. With their purchase of the government's pipelines running from Texas across its borders in 1947, they moved into the oil and gas business, and they wanted no union labor in any of their enterprises. All this was not exactly about the New Deal's agenda for lifting up the South and West. But neither was it simply about Johnson's (or Corcoran's) financial needs. It's more fully accurate to say, as Jordan Schwarz wrote, that by 1940, "Lyndon Johnson had seen the future of American politics. . . .: Public works projects could help elect congressmen, but defense contracts could become public works." It's also true that one way and then another fierce antilabor sentiment in Texas, and Johnson's problems in working around it with national union leaders, hindered his political career into the 1960s.[23]

At the same time, what Johnson was not was just another congressman, or just another vulnerable New Dealer. Roosevelt set him up as a Washington insider with a path to national aspirations and political protection, thanks to the national defense issue. The green congressman made the most of the gift. His friends among the Rooseveltians, practiced in split vision about FDR and about themselves, securing their own post-New Deal destinies, understood his need to develop a base for himself that could survive the impact of Roosevelt's removal from the scene on his, and their, fortunes. They looked at Johnson in a variation on the way Alvin Wirtz did: first as an uncommonly able operator, second as an ideological brother.

. . .

They ran all sorts of political interference for him. In the heat of Johnson's bid for the Senate in 1948, Corcoran sent Douglas a memorandum (probably he or Jim Rowe authored it) stating that "Lyndon . . . can still win in Texas," but that labor was angry at his votes in support of the Taft-Hartley Act. (The memo noted that Johnson's votes were "damn fool moves if he intended to run at large in Texas . . .") Would Douglas join Corcoran in calling Reuther to get him to move "quietly and without any formal endorsement which would be the kiss of death . . . to point out to his own people that whatever sins Lyndon has committed on the Taft-Hartley bill, he is the lesser of evils"?

This was the message that declared that "Lyndon . . . is very important from many points of view." What did that "many" cover, overriding Congressman Johnson's deviation from the New Deal line in his voting record? Not, obviously, anything like a scholarly orientation to legal realism or Keynesian economic theory; the links that brought so many of the Second New Dealers together.[24]

The fact was that Texas was a primary strategic link in the New Deal coalition. The deal that made Governor Roosevelt of New York the presidential nominee at the 1932 Democratic convention turned on his taking Speaker Garner of Texas as his running mate. In 1937 Sam Rayburn of Texas became House Democratic leader and then speaker. A steady flow of Texas senators and congressmen chaired important congressional committees; a total of twelve in the late 1930s. For all these reasons New Deal public power projects and other patronage investments in Texas were immense.[25]

And Texas, unlike the rest of the South, was not locked into racial politics. In his last year as vice president, preparing a backstage bid for the 1940 presidential nomination, Garner astonished Roosevelt by offering privately to help him orchestrate passage of antilynching legislation because "it was necessary to do something to hold the Negro vote in the Democratic Party" institutionally, beyond Roosevelt's own success as "the only Democrat who had ever been able to attract that vote." The riddle of Texas since Sam Houston tried to keep it out of the Confederacy, which became the riddle of Johnson's own career, was whether it was Southern or Western.[26]

For this conglomeration of reasons, Johnson's Rooseveltian friends saw that he was beginning to look like their best bet as a replacement of Douglas for the role of heir to FDR.

. . .

Johnson's famous "landslide Lyndon" election to the Senate in 1948 by a dubious primary margin of eighty-seven votes, contested all the way to the U.S. Supreme Court, brought the Rooseveltian team into an emergency huddle.

Managing Johnson's case were Wirtz in Texas coordinating with another of Ickes's undersecretaries of the Interior, Abe Fortas, by then building his Washington law firm on the Corcoran plan. Also on the Washington team were Corcoran, former attorney general Francis Biddle, Ben Cohen, Fortas's partners Paul Porter and Thurman Arnold; influential Roosevelt appointees and advisers all. Johnson's conservative opponent, Governor Coke Stevenson, was appealing the election through federal courts. That made it appropriate for Johnson's Washington team to take the case to their and Johnson's friend and Roosevelt's first Supreme Court appointee, Hugo Black of Alabama. Justice Black had oversight of the regional circuit court in question. Corcoran told Johnson years later that Black had confided in him then that the embattled Texas candidate personified "his hope both for American liberalism and a new South." Possibly that was Corcoran on the accordian; in any case, Black knew from his senatorial days just what a contested Southern Democratic Party primary election was.[27]

The rest is history. On the justice's eightieth birthday, in 1966, President and Mrs. Johnson gave him a party at the White House, and LBJ remarked in his toast, "If it weren't for Mr. Justice Black at one time, we might well be having this party. . . . But one thing I know for sure, we wouldn't be having it here."[28]

"Both sides stole" is the conclusion of most historians. Johnson's friends' version, the one I heard at home, was that whatever the degree of theft in the 1948 race, it was Johnson's turn, fair and square. He, Wirtz, Rayburn, Allred, and the other Texas New Dealers had suffered the 1941 special Senate election to be stolen by the same conservative forces that conspired to pull Texas away from Roosevelt in 1944 and that were prepared to steal the 1948 Senate election. Two successful thefts would make them look like fools. Fools they were not.[29]

And anyway Texas was Texas. A story among Johnson staffers was of a 1948 primary election night call to John Connally from the boss of one of the vast South Texas counties on the Rio Grande, in a position to bring Mexicans across the border in bulk and "vote" them. "Jawn," he'd supposedly purred to Connally, "the moon is high and the river is low; how many votes do you need?"[30]

. . .

Seven years after his 1948 "landslide," Johnson became Senate majority leader. In partnership with his venerable friend Speaker Rayburn, he led a formidable congressional Democratic Party through the Eisenhower years, the first Republican presidency since 1933.

By 1958 Johnson was regularly referred to as "the second most powerful man in the United States," and the ablest Senate majority leader in history. His legislative skill was compared to that of Henry Clay, advancing national interests through mastery of flexible regional alliances and personal persuasion. The testimony of his colleagues (in many cases resentful, and not until years later, in oral histories) was of the way he deployed physical presence and energy, persuasion and command of under-the-counter intelligence data, literally to overpower them. But public caution—he called it "moderation"—and private fear inhibited his maneuvers. Along with "Landslide Lyndon," his critics' nickname for him was "Lying-down Lyndon."

His strategies focused on protection: of the national Democratic Party against red-baiting, and against the enormous popularity of Dwight Eisenhower (once of Abilene, Texas). And of his own political base at home against post-New Deal, boom-time conservatism.

Periodically Johnson led his troops on daring, morale-boosting raids over public power or farm policy, or ran a mission solo, or forged a historic alliance with Republican moderates. Though he waited too long in the eyes of many liberals in moving in on Joe McCarthy, he orchestrated the Senate's censure of him in 1954 so as to end one of the most reckless witch-hunts in American history once and for all. The same year he helped force a behind-the-scenes veto of Secretary of State John Foster Dulles's desire to rescue the French troops at Dienbienphu in Vietnam.[31]

In the 1950s, as in the 1940s, he found the safest way to strike a national posture, while also positioning himself adroitly in Texas, through defense and military preparedness issues. Fresh from the publication of his own history of Roosevelt's administration of the war, my father wrote a piece about Johnson's chairmanship of the Senate's "watchdog" defense preparedness subcommittee for the *New York Times Magazine* in 1951.

Johnson, he wrote, was a "restless 'doer' . . . tall, dark and handsome, tense, a natural generator and transmitter of enormous nervous energy, normally soft-spoken but on occasion, aggressively emphatic and devastatingly sarcastic." (Donald Cook, about to become Truman's SEC chairman, once again took time out to run Johnson's investigation. Cook's staff reports, my father wrote, were "definitive, more often than not they are devastating; above all they produce results.")

Johnson wrote,

Dear Eliot
We have seen the Magazine section of tomorrow's *New York Times*.
Collier's tried—it was adolescent.
Saturday Evening Post improved, but I guess it is always difficult to satisfy the subject.
You did, however, and thanks a million . . . [32]

. . .

Back home in Austin, the sudden death of Alvin Wirtz that autumn cost Johnson more than a wise and savvy mentor, adroit and powerful in his ability to help protect Johnson in his political base and guide him in building his and Lady Bird's private broadcasting properties. Wirtz's versatility and force in his multiple past roles—leader of the Roosevelt forces in Texas in the 1930s and forties, state capitol power broker and sophisticated emissary to Washington, political architect of the dams and public utilities the New Deal fostered, lawyer for Brown and Root, the construction firm that built them, and for the new, independent oil producers, synthesizer of all these strands as Ickes's undersecretary of the interior, and much more—were outsized.

Wirtz was sixty-three at his death. Johnson was forty-three, no longer a cub. His loss, said Lady Bird, was "one of the final blows that ushered us into having to stand on our own"; it meant that "there was nobody to go to really." It also meant that Johnson was much more naked and visible than he'd been as he acted out his political fears, which extended from accommodation of the forces of reaction to anxiety about his own financial security if he lost his public office. He was, indeed, the lament of his oldest friends as much as of liberal critics of his Senate leadership for the ways that his craftiness blurred with timidity, as well as for his private financial preoccupations. That was a mark of a number of his relationships with friends from the New Deal years.[33]

Jim Rowe called Johnson to account for ducking the civil rights issue as early as 1943. To Ed Weisl, Cook, Douglas, and other practitioners on the Johnson case, my father would complain about Johnson's reluctance to take on Eisenhower on economic and fiscal policy and speak of his "yellow" streak. In 1956 Eisenhower briefly appeared vulnerable for reelection—he'd suffered a bad heart attack, then toyed with dumping the ambitious, unpopular Nixon as his running mate. Sitting with Johnson just off the Senate floor one day in 1956, my father urged him to make a serious run for the Democratic presidential nomination.

"What are you trying to do?" Johnson complained. "Destroy me?"[34]

Sometime in the mid-1950s my father was brokering a possible deal to sell off one of the Johnson broadcast properties in Texas at what appeared to be an astronomical figure. He directed me to listen in on another phone as a relay team of long-distance telephone operators found Johnson at the LBJ ranch. The U.S. Senate majority leader, "second-most powerful man in the nation," absorbed the details of the offer attentively; then a long-distance beat, then a return to the handsome bottom line: "Is that befo' or after taxes?" he murmured.

To my father the question was self-satire after Molière: our populist country cousin turned greedy bourgeois operator. "Is that befo' or after taxes?" became one of his taglines for suggesting one of the backstage moods of Lyndon Johnson.

But most of the time he appreciated the overall Johnson political enterprise and defended Johnson stoutly for his unmatched effectiveness to anyone but intimate co-conspirators. He was, after all, deeply invested in Johnson, as were the other partners. Complaints about Johnson to a co-conspirator like Weisl or Douglas were in the context of their shared frustration in programming the restless senator of many faces. But as befits a partner in a trust, advancing the interests of the devil you knew meant hinting now and then at just how *much* you knew.

. . .

The Supreme Court's school desegregation decision of 1954 made civil rights the issue that could no longer be denied nationally. But the power of the old congressional Southern Democratic bloc, which in the Senate numbered votes sufficient to defy efforts to close down filibusters, blocked action as it had since the end of Reconstruction.

So, it seemed, did Johnson and Rayburn. As Texans they were thought to be effectively men of the South. As national Democratic leaders they feared (as had Roosevelt) their party splitting apart on the race issue. And the Senate's Southern high command led by Richard Russell of Georgia had sponsored Johnson's rise through the leadership hierarchy. But Johnson's web of relationships went left as well as right.[35]

By 1956 the Eisenhower administration was gearing up on the civil rights front. The iron Southern-Republican coalition of interests that stalemated New Deal and Fair Deal legislation after 1938 was coming apart; the black vote was up for grabs. Republican politicos led by Attorney General Herbert Brownell and Vice President Nixon saw the Democrats' discomfiture and pressed legislation to enforce voting rights and expand Justice Department powers. In the South civil rights protests and abuses mounted. The House passed a weak bill. Johnson saw nowhere to go in an election year but to postponement.

In 1957 he had the choice of seeking shelter where Democrats traditionally found it—in acquiescence to the Southern veto—or in mapping a new path. A new adviser, Dean Acheson, along with Fortas, Ben Cohen, and Rowe, was helping Johnson with legislative draftmanship. Acheson, a moderate on race, recalled asking Johnson, "Would it make any difference to you to enlarge your electorate by some large percentage with Negroes?" Johnson, he said, was candid in response: "Of course it would. . . . With 600,000 more [Texas] Negroes voting I'd be in a much better position. They're citizens; I want them to vote."[36]

For Johnson of Texas especially, more than for imprisoned closet liberals in the deep South like Fulbright of Arkansas and Hill of Alabama, the conjunction of ideal and interest was so close he could touch it. Even his friend Senator Russell of Georgia, who dearly wanted to see him in the White House, accepted that there was no escape from Texas or Congress into a national political candidacy if Johnson continued to preside over evasion of the civil rights issue.[37]

Johnson's private views on the subject were distinctive—inaudible to critics who heard only the public ones of a one-time Texas New Dealer running very scared. He told one of his aides in the late 1940s that blacks, having fought in the front lines of Word War II, were "not gonna keep taking the shit we're dishing out." In 1954, the year of *Brown vs. Board of Education*, he told a close Washington friend, Tex Goldschmidt, that "it's too bad" the Supreme Court hadn't continued to make a frontal attack on segregation through voting rights law after the 1944 "white primary" decision, the reform of which (he argued accurately) would have empowered more advancement of civil rights faster than did the strategy of attacking segregated education.[38]

Showing his hand only covertly three years later, gradually confident of his command of the Senate's levers (but less so of his own standing in Texas), gauging the flow of the civil rights tide, Johnson orchestrated passage of the first Civil Rights Bill since the Reconstruction era. In the eyes of his liberal critics, the 1957 bill was small beer, badly watered down; and/or a hoax to position Johnson for a bid for the Democratic presidential nomination in 1960.

These were credible objections. But the fact remains that Johnson's maneuvering had broken—once and for all—the Southern bloc's veto over civil rights legislation. With every civil rights bill that followed, and he masterminded each one (in 1959, 1960, and through the years of his own presidency), Johnson built upon that base to tear down the fabric of de jure and de facto racial segregation in the United States.[39]

. . .

To Corcoran, Douglas, Fortas, Rowe, and my parents, Johnson, for all his personal flaws, was demonstrating on a grand scale the extraordinary political gifts they'd sensed in him as a young Roosevelt protégé. (Fortas, whose cautious instincts mirrored Johnson's, told Rowe—who passed it on to Johnson—that, while it sounded "cynical" to say it, "Lyndon gives too much weight to accomplishment. He should be . . . Majority Leader, and stop [trying to be] Prime Minister.") Johnson did zigzag between caution and daring, but in the fights he waged in earnest in the 1950s—giving Eisenhower a run for his money on public power, farm policy, military preparedness, and other issues he could unite the Democrats on, putting Joe McCarthy out of business, enacting civil rights laws—he delivered.[40]

He and Speaker Rayburn finally had the Texas Democratic party more or less under their control, though only with major concessions to the "Republicrat" conservatives. ("Lyndon loves me this I know / 'Cuz Sam Rayburn told me so," sang the Texas liberals, sarcastically, to the tune of "Jesus Loves Me.") Johnson's three predecessors as Democratic Senate leaders had lost their seats by becoming perceived as "too national" at home, but his and Rayburn's maneuvers in Texas made him modestly more daring in Washington. The national press corps became fascinated with Johnson, impressed by his clout and entertained by his extravagant personality and quirks. He had nowhere to go but up. His Rooseveltian fraternity was one of his natural instruments for repositioning himself with something like the confidence he'd lost after Roosevelt's death.

As talk began of the Democratic presidential nomination being within his reach, Johnson moved a notch toward reestablishing his New Deal credentials. He hired FDR's last personal secretary, Grace Tully (she of the 1944 *happy-to-run-with-Truman-or-Douglas/Douglas-or-Truman* letter) in the majority leadership office, and several thoughtful liberals to his Senate staff. He advertised his "kitchen cabinet" of New Deal Washington lawyers; Corcoran's partner Jim Rowe joined his staff full time for a period. He was more open to my father's bridge building to Walter Reuther, increasingly a power in the Michigan and national Democratic Party as well as in organized labor. He wooed a skeptical Eleanor Roosevelt with congressional measures to honor FDR's memory.[41]

In 1959 forty of Douglas's close friends gave him a dinner on the occasion of the twentieth anniversary of his appointment to the Supreme Court. Tommy Corcoran, Abe Fortas, Jim Rowe, and my father were there, together with Douglas protégés and friends from the law, journalism, and academic life. Johnson was the only elected official, and one of three speakers, with the satirical Thurman Arnold and a more reverential Ben Cohen. With a bit of self-mockery of the two faces he employed for Texas consumption Johnson said to the group,

> A lot of Texans have told me—"That fellow Douglas ought not to be on the Court." I can always say back to them in good conscience— "I have tried for fifteen years to get him off the Court." And I have. I would have liked—and still would like—to see this man's talents used in the highest executive positions of the land.[42]

For skeptics who looked at Johnson in a prosecutorial manner, these were the token gestures of a clever, cynical chameleon. To those who looked at him and saw progressive possibilities surrounded by constraint and outright fear, the signs were promising.

. . .

But to be in relationship with Johnson was to deal with the jarring contradictions in his nature and in his political position. National ambition dating from Roosevelt's patronage of him, and the hurricane force with which he came to dominate the Senate and its members, were at odds with his deep insecurity about the vulnerability of his base in Texas, forever dramatized by the disputed 1948 Senate election. Deeper down were his darker demons. His natural gregariousness and instinct for the great game of politics were interchangeable with sullen self-pity.

In turn, Johnson's Rooseveltian intimates had relationships with him that reflected the differences in their own natures and the courses their careers took after 1945. In the 1950s Corcoran was the elder, but his "fixer" image rendered political intimates like Johnson vulnerable to guilt by association; a friend to keep at a distance. Corcoran's partner Jim Rowe was closer to Johnson in age; his liberal credentials remained in order after Corcoran's became tarnished. And Rowe's knack for standing up to Johnson without alienating him made him popular with Johnson's often intimidated staff.

Fortas adopted the policy that though he, Johnson, and the others had all been young comrades in arms together, Johnson's emergence as a national figure meant that they needed to be in his service as they'd been in Roosevelt's; loyal to their friend, sympathetic to the pressures on him, and deferential to his interests. Clark Clifford fell between these positions, sometimes seeming interchangeable with Fortas in deference. (Yet in the historic last act in 1968, Clifford led the way in forcing Johnson to turn around in Vietnam, while Fortas, as if deaf to the swiftly changing mood of the country, remained a fierce echo of Johnson's most willful, stubborn impulses.)[43]

The lawyers in this brotherhood also divied up various pieces of Johnson's personal and legal business as they had Bill Douglas's, with Ed Weisl as an addition to the team. Weisl was a board director of one of his own most important clients, Lehman Brothers. With Weisl's hand on the levers and sometimes consulting with my father, Lehman Brothers managed the Johnsons' investments.[44]

From the distance of New York, Weisl also played elder and, with my father, recipient of cries for long-distance help, which came in forms as various as securing advertisers for the Johnsons' radio and television stations and lining up managers of Texas movie theaters controlled by Weisl's client Paramount Pictures in campaign seasons. Another Weisl client, the Hearst empire, owned a newspaper of special importance to Johnson, the *San Antonio Light*. My father's contact points in business, labor, political, and press circles in New York and nationally were more various. His intimacy with Weisl meant that the resulting traffic between the two of them in New York, and around what might be called "the Johnson zone" in Washington and Texas, was intense.

In the wake of the Soviet Sputnik launch in 1957, Corcoran (visiting Johnson at his ranch), Weisl, Donald Cook, and my father joined to prompt Johnson to respond dramatically. With his crisp young partner Cyrus Vance in tow, Weisl went to Washington to run Johnson's Senate investigation of U.S. policy on outer space and missile technology.[45]

. . .

In aligning himself so closely to Johnson, my father was indeed looking for payback. He sought this not in the usual Washington commodity of intervention with a regulatory agency or for a legislative or tax break, but in receptivity to his views and spurs to action on policy.

His own stock-in-trade remained unorthodox insight into problems in the political economy, and remedies for them. For him, a romance with a shrewd politician was about connecting up his own ability "to give ideas legs" and a politico's direct hand on power. Thus to steal the scene, control the play, and the next one . . . And by the 1950s his ability to demonstrate

political influence was also tied to his success in selling himself to business
clients and getting his pronouncements and predictions quoted in the press.

Johnson blew hot and cold in this relationship, as he did in so many
aspects of his life. He owed my father for many favors in the early years;
especially the out-of-state money, favorable publicity, and access to an unusual network. Johnson generally found the raw data my father relayed to
him about market trends and their political implications unique, expert,
and useful. By mid-1958 the messages between him and Johnson and his
entourage were practically on a daily basis. A typical example: with the
"Eisenhower recession" causing distress, my father wrote Johnson in the fall
of 1959,

> Republicans who talk about civil rights [do not] realize that the Negro
> is the first to be deprived of his right to credit during a money squeeze.
> I mention this now because repercussions [on automobile loans] and
> foreclosures on houses are on the rise, and this has a sensitive bearing
> on the Civil Rights issue.

Thanking him for the tip, Johnson responded immediately asking "if you
could supply me with some figures to demonstrate the point. That would
be useful."[46]

Earlier that year, after a frenzied round over the state of the economy,
Johnson wrote,

> Dear Eliot:
> While we have talked several times in the last few days, I do not
> know that I have adequately expressed my gratitude for the construc-
> tive ideas and suggestions you furnished us prior to the unemployment
> speech.
> The suggestions were excellent and of course, as you know, a num-
> ber of your thoughts were used.
> I am deeply appreciative of all the time and energy you put forth
> on my behalf.

This was an acknowledgment of substance from one difficult man to another. Roosevelt, his closest allies and most loyal aides agreed, never thanked
them.[47]

The "us" in Johnson's first sentence was instructive. Johnson had become
much more than a powerful senator. Dealing with the Senate majority
leader had come to mean dealing with various of his top aides, some of
whom were quick and able, and at times much more inclined to liberal
activism than Johnson. My father began to supplement his bombardment
of advice to Johnson with secondary campaigns through these assistants,
who in turn (the Johnson Library file copies of the correspondence indicate)
were often the actual drafters of Johnson's letters as they processed the
information exchange. The old one-on-one relationship had become a kind

of small business, the informational trade through it helping fuel the engine of Johnson's management of his agenda.[48]

But periodically Johnson's guard went up against my father's steady pressure to act on his advice, and especially against deploying his growing clout as Senate majority leader against the popular Eisenhower and his conservative economic policies. In 1957 Ike took as his second secretary of the treasury Robert Anderson, an influential Texan linked to Johnson and Rayburn. To my father's and many Democrats' dismay, Anderson brought fresh inhibition to Johnson's fighting instincts. Harassing Johnson and his staff, he sent word that the senator was "underwriting" Anderson's "asinine . . . attitude of 'tough-minded confidence towards the [economic] slump'" of 1957–1958, which amounted to "Do-Nothing-ism."[49]

At times my father's appeals to Johnson in the 1950s to play from his strengths and confront Eisenhower appealed to the majority leader's sense of ambition, enterprise, and association with the Rooseveltian legacy. At other times Johnson simply grew impatient with this interpretation of the balance of power between them. The path of Johnson's career was from privileged position in the New Deal years to mid-career political vulnerability, and he interpreted pressure on him as trouble. His personal insecurities led him to exaggerate that vulnerability. But he wasn't wrong about the growth of reactionary venom against all things "liberal" in parts of Texas. He and the people around him associated the assassination of John F. Kennedy in Dallas just a few years later with the climate of hate there as much as northerners did.[50]

This was a case of occasional abrasion arising from my father's close-in experience of power never having included the burden of out-front responsibility for decisions. He never personally faced the kinds of painful choices between appeasement and confrontation that public officeholders must manage every day. In contrast to Abe Fortas's silky style of managing a partnership, my father's approach could trigger Johnson's suspicion of being used by "friends" no less ambitious and insightful than he, authoritatively pressing agendas that might or might not jibe with his.

But before 1960 these tensions between them were latent. On the surface the relationship was one of great mutual regard and reciprocal use.

. . .

In the 1950s my parents would take by brother Bill and me along with them on Washington trips when school was out. They'd book a suite with at least two phone lines in it at what is now the Sheraton Carlton Hotel and lay down a barrage of calls. My mother and I fielded the returns on one line while my father did business and made dates on the other.

A call on Hugo Black and his wife Josephine in Alexandria, a tour of Josephine's airy painter's studio, a visit with Ben Cohen, with his trademark mix of frailty and incisive bite. I remember Douglas dropping by the hotel for a drink on his way home from the Supreme Court, this legendary figure in family lore, touchingly alone, fedora in hand, exchanging a warm, face-front kiss with my mother as she opened the door to the suite. He was flinty and witty, dry and offhand. You could see stature, but also a kind of ab-senting of himself, into himself.

Up to the Capitol for a visit with the Senate majority leader. All four of us seated round his desk with its view out to the Capital grounds. Tall and grave, suave and groomed, it was clear that this kind of time for old friends was not offered lightly. The mood was relaxed; compliments and a bit of business back and forth. (Johnson, who years before claimed my mother's novels had "broken the spell" whereby he'd never read a book to the end, seemed to enjoy being lobbied by her about copyright law on behalf of the Author's Guild.) Then, "Well, anything Bird or Ah can do while you're here . . ."; hugs and hearty handshakes.[51]

⇒ IO ⇐

1960—Checkmate

"LOOKING BACK,

THE RESULT WAS INEVITABLE"

In the 1950s, associating his own success in leading the Senate out of stalemate with that of his hero, Majority Leader Lyndon Johnson would recall details of Franklin Roosevelt's rescue of the nation from governmental paralysis in 1933. As a young staffer in the office of Texas Representative Richard Kleberg, he had firsthand recollections of the way Roosevelt matched physical presence to words and actions in the hundred days after he took office.

One day in March 1958, moving to take advantage of the power vacuum flowing from President Eisenhower's sloth in responding to the challenges of that year—a recession and the Soviet Union's success in launching the Sputnik space satellite, Johnson spoke in the Senate of having seen with his own eyes "the Republic almost fall" because of the "wait until tomorrow" stance of the Hoover administration. "I saw a brave man come down Pennsylvania Avenue and throw out his chin and say: 'The only thing we have to fear is fear itself.'" Recalling the accomplishments of the first hundred days of the New Deal, Johnson intoned, "We needed action, and we got it. . . . Mr. President, sometimes I wonder if this is not where I came in. The events of that day are strikingly similar to what is taking place today."[1]

Such chords played well with the press, which ran lists of Johnson's closest friends and advisers cut from New Deal cloth. That the principal alternative candidate for the Democratic presidential nomination in 1960 looked to be the son of Joseph P. Kennedy, who turned from Roosevelt and the New Deal to unbridled reaction and support for Joseph McCarthy, reinforced the iconography, at least in public. (In private Corcoran and Douglas worked hard for Johnson for president while maintaining friendships with Joe and Jack Kennedy.)[2]

. . .

In June 1958, as I prepared to enter college in the fall, my father arranged with Johnson for a summer job for me; a bit of parental transfer of privilege and entre. Every day the Senate was in session I was one of a dozen or so doormen for the visitors' galleries. On days of adjournment I was one of a half-dozen staffers drafting replies to Johnson's mail. On doorman duty I would sometimes see Johnson stride down the corridor from the elevators to his Capitol Hill office (he had several outlying ones in the Senate office buildings), tall, heavy, smoothly groomed, hands in the pockets of his buttoned suit, and acknowledge me: "How you gettin' along?" or "Spoke to your daddy today . . ." When it served the purpose of claims for the cosmopolitan makeup of his staff he'd tell someone that not only had he attracted his new flock of brainy full-time assistants, "This wonderful boy has come all the way down from Harvard to help me out." From the gallery I studied his posture and body language on the Senate floor. He was at home with the "whales" as he called them (Richard Russell, Robert Kerr, Lister Hill, Warren Magnuson, Everett Dirksen, Hubert Humphrey; others), but not with the "minnows." The whales and the minnows were constants. Johnson was not. Moving among them, he might be formal and commanding or slouched, conspiratorial, and intimate. Many faces indeed.[3]

There followed for me hours of observation of live drama, some history, some comic opera, and of course tedium; but above all, absorption into the Johnsonian orbit, which included a few young staffers from Texas of extraordinary talent, soon to make names for themselves, including Bill Moyers, Harry McPherson, and Bill Brammer. They became my summertime tutors. Johnson's chief aide on the Senate floor, Bobby Baker of South Carolina, sleek, smart, charming, and witty, his roguishness still in check, was another member of that group. At a far pole of the Washington scene, and outside my father's circle, I had a chance social encounter with Dean Acheson, who didn't know Johnson well and was interested in hearing more about him; a mentor-protégé friendship ensued.

That summer of my nineteenth year, and for four more after it working in the Senate, I took a step in from the sidelines, closer to participation in the political environment in which I'd been reared. Thereafter my own path took another course, in journalism (another form of observation, another story). But, for a time, I was taken inside to witness some of the circumstances of my father's and his friends' world as it spun back and forth, in and out of their control.

Running through those glimpses is the theme of conflict within Lyndon Johnson; conflict and irony. For the political environment shifted dramatically for him and his colleagues in the fall of 1958. With the help of the

"Eisenhower recession," the Democrats swept the congressional elections that year. Their 49–47 margin in the Senate widened to 62–34. Then came Alaska and Hawaii's entry into the union (another erosion of Southern veto power in the Senate, stage-managed by Johnson), which yielded four new senators—all Democrats. Nineteen-forty was the last year the Democrats held such a Senate majority.[4]

To the Senate came such new faces and crisp minds as Edmund Muskie of Maine, Eugene McCarthy of Minnesota, and Philip Hart of Michigan, at the head of their class. This infusion of talent changed the culture of the Senate and forced a shift in its management.[5]

The narrow Democratic edge before 1958 gave Johnson an instrument with which to induce compromise and cooperation; to dominate from the middle. The new numbers gave the strengthened liberal group less reason to yield to Johnson's designs. That weakened his hand at the wheel-and-deal stage. Accordingly, tensions between Johnson and liberals who wanted a more militant challenge to the Republicans accelerated.[6]

On the other hand, with the end of the Eisenhower years coming into view, so was the pull between Johnson and the very center of the political stage. Bill Brammer, who was working after hours in Johnson's office on his fine novel about Texas politics, *The Gay Place*, mixed an antic sense of humor and appreciation of our employer on and off the page. "Sweet Daddy Grace," he sometimes called Johnson in conversation, after the outlandish black evangelist of the 1930s. This was Brammer's way of suggesting Johnson's extremes, between shrewd political mastery and raw vaudeville, between near paranoia and overbearing exuberance, especially when he moved from the cockpit of the Senate to the national stage. And Johnson's performance style did veer from back-alley suspicion to suave polish to brazen provincial corn.

Sometimes this display of alternative personalities was for the benefit of the Senate, sometimes for public audiences, sometimes for the purpose of mesmerizing accomplished journalists like James Reston and the Alsop brothers (not to mention more impressionable ones) in his lavishly refurbished office in the Capitol, dubbed by some reporters and staffers the "Taj Mahal" and by others a "Turkish whorehouse." Next door, on the Senate floor, he would solemnly invoke Old Testament wisdom (Isaiah: "Come now, and let us reason together"). Unchained and unbuttoned, railing at the vile accusations of his critics, he'd intone in a stump speech back home, "We've got a saying in Texas, 'Forgive them, for they know not what they do,'" cavalierly taking on the role of Jesus Christ. Brammer distilled the Johnson style from nature to art in the character of Texas Governor Arthur Fenstemaker, waking up a state legislator with an early morning call:

"What're you doin'?" Fenstemaker boomed.
"Sleeping," Roy Sherwood said. "Real good, too."

"Hell of a note," Fenstemaker said. "World's cavin' in all round us; rocket ships blastin' off to the moon; poisonous gas in our environment. . . . Sinful goddam nation . . . laden with iniquity, offspring of evildoers. My princes are rebels and companions of thieves . . ."

"Who the hell is this?"

"Isaiah," Fenstemaker said. "The Prophet Isaiah. . . ."

"Who the hell is this?"

"Arthur Goddam Fenstemaker. Hah yew?"[7]

As Brammer's portrayal suggests, it was hard to know with Johnson what part of this was ingenuous, what part disingenuous. The indication was that he didn't know himself.

Another persistent note was his ambivalence about reaching for still higher station. As Senate majority leader, Johnson made appearances around the country for Democratic Party worthies, addressing their testimonial dinners, and this brought him now and then to New York. Unstated but obvious was that he was presenting himself for inspection outside the domains he controlled (and doing so especially in New York, capital of liberal and press elites) as a presidential candidate.

For the moment the presidential issue was merely implied; no bands or hoopla. So these were stiff, official rituals, invoking the memories of Al Smith and FDR, paying homage to such latter-day tribunes as Averell Harriman, Carmine De Sapio, and Brooklyn Congressmen Emmanuel Celler and Eugene Keogh. (Johnson's own favorite New York politician was undoubtedly Adam Clayton Powell of Harlem. Powell would occasionally wander onto the Senate floor for a bit of deal cutting with Johnson, and you could see the two of them go into a hugging, whispering, schmoozey embrace, political hams, each enjoying the theater of it and the knowledge of the other's number.) Present at several of these New York political circuit events on weekends home from college, I would go up to the dais to pay my respects. In response Johnson was appreciative and sad-eyed as a spaniel. These were roles to be endured, not savored.[8]

Occasionally he took an evening off. One night in 1959 Ed and Alice Weisl, my parents, and I joined the Johnsons for dinner at Toots Shor's. Johnson was stonily self-preoccupied ("He wants his belly rubbed," my mother whispered to me) and, after some desultory talk, focused on his food, shoveling it in steadily. Inevitably my father took up the slack and started opining. After a few minutes my mother caught sight of a glamorous older woman in evening dress trying vainly to get our eminent friend's attention: "Oh, Mr. Johnson . . . Senator Johnson?"

My mother could be dead-eye on a piece of unfolding drama. "That," she whispered to the Weisls and Lady Bird, "is Cobina Wright. Cobina Wright, *Senior*, as she calls herself." Cobina Wright was a café society personage and sometime Hollywood gossip columnist. "She's *important*," my mother instructed them. She meant that—for Christ's sake—this was New York, Johnson was very visible at Toots Shor's, he was preparing to become a *presidential candidate* . . . You don't expose yourself in that combination of circumstances and refuse to acknowledge somebody like Cobina Wright, who knows where to put out the word that Lyndon Johnson of Texas is a rube, and rude in the bargain. His dark mood was deep; neither Cobina Wright, Senior, nor my mother prevailed.

. . .

As Johnson peaked in his leadership of the Senate in the late 1950s, so there had to be a next act. Enter the Kennedy family.

The story of the 1960 Democratic Convention and the formation of the Kennedy-Johnson ticket has been told often, though its most interior recesses may never be known. While Theodore White's initial and legendary version (*The Making of the President 1960*) has its fairy-tale aspects with respect to the Kennedys' campaign, it fairly captures Johnson's.[9]

Even to a young staff enthusiast the Johnson campaign for the 1960 Democratic nomination was feeble, parochial, late, and directionless at the top. He had been celebrated for several years by the national press as a supremely accomplished legislative leader, as a shrewd healer of a great party on the march again as the Eisenhower era played out. In equal portions Johnson savored the kudos, and feared trying for the presidential nomination and suffering humiliation in defeat. Publicly he would question whether a man "from my part of the country" could be nominated; then suffer the fires of his ambition to be stoked. One day he was a candidate, authorizing national appearances and contacts. The next day, to the rage of his aides and supporters, he would cancel them. The truth, even his best friends told him and each other after the fact, was that he remained the prisoner not only of his Texas constituency but of his special fear of Texas turning on him. The constant reel replaying in his mind was of the youthful pride of the New Deal, humiliated in his 1941 Senate defeat, tarnished by his disputed 1948 victory; both of them all-out, left-right contests.[10]

The irony was that for his old New Deal friends Johnson in 1960 was the only candidate with authentic links to Roosevelt. He was only fifty-one as that year began—the same age as Roosevelt upon taking office in 1933. So their concept was not of a restoration but of a resumption, a "recapturing" of the "spirit of firm, tough-minded, and fearless approach to . . . the world of politics and the desperately pressing problems of economics. . . . I am for Lyndon Johnson because I see in him the best hope of re-capturing" that spirit. So my mother expressed the case in a letter to Eleanor Roosevelt, whom she'd written about and visited with, in June 1960.

Reflecting Johnson's problem, Mrs. Roosevelt, like many liberals, knew the cautious, public Johnson, not her husband's protégés' comrade in arms.

She was dubious: "The New Deal is now old fashioned," she wrote back to my mother. "We need some fresh thinking. The New Deal was not simple at the time. Fortunately, it is now!" She meant, it had met contemporary challenges but was not necessarily relevant to new ones.[11]

But the partners were serious. My father and Jim Rowe raised money for Hubert Humphrey, Johnson's surrogate against Kennedy in the West Virginia primary. Douglas made noise about leaving the Court to help make Johnson president, if the senator would commit to a serious run. For a long time Corcoran had been talking with Joe Kennedy about financing a Johnson-Kennedy ticket, designed to moot the Catholic issue and ease Jack into the presidency thereafter.[12]

Johnson's inability to resolve his course took the contorted form of campaigning nationally by playing the familiar role of dutiful Senate leader. Corcoran: "I told him, 'For Christ's sake, Lyndon, hook up with Joe Kennedy and run with Jack [that is, with Kennedy as the vice presidential candidate]. He's been your friend in the Senate when you needed him. This is a national alliance. Let's win the election and pass the bills next year.'"[13]

Johnson's friends became distraught. Ed Weisl and my father spoke of switching their support to another old friend, Senator Stuart Symington of Missouri. Corcoran's law partner Jim Rowe signed on officially with Hubert Humphrey and Dean Acheson with Symington, but only because Johnson had equivocated for so long. Was Johnson running or not? Jack Kennedy asked Corcoran. Corcoran replied, "Is he running? Does a fish swim? Of course he is. He may not think he is. And certainly he's saying he isn't. But I know God damned well he is. I'm sorry that he doesn't know it."[14]*

My father was bearing messages and pounding on Johnson to announce. Mayor Wagner of New York was "dying" to be Johnson's running mate; Governor Robert Meyner of New Jersey was pro-Johnson and would make a good attorney general; a heavily pressured Hubert Humphrey was holding out against Kennedy pressures. (My father to Johnson's chief Senate aide,

---

*Though Corcoran placed these two conversations, with Johnson and with Kennedy, in late 1959 or early 1960 in his unpublished memoir, the scrupulously careful Robert Dallek has made the case in *Lone Star Rising*, the first volume of his biography of Johnson, that Corcoran's memory had blurred and that they occurred in 1955–1956, with reference to the contest for the nomination that year. (Robert Caro follows Dallek's lead in his third volume on Johnson, *Master of the Senate*.) Based on my own research in Corcoran's papers, I believe he elided two sets of conversations with several Kennedy family members and Johnson, one set in 1955–1956, the second in 1959–1960. The contextual indications of the quotes and the further internal evidence in the memoir itself persuade me that the conversations noted here did occur in 1959–1960, as Corcoran stated, as a follow-on to conversations four years earlier. Professor Dallek finds my conclusion plausible. See also note 37 to this chapter, pages 262–263.

Walter Jenkins: "I said to him, 'Hubert, they are saying you are for sale [to the Kennedys] and I have been denying it. They are talking about you being for sale for $500,000.'")[15]

Walter Reuther, in control of the Michigan Democratic Party and influential in labor circles across the country, was still "neutral". At least, "Reuther said I could tell Lyndon that anyone that was trying to say that [Johnson] was not acceptable—well, that just isn't true," my father advised Jenkins in May 1960. Douglas was intervening with Reuther as well. But none of these angles could be played, or the Kennedy juggernaut held off, if Johnson wouldn't declare. "I just don't know how long we can hold things together," my father complained to Jenkins. "Our problem is not with Reuther, with [California Governor] Pat Brown or the others—our problem is with Lyndon Johnson and you know it."[16]

A few days later he resorted to prodding Johnson in his client newsletter, scolding the majority leader for campaigning from "the Senate cloakroom." Those were fighting words for a candidate deep in the grip of inner conflict, and Johnson, on the mailing list, paused to write back, partly in hand,

> Dear Eliot:
>   I have not been in the Cloakroom in a year. I operate from the first seat on the front row on the Floor five days a week with the press spotlight constantly in my eyes. Then I speak my lungs out in four or five states each weekend.
>   You write like Rip Van Winkle, but I'm so grateful for your friendship and I do love you.[17]

He wanted the nomination to come to him. Then, on the eve of the Democratic Convention, Johnson announced with stirring words ("Since Woodrow Wilson, the American Presidency has been looked to as the world's chief office of peacemaking and leadership for freedom"). My parents wired him, "YOU WERE MAGNIFICENT YOU ARE ON YOUR WAY." But it was way too late.[18]

. . .

I was one of an odd lot of junior Johnson staffers picked for what wound up as inconsequential convention duty in Los Angeles. (A number of senior aides were left in charge of the store.) Our cohort flew west in the small company plane of one of Johnson's "new money" Texas backers, touching down for fuel in Alabama, west Texas, and Arizona. We were the secretaries, lesser press staff, and willing gofers; only one or two could claim professional political experience, none of it national.

The campaign office in Los Angeles was loosely led by provincials from the Texas statehouse scene. Often our assignments were vague. One of mine was to manage the AP ticker and get relevant news items to the right desks. The maneuvering at this contested convention was nonstop. But at the end of one day, without thinking, I turned the Associated Press ticker off for the night, losing us twelve hours of AP take: my contribution to the campaign's amateurism.

A slightly more heroic moment came when the schedule called for Senator Eugene McCarthy to place Adlai Stevenson's name in nomination. The Johnson and Stevenson forces were deeply in league to try to hold Kennedy from a first-ballot nomination in the hope of forcing a brokered convention in which they would hold the cards. Along with a handful of other Johnson staffers, I was sent with an official pass to the convention gallery to hold the doors open for hordes of uncredentialed Stevenson volunteers who filled the galleries, cheered McCarthy's speech wildly, and triggered what was intended to be a convention-stopping floor demonstration for Adlai.[19]

My parents, seasoned Democratic Convention attendees, were in Los Angeles. My father whisked by one day in convention badges, dispatched by the Texans at that moment to speak on Johnson's behalf, oddly, to the North Dakota delegation. Another day, passing before an office TV set, I caught an unexpected flash of my parents on an interview show, my father pronouncing on Roosevelt's removal of the pro-appeasement, fascist-leaning Joseph Kennedy from his post as ambassador to Britain in 1940 because of the latter's failure of responsibility in the world's worst crisis, or words to that effect.

This family moment was prelude to Johnson's own last effort, a challenge to Kennedy to a joint appearance before the Texas and Massachusetts delegations, which Kennedy gamely accepted. There Johnson too attacked Joe Kennedy as a pre-war appeaser and apologist for the Nazis, crying "I wasn't any Chamberlain umbrella-policy man! . . . I never thought Hitler was right!" Standing at the edge of the proceedings, I thought he seemed finally alive; I'd never seen such fire in him on the floor of the Senate. His agent John Connally hit harder, charging—a truth held to be a below-the-belt allegation at the time—that Kennedy suffered from Addison's disease.[20]

Then it was over. The night and day after Kennedy's survival of these attacks, and of McCarthy's elegant speech meant to trigger a Stevenson stampede, were grim for our small group. The class act in defeat was Lynda Bird Johnson, sixteen years old that year, delivering a graceful short talk of thanks to the campaign staff.

The next day I was a gofer in Johnson's hotel suite during the hours that Kennedy moved to bring Johnson onto the ticket with him. Friends came to harsh words. Corcoran, one of a cadre of back-channel brokers of the deal, pushed it hard. Johnson told him he'd have to get Sam Rayburn to go along, and, Johnson added, "He hates Kennedys." Senator Kerr of Oklahoma, ornery and hard, slapped Bobby Baker across the face when his and Johnson's young protégé tried to calm his rage at the news. John Connally fought the move bitterly; white-faced with fury, my father stood with

Connally. At one point, my father claimed, he, Connally, and Lady Bird retired to one of the suite's bathrooms where she agonized over how "trapped" she and Lyndon felt.[21]

Rayburn, various senators, congressmen, and governors came and went, debating the merits of Johnson taking the vice presidential nomination. Corcoran argued that Johnson could be on the ballot for both vice president and reelection to the Senate, and so had leverage with the Kennedys: if the ticket won and if by January 1961 they hadn't guaranteed him real power in the administration, Johnson could stay in the Senate! (That sounded like Corcoran's style, but not the Kennedys'.) John Connally put his big hand on my neck and whispered some command in my ear. The air was heavy; these were powerful men, deprived of their power.[22]

"Ed Weisl says <u>no</u>," begin Lady Bird Johnson's handwritten notes from an emotional phone conversation as word of Johnson's decision to become Kennedy's running mate began to spread around Los Angeles on July 14, 1960:

> Would have to kill himself—violates every principle he holds near and dear. . . . South would consider him traitor and so would he . . . if thought Lyndon would *dream* of doing this would never have done what he did [to help Johnson]. It is unthinkable—sellout. . . . Kennedy only using him and would destroy him.[23]

Waiting for the hotel elevator on my way back to the campaign office, Lady Bird appeared, purposeful in a tailored dark suit. Naturally shy, appreciative of my parents' friendship over the years, she had always been warm and outgoing when I saw her. "How are *you* doing?" I asked with emphasis, knowing at least some of what the tensions in the room were. (Philip Graham, chronicler of all the maneuvering as the key Kennedy-Johnson go-between, called her own position on whether Johnson should run with Kennedy "something between negative and neutral.") She smiled wanly. "Well, Ah'll be all right someday, mah friend," she said with her pronounced twang and drawl, her words letting her usually politic guard down low.[24]

By that time the peculiar drama whereby Robert Kennedy undercut his brother's offer to Johnson was in motion. My mother analyzed this as a cold ploy to make Johnson want what he didn't want—becoming a shadow behind Jack Kennedy—by adding insult to injury, one that only Jack could undo—and in undoing bind the suddenly impotent Johnson to him. Stage management or pure hatred of Johnson on Bobby Kennedy's part, it was working. Fearing a worse humiliation than he'd imagined in reaching for the presidential nomination, Johnson now sought to rally support for himself for the vice presidency and asked my father to get in touch with Reuther. "Do it yourself," my father claimed he replied, and left the suite.[25]

The conflicts for Lyndon and Lady Bird Johnson swirled deeper and deeper. When they went out of their hotel suite for the formal announcement that the Senate majority leader was accepting his junior colleague's offer they looked, Phil Graham remembered, "as though they had just survived an airplane crash."[26]

. . .

A handwritten note from Douglas to my father on Supreme Court notepaper as the convention ended reads:

Dear Eliot:

I've been watching television and conclude that during the last three or four months we would have done just as well if we had talked only to each other.

As ever,
Bill[27]

The House of Roosevelt came together for Johnson, but, as Douglas's note suggested, it looked like ancient history. And it was showing signs of breakage under strain.

Corcoran, who had been figuring the possible angles of the Kennedy-Johnson ticket his own way, took a characteristically upbeat view: "I think Lyndon did the right thing but I'm not sure a lot of other people think so," he wrote Douglas at his Washington State retreat on August 1. "Ben [Cohen], who was against it at first, agrees with me."[28]

Always solicitous of Johnson, Abe Fortas wrote him across town that "you have done a noble act" in settling for the vice presidential nomination, and offering "anything I can do to be of assistance." But the same day he wrote Douglas in the West, in disconsolate pessimism:

Dear Bill,

Looking back, the result was inevitable. The plain fact of the matter is that Lyndon was unable to bring himself to do what was necessary months ago, when it might have been possible. Incidentally, Eliott [sic] did him a lot of damage.

The Hell of it is that we must go on from where we are, and not from where we might have been. I think that the wreckage at this moment is fantastic and perhaps beyond repair; and there is no basis for assuming that the young man [JFK] can repair it.[29]

"Eliott did him a lot of damage" meant that from Fortas's Washington viewpoint one didn't fight a war more aggressively than suited one's leader. My father had raged against the Kennedys on Johnson's behalf and wouldn't stop. From Fortas's standpoint he was being impolitic when what was indicated was management of a difficult situation. My father was no less acid in his notes to Douglas and others about Fortas's stance. In the past he and Douglas had reserved a high, sarcastic style for moments like this; thus my father wrote,

Dear Bill,

Yours of July 14, on your reaction to what was visible at Los Angeles over television, surprised me because it indicated that you were not privy to what was fundamentally at stake. . . . The Fortas firm, after all, had accumulated a large stake in being "in." . . . Playing the game cool and with judgment and a sense of responsibility necessarily precluded the running of risks and the provoking of resentments which might have . . . cast a cloud on the cumulative "in" or, of course, on its potential during the ripe years ahead.[30]

In other words, Johnson as vice president was an excellent commercial indicator for his principal Washington attorneys, Arnold, Fortas and Porter. My father's trademarked cynicism and social satire, stamped by youthful immersion in Molière and Marx, were on display. He had a piece of a point. On the one hand, Fortas disliked the Kennedys too, and a powerful Johnson in the Senate majority leadership was a better rainmaker for his firm than a politically marginalized Johnson in the vice presidency. Nevertheless, straight off Fortas managed the controversial Texas ballot arrangements that locked in for the anxious senator a green light to run simultaneously for reelection to the Senate and for the vice presidency. And after January the cases of people with difficulties in Washington who asked the advice of the vice president were steered where so many of his own legal needs were dealt with, to Abe Fortas.[31]

Douglas's traffic in wisecracks and highlighted news items like "Many Past 90 Sexually Active, Study Indicates" with my father and the others resumed its pace. The foxy Supreme Court justice they'd all worked to get into the vice presidency in 1944 and the presidency four years later, and to whom they all reported in as they had in past political seasons, offered no further written comment that season on what his closest friends were fighting about.[32]

. . .

The new wisdom held that running with Jack Kennedy was Johnson's last chance to "go national" and transcend Texas; that the worse fate would have been for him to go back to the Senate and be majority leader during a Kennedy administration, without the independence he'd had under President Eisenhower. (That scenario, of course, assumed Kennedy would have won without Johnson as his running mate.)[33]

No one was more rapturous on this theme than Tommy Corcoran. In a "pep talk" letter to Lyndon and Lady Bird Johnson on election day 1960, the man who, at FDR's signal, ushered the freshly minted young Texas congressman into the New Deal's inner councils in 1937 referred to the crowd of Dallas right-wingers who roughed up the Johnsons and spat at them in a hotel lobby four days before the 1960 election, and waxed avuncular:

> I know you didn't like what I said to you [several months earlier] about escaping from the cage of Texas but your subconscious knew even then it was true. People like that Dallas suburbanite crowd— opportunistic carpetbaggers from anywhere except the soil and soul of *your* Texas—are the reason you couldn't do what you had to do from two years back to win at Los Angeles. Trying to keep the false friendship of that kind of "Texan" you couldn't in time take the positions you had to take to make the North believe in you. . . . These were your real enemies—these Dallas "Texans"—not FDR's followers in New York or Pennsylvania or Massachusetts or even Michigan. . . .
>
> No matter how the votes fall today, *you* are a free force in the world, free to be right, free to be a *national* statesman, free to be a *world* statesman, free to free the greatness that FDR saw in you.[34]

Corcoran wrote a month after his law partner and comrade in so many rounds with Johnson, Jim Rowe, unleashed a message in dramatically different tones. Rowe had been present in Los Angeles to help handle the turbulence within Johnson and around him as he became Kennedy's running mate, counseling him that John Connally was the right *hombre*, "fully as 'hard-nosed' as Bobby," to manage the vice presidential campaign and deal with the tensions between Johnson and the Kennedys. Rowe's efforts to be helpful in the weeks thereafter ran up against Johnson's behavior in what was becoming a personal crisis for him. The hot-and-cold running impulses that haunted his attempt for the presidential nomination over the preceding year, his humiliation in Los Angeles having tried and failed, the continuing incompetence of his national campaign apparatus, his terror that Kennedy and he would fail to carry Texas, the lifelong splits within him between daring aspiration and fearful, truculent self-protection; all these were on display for the Johnson entourage. They were a foretaste, in fact, of the final act of his presidency, as failure of his Vietnam policies became a monumental political disaster and a personal one as well. Rowe's letter, hammered out on a weekend halfway through the fall presidential campaign on his own typewriter replete with errors x-ed out, has not previously been available, though the fact that he confronted Johnson was known. Because these were crucial weeks in national political history, and painful ones in Johnson's personal evolution, because the letter touches on behavior patterns that Johnson would in some cases manage better as president, in others even worse, it deserves to be quoted at length.[35]

Rowe began, factually, by enclosing rave reviews for Johnson's performance at two New York conclaves of liberals supporting the ticket; dates he'd been cranky about agreeing to. The meetings, growled Rowe,

> both of which I had urged for weeks and both of which you held up until the last damn minute[,] show what you can do and how eagerly these people will come nine-tenths of the way if Lyndon Johnson will condescend to come one-tenth . . .
>
> Of course it completely escaped your attention but I have been in a *cold fury* about the way you [otherwise] *wasted* your time in New York. It may be useful for [New York public relations man Thomas Deegan, hired for the campaign] to have you appear at a Catholic girl's [*sic*] school, of which Mrs. Deegan is an alumna trustee, but . . . Kennedy does not need one bit of help on the Catholic vote. (He does with negroes and Jews in New York). And it may be useful for Tom Deegan to have LBJ go to Greenwich Connecticut to meet 75 "opinion makers," all of whom by some odd coincidence live in Greenwich, some of whom are Deegan's clients and others will be after *that* performance.
>
> But how it helped *my* Democratic Party escapes me. It also escaped [New York Democratic organization leader Carmine De] Sapio, the Liberal Party people and the Reform group, all of whom quietly asked me who the hell arranged that schedule. . . .
>
> You asked me months ago to check out Tom Deegan. I did and gave Walter [Jenkins] the report. I guess you never saw it. "Con man" is too rough language but it was applied several times. And you certainly were taken, like a country boy.
>
> Lyndon, I know you don't like this kind of remark.

From facts Rowe here moves to the issue of personal interaction with Johnson. As he notes, the problem has nothing to do with his own views as a liberal, or with his own tough nature, because it applies equally with the even tougher conservative in the senator's inner council, Johnson's former aide John Connally:

> But by God, somebody ought to tell you the truth occasionally— and there is no one around who *dares*.
>
> I would tell you [all this] to your face but I have learned I can't get one word in edgewise with you—or we end up in a yelling match. I get bored being an audience and I don't really like yelling. So I am doing it this way.
>
> And don't think for one second that this is being written by a man who no longer loves you or is no longer loyal to you . . .
>
> Don't you ever pause for a moment and wonder why such old and devoted friends—at least a quarter of a century apiece—like John Connally and Jim Rowe find it impossible to work for you?
>
> It would make me wonder.

I don't think John and I agree on anything in substance—except that we both love our country as much as Lyndon Johnson. But we disagree as rational men, with respect for each other's opinions and judgment.

Rowe then gives Johnson high grades on his public campaigning (of an appearance in New Jersey: "FDR would have topped it. But Kennedy, Stevenson, Truman or Kefauver could not"), the internal problems notwithstanding. Even some of the parochial Texan staffers are performing well against odds and "*despite* you," he observes, and then puts the mirror to Johnson's face about his treatment of his staff:

Have you completely forgotten that there is . . . a carrot as well as a stick? I have not seen you pay one compliment, thank one person, be the sweet and kind and attractive Lyndon I used to know in all the time I have travelled [*sic*] with you. I have seen you do nothing but yell at them, every single one of them.

And most of the time, you, LBJ, are wrong and they are right. Maybe you do not know it—but I do—the morale of your staff is awful. They . . . are beginning to dislike you intensely. They cannot do anything right, they don't dare make a decision about where to hang your clothes even, and they bend their heads and wait for the blows to fall—like obdurate mules who know the blow is coming.

It makes me so goddam mad I'd like to sock you in the jaw! . . .

As John Connally and I said to each other in New York—"Where is that wonderful guy of ten years ago we used to know?" What the hell do you think you are—a Mongol emperor, a feudal overlord?

These are people, Lyndon, human beings . . .

Please—one day a week, go up and down that plane and tell George Reedy and Bill Moyers, and the stenographers and the advancemen and Walter Jenkins . . . that you appreciate what they are doing for you, that you are under tremendous strain and have to blow your top at them, but that you love them—which you do, dammit . . .

With his mention of "tremendous strain," Rowe brings Johnson's psychological demons, his struggle to deal with his conflicts of sensibility and role, the embarrassment of old friends turning on him in Los Angeles, to the table. But in contrast to Corcoran and Fortas, he will not stop short at solicitousness and empathy. He goes near the split that had driven Johnson's closest friends and strongest supporters to distraction for years, and would help destroy his own presidency: the struggle between his driving self-confidence (requiring adulation and confirmation), fueling his instinct for power; and his devastating anxieties. As evidenced, finally, in the eyes of the world in the Vietnam years, that struggle sent him at times into shrewd, probing, strategic plotting, at times into a kind of paralysis, and at times into raging frustration taking the form of abuse of others. Anxieties trumped confidence, and he became his own worst enemy.

Rowe does not refer directly to Franklin Roosevelt in this passage, but in demanding that Johnson hold himself to a higher standard of performance than he is displaying, he speaks from the web of experience the two shared as young men uncommonly close to FDR:

> Yes, of course I have some understanding of the strain you are under. I know you must feel that you are all alone, that your friends are deserting you, that no one really can understand the pressure you are undergoing. Well, I guess no man can, Lyndon. But this is always true of men in your position. And they have been able to do it, even if it is lonely.
>
> Perhaps I don't really understand. But I have a feeling that at present your [*sic*] are caught between tremendous vanity—yes, Lyndon, the boys are right when they write this—and a curious lack of self confidence about your judgment of men. You give me the feeling quite often that you are not sure you can trust anyone and therefore must do it all yourself. You can't . . .
>
> You won't believe it, but this is written from the affection I have had for you for so many years . . .
>
> This is probably the end of an old friendship.[36]

There was more. And the Johnson-Rowe friendship did go on ice for three years.

Of course, letters to Johnson from his closest friends were on occasion intended in part as paramedical interventions—feel-good therapy like Corcoran's, deliberate shock therapy like Rowe's. My father's position, which had partaken of both those models, became simply perverse and irreconcilable. But even in his fury at the Kennedys' takeover, reportorial networking was central to his own operations, and he had a long talk with Connecticut Democratic chairman John Bailey, his old friend and co-conspirator, since Kennedy's nomination the Democratic national chairman, a straight shooter. He talked with Corcoran and Douglas, who knew all the players; with Ed Weisl and John Connally. The net take: as early as 1955 Joe Kennedy had talked to Corcoran and perhaps Johnson about financing the right kind of ticket (Johnson-Kennedy in 1956, to bring Jack along as FDR had been brought along as the losing candidate for vice president in 1920). In the process, he'd said, " 'I'll make you rich, Tommy.' And he told me about oil in place and he told me about real estate and . . . a lot of things." This time, Joe Kennedy worked Johnson over on the back channel—the two knew how to talk to each other without regard to heated, ad hominem campaign rhetoric about each other—with his own vision of the future, whereby "these boys" are not ready to run the country, which means that "you and I, Lyndon" are going to have to run it for them. Then, my father claimed Jack Kennedy's man John Bailey told him, Joe offered the Senate majority leader $1 million to settle Johnson's campaign debts.* Offer accepted.

Plausible; at any rate he claimed to have reported it authoritatively.[37]

. . .

But what was the source of my father's *rage* about the Kennedys? Douglas, Corcoran, and Clifford accepted the Kennedy family takeover and did business with them. Fortas felt about Joe Kennedy more or less as my father did but never put his relationship with Johnson on the line over it.

Instead of healing, this fury deepened. My father traded in the worst scandal about Jack Kennedy, whom he'd viewed in rather sporting terms in his first years in politics, and began casually to refer to him with words like "that degenerate little cripple in the White House." On the one hand, history has shown us that some of the most unsavory gossip about Kennedy was based in fact. On the other hand, on this score, my father hurled his inside information at you with a venom reminiscent of the Roosevelt haters of the 1930s who spread rumors that FDR's disability was syphilis.

My father's stated grounds for bitterness were clinical and for once (apocalyptically) moral: Joe Kennedy "bought" the nomination and then the election, as if this were the age of the robber barons. He bought Johnson too. Corruption was everywhere: that his old Rooseveltian partners, however reluctantly, were in effect reconciled to Johnson's deal with the Kennedys meant the prevailing value had become, "The game must go on!" The press, falling for Kennedy's "style" when his victory was about his father's money and shady alliances, was worse. Kennedy's appointment of his brother as attorney general (all the Rooseveltians, and especially Clark Clifford, who played a curious role in the drama, knew that had been Joe Kennedy's personal *diktat*) proved the family was shameless.[38]

Digging deeper, his only co-conspirator with comparably unreconcilable loathing for the Kennedys was Ed Weisl. In his role as a leading corporate lawyer Weisl had some years earlier been on the defending side of a hostile fight with Joe Kennedy over control of Paramount Pictures. Normally disinclined to make enemies, Weisl always said that in that set-to he'd experienced firsthand Joe's antisemitism and learned details on his traffic with the mob. J. Edgar Hoover and Roy Cohn, both of whom despised the Kennedys, fed Weisl their worst dirt on them. With whatever tribal reasons

---

*If my father was right in this account as well as in his memory of Joseph Kennedy offering the same figure to help Douglas's supporters stalemate the 1944 Democratic National Convention until they could put him across, Kennedy had neglected the rate of inflation. (See page 56.)

for solidarity with Weisl, my father began to speak of the Kennedys as a menace to democracy in phrases that drew from those of his friend.[39]

My father regularly quoted Veblen, Voltaire, Talleyrand, and Proust on naïveté. At one level he was furious that his team, the Rooseveltian insiders who as a function of their sophistication had a strong market position in cynicism, had been made to look like naïfs by the even more cynical Joe and Jack Kennedy. But at root I think he recognized checkmate. He saw any House of Roosevelt worth preserving in free fall.

For Joe, Jack, and Bobby Kennedy represented—again, as in a nineteenth-century saga—a new, potent, and cold-blooded force. It was built on understandings of power similar to that of the Rooseveltians, but minus its pretense of, or connection to, reform causes. First and last, the House of Kennedy *would* dominate the environment of power. Unlike Douglas reluctant to risk his seat on the Supreme Court for an overt reach for national elective office, or Johnson in his hesitancy to risk what he'd won in the Senate in a run for the presidency, there was nothing whatsoever equivocal about the Kennedys' project: It was, and they had, control. The Rooseveltians' decades-old venture in brokering ideas and power appeared to be over.

Even Weisl healed the breach with Johnson, though never with a good word for Kennedys. Weisl was a counselor and a survivor; no warrior or innovator. But for my father, who had as a youthful freelancer aspired to rewrite Marx, then as a young journalist felt empowered to edit the New Deal, here was a professional catastrophe.

. . .

When Kennedy rolled over Johnson at the 1960 Democratic Convention, Fortas had included in his dire report to Douglas that rather than "trying to regain a position of 'leadership'" in the world, given the "wreckage" and given the implausibility of "the young man" nominated for president, it might be time "for the United States to attempt to work out an international mechanism through the United Nations."[40]

Early in 1962, at Douglas's suggestion, Fortas hatched a cozier plan for coping with the new order of power, which so far featured their man Johnson on the outside looking in. The vice president's assignments were of the second order and left him subject to the petty disdain of Robert Kennedy, and of former Kennedy Senate aides, previously inconsequential peasants on the far reaches of the estate of the mighty majority leader, like Kenneth O'Donnell.[41]

Fortas's proposed arrangement, to be sold to Kennedy, would assure that Johnson "is loaded with work—overloaded," as Fortas put it. He wrote Douglas,

This will serve his own peace of mind and it will also avoid the waste of his extraordinary talents.

Apart from the special case of LBJ, it would be a notable contribution to our Government if a pattern could be found within which Vice Presidents can function.

Fortas's plan imagined Johnson as coordinator of policy and programs involving youth, transportation, and foreign aid, policies where his can-do instincts would be engaged. Nonetheless he concluded with an emphasis on the ceremonial and the hierarchical. Henceforth, Fortas proposed, "portions of the Presidential staff (sometimes, perhaps, even the Budget Bureau!), and heads of agencies, could be asked to report to the President through the Vice President." Furthermore, Johnson needed to step out of Washington's shadows to an office in the White House, a move that "would have considerable symbolic significance." (Vice presidents had offices at the Capitol and in the Executive Office Building but not in the Executive Mansion, until Jimmy Carter gave one to Walter Mondale in 1977.)[42]

Given what was known even then about Robert Kennedy's influence in his brother's White House, as well as what his and Johnson's relations were and where they seemed headed, this was idly naive thinking coming from such a consummate insider. Johnson was stuck. Even his old domain, the Senate, was riddled with land mines.

Mournful and idle, he would sometimes wander onto the Senate floor, where once members and staff snapped to attention at his every word or gesture "as if they were school kids" and Johnson a formidable teacher, in his chief legislative aide Harry McPherson's image. In Johnson's reduced state, though, "nothing happened. . . . He was no longer a member of the club." McPherson stayed on for two years with the new majority leader, Mike Mansfield. I was hired to their summer staff in 1961 and 1962, and was on hand for some of these mournful Johnsonian moments. The vice president would take a long, slow amble around the rear of the chamber, jangling keys and change in his pockets, sizing up the action and calculating whether to climb the podium and play presiding officer for lack of anything more pressing to do. Perhaps one of his old intimates might be around.[43]

One day in the summer of 1962 this path led him to a chair near the front of the half-circle of Senate seats facing the podium, to the left of his old friend and ally Robert Kerr of Oklahoma. Kerr had, that season, moved into the vacuum created by Johnson's departure as majority leader, and by Mike Mansfield's minimalist approach to the role. The press was full of admiring profiles and cover stories about Kerr that recorded these facts, echoing the Kennedy White House's sarcastic line, "Whatever happened to Lyndon Johnson?"[44]

The chamber was almost empty. I was the only staffer at the desk in front of the podium, looking directly at the senatorial lineup, my appointed post. Kerr was tough, wily, able, and something of a bully. (Dean Acheson, master of the lethal thumbnail sketch, wrote to me acidly of Senator Kerr that year, "Though I have sensed his power and capacity—and, generally speaking like people who are straightforward and strong . . . he seems to me . . . a meager and shoddy personality, a Buonaparte without even the second-rate quality of the 'empire' style.")[45]

Kerr, deep in heavy trading with a colleague seated on his left, did not at first notice the gloomy vice president on his right, massaging his face and jowls with a big, beefy hand, eyeballing the Senate chamber ceiling. At one point Johnson gave me a tight smile of acknowledgment; I smiled back.

Finally Kerr's trading was done and his lesser colleague dispatched. He became aware of Johnson. Embarrassed at having ignored his friend and surely aware that his own season of stardom in the press was the flip side of Johnson's eclipse, he turned, put out a hand, and exclaimed too loudly, "Whuh, *hello*, Lyndon!" Johnson gave it a beat of two or so, let his eye linger on me for a moment (yes, he had a witness), then slowly pulled his hand down his face and over into Kerr's grasp, turning a big, crinkly eyed, insincere smile on him.

"Hel-loo Bob," murmured the once-and-future master from the depth of his self-pity. "Ah jest sat down here because ah wanted to learn a little something about runnin' the Senate." Kerr smiled weakly. Moments passed. After a while Kerr thought of something to say. Johnson grunted, and after a minute or so got up and lumbered slowly, heavily out, a languorous look around, jangling his keys.

Figure 18. The morning after John F. Kennedy and Johnson were nominated in 1960. *Left to right:* Leroy Collins, JFK (behind him, Eugene McCarthy), LBJ, Edmund Muskie, Sam Rayburn, James Roosevelt, Lady Bird Johnson, Ernest ("Fritz") Hollings (behind Mrs. Johnson), Adlai Stevenson, Hubert Humphrey, Stuart Symington, Ernest Gruening. The author is seated three rows back (above JFK and Collins), in bow tie, with Geraldine Williams of the LBJ staff. *AP/Wide World Photos*

Figure 19. LBJ toasted Hugo Black at the White House in 1966: "If it weren't for Mr. Justice Black" ruling on the contested 1948 Texas Democratic primary, "we might well be having this party. But . . . we wouldn't be having it here." *Frank Wolfe / LBJ Library*

Figure 20. Clark Clifford and Abe Fortas "divied up various pieces of Johnson's personal and legal business as they had Bill Douglas's," and became the principals of LBJ's White House kitchen cabinet. *Yoichi Okamoto / LBJ Library*

Figure 21. Johnson and Douglas at the LBJ ranch in 1965: Douglas wrote, "Lyndon knew no barriers where friends were involved. In spite of our disagreements he clung tightly to me, for he knew I would never make an unfriendly move against him." *Yoichi Okamoto / LBJ Library*

Figure 22. Tommy Corcoran greets Johnson at the White House in 1964, James Madison looking on: LBJ's presidential rhetoric "makes my heart to sing again as in the Thirties," wrote Corcoran to his old friend. *LBJ Library*

Figure 23. Johnson gestures at North Carolina governor Terry Sanford in the oval office, Jim Rowe looks on: healing a breach, LBJ told Rowe there, after the Kennedy assassination, "Be content to be the first man to whom the 36th president of the United States has offered his apologies!" *LBJ Library*

Figure 24. Walter Reuther and LBJ share a laugh in the oval office with White House aide Joseph Califano: during the wartime scarcity of Washington hotel rooms, my father found a bed for Reuther on the Johnsons' sofa. *Yoichi Okamoto / LBJ Library*

Figure 25. Tommy Corcoran, Hubert Humphrey, Jim Rowe, and Ben Cohen in 1977: Old associations with these men were part of the reason LBJ "never really liked the term Great Society. . . as much as he liked the New Deal." *AP/Wide World Photos*

Figure 26. "I find myself, again, at . . . the center of events and intrigues," said my father late in life. Here he counsels Governor Jimmy Carter in 1975. *Leviton-Atlanta / TimePix*

Figure 27. LBJ at his ranch, his hair grown long, health failing, with Tommy Corcoran and former house speaker John McCormack in 1972: "I'm kind of ashamed of myself that I had six years [as president] and couldn't do more than I did," he pronounced at a civil rights symposium four months later, shortly before his death. *LBJ Library*

Figure 28. My mother and father on a talk show, 1975. *People* magazine called them "idea brokers whose time has come." *Leviton-Atlanta/TimePix*

Figure 29. Carol Fortas to her husband, pleading with him to resign from the Supreme Court under the glare of scandal in 1969: "Abe, it's too much. The hell with it. It's not worth it to live this way." Here the Fortases stand outside the Court in 1982, where Abe has just pled a case. *Associated Press/Wide World Photo*

Figure 30. Clark Clifford, last of the power brokers who bridged the Roosevelt-Truman era and the Johnson years, his career ruined by an international banking scandal in the 1990s. *Doug Mills-AP/Wide World Photos*

❧ 11 ❧

President of All the People

"YOU CAN'T DEAL WITH HIM

ANY LONGER"

T hat there were two Lyndon Johnsons (at least two) had been privately documented, and sometimes noted in the press, for years. Johnson's friends from New Deal days had long ago learned that his bold, make-things-happen impresario side and his profoundly depressive one were connected; that satisfaction of the furies within Johnson was part of the fuel line driving him to original accomplishment, superb performance.

Jim Rowe's blast of a letter of October 1960 made the case that it was not the targets of Johnson's rages who were at fault; rather, "LBJ is the trouble." My father had said the same to Walter Jenkins about Johnson's presidential candidacy in the spring. Johnson encountered generally unrelieved political shocks and traumas in 1960, and more as vice president, which, evident to those around him, affected him profoundly. He put on weight, drank far too much, was depressed; a figure of fun for the Kennedy entourage and for the press. If, as there has been reason for some of his aides and some historians to speculate, he suffered a degree of disintegration of personality in the presidency, the roots for it lay far back. But they were severely aggravated between the summer of 1960 and November 22, 1963.[1]

But, previously in his career, the chemistry of his inner conflicts sent him at least as often into forceful, capable response to challenge as it did into retreat and depression. As has been recorded in all accounts, the first Johnson snapped into place at the moment of the assassination of John F. Kennedy—and stayed in place for months to come. He was master of himself, the nation, its international position, the situation. "He has not put a foot wrong," the ever critical Dean Acheson wrote me a month after Johnson took office.[2]

Harry McPherson witnessed one odd and crucial moment in the first days after the assassination, to which he has added for the account here. As an assistant to Johnson in the Senate, he had introduced the Johnsons to the Reverend Bill Baxter, the liberal, literary-minded young minister of St. Mark's Episcopal Church, two blocks from the Capitol. Lady Bird Johnson took a particular shine to Baxter, and it was to St. Mark's that the Johnsons chose to go for Sunday services on November 24, 1963. There Baxter spoke movingly of the awful events, of fleeting unity in national tragedy; the congregation sang "America," and there were tears. Baxter asked for prayers for the new president.

McPherson had moved from Senate Majority Leader Mike Mansfield's office to a Pentagon position, on his way back onto Johnson's staff in the White House some months hence, but had stayed in touch with the vice president. St. Mark's "was swarming with Secret Service agents," he recalled. "God, there must have been twenty in the church, and there were cops on the top of the Library of Congress Annex with rifles, and a massive crowd outdoors." The two men talked inconsequentially for some minutes after the service. McPherson asked Johnson how he was bearing up. Suddenly, one of the Secret Service men appeared and whispered something in the president's ear. McPherson saw Johnson sag visibly for a split second, then recover. "I've got to go," he said. At the door of the church, the agents "just took him by the elbow and very strong, with great strength, moved him right down those stairs," Mrs. Johnson too, and into the presidential limousine.

It was just after 12:30 P.M., Washington time. Except for the Secret Service, the church parish hall was secluded, cut off from the turmoil of the world. McPherson has always assumed that the word from the agent into Johnson's ear moments earlier was part of the first signal that—at 11:21 Dallas time—Lee Harvey Oswald had been shot while in the custody of the Dallas police, visible to viewers of television nationwide. Hours and days later McPherson could only imagine what nightmares Johnson had to process as the Secret Service signaled to him this latest shock to the nation's, and his own, system; the specter of further chaos, playing out as Kennedy's assassination had on his own, seemingly outlaw, home turf. What stayed with McPherson was the way that Johnson, handling the shock, remained completely in charge of himself.[3]

A week later the Johnsons returned to St. Mark's. That day the president took McPherson back to the White House with him, and into the Oval Office, where Tommy Corcoran and Jim Rowe were waiting. McPherson was a "fly on the wall" as Johnson directed remarks to Rowe: "I've been thinking back over 1960 and thinking of where I am now; and I need friends." It was his fault, said Johnson, that the two "drift[ed] apart. . . . I was foolish and short-sighted and I hope that you'll forgive me."

Thrown for a loop, Rowe responded: "My God, Mr. President, it wasn't your fault"—Rowe was taking the blame for confronting Johnson as he had with his angry letter in the fall of 1960. But since no one but the two of them (and Corcoran) knew of the letter, McPherson was in the dark about the background of their quarrel.

"Yes, it was," said Johnson; "Don't argue with me. Just be content to be the first man to whom the 36th President of the United States has offered his apologies!"[4]

For the moment, the circle seemed closed. Lyndon Johnson was where he was meant to be, exhibiting privately—with witnesses!—contrition along with grace under pressure; acting publicly as a great leader in a time of crisis.

. . .

Immediately after the assassination, my father assumed a clean slate. Knowing of his long relationship with Johnson, reporters sought his views. The Monday after the assassination the *New York Times* quoted him predicting (for once not hyperbolically) that Johnson's effectiveness would trigger the New York Stock Exchange's reversal of sharp losses on Friday, November 22 "not in weeks or months but in a few trading sessions."[5]

With many banks and markets closed in mourning and uncertain about Johnson (the new president was an unknown factor abroad), my father labored behind the scenes in New York with Ed Weisl, and Weisl's client Lehman Brothers, to build confidence. Weisl got the firm's powerhouse Robert Lehman "to call up the principal factors in the European firms and say Johnson was all right and we knew him and he was our friend and we [Lehman's] handled his money . . . and Johnson was going to be good for business and good for the market." (This is my father's account, confirmed by Weisl in his LBJ Library oral history.) The U.S. Postal system was also closed, "so that no margin calls could be delivered. . . . The margin calls were all backed up." By the time everyone was open again for business, in my father's telling, "we had something like a 25% premium built into American stocks traded in Europe." (A characteristically acid postscript from my father: "Bobby Lehman was a very generous man [but he] always complained to the day of his death that Johnson never even thanked him.")[6]

Addressing business executives in Detroit ten days after the assassination, he remarked that Johnson "will need three Cabinets, one with each shift of the day to keep up with him." The new president, he said saltily, "is not an omnivorous, or even a functional reader, but oh boy, can he count. . . . He will get this country moving, by getting the machinery of Congress moving again."[7]

The *Ladies Home Journal* commissioned my mother to write a piece about

Lady Bird. Lunch at the White House and a long talk with "my friend Bird Johnson" about her self-disciplined response to a lonely childhood and early years shaped a portrait that emphasized the new First Lady's seriousness, warmth, and humor.[8]

Johnson and Weisl were back in business after the latter's emphatic disgust ("unthinkable . . . sell-out") with the 1960 Democratic National Convention. But the new president's anger about the way my father handled his reaction to the deal with the Kennedys was long-term. A series of ostensibly pleasant notes was exchanged; Johnson's drafted for his signature by senior staff. But months passed; no summons for advice or anything else came from the White House.[9]

My father was unrepentant. In his view Johnson, on his way to complete emasculation by the Kennedys before November 22, 1963, should have been grateful for friends who'd showed independence in 1960 and could help him chart his own way now. He assumed Johnson was sulking, as he did so often, and communicated through intermediaries and staff. He delivered advice and reports of his service in bolstering the new president's standing in the eyes of Wall Street and the corporate world—dressing them with tartness, soon to become sarcasm, about Johnson's lack of gratitude. As the weeks wore on, less mutedly than other longtime Johnson allies like Senator Richard Russell and Ed Weisl, he implored Johnson's aides to put a lid on the lavish homage the president was paying to Kennedy's memory, and to get him to start sounding his own trumpet and appointing his own men.[10]

Such tactics in the past generally worked, or else Johnson's mood swings and shifting sense of which allies he needed for which fresh issue cleared the air. But the world had turned: our shrewd country cousin, so long a striving loner reliant on insider networks beginning with the Rooseveltian brotherhood, no longer had any lack of advisers and allies.

. . .

In brash naïveté I tried to write something about Johnson from my perspective; too soon. Out of college, I'd just finished basic training in the Army Reserve six-months program. I went to see Tommy Corcoran, white-haired and stout but still conveying a top-of-the-world confidence. He took me on a walk around Washington and told me stories:

Aubrey Williams, the liberal head of Roosevelt's National Youth Administration, called him in 1937 to say that he was about to lose his best state director, Lyndon Johnson. Could Corcoran do anything to help him persuade Johnson that running the NYA in Texas was more important than being a congressman? Corcoran said such a job description was in fact accurate in Illinois where the state director, William Campbell, later an influential federal judge, was the clearinghouse for the old-line Chicago Democratic machine, the progressive Roman Catholic archdiocese, labor, and the New Deal.

But Johnson was determined to get to Washington. Roosevelt's order to Corcoran was, "Here's a wonderful boy who's stuck his neck out for us, so lets do what we can for him."

Corcoran's account tracked his, and Johnson's, evolution from New Deal reformers to Washington middlemen. The closing of agricultural export markets and fall-off in support for the New Deal's reciprocal trade policies, Corcoran recalled, coincided with the rise of oil to dominance in the Southwest. He and Harold Ickes "fought like hell" to give Texas, with its strong Democratic establishment, a deal on access to tidelands oil sufficient to keep moderates like Texas Senator Tom Connally, let alone New Dealers like Johnson, safe in their congressional seats. But "the oilmen wanted it all." They scared Connally, chairman of the Senate Foreign Relations Committee, into retirement and replaced him with the weak governor, Price Daniel, saying they wanted "an oil man, pure and simple." Corcoran smiled, the tribal sage with his saga: "No wonder Lyndon was nervous."

Now life had come full circle. Corcoran described a summons to the White House for a small ceremony early in 1964 to mark the placement of FDR's portrait in the Cabinet Room. Johnson turned to him as the painting went up and whispered, "The transition is over."[11]

Aubrey Williams and Milo Perkins, Roosevelt's head of the Farm Security Administration, gave me their impressions of Johnson in the 1930s. Williams was in bed, dying of cancer; Perkins was still active on the Washington scene. Their accounts featured Johnson's insistence on helping black farmers and laborers in Texas as a young New Deal official and congressman. The profound influence of Roosevelt on Johnson, Williams told me, had to do with "concept of government—that whatever happens to people is a concern of government; that government is something much more than collecting taxes and keeping the peace."[12]

I visited Justice Douglas at the Supreme Court. He'd written me a *pensée* about Johnson designed to stress shared radical impulses when young: "Lyndon is an old friend and I admire him greatly. He was the only person elected to Congress on Roosevelt's court-packing plan. . . . That was the beginning of my pride in him and for him."[13]

Douglas was ruminative, having a good season. Whatever his regrets in the summer of 1960, he was, after all, wired on both sides of the Kennedy-Johnson divide. Johnson in the prelude to 1960 and Joe Kennedy at the end of that year had told him they wanted him to become secretary of state. Not in the cards, but he retained the several connections and added another. His link to the Kennedys centered on Joe, "the patriarch," but at Joe's request Douglas had taken Robert Kennedy on trips abroad with him in the early 1950s. They were friends, of a sort. (During a 1961 visit to him, Douglas had told me in words of one syllable to tell my father, who despised Bobby above all Kennedys, that the new attorney general "will be o.k.")[14]

Corcoran, Douglas, Williams, and Perkins pressed their sense that Johnson as president would be an energetic force for social reform. Donald Cook offered an alternative angle. He recalled his wartime days on the staff of the House Naval Affairs Committee, and of James Forrestal's arrangement through Cook for Johnson to attack the Navy Department for inefficiencies in such a way as to make himself look good, while also arming Forrestal to do what he wanted to do. These were, Cook, concluded, "stories of the interplay of *careful* men, trying to get things done."[15]

It took a while to see that, though Vice President Johnson had remained kindly disposed toward me, President Johnson commanded fresh heights. One way and another, the terrain between him and my father was becoming a minefield onto which it was dangerous to venture. The president sent chilly signals about my project through Jenkins. My interview notes went into a file, and I went into journalism.

. . .

Abe Fortas emerged front and center among the confidants from the old days. Visiting older friends in Washington early in 1964, I was taken to a black-tie dance party that drew from the city's ruling tribes. There were the Fortases, among others. Fortas had become prosperous, bought an expensive new house in Georgetown; tooled with Carol to and from their weekend home in Westport, Connecticut in a handsome Rolls Royce. Once lithe, he'd put on weight yet remained sleek. He exuded the "physicality of menace" his biographer notes, demonstrating force that evening by the way he said and did almost nothing, while drawing the side-glances of the power-conscious other guests. A neutral handshake; guarded words; "How's your father?" The two had not spoken in a long time.[16]

Carol Fortas, svelte and assured, smoked one of her signature, cigarette-sized cigars and talked about a midnight raid by "Lyndon" on Sheldon Cohen, one of her protégés in the tax law ranks of Arnold, Fortas and Porter, for duty at the Internal Revenue Service.

A number of men around Washington that season, including Johnson's once and future aides Bill Moyers and Harry McPherson as well as Anthony Lewis of the *New York Times*, thought well of both Johnson and Robert Kennedy and imagined that some sort of truce between them was still possible. They sought to be backstage conciliators. McPherson and Lewis were present that evening, but memories among us fail as to which one just then sought a private word with Fortas about detente between the two camps. I remember that the two stepped away, and that Carol Fortas took a draw on her diminutive cigar and purred, working against her own stylish presence, "How'd you like to talk to an old bag about the old days?" Some chat and a fox-trot, then back to the others. Fortas's mouth was drawn wide, something between a smile and a frown—definitely not "puckish," as in the youthful descriptions of him. The signal was that as for a bridge between the new president and his bitter, inherited attorney general: no dice.

The values of some of the old Rooseveltians had themselves become conflicted. This was in fact the season in which Johnson wanted Fortas, Clark Clifford, or Ed Weisl to become attorney general and wrest the department away from Robert Kennedy's surrogates. Carol Fortas was even more adamant than her husband that the priority for him at age fifty-five was to lock in some additional good years of lucrative law practice. Then, perhaps, the Supreme Court. When Johnson drafted a deeply ambivalent Fortas for the Court a year later, he called Carol to ease what he knew to be her ire at his haste. "You don't treat friends that way," she said to the president, and hung up on him. ("She said her life had been ruined," Johnson told Senator Mansfield in his mordant mode. "I don't know— these women! Their lives get ruined mighty easy!") It would emerge that Carol Fortas had a point.[17]

. . .

The 1964 election loomed. The "for Johnson before Los Angeles" group was as eager for the president to get Bobby Kennedy out of the way as LBJ himself was, no two of them more fervent on that score than Ed Weisl and my father. They sent message after message urging him to take his own man for vice president, and to beware of anyone Bobby could manipulate. They included the warm, genial, ultimately malleable Hubert Humphrey in that category and were aware that Kennedy holdovers in the White House and the Democratic National Committee wanted Humphrey if Bobby was out.[18]

Despite warm friendship and campaign donations to Humphrey over the years, my father was pushing Minnesota's other senator, Eugene McCarthy. Clark Clifford thought McCarthy was ahead of Humphrey for a while that spring in Johnson's reckoning, and had Lady Bird's vote. Tommy Corcoran and Bill Moyers both said John Connally favored McCarthy, and that this was a strong indicator of where the president would wind up. Though Johnson genuinely liked McCarthy, and the feeling was mutual, with a nose to the wind in mid-summer and perhaps mischievous, he told Connally— no enemy of the oil industry—that McCarthy would "get a lot of smear. He votes the oil and gas companies. . . . He's kind of regarded as a liberal renegade."[19]

Whatever cards he was playing, McCarthy had the potential for headstrong independence, as he'd shown in trying to rally the 1960 Democratic Convention for Stevenson and against Kennedy, in close collusion with the Johnson camp. In the spring of 1964, Johnson gave McCarthy reason to believe that he was in the race for the vice presidential nomination, for real.[20]

But at the eleventh hour McCarthy decided that Johnson had made his decision in favor of Humphrey and that he was being used as a foil—to keep a Roman Catholic in the race until Humphrey's selection was for-

malized as a backstop to any Kennedy camp effort to stir the pot of religion. To Johnson's intense annoyance, McCarthy pulled out just before
Humphrey's designation was made official. (Johnson threw other Catholic
names in, but everyone was on to the game by then.) As word of
Humphrey's selection began to leak out, I happened to have dropped by
my father's office. He was on the phone to McCarthy: somber, elegiac
words. "Tough," he said when he hung up. He was referring to McCarthy,
not to his luck. "He'll be heard from."[21]

. . .

The enormity of Johnson's dominance of the collective imagination of the
country in the first two years of his presidency (not counting those of the
Kennedy circle who saw him as instant antichrist) is hard to call up now,
so permanent is the imprint of his plunge into disaster in Vietnam. You
didn't have to love Johnson in 1964 and 1965 to appreciate the creative
energy for social progress he unleashed. You didn't have to like Johnson's
"style," however assiduously those who idealized Kennedy worked to high-
light measurement of the two men by that dubious standard, to see that he
had the potential to earn a major place in history because of the combination of his effectiveness—when he was on his game, arguably as great as
Roosevelt's—with his passion—indisputably greater than Kennedy's.

With a display of personal daring and inspired, unbridled departure from
text he confronted Southern racism at the source in a New Orleans campaign speech in October 1964. He whipped out an anecdote about an old
Mississippi-born senator who said to Sam Rayburn at the end of his career
that he wished he felt well enough to go home "and make them one more
Democratic speech. . . . Poor old Mississippi, they haven't heard a Democratic speech in thirty years." Johnson waved his arms as he pounded out
the punch line: "All they ever hear at election time is 'Nigger, Nigger,
Nigger!'"[22]

Five months later, as Martin Luther King marched in Alabama, Johnson's magnificent "We shall overcome" speech to Congress married the
government of the United States to the language of the civil rights movement. Johnson proclaimed, "The real hero of this struggle is the American
Negro," whose "protests, . . . courage to risk safety and even to risk his life,
have awakened the conscience of this Nation." He recalled the poor Latino
students he'd taught in the late 1920s and said, "It never even occurred to
me in my fondest dreams that I might have the chance to help . . . people
like them all over this country. But now I do have that chance—and I'll let
you in on a secret—I mean to use it." Watching Johnson on television in
Birmingham, King wept. The speech is still deeply moving to read.[23]

But Johnson's fears were greater than his gift for handling power and
seizing the day. He let the sneers from the Kennedy types and jokes about

his style infuriate and humiliate him. He never treated them, as Roosevelt did the foul jokes of Social Registerites, as expressions of relative power-lessness that he could maneuver around and overcome, even exploit. A day or two after the 1964 election, in which he surpassed Roosevelt's greatest majorities, Johnson complained to Ed Weisl, who promptly related the con-versation to my father, that he was not fully satisfied. The numbers were indeed extraordinary, but the press and the Kennedy partisans were saying (as the White House tapes picked up the conversation for posterity), "They're just voting against Goldwater," and "Johnson didn't have any rapport, and he didn't have any style," and the rest of the sad refrain. Johnson, said Weisl, wanted him to talk to Doyle, Dane and Bernbach, the New York ad agency retained by the White House in the late campaign, about staying on the account (as Weisl relayed Johnson's words to my father) "to make the people love me."[24]

But even if he suffered from insufficient public adoration, Johnson for a few seasons commanded the full political scene, co-opting his opposition as no one since Franklin Roosevelt had (and no one, including Ronald Reagan, would again to this time). His shrewder critics were able to move past a monolithic view of Johnson and catch the duality. One of the best was Jules Feiffer's period piece cartoon in the *Village Voice* featuring Johnson's boots dangling in the upper portions of the panel as he answered the plaintive cries of the citizenry ("O, what do you see, Mr. President-of-all-the-people?"):

I see a land where love reigns. I see great farms and giant cities. I see men at work, children at play, women at peace . . .

And on through the panels of the cartoon:

I see the end of divisiveness and contrariness. I see small men growing large and closed minds opening wide. . . . I see black and white in final harmony. . . . I see the determined faces of millions, fat and skinny, tall and short, bold and shy, crying as one: "ONWARD TO THE GREAT SOCIETY!"

In the last panel the citizens ask, "And how will all this come about, Mr. President-of-all-the-people?" Johnson's voice from the sky responds, "I shall wheel and deal."[25]

This kind of satire was to Johnson worse than the calumny of the right-wing haters, because it *got* him; such critics had cracked the code. At the same time it reflected the totality of his success as a political presence in what could have been at that time an utterly unstable environment. It was more positive than Republican journalist William Allen White's edged trib-ute to Roosevelt in the late 1930s: "Mr. President, we who hate your gaudy guts, salute you."[26]

. . .

The New Deal informed Johnson's presidency symbolically. In the White House he relied, as he always had in his most difficult hours, on selected remnants of the House of Roosevelt. Some, like Fortas, played to his cagey side. Corcoran entered a note, after Johnson's inauguration in his own right in early 1965, that reflected the president's opposite, passionate persona. First he complimented Johnson's rhetoric of late, which "makes my heart to sing again as in the Thirties." Then, with a characteristic reference to St. Augustine on Christianity ("The greatest miracle of all is that so many believe it"), Corcoran wrote,

> Skeptic Holmes once told me that no man could be intellectually honest that he was more than right 51% about anything. I told that story to Brandeis. I have never forgotten his reply:
> "Holmes may be philosophically right. But in the world of action no man can lead other men who cannot himself believe, and make other men believe, that he is right 300% . . ."
> At the Inaugural I sat right under your nose with my daughter Margaret in the lovely seats Lady Bird gave us. . . . And as I listened to you vibrate 300% conviction almost thou madest me a Christian.[27]

The unchained exuberance Johnson brought to his domestic programs did indeed have personal roots deep in his participation in the great days of the New Deal. Abe Fortas alluded to them in the summer of 1960 and anticipated some of Johnson's broad-brush presidential posture in posing the Great Society as the heir, at least in spirit, to the New Deal. He urged Johnson then, as Kennedy's vice presidential candidate charged with holding the South for the Democrats, to propose "a new, dramatically conceived and dramatically launched program for economic development in the Southern states" as an alternative to getting bogged down in racial politics. "The Southern states, by and large, are still the have-not states," wrote Fortas, echoing New Deal–era analyses and Roosevelt's own rhetoric about the region. The plan should, he told his friend, "coupl[e] resource development, industrialization, improvement of agricultural income, disbursal of defense facilities," all on the New Deal model, and be accompanied by "parallel programs" for "other lagging segments of the country." But, ironically, neither the New Deal nor the New Dealers had much direct, creative bearing on the details of the freshly coined Great Society initiatives. Those came from the Kennedy bureaucracy, and their fate became a subset of Johnson's strategy in his homefront guerrilla war with Robert Kennedy.[28]

When Johnson thought about the Great Society and the war on poverty, Bill Moyers told Johnson's biographer Robert Dallek in 1997, he thought about "fulfilling FDR's mission." Indeed, Moyers claimed, he "never really liked the term Great Society. . . . He didn't like it as much as he liked the New Deal." His instinct was to fold the dissonant antipoverty initiatives hatched in the several branches of the Kennedy-staffed bureaucracies in with the unfinished Roosevelt and Truman agendas, and with mainstream social and economic initiatives—job training, urban development, deliver them in one passionate outpouring of reform as the grand *Johnsonian* achievement, and sort out the details later.[29]

On a larger canvas still, the trauma of the Kennedy assassination and Johnson's initial success in guiding the country past it, an emerging (alas, not-long-lived) spirit of corporate social responsibility about ghetto poverty, the narrow base of the Goldwater candidacy and his own hunger for unified support and aversion to close, confrontational face-offs combined to give him a basis for mounting the Great Society as "President of all the people." The chord of memory of the momentum Roosevelt orchestrated as activist *national* leader in the emergency of 1933 ("I saw a brave man come down Pennsylvania Avenue"), and rode for two years in the consensus-oriented First New Deal, chimed in as well.

What happened next has been well chronicled by a sequence of witnesses and historians: in 1964 enthusiastic policy makers who came together in the Kennedy years wove the somewhat fuzzy theory of "community action," embracing "maximum feasible participation" by the poor in programs designed to benefit them, into the legislation that enacted the Office of Economic Opportunity (OEO), the antipoverty program.[30]

But what did "community action" mean? At least four readings were possible, Daniel Patrick Moynihan, present at the creation as assistant secretary of labor, concluded with some battle fatigue at the end of the 1960s. Each brought its own ideological and bureaucratic provenance to bear: "organizing the power structure, . . . expanding the power structure, . . . confronting the power structure, . . . and finally, assisting the power structure." Failure to clarify which were operative, he concluded, resulted in "maximum feasible misunderstanding."[31]

"My own political science discipline was muddle-headed" in trying to manage direct democracy in a federal context, remarked urban expert Robert Wood, another Great Society bureaucrat, some years later: "We advocated Rousseau and Madison simultaneously." A third academician serving in the Johnson administration, Henry J. Aaron, discounted the factor of passing-grade intellectual coherence. Aaron argued that the real problem with the community action initiatives was that "their objectives were vague and inflated beyond hope of fulfillment by flamboyant rhetoric," and that they "pursued the inherently divisive objective of increasing the power of the poor by wresting it from others."[32]

The New Deal, in Roosevelt's deployment of its competing factions, managed such disparate missions, even on some fronts after its congressional momentum came to a halt in 1938. But it did so through two presidential terms dominated by acute economic crisis, when uneasy barons of the power structure were receptive to changes in the rules.

Johnson, by contrast, was directing domestic policy in times of high prosperity in the name of justice and reform, not as a Depression-era crisis manager. Intent on making his mark on history and on outdoing Roosevelt, Truman, and Kennedy, driven by his uniquely acute sense of timing about how to get things done in Washington, Johnson remarked again and again that speed, not refinement of policy niceties, was of the essence. (With Congress, Johnson told McPherson in 1965, after his landslide election victory, "You've got just one year when they treat you right, and before they start worrying about themselves. . . . A lot of our people don't belong here, they're in Republican seats, and the Republicans will get them back.") And as "fulfilling FDR's mission" was one of Johnson's *idée fixes*, its converse for him was to govern on the waves of consensus. His imperative was to deflect the kinds of resurgent business and conservative resistance that stalemated the New Deal in Congress in its sixth year, and reverberated in Texas in the 1940s and fifties, traumatizing him for life about his political base there. A third imperative was to out-maneuver Robert Kennedy, feeding the press and along with it (Johnson raged in 1964) "laying for us."[33]

John Kennedy had some interest in FDR but not much in the New Deal; Robert Kennedy had less. Members of their entourages tended to echo the sentiment. "The New Deal was ending in a kind of generalized disappointment," recalled Moynihan. "Nothing better seemed likely to follow." By contrast with the established government agencies' "long list of programs that hadn't quite made the cut for the New Deal," wrote Nicholas Lemann, community action "had the excitement of a new idea; it seemed fresh and vigorous" and it responded to "the deep-seated chord of dissatisfaction with the New Deal approach to government that was floating around in the Kennedy Administration."[34]

Robert Kennedy's own ideas, influenced more heavily than were those of his brother by their father, faced directly away from Rooseveltian, social welfare, top-down national government. It is impossible to resolve the mountain of speculation whether, from the moralistic Catholic conservatism that drew him to Joe McCarthy's side in his youth and drove his campaigns against Jimmy Hoffa and Fidel Castro later, he genuinely turned for the long-term into some sort of existential "rebel" after 1963. The issue is too clouded by the dynamics of the younger Kennedy's links to his father, idolization of his brother, and demonization of Lyndon Johnson; by the romanticization of him by commentators while he lived, and by his own assassination in 1968. What does seem clear is that within the idea of community action in Robert Kennedy's mind was a mystique about individualism and empowerment that connected to projects like the Peace Corps, perhaps even the Kennedys' much-favored Green Berets. Such values had almost nothing to do with the moderate collectivism of the New Deal agencies Johnson knew so well and identified himself so closely with—the National Youth Administration, Rural Electrification Administration, Civilian Conservation Corps, and Public Works Administration.[35]

Johnson saw in the community action concept the danger of self-inflicted wounds, and first said no. Then, judging that keeping the peace with the Kennedy entourage was the better part of wisdom for the season, he accepted the proposition dubiously. Thereafter the policy and programmatic fine points were secondary to the politics of the situation. Craftily, he made the Kennedys' brother-in-law Sargent Shriver his OEO director. Shriver kept the lid on the instability inherent in the possibilities of multiple interpretation only as long as it took to pass the legislation in the summer of 1965.[36]

Any and all of the professorial theories about what was wrong from the start applied to what happened next. In short order Mayor Daley of Chicago, outraged by translations of the idealism of "community action" into a mandate to wage war on City Hall, was only the most powerful player to storm directly at Johnson and his inner circle. "What the hell are you people doing?" demanded Daley. "You know what Daley said to me?" an irritated Johnson told an aide, as if to the slow-witted: "He said he could be difficult."[37]

Daley was echoed by a host of less powerful mayors and governors, and by two close friends of Johnson's from New Deal days, both still liberals, Elizabeth Wickenden, whose background was in social welfare policy, and, once again, Jim Rowe, who had been one of those at Johnson's side in his Senate days drafting civil rights legislation. They warned Johnson privately about the community action centerpiece of the antipoverty program, early and subsequently. Wickenden, like Robert Wood in retrospect, saw an inherent flaw in a "small is beautiful" approach to so profound a national problem and predicted that, by the same token, "a federal agency would be short-circuiting the normal channels of relationship to states and localities in their own areas of responsibility."[38]

Then came the results: Rowe alerted Johnson in June 1965 that "something quite odd is going on! . . . The national headquarters of the Office of Economic Opportunity (Sarge Shriver's own headquarters) is giving instructions and grants to local [Washington] private groups for the purpose of training the Negro poor on how to conduct sit-ins and protest meetings against government agencies, federal, state and local." As a liberal, Rowe meant that procedurally, "community action" was generating political trouble.[39]

The poverty program represents at best turmoil in the annals of Johnson's ambitions for "fulfilling FDR's mission." No more happy was the fate down the road of his most heartfelt Supreme Court appointment, influenced as it was by another legacy of the history of the New Deal.

In 1965 Johnson reminisced to his cabinet that Roosevelt's response to a reactionary Supreme Court's provocations in striking down New Deal legislation—his aborted "court packing bill" of 1937—cost him his legislative momentum, "and from that Congress to this, no really major social legislation was enacted."[40]

Mindful of Roosevelt's problems with the judicial branch, seeking a direct line into Supreme Court business generally, Johnson made Abe Fortas an associate justice that year. (Fortas being ambivalent, the impatient president enlisted Bill Douglas to close the deal.) So intent was he on a preemptive strike on the Court that he maneuvered a sitting justice (Arthur Goldberg) into a lesser post (ambassador to the United Nations, with illusory promises of influence) to make room for Fortas. The stage was set for a debacle before which FDR's failure to pack the Supreme Court paled.[41]

. . .

Word of how Johnson's support began to erode after the peak of his dominance came in many flavors. At first the word *Vietnam* was not at the center of every conversation on the topic of Johnson's standing in the country. The genuineness of Johnson's commitment in promising that "We shall overcome" racial injustice had been real. But on other fronts—the Dominican Republic crowded out Vietnam for a period—he seemed to be saying, "We shall work our will" and, in Vietnam, dissembling about what that meant. The Kennedy claque never let up on the subject of his "style"; that and his "credibility" became press themes. In reply to Johnson's question "Why don't people like me?" the steely Dean Acheson had been reported to reply, "Because, Mr. President, you're not a very likeable man." Acheson wrote me in 1966, in response to a question about the line attributed to him, "I have no recollection of having said it. I have often thought it—and the opposite too. A strange man, for whom I do not wish to work."[42]

Then Vietnam became the only topic. At the doveish end of the Democratic coalition Senator McGovern of South Dakota told me off the record (I was reporting a piece for the *Atlantic*, where I was an editor, about growing antiwar sentiment) a tale of bringing the president a background memo he'd prepared, sometime in 1966 or 1967, arguing for disentanglement in Vietnam. Seated at his desk, the president first promised to read it, along with the stack of memos he had from "Professor Mansfield" and "Professor Lippmann." Then, said McGovern, he pulled out a drawer at his desk and tossed several Top Secret briefing papers from the intelligence agencies across the desk. These reported on various Soviet and Chinese Communist activities around the world. "Here's what they're doing in Asia, in Africa," Johnson growled, pointing at the papers. "Here's what they're doing in Latin America. . . . They're everywhere." At that point, McGovern said, he decided there was no way to pursue the conversation.[43]

Johnson had already aroused extraordinary, forbidden fears among several of his closest aides about erosion of his emotional stability. The more he thought and talked as he did to McGovern, the more he aroused the concerns of the kinds of mainstream, thinking citizens and opinion leaders that presidents had been able to count on since Roosevelt resolved the issue of American world responsibility in 1940–1941.[44]

Reflecting the collapse of consensus nationally, the Rooseveltians split deeply. Fortas and Jim Rowe on the inside, their respective law partners Thurman Arnold and Corcoran on the fringe, saw Vietnam as Johnson did, as a 1930s-style armed challenge to American abilities to respond adroitly. Douglas and Ben Cohen from the start, echoed by Johnson's old Senate friends Mike Mansfield and William Fulbright, saw the flaws in the analogy. My mother recalled Cohen coming to lunch in New York late in 1961 in a rainstorm ("his little blue beret was getting soaked"), bringing alarm "in that creaky voice of his . . . about all this business in Vietnam," and about the dangers of the buildup of American presence there. Cohen asked a Kennedy White House aide in the same months, "What on earth does our government think it's doing in Vietnam?" Lifelong friendships among some of the Rooseveltians were broken. In his memoirs Douglas recalled a visit to Johnson at the White House in the late 1960s on "a conservation matter" and an exchange that led first to the Vietnam War, then to candidates for a Supreme Court vacancy.

> He mentioned names and I commented on them. Regarding one, I said, "He will be very conservative on economic matters, and occasionally for liberty and justice on other matters."
>
> "Liberty and justice," he said, "that's all you apparently think of. And when you pass over the last hill, I suppose you will be shouting 'Liberty and justice!'"
>
> "You're goddamn right, Mr. President," I replied as I left by one door and he by another.[45]

Douglas's benediction, composed after he suffered a devastating stroke, reflects the chilly ambivalence deep in his own nature, even as he tried in a sequence of musings to capture Johnson's inner conflicts. "Knowing the man and loving him for all his good points, I became physically ill to see his world collapse publicly on TV," wrote Douglas at one point in his memoirs. Nevertheless (some pages later), "mostly he was a fair-weather friend." Nevertheless (some more pages later), "Lyndon knew no barriers where friends were involved. In spite of our disagreements he clung tightly to me, for he knew I would never make an unfriendly move against him."[46]

. . .

While Johnson let establishment thinking dominate his course in Vietnam, he was from the start suspicious of those, especially those in uniform, who urged him on. He needed the allegiance of Kennedy's hawkish "best and brightest" and their press admirers. But he found special solace in the solidarity of his most intimate Rooseveltian kitchen cabinet members—Fortas, Clifford (as long as Clifford agreed to be a hawk), and Rowe. Fortas's maverick partner Thurman Arnold defended the Vietnam policy to old liberal friends like Rex Tugwell, writing one of them in 1967 that if Johnson were defeated the next year, "as he may well be, he will go down as one of our greatest Presidents." Their support for his war policy in the years of escalation signified to Johnson, at least a little, that he hadn't abandoned the Great Society, hadn't sacrificed "Dr. New Deal" for "Dr. Win the War."[47]

As late as March 12, 1968, *after* the Tet Offensive, Fortas was urging Johnson to end

> totally, for the time being, the "what-can-we-do-to-get-them-to-negotiate" nonsense . . . and [carry] the war to North Vietnam—without explanation or apology. . . . Unless we "win" in Vietnam, our total national personality will, in my opinion, change—and for the worse[48]

For reasons impossible to fathom now, Fortas and my father picked just this moment to proclaim auld lang syne. On the eve of the New Hampshire primary in which Eugene McCarthy's strong showing sent shock waves into the political atmosphere, my parents went to dinner at the Fortases with the justice's Supreme Court "brethren" Douglas, William Brennan, Thurgood Marshall, and their wives. Fortas, my father recalled for his oral history in rhetorical overdrive mode, "was droning on about the boss and he'd never seen the boss more in command of the situation. . . . Fortas was talking . . . as if we didn't know poor Johnson was crazy—maybe Brennan and Marshall didn't know, but Douglas and I knew—talking about him as if he were Superman."[49]

Fortas's hawkishness was too much for Jim Rowe, back on board from his and Corcoran's firm to direct Johnson's 1968 reelection campaign. "A week after Fortas counseled Johnson to harden his stance, Rowe wrote the president "with the frankness that, I think, has existed between us," urging him to leave off "the hard line. I am shocked by the number of calls I received today in protest" against the president's call in Minnesota two days earlier for "*a total national effort* to win the war."[50]

The collapse of Johnson's Vietnam policy and of his presidency in 1968, and the disastrous Democratic National Convention in Chicago in August, marked the end of the Rooseveltians as a force as well. Johnson's men Richard Daley and John Connally enforced the presidential will on behalf of Hubert Humphrey's nomination and against dissent—but only after Johnson toyed with the idea of reentering the race himself. From the sidelines, just before the convention, Corcoran, a die-hard Johnson loyalist, wrote the president in parable form:

A commentary on whispers I hear these days:

I was unofficial treasurer for FDR's Third Term [in the pre-campaign phase]. I was sent to a potential contributor in New York to get $50,000.

When I mentioned the amount I was greeted with "$50,000! The son-of-a-bitch! And he is a son-of-a-bitch! You know it don't you?" For one hour I listened to my excited informant's "proof"—with pacing of floors and gestures—from his first acquaintance with FDR down to date.

When he was exhausted I quietly chirruped, "Well, I certainly now know how *you* feel. . . . [But] I'm just an innocent boy sent to get a job done. Can I go back saying I got the job done or no?"

A pause—a reply: "When you came into this room, boy, you didn't have a chance in hell of leaving here with $50,000. But you've let me talk myself into it. . . . He is a son-of-a-bitch, but I'm afraid *the times require a son-of-a-bitch!!*" . . .

If you want me, I'll be doggo at the Lake Shore Drive Hotel.[51]

But that was an echo from what were already the ruins of the House of Roosevelt. The old brotherhood had lost not only the knack of effective operation but the tide of history. Tragically, for the country in the course of the debacle, what FDR had done—in Churchill's words—to bring "help and comfort from the New World to the Old," to make the United States the heroic leader of the West, faded before the spectacle of the U.S. as the villain in the East.[52]

. . .

By 1965 my father had begun moving to turn his break with Johnson into an adventure in antiwar insurgency. Always an effective sleuth, he developed an indictment of Johnson's decision to underfund the Vietnam War so as to keep its escalating magnitude out of view, and of the inflationary effects of that sleight of hand. He wrote a book examining the ways all previous wars that touched the United States fueled economic expansion, and argued that this one wouldn't.[53]

With such argument and data supporting it he fed the opposition of congressional doves, some of whom had been close allies of Johnson's before Vietnam alienated them, including Senators Fulbright, Mansfield, Church, Morse, and McCarthy. His special agent in the Senate was Vance Hartke of Indiana, another former LBJ intimate. Hartke was no towering figure in the Senate, more like a vintage Sinclair Lewis character, but he had a knack for linking his increasingly concerned colleagues up with each other. With his small-town style he helped the more cultivated Fulbright, Mansfield, Church, McCarthy, and Morse connect on Vietnam-related issues with less articulate, more frankly political colleagues. He would organize senatorial gatherings at which my father and experts from other fields—shades of the young New Dealers' "seminar" evenings in the 1930s—would fly in and help build the Senate doves' case against the administration.[54]

The Washington columnist Robert Novak picked up the scent of these intrigues and wrote about them. Novak liked to call my father "an East Coast Lyndon Johnson." In a conversation he commented bemusedly on my father's familiar device of identification ("We're going to get Hubert some dough. . ."): "It's always a riddle who your father means when he says 'we' . . ."

Once or more in those years my father traveled with several of these senators in Europe, introducing them to businessmen and politicians who could add to their sophistication about such dimensions of the American position as the status of the dollar and the international balance of payments. Through middlemen he made a new friend, Prime Minister Harold Wilson of Britain, emerging as a troublesome Vietnam War critic. He became more public in condemnations of Johnson's policies on these outings, and in speeches and his syndicated newspaper column. As someone who'd known the president for more than twenty-five years, he was here to tell you the ways that, though Johnson was as smart as they come, he was deceptive as the day is long.[55]

The sentiments appeared to have been reciprocated well before that. In 1965 Johnson considered and rejected a friendly gesture: appointment of my mother to the board of the new National Endowment for the Arts. The routine FBI background check came back to the White House in the form of a three-page letter from J. Edgar Hoover to one of Johnson's hard-rock conservative assistants, Marvin Watson, skimming from the accumulated files on my father the cream of his Communist associations from 1931 to 1934 and the dates of his travel to and from the Soviet Union.

Watson's covering note maintained the spirit of the enclosure.

November 5, 1965

Mr. President:
    Thought you might like to see the FBI report on Mr. Eliot Janeway. You will note that there is nothing in recent years but his background is interesting.

Marvin[56]

My father and Johnson *were*, as Novak and others observed, similar as personalities. Perhaps he had touched early in their friendship in the 1930s, or along the way, on his radical fling; maybe Johnson knew about his run-in with the FBI in 1941 and appeals for help to mutual Roosevelt administration friends. (In Johnson's own *épater les bourgeois* mode, he used to tell White House aides that he'd known every Communist in Washington in the New Deal years.)[57]

As opposite as they could be in background, in intellectual training and

orientation, they shared the attributes of shrewd intelligence, vast information banks and long memories, crafty sense of tactics, pride in the extent
to which they'd been self-made boy wonders, the need to dominate, mesmerizing skill at doing so, ability to manipulate subtly as well as with obvious
force; dark, satiric wit—to name a few.

Each of them could lean, even be pushed, in the direction of nuance,
broad view, a cautious and creative balance in their exercise of power. Or
they could go the other way, toward stubborn self-righteousness and single-
minded will.

Distinctions between the outer and inner natures of such men emphasize
the overbearing force that identifies them publicly and the subtleties of their
powers of persuasion in intimate settings. In fact, to be close, truly close to
either Johnson or my father at a staff or protégé level was to be essentially
a creature in the maw of power: an instrument or an audience. As Johnson's
younger wise man, Harry McPherson, recalled the president's cumulative
impact on him in a 1969 oral history interview for the Johnson Library, by
1966

> I was in danger just like everyone around him of capitulating to what
> you might call the [Jack] Valenti syndrome, which was to judge myself
> as a person by his judgment. . . . When I was in favor, I was on top of
> the world; when I was out of favor, I was in the dumps. . . . [So] I
> made a number of efforts to pull back . . . from a relationship, an
> intense relationship with him. It has saved my sanity and judgment
> . . . and made me a good deal more self-confident and steady in my
> relationship with him.

Only by such self-discipline could McPherson, holding the "counsel to the
president" position that Clark Clifford held in the Truman White House,
have been able to risk his relationship with Johnson by becoming what
Clifford called "my closest ally in the White House . . . 'my silent partner'"
in the struggle to stop the escalation in Vietnam after the Tet Offensive in
1968.[58]

Bogging down in Vietnam and against domestic opposition to the war,
Johnson was powerful, Johnson was frustrated; so Johnson exerted more
power, and heated rhetoric, to dislodge his opposition and ease his frustration. Instead, he caused both the opposition and his own frustration to
mount. Such was the wiring of my father's will too, as he turned on his old
friend.

When in late 1967 Eugene McCarthy was ready to mount his challenge
to Johnson for the Democratic presidential nomination, my father was behind him. He brought McCarthy one of his key financial backers, Howard
Stein of the Dreyfus Fund. The senator's shrewd wife Abigail wrote later,
"Eliot had acquired . . . a touching faith in my organizing ability" and was
regularly checking in with advice such as, before the New Hampshire pri-

mary, "You can buy it . . . buy it the way Kennedy bought West Virginia" in 1960.[59]

Later he claimed he also told her that McCarthy "doesn't have to be a martyr to get rid of Lyndon. Lyndon will get rid of himself" and that, if McCarthy eliminated Johnson, institutional Democratic Party reaction to his success would mean that "he'll never be nominated and he'll never be President." But, "if you insist on doing it, it'll get rid of Lyndon faster, so I'll help you because Lyndon shouldn't be there. He's not of sound mind any longer and you can't deal with him."[60]

Characteristically over the top; the details probably laced in the retelling with wisdom of hindsight. On the other hand, that's what Johnson's Senate critics like Mansfield, Fulbright, and Wayne Morse, and their friend Justice Douglas, men who'd known him very, very well for years, really thought too: "you can't deal with him," not any more. *Deal*: that was supposed to be what Johnson did.

. . .

The end of the Johnson presidency brought no lightening of tone to anyone looking for a return to a balanced view of the man. This was the end of what Johnson's friend Don Cook described in 1964 as "the interplay between careful men," the management of power on the part of those who understood it to its core.[61]

Johnson's first motivation in Vietnam had been to take cover against a replay of the "who lost China?" attacks on Truman and Acheson, persuading himself that "careful" was his watchword. "I know what pressure you're under from McNamara and the military," Clifford told him optimistically early on, "but if you handle it carefully, you don't have to commit yourself and the nation." He took care to question the military long and hard, and maintained deep skepticism about, for example, the efficacy of bombing his way to a solution. ("Airplanes ain't worth a *damn*, Dick," he said to Senator Russell in 1965; "They just scare their prime ministers.") He persuaded himself, some of the time, that he'd taken care to protect his Great Society programs as the Vietnam War escalated, rather than throwing them over, as Roosevelt had the New Deal. (In fact, he'd banked on a quick war. His ex post facto version of events, to Doris Kearns Goodwin, was that "I knew from the start . . . [that] if I left the woman I really loved—the Great Society—in order to get involved with that bitch of a war . . . I would lose everything at home.")[62]

He had nothing to show for this carefulness. Instead, his exercise of power looked to the country like blind willfulness. It took the daring declaration of will on the part of two men who knew Johnson better perhaps than he knew himself at that point in the proceedings, Gene McCarthy and Clark Clifford, to undo Johnson's illusion that he was being careful.

Behind Clifford (who yielded to Johnson's plea that he replace a demoralized Robert McNamara as secretary of defense early in 1968, as McCarthy's presidential challenge went into high gear) stood Dean Acheson. Earlier disinclinations notwithstanding, Acheson took one last assignment, to evaluate the Vietnam situation based on his own analysis of the best intelligence available to the government. This exercise swung him, and was decisive in swinging Clifford, to the conclusion that the escalation hadn't worked and that our Vietnam policy was bankrupt. ("Who poisoned the well with these guys?" Johnson asked Clifford and Dean Rusk, of the defection of his Wise Men from their support for Johnson's course in Vietnam.)[63]

When Clifford mounted his inside charge in the first months of 1968, "It was like being in a John Ford movie," his White House staff ally Harry McPherson mused. "It was like the calvary rode in"—except that, as McPherson also noted, Clifford developed his challenge to Vietnam policy for so many weeks alone, without powerful allies and cut off from his friend the president—"the most extraordinary demonstration of personal courage and perseverance that I have ever seen in government or out." (Meanwhile Clifford's trusted law partner Thomas Finney was functioning as one of McCarthy's ablest lieutenants in the outside insurgency.) When Acheson and other elders fell in, the president folded, virtually overnight. The nuances of the Tet Offensive and McCarthy's strong showing in the New Hampshire primary may be debated even more than they have been, but men like Clifford and Johnson knew what they meant. On the last day of March, a shadow of the man Franklin Roosevelt and his ablest acolytes took to, Johnson announced the termination of his career.[64]

But not before a final affront by Robert Kennedy. On March 14 Senator Kennedy and Theodore Sorenson pitched a deal to Clifford: have Johnson appoint "a commission to review Vietnam policy," the membership of which Kennedy would effectively name and control. Otherwise, to "correct the policy," Kennedy would announce his candidacy for president. Johnson, meeting with Clifford, Fortas, and Humphrey, swatted the idea down.[65]

Did Johnson recall his and the other Rooseveltians' urgent midnight exchanges about whether Bill Douglas should become Truman's secretary of the interior in February 1946? That was the deal whereby Douglas, not the White House (as Johnson had made the case to Corcoran), would be "calling the signals" because "somebody's got to do it," because "we've got to have some brains in there," because "you know how bad off we [congressional Democrats] are, don't you?" Such a view of the Johnson White House was, in comparable terms, the one in play twenty-two years later in Democratic congressional circles.[66]

Johnson waged one last all-out fight, a final link back to the Rooseveltians' great days—to make Abe Fortas chief justice of the Supreme Court. In Clifford's words, that ended in "tragedy not only for Abe Fortas, but for the nation," and led ultimately to Fortas's forced resignation from the Court in disgrace the next year. (Johnson's own epitaph after Fortas withdrew from the Court echoed more somberly still: "I made him take the justiceship" in 1965 in the first place, he said. "In that way, I ruined his life.")[67]

Johnson took his spite and frustration out on the loyal Hubert Humphrey, spoke ill of him to friends and reporters ("He cries too much"), frustrating and punishing him for indications of independence—indications that in turn were the only way for Humphrey to defeat Richard Nixon. When Nixon won, one view was that Johnson wasn't sorry: Nixon now owed him.[68]

At Christmastime 1969 Clark Clifford held a party at his house in Chevy Chase for his comrades in arms during his brief tenure as secretary of defense. I was down from Boston visiting Harry McPherson, who brought me along to the celebration. Clifford was the model of great man as generous host, happy warrior, or rather victor, in the fight for policy sanity during the previous winter. He'd contracted hepatitis on an official trip to Asia in the late 1960s and could no longer drink, but he mixed cocktails with what can only be called charisma. "There," he enthused, holding up a bourbon old-fashioned for a guest, its slice of fresh orange radiating health in December, "looks too pretty to drink, doesn't it?"

Clifford, the ultimate manipulator, might be said to have saved Johnson from himself. He might also be seen—and he was, by LBJ and his hardcore partisans—to have been disloyal to his intimate friend the president, triggering Johnson's political collapse. Either way, despite what he called "the chill" that had fallen on his once intimate relations with Johnson, Clifford was the toast of Washington in 1969 and for many seasons to come for having combined statesmanship and insider political skill to tremendous effect in his brief term as Lyndon Johnson's ablest cabinet member.[69]

The atmosphere of the party was oddly upbeat; an anomaly. (Most of Washington had been torn apart in the Johnson years—was in mourning: *President* Nixon?) This was a group of men and women deservedly celebrating the success of a patriotic conspiracy that Clifford himself compared to those of the French Revolution. Formal funerals commemorating the end of both the Johnson and Roosevelt eras would follow all to quickly.[70]

. . .

In 1971 Lyndon Johnson published his memoir, *The Vantage Point*. Some months afterward, I was sitting with my father in his study when the subject of Johnson's book came up. Had he looked at it? No, he said, though the publisher had sent it to him, and he nodded in the direction of his overflowing shelves. Then he reached for it and opened it, for the first time.

On the flyleaf was an inscription in ink: "For Eliot Janeway, who helped me in my youth—Lyndon B. Johnson." A moment of silent absorption of Johnson's gesture, a low smolder of emotion, and then he *threw* the book at a sofa across the room, growling, "Son of a bitch. *Son of a bitch!*"

They had been many places together, seen the workings of politics much more shrewdly than their contemporaries. That the Johnson era was over Johnson seemed to have accepted in a snap, even if he had trouble accepting the reasons. Along with several others among the Rooseveltians, my father's last round featured less recognition of the stages of life than Johnson, for all his weaknesses, had managed.

⊱ 12 ⊰

Last Act

I had found it odd in the 1960s and seventies that my father had not been more rocked than he seemed to be by the disasters involving financial arrangements with dubious outside benefactors that befell his friends Justices Abe Fortas and Bill Douglas. His comments at first were acerbic, to the effect that his intimates from another time had been both chintzy and foolish.

With Nixon and John Mitchell at the controls, leaking damaging details to members of Congress and the press, Fortas was driven from the scene in May 1969. Ironically disparate character traits prevailed. In this face-off Douglas, the fighter (fierce opponent of the Vietnam War from the start), took the hawkish position. Arguing that he'd been weathering similar attacks, he implored Fortas to stand fast. The ever insecure Fortas (intransigently hawkish voice in Johnson's ear on Vietnam the previous year), counseled in turn by Clifford (back from his months of insurgency against the war as secretary of defense to his familiar role as accommodater), folded. Carol Fortas prodded her husband: "Abe, it's too much," she said; "the hell with it. It's not worth it to live this way."[1]

In the wake of Fortas's resignation from the Supreme Court, Douglas wrote one friend that "The powers behind" the charges against him of inappropriate financial arrangements, Nixon's "Department of Justice—have incorrectly figured out how to get rid of me." He told Earl Warren (who told my father) that Nixon's attorney general John Mitchell sent word that "we got Fortas. We got your man. If you know what's good for you, you'll resign too." As the story goes, Douglas replied, "Well, saddle your horses . . ."[2]

Meanwhile Corcoran's last years saw him ever more indelibly stamped a "fixer"—but fumbling. Thomas Eagleton of Missouri, newly arrived in the Senate in 1969, recalled being invited with his wife to dinner by the old master at the apartment of Anna Chenault, Corcoran's companion since the death of his wife and veteran of the China lobby. "When we entered, we saw only elderly Southerners": John Stennis of Mississippi, Allen Ellender of Louisiana, Spessard Holland of Florida, and the somewhat younger Harry Byrd Jr. of Virginia. "What the hell were we doing there?" The evening, it seems, was meant to help rally the old guard against recognition of Communist China; ironically, Eagleton was on record as supporting recognition. The explanation: "It turns out my name was immediately above [James] Eastland [of Mississippi] on the list of senators and a secretary addressing the envelopes made a mistake."[3]

More seriously, Corcoran's recklessness was out of control. That same year, a season after he wrote Johnson about lessons learned in the service of FDR, it became known that he'd crossed a line the more remarkable because he'd started in the service of the incorruptible Oliver Wendell Holmes. He tried to lobby Justices Hugo Black and William Brennan in their offices on behalf of a private utility client, El Paso Natural Gas Company. This backfired badly; as well, it shattered his relationship with Black (who had taken Corcoran's daughter Margaret as his law clerk) and caused fresh damage to his friendship with Douglas. There had been no closer operative alliances among the Rooseveltians.[4]

Perhaps my father's vacant response to his friends' Fortas's and Douglas's troubles simply denied the disturbing extent to which they echoed his own, while Corcoran's haunted the whole house. On the other hand, having drifted apart from them, he grew close to them again. In the 1970s he and my mother would drive out to Westport to visit with the exiled Fortases. Douglas's discourse on the Constitution in a long television interview with Eric Sevareid was "the most eloquent and meaningful" of its kind "since Nixon had his first shave," he wrote the Justice in 1972.

Succeeding in his resolve to outlast Nixon, Douglas stayed on the Court until a crippling stroke drove him into retirement late in 1975. My father visited Douglas often at the Rusk Institute of Rehabilitation Medicine in New York and in Washington until Douglas's death. In November 1978, seeking to heal wounds and rekindle the embers, he staged a lunch for Corcoran, Douglas (reduced to a wheelchair), and himself at the Cosmos Club in Washington. Over lunch Douglas yielded to the spirit of the occasion and volunteered, "Tommy, I guess I always knew you were my best friend." (Douglas's last letter to my father, as if starting over as an operator, featured an effort to broker a meeting between him and the last Kennedy, Ted. Stranger connections had been made since the 1930s along their respective paths.) He and my mother took warmly to Douglas's last wife, Cathy, an able lawyer, and made her welcome in New York before and after Douglas died in 1980.[5]

My father joined the other survivors at Corcoran's funeral the same year, where time healed wounds. He and Lady Bird talked about the good times. Fortas died of a ruptured aorta in the night in April 1982. Douglas and Corcoran had been eighty-one and eighty, respectively; Fortas only seventy-one. The next morning Jim Rowe called my father and the other survivors of the New Deal brotherhood with the news, and a round of nostalgic reflections. Ben Cohen, eighty-eight, died the next year; Rowe, seventy-five, in 1984.

. . .

There was not a lot of reflection among the Rooseveltians at the end. They'd been interviewed, up to a point, by the historians and biographers. Tommy Corcoran tried to write a memoir. It was rich in anecdote, short on fresh insight. There were anniversaries—Franklin Roosevelt's centennial in 1982—and, the next year, attempts to make the most of the fortieth commemoration of the launching of the New Deal while there were still some New Dealers around. That season, as an editor at the *Boston Globe,* I invited Jim Rowe to put his thoughts about Roosevelt on paper. He replied, "I have been speaking about him a lot the last year"; had reviewed a new biography of him but thought his own piece "so bad [that] I think I'm written out on FDR."[6]

In fact, two little-noticed reminiscences had come more than a decade earlier from Abe Fortas—and from Lyndon Johnson. Forced from the Supreme Court in disgrace, barred from rejoining the law firm he built by a revolt against that idea in its ranks, hanging out his shingle alone, remembering his late law partner Thurman Arnold for the *Yale Law Journal* in the spring of 1970, Fortas drew a straight line from the New Deal to the design of his and Arnold's lucrative corporate law practice after World War II.

In Washington in the mid-1940s, wrote Fortas,

> The Nation's business was struggling under the mass of rules, regulations and restrictions which World War II had spawned. . . . Washington know-how was in demand, and the proliferation of Washington law firms had not yet taken place. Lawyers who were veterans of the New Deal and government service were presumed to be qualified to find their way through the maze, to guide and assist companies which had unfamiliar problems.

Then came the anticommunist "hysteria," Fortas continued. His and Arnold's response was a "product of time and place, and of the background and ideological identification of the members of the firm. We were 'liberals.' We were New Dealers." So he and his partners helped organize "the resistance to McCarthyism."[7]

For the sake of argument, continue the line from there, to Fortas's celebrated success in securing the right of legal representation for indigent defendants in his advocacy of *Gideon v. Wainright* before the Supreme Court in

1962 . . . to his blitheness in accumulating conflicts of interest in the service of his friend and former client Lyndon Johnson after 1965, while sitting on the Supreme Court (and taking inappropriate fees on the side to cushion his financial sacrifice in leaving private practice), to the end of the story. To historians' attempts to make sense of it.

Pause for a moment on the extraordinary last hurrah Lyndon Johnson managed about a month before his death at sixty-four, in 1973. Despondence and, as Elizabeth Wickenden put it to Fortas after visiting the Johnsons, "deep withdrawl," had been Johnson's prevailing moods. Heavy into self-destructive eating, drinking, and smoking, he had found it hard to imagine a post-presidential life. Against his doctor's orders, chewing a digitalis now and then for his worsening heart condition, he roused himself to speak to a gathering of notables in Austin in December 1972 for the opening of the LBJ Library's civil rights archives spanning his career. Out in the land, because of Vietnam, he was hated and distrusted, a figure of scorn.[8]

That day in Austin Johnson was elegiac; he was humble. "I do not want to say that I've always seen this matter, in terms of the special plight of the black man, as I came to see it," he acknowledged toward the start of his remarks. "I don't want this symposium to come here and spend two days talking about what we have done—the progress has been much too small, we haven't done nearly enough. I'm kind of ashamed of myself that I had six years and couldn't do more than I did."[9]

Johnson spoke of the "unequal history" whereby "whites stand on history's mountain and blacks stand in history's hollow" and of "a lifetime of listening to the language of evasion" about race. "All that I hear now" about affirmative action proposals, he cried,

> I have heard . . . for forty years. . . . Give them the vote? I saw murder almost committed because I said that in '37. Most people said, unthinkable! Give them the right to sit wherever they wish on the bus? Impossible! Give them the privilege of staying at the same hotel, using the same restroom, eating at the same hotel, using the same restroom? Never! Never!

He went on, and on. He counseled the assemblage of civil rights leaders, members of Congress, and former government officials in his and Kennedy's service on ways to propel the cause forward even if the Nixon administration proved hostile to it. Worried about his physical condition, Lady Bird tried to get him to stop. "We know there's injustice," he concluded.

> We know there's intolerance. We know there's discrimination and hate and suspicion. And we know there's division among us. But there is a larger truth. We have proved that progress is possible. We know how much remains to be done. And if our efforts continue, and if our will is strong, and if our hearts are right . . . I am confident we shall overcome.

Standing ovation! Johnson left the podium—then came back for more. And spent the next two days in bed, in pain, taking oxygen. Less than six weeks later, on January 22, 1973, he was dead.[10]

We have proved that progress is possible. Put the Vietnam War to the side—he hated it, but he saw no way around it. Or don't put it aside. It becomes clearer that, in Fortas's mind and Johnson's too, given his and Johnson's undeniable, monumental (in Johnson's case) contributions to the commonweal, all they had achieved, all the great deeds and all the dreadful decisions, the ones that tarnished them, were part of a seamless web. All were judgments, shrewd or misguided, heroic or tragic, generous or selfish, pragmatic or counterproductive, made in the interest of surviving to fight another day—on which day work on the great deeds could be resumed. *We were "liberals." We were New Dealers.* Yes, and *we get the job done. Thus is progress possible.*

. . .

Having staked out a post–House of Roosevelt position of influence, my father began in the 1960s and seventies to add to his entrepreneurial insider networking, consulting, newsletters, newspaper column, lecturing, and the rest of it, a "cult of self" as a political-economic guru. He added a fast-cash sideline, delivering testimonials in print and television advertisements for items like Mazda cars and Glenfiddich Scotch whiskey (Well-Known Iconoclast Touts Offbeat Product). My brother Bill's theory was that this was in part a belated gratification corresponding to the kind of public recognition friends in high public office enjoyed; a gratification his radical past probably ruled out politically in the Cold War era. On the face of it, his go-it-alone, retail approach to marketing his information brokerage energies was shrewd. But the ground on which he stood—and on which he based his proprietary claim to insight into "the way the world works"—was shifting.

He continued to be capable of startlingly original and acute insights, though his increasing indulgence of hyperbole and cynicism in communicating them put people off. He was highly quotable. As a contrarian seer he was a godsend for a reporter in need of a bit of background to lift his story from the tedium of the familiar, for an editor looking to be better informed than the reporters, for a politician moving around. He became synonymous with the dark forecast, and the need to take defensive investment positions against it. His press and television talk show handles—Johnny Carson made him a featured guest for a while—were "Cassandra" and "Calamity Janeway." This casting of shadow was part of his way of getting and holding attention, but also went deep in his nature.

His view had become something like this: *if the smart people no longer control the levers of power—and they don't, otherwise I and my friends would be wielding it decisively instead of manipulating it at the margins—then matters are in the hands, at best, of those who do not understand how the world works and, more often, of fools. Therefore, disaster is inevitable.*

But he held on to an audience, and to friends who valued his critical eye. In my thirties, back in my parents' New York townhouse overnight in the early 1970s, I witness a typical breakfast ritual: Sipping his coffee, combing the *New York Times* with arched eyebrows, glasses down his nose, he picks up the phone and without lifting his eyes from the paper, tells his switchboard receptionist to get him Harrison Salisbury, then a top editor at the *Times*. A moment or two later he murmurs, bemused teacher to well-meaning student, "Har-ri-son . . . Your boys still haven't got the story straight." Another day begins.[11]

. . .

Alas, a dark star dogged his designs for securing, finally, solid and lasting wealth, as distinct from the handsome cash flow he could generate. Here a curious syndrome was his judgment in business partners. Upstart entrepreneurs would present themselves, intriguing him with their brash schemes. They were interested in his connections. Co-ventures would ensue, take flight, became dubious, crash, or fade away.

My brother's theory was that he was susceptible to a side effect of his once Marxist, always sardonic critique of capitalism. That is, his contempt for the general run of the business establishment blinded him to the warning lights on some of the ambitious entrepreneurs with whom he trafficked, characters most sensible people would never have let into their offices.

On the upside, *People* magazine, plaything of my father's alma mater Time, Inc., ran a piece on my parents as "idea brokers whose time has come." The photo spread featured them on a talk show, at work in the "Edwardian splendor" of their Manhattan town house, and my father counseling an attentive Georgia governor Jimmy Carter at his statehouse office. Chroniclers of the Roosevelt era interested in Corcoran, Cohen, Ickes, and Frank, biographers of Johnson, Forrestal, Luce, Douglas, and Fortas began to call at the townhouse for interviews. Less auspiciously, *Esquire* published an investigative cover story on him dipped in acid, highlighting his egocentricity, financial reverses, and mixed scorecard of predictions. Johnny Carson began to do send-ups of him.[12]

My father, younger than his New Deal friends, continued to pop up unexpectedly in the middle of odd political fandangos and media attention. "I find myself, again, at . . . the center of events and intrigues," he remarked in one of his oral history interviews in the spring of 1988. Wearing tinted glasses against glaucoma, there he was that season with Clark Clifford, Robert Strauss, and Bert Lance in a publicized "getting to know you" sit-down of Democratic Party elders with Jesse Jackson. With Corcoran, Douglas, Fortas, and Rowe all gone, a fringe of white hair around a now greatly aged face, there he was in the fall of 1991 as one of the only surviving New Deal confreres telling stories from the old days on the fine "American Experience" documentary profile of Lyndon Johnson.[13]

That fall I shared a podium at a regional press association event in Chicago with Arkansas governor Bill Clinton. "Any relation to ? . . ." he asked me. A conversation. "He calls me up," said Clinton; "gives me a lot of advice. Some of it's pretty good."

The facade stood, just.

. . .

As always, my mother took her perceptions and concerns to her typewriter—this time by way of the library. In the 1960s she turned from fiction to research and reflection on the themes of gender, myth, and power. This work was steeped in thoughtful readings of sociology, anthropology, political theory, and cultural history, and emphasized the living reality and force of "myths" of gender roles and power relationships. Much of it was highly generalized, but at root she was, I think, working through her relationship with my father.

What men fear in women and women fear in men, she wrote in *Man's World, Woman's Place* (1971) is roughly parallel: traditional roles turning negative. "In the case of women," she wrote,

> this means a reversal of behavior from docility to dominance. For men, it means the increase of the dominance they wield already until their power grows so great that they are answerable to no one. The shadow role of the dominant male is the ogre.

For illustration, she picked none other than her and my father's old friend Lyndon Johnson, who broke

> out of the relationship which must bind the President to the public, and [ceased] to make what he was doing explicable. . . . From being "Big Daddy," a figure of authority who could be understood though not loved, Johnson passed into being the shadow behind Big Daddy, which (as the fairy stories make clear) is the ogre who eats the young.[14]

My mother developed the theme of power as a two-way relationship in *Powers of the Weak* (1980), again with Johnson (now joined by Nixon) as a negative model. "Power, say the powerful, belongs to us because we . . . know how to use it," she wrote. But in the politics of the state as in that of men and women, power must be "more than merely domination and subordination"; it must be "seen as a relationship [rather than] as an attribute of the powerful," or it provokes rebellion. For example, Johnson's "assumption that the presidency was a tool that he could use at will—an assumption that he had never made about the power he had wielded in the Senate— [caused a] reversal of his standing with the country . . . as dramatic as any in myth or legend."[15]

Critics and experts in the disciplines on which she drew for these and three more books praised her for "important insights" (Bruno Bettelheim), "compassion and wisdom and knowledge" (Jane Jacobs), and "absolute sociological pitch [and] disciplined mind" (Robert Merton). Reviewing *Man's World, Woman's Place* in the *New York Times*, Margaret Mead called it "a lucid and fascinating book" that "draws so skillfully on the best of our fragmented social science, that, as a social scientist, it gives me renewed faith that we may, in time, produce an integrated understanding of the world."[16]

She'd won a new level of acclaim and of standing in the world in relation to that of my father. Younger women writers became her close friends and acolytes. (Small world; in the mid-1970s she wrote Bill Douglas, still on the Supreme Court, urging him to make time for one of them, Erica Jong, who "has written a very funny novel called FEAR OF FLYING, which you would enjoy, though it might shake up Potter Stewart a bit.")[17]

Midway through the sequence of these books about gender and power my mother said in an interview, "I should say once and for all that my husband has been the greatest force in my life, encouraging me to write, to respect and take seriously whatever talent I have and to live up to my potential for action and thought." This was a mixed message. Deep in her being and in her texts was an acceptance of the imbalance of power as natural—and a need for protection in a much harsher environment than she'd known as a child. My parents' arrangement, their "bargain," liberated her from the genteel world of what she called "Thither Brooklyn" where she'd grown up, where women like her mother and aunts had views but no way to exercise them. That world was in any event destroyed by the Depression. My father offered her a substitute security as well as liberation.[18]

But her need for that bargain held. On the same page as one of her insights into Lyndon Johnson's hubris in *Powers of the Weak* she wrote,

> In personal situations, the weaker member will give up some initiative in return for reciprocal advantages—they may be emotional, or financial, or social (and they may of course be overvalued)—but they will be accepted as sufficient, *and the acceptance will sustain the relationship* (emphasis added).[19]

She'd adjusted the balance of force between her and my father. But in their bargain she'd had no real sanction on his power as it grew and faded, other than the power to leave. My brother and I understood this had been contemplated at one point or another. There had been through the years several attractive, smart young women in his office entourage to whom he'd dictate pieces of his oeuvre—his newsletter, correspondence, speeches, book manuscripts—late into the evening and on weekends. It seemed clear that one or more of them had been folded in from the seamless buffet lifestyle of his office and their home, first as charming, witty protégés or muses and then into something more—a kind of European baronial arrangement. At least one of them ended with a bit of fuss.

. . .

"Other people's money" was one of Justice Brandeis's great phrases, appropriated by Roosevelt and the young New Dealers in their rhetoric. It referred to unconstrained license and greed on the part of capitalist financiers.

Fortas's, Douglas's, and Corcoran's ends smacked of such excess. Then, at the start of the 1990s, came the catastrophic ruination of Clark Clifford, a power broker who made the others look like pikers, in an international banking scandal. None of these Rooseveltians, men who had once had such enormous influence, seemed to know how to leave their active association with power. The Rooseveltians' great chain of dealing had become its own end. Lyndon Johnson, more or less willing the end of his life on his ranch, was the perverse exception.[20]

Like Clifford, my father continued on as if age, and the collapse of the networks in which he'd been so influential, could be denied. Also like Clifford, he'd added traffic in other people's money to his repertoire: he'd become an investor of clients' and friends' savings, pooling these resources for greater leverage in making deals. For a while he managed them with a decent return, but in the 1970s he began to falter. The more he did, the less he could admit to himself what was happening. Large amounts of these clients' investments vaporized. So simultaneously did most of his. He engineered increasingly stretched credit arrangements with obscure banks—on Long Island and, after he and Jimmy Carter's sidekick Bert Lance discovered each other, in out-of-the-way parts of the South.

My parents still entertained in style. The townhouse on East 80th Street remained a living monument to their professional achievement, if you didn't check the underpinnings and back bills. "Vienna," my brother called it, suggesting the charadelike effort to hang on to the great days. From some forgotten corner my mother found a sketch of my father in his radical student days in London and framed it: clear eye, wavy hair, worlds to be conquered in short order.

But he was no longer smiling ironically as he toiled at the pulling of strings. He was fighting for solvency and new toeholds and, as the debts mounted, he was losing. The mortgages on the townhouse grew in number and amount. The chauffeured Cadillac was long gone.

For decades he'd dazzled others as he mixed his cocktails of skepticism and airstrike, telling them when and where to move. Against the tide of aggressive Asian and European trade initiatives and OPEC oil pricing he tried to mount a campaign for tough, tit-for-tat American export policies. Some of his Democratic cohort liked it and, among his older friends, so did John Connally, lately Richard Nixon's secretary of the treasury and prince regent. But the mood of the country was recessional.

One heard from him ever more unbridled exaggeration of the virtues of his favorites and intemperate vituperation for those who did not meet that standard, or with whom he'd broken. A prominent banker was "a stuffed shirt, expensive counter," Jim Forrestal's wife Josephine "a venomous alcoholic." His old friend Johnson was "a slob," Hubert Humphrey was "Johnson's lapdog." These characterizations were not utterly without truth. But they issued in the voice of a Shakespearean chorus of utter negation gone round the bend: a verbal violence, signaling the decline of the influence that had been his second nature.[21]

He continued to behave as if he could get it all back; he'd jump-started his career when he left Time, Inc. and went out on his own; hustled clients ever since. "Retirement" was not a word in his vocabulary. He had little interest in his grandchildren, beyond their potential as a new audience for monologues. Faith in oneself and one's unique performance in action, one's commanding role in the partnerships, had triumphed again and again. Roosevelt had died thirty-five years ago. What other gospel was there?

. . .

Meanwhile, more and more of the elements of the environment in which my father and his friends established themselves in the 1930s and 1940s began to disintegrate too. Like vinegar separating from oil, you saw them each in clinical relief. Reagan's "Morning in America," out of the ashes of Vietnam, Watergate, the inflation of the 1970s, and the rustbelt, worked for those for whom it worked. For others, postmodernism had arrived, and it was difficult for adults to explain to the young just what New Deal–era political modernism—the idea that problems were there to be analyzed critically and then solved, and that they *were* solved, up to a point—had meant.

The government had become an amorphous bureaucratic grid. Politicians did what their pollster-media consultants told them to do. There was action, to be sure, for clients of the lobbyists' Army of the Potomac. A Rupert Murdoch (for a season he and my father dallied with each other) could come to town and seize a piece of the government's plumbing. But with a few exceptions like Senator Sam Nunn and Tony Coelho, formerly House Democratic whip, relocated to Wall Street, the autumnal network in my father's last act featured a crew of faceless timeservers. Two of his favorites in fleeting authority were consumed by disasters of their own making: Wilbur Mills and Bert Lance. In Texas John and Nellie Connally put their property up in a bankruptcy sale. None of it seemed to matter.

And the information trading house was itself undergoing transformation. The world was decentralizing, power becoming more diffuse and information about it more fluid, less centrally manageable. My father's information brokerage strategy, ahead of its time in the 1940s and 1950s, depended on a network of regional elites and authoritative connections beyond the ken of the average reporter. The proliferation and speed of the new, computer-driven trading and information systems, the penetration of the American heartland by vast overseas firms, superseding indigenous local elites; the disappearance of the old political organizations, and of influential regional newspapers into homogenized corporate chains. . . all these worked against my father's brand of networking and command of the kingdom of information.

. . .

Henry Luce, in his inarticulate way, was perhaps worrying about power corrupting, or at least about it coming apart, in remarking to my mother in 1946 that "Eliot knows too much." But for years the point about my father seemed defined by performance, energy, tour de force: how uncannily he found his way to centers of power and deployed his instruments of influence upon them; on the side, offering up thrilling, or chilling, accounts of *how it works* there. How, given the mix of insight and action, could you "know too much"?

The point becomes moot. A series of strokes erodes his memory and speech, diabetes destroys his eyesight and mobility. At his side a worshipful doctor promises him time. Like Faulkner's Sutpen, he tries to control even nature. "Your father is a fighter," my mother remarks, several times over.

He claims to have one last deal in the works that will pull him out of debt and put him back on top. The deal, as if from a darkly satirical script, involves a close-action military aircraft for the third world. Its promoters have come to him because, a thread of the network holding, his friend Sam Nunn, chairman of the Senate Armed Services Committee, could encourage its procurement. Clinton's election in 1992 promises an improvement in the climate for leverage . . .

My brother Bill, a successful investment banker in New York, tries to persuade our father to accept some measure of reality. Anxious and upset, in agreement but oddly distanced from the frontline of the disaster, our mother is a frail ally. She does make a noise about "leaving" if our father fails to see reason, telling him that he needs to do so for her sake; managing the grand 80th Street townhouse has become too much. My brother covers the astounding debts, then forces the issue of feeding them.

My father now must give up what's left of the baronial lifestyle, move with my mother and a fraction of the staff to a cramped apartment and office space adjacent to the townhouse. On a visit from Chicago, where I live and work, I converge with Bill upon the house for triage of a sacred remaining asset: *the books!* My father refuses to cooperate. In his study, just past the portrait of him in revolutionary youth, he answers my mother's call from the next room—"Eliot, what are you *doing*?"—in an affectless monotone. "Writing a book."

My father, just turned eighty, dies in February of 1993. I fly in again. (At my parents' apartment the last retainer is taking a call from Sam Nunn's

office. "The Senator was out of the country and was shocked to hear . . .")
My brother and mother, all too close at hand, are too emotionally exhausted
to view the remains.[22]

Alone with my father's body at the funeral parlor, I say there are two
riddles of his youth and the end of his life that haunt me: his suppression
of his Jewishness, and of any meaning or legacy it might hold for me or my
brother; and his failure, even in his loneliness and isolation, to try to connect
with his grandchildren, my son and daughter, now joined by a son of Bill's.

But these, of course, are the questions a sentimentalist, anyone at all,
would ask; ordinary questions to an ordinary father. I feel better for asking
them, but their irrelevance is as absurd as my timing.

Then I see, beyond the surface scars of hospital life-support tubes on
mouth and nose, two enduring images: a wizened face from the shtetls of
Europe, wise and almost Oriental in its impassiveness. And, despite the last
surrender of power, total will.

Epilogue

Perhaps I've brought the two sets of memory—one public, the other private, the second blurring with the first—into register. Perhaps not. Perhaps it depends on how you're inclined to factor the personalities of the powerful into the way you think about how history unfolds—and how much any of us, however privileged (and thus skewed) our perspective, really knows what goes on inside the minds of others.

There is the issue of outsized personalities, like Johnson's, Corcoran's, and my father's, that fit no molds, and fall into fatal excess or dysfunction. On the other hand, how do we dare to break molds? Conceive, as Roosevelt and Corcoran did before and after 1940, of the need for a fundamentally, functionally reformed political party system in the United States, and of a way to pursue it? Argue, as Tugwell, Corcoran, Douglas, Frank, Ickes, and my father did in 1941, that wars cannot be fought without coherent ideas behind them that men and women believe in on a critically reasoned basis as well as salute?

Does the model the Rooseveltians collaborated on recommend itself to us as a relevant one for the future? There are many reasons to say no. One is that the men of the New Deal shaped an activist government but fell short of building a social democracy to engage with it (a Great Society). Then, in all too many respects, government evolved into Theodore Lowi's "ungovernable" bureaucratic morass. The Rooseveltians' sad last chapters, individually and collectively, also argue against using the New Deal model for contemporary purposes.[1]

After all, the idea of assembling brilliant, dedicated reformers in Washington to attack social, economic, technological, and international dilemmas has been adapted with mixed results several times since the New Deal. As we have seen, the list includes Kennedy's "best and brightest," academicians and technocrats, so crucial to the unleashing of disaster in Vietnam . . . Their colleagues who hatched what became Johnson's antipoverty initiative, crisply applying "McNamara Whiz Kid" cost-benefit analysis at the Office of Economic Opportunity . . . Clinton's health care planners . . . [2]

The Truman administration's Wise Men, as noted, is a different model altogether, composed of senior, veteran public officials from the halls of foreign and defense policy making, not different from "government of all talents" coalition or "privy council" European models in earlier centuries, and by no means defined by commitment to reform. The same is true for Kennedy's "ExCom" in the Cuban Missile Crisis.

Then we have the alternative model of those who mounted a successful attack on the New Deal and the Great Society: the neo-conservatives and libertarians, who found their man and moment with Ronald Reagan, promising on the eve of his defeat of President Jimmy Carter a "crusade . . . to take government off the backs of the great people of this country." It is true, as Sidney Blumenthal has written, that Reaganism was built in great part on a mythology of restoration of an American past, filmlike "dreams of what never happened." But the success of the "Reagan Revolution" had to do as well with the convergence of serious ideas and power. The fusion of the critique of modern government by free-market thinkers like Friedrich Hayek and Milton Friedman together with the factual bases for widespread disaffection from official bureaucracy (examined by searching liberal critics like Lowi and Michael Sandel as well as by the free-marketeers) gave Reaganism a force far beyond what it could have found in dreamy myth.[3]

Thus Reaganism resembles the New Deal example, and differs from other post–New Deal ones, in one important respect: in how it has constituted something of a mass movement, an idea whose time did come. Like the other models, it featured its elite cadre of theorists and self-important technocrats in crisp parade formation in Washington, burning lights late in positions requiring top security clearance. But undeniably, neo-conservatism and associated creeds have attained deep and organized roots out in the country, on campuses, in communities, among people who care as much about values and ideas as do progressive reformers.

As the Reagan Revolution gives us a modern counter–New Deal case in point, so it brings us to the question of the impact of television—of the stage business and manipulations of the media age—on efforts to bring ideas and power together. Efforts by academicians and public-minded television managers to try to make that medium work in the direction of John Deweyesque participatory, "good government" politics have been attempted, but appear largely quixotic to date.

Television is one of the channels both fueling and mediating widespread public alienation from politics in recent decades. The harnessing of it for the politics of progressive reform and governmental activism is finally a more difficult business than employing it for the politics of rolling back reform and government.[4]

. . .

Two salient criteria distinguish the New Deal model of concerted reform from the Kennedy, Johnson, and Clinton ones. The first is that the post-Rooseveltian versions were hatched in isolation from congressional and other elective politics and politicians—in some cases, fatally so. The Wise Men of Truman's postwar containment policy made a shrewd pact with Senate Republican and Democratic leaders, but that, again, was its own model (or rather, the old European model), not the Rooseveltian one. Johnson counseled privately with a few old senatorial confidants full of doubts about the Vietnam War, especially Richard Russell and Mike Mansfield, from the start to the end of his presidency. But the purpose of the retooling of the Wise Men concept in the Vietnam years was specifically to yield the administration a compact, effective distillation of the foreign policy establishment. Guided at the start by McGeorge Bundy and manned by senior former cabinet, White House, and Pentagon officials unconnected to politics, it was the less prescient for its haughty distance from Vietnam War skeptics on Capitol Hill. (Again, the "Reagan Revolution" more closely resembles the New Deal one; not a little of its brainpower and energy came from the David Stockmans and Richard Perles who served and worked in Congress.)[5]

By contrast, though some cerebral New Dealers looked down their noses at the other end of Pennsylvania Avenue, others, like Corcoran, Cohen, and Douglas, operated on the opposite premise. Congressional figures including Sam Rayburn, Robert La Follette, Robert Wagner, George Norris, James Byrnes, Burton Wheeler, Hugo Black, Claude Pepper, the young Lyndon Johnson, and many others collaborated on the genesis and development of all the major New Deal initiatives: emergency recovery and economic reform in the worst of the Depression crisis in 1933 and thereafter; the fights to regulate markets, utilities, wages, hours, and prices, and to protect the rights of workers to organize and strike; to harness energy, to build public utilities and to develop the American South and West; to modernize tax and fiscal policy and the courts; to mobilize for war and plan for postwar full employment; and on and on.

"Roosevelt began to realize in 1938 that the country was drifting into a European cartel system," Thurman Arnold wrote some years later, with "big business . . . dividing the markets of the world, as well as those in the United States." In this view the grip of trusts and cartels controlling prices and markets was an ominous common thread in German and Italian fascism and in European and American capitalist democracies alike. Linking domestic and international concerns on the eve of war, Roosevelt unleashed the American tradition of antitrust policy on the syndrome, with Arnold at the Justice Department in charge. (Under pressure from the military and war agencies, which wanted order, the president allowed the antitrust initiative to be stalemated a year into the war. Nevertheless, in his forceful if inconstant way he'd made the point about cartels, to be taken up in peacetime.) And Roosevelt simultaneously orchestrated an unusual, ambitious, joint congressional and executive branch inquiry, the Temporary National Economic Committee (TNEC), chaired by an antimonopoly New Dealer, Senator Joseph O'Mahoney of Wyoming, in collaboration with a cohort of New Deal economists and lawyers including Douglas, Arnold, and Frank. (A set of research assignments from the TNEC was my father's first formal collaboration with the New Dealers.)[6]

The TNEC took the stage under bright lights, conducted prodigious research into the structure of American industries, had limited immediate impact on the eve of World War II, but helped ratify modern fiscal policy—Keynesianism and associated ideas—and New Deal principles of regulation. "TNEC ideas," as Alan Brinkley has written, reached "well beyond the hearing rooms and offices of the committee itself." In any discussion of models for effective policy development, it remains suggestive.[7]

It is true that the New Dealers were constrained by the decision from the top that reform legislation, and election results to further it, required compromise with conservative congressional barons and big city bosses. And that after 1938 those forces tended to prevail.[8]

On the other hand, recall Moynihan's diagnosis of "maximum feasible misunderstanding" of the community action concept in the War on Poverty in the 1960s—whereby no one paused to sort out whether community action meant organizing, expanding, confronting, or assisting the power structure. That meant that in the inevitable confrontation adversaries like Mayor Daley, who had such questions sorted out, trumped the reformers. By contrast, the New Deal in the end is defined by its roster of lasting successes in reforming the power structure in all four of Moynihan's specified ways: for example, in organizing labor, and new political coalitions; in expanding wage and old-age security, and building the economic infrastructure of the South and West; in confronting selfish corporations' prerogatives to operate free of rational regulation; in assisting government to adopt sophisticated tools for fiscal and monetary management. The essence of those gains was preserved in World War II and, in contrast to the previous war, in the peace that followed.[9]

. . .

The second characteristic distinguishing the Rooseveltians from subsequent "president's men" was that the Roosevelt years were times of crisis paralyzing the nation and threatening democracy itself. It is tempting, looking prospectively for solutions to drift and impasse, and trying to make sense of disorderly history as well, to view crisis at its most climactic as a cathartic force that, finally, brings unfocused agendas together. Against such a tidy formulation it has been argued that crisis was the enemy of coherence in the New Deal and a key instead to "its monumental confusions." From either viewpoint the tides of radical reform and defense of democracy against fascism did run in Congress in the 1930s and forties, and in the campaigns that sent men and women there, as well as in New Deal executive branch circles, and then on the Roosevelt Supreme Court, as they do not in more secure or serene times. From challenges to the status quo they evolved into policy action and in some cases gradually into new consensus, as for government intervention in the economy and against isolationism, across the branches of government.[10]

(At this point of comparison the Reagan Revolution becomes problematic. Reagan's and key aides' conviction that they too confronted a crisis, and threats to democracy, provoked deep division, especially in Congress, rather than consensus. On the other hand, paralleling the New Deal's afterlife in the form of the Warren Court in the 1950s and sixties, the Reagan Revolution did succeed in yielding a continuity of deeply conservative control over the Supreme Court up through the present.)

Each of our great national parties owes a portion of its roots to a crisis—understood as economic, societal, or political breakdown—which, together, add up to what Bruce Ackerman describes as the "crucial transformative periods" in which our eighteenth-century Constitution was modernized.

> The first is the Republican reconstruction of the Union after the Civil War. The second is the Democrats' legitimation of activist national government during and after the Great Depression.
>
> As with the original Founding, neither of these sweeping changes came about overnight. Each was preceded by a generation and more of political agitation that prepared the way for a decade of decisive change.

The "agonies" (Ackerman's term) that were required before the courts could accept slavery as unconstitutional in the 1860s, or government intervention in the economy as constitutional in the 1930s, were devastating to the nation, to its people. But from those crises came renewal.[11]

The enormity of the terrorist attacks on New York and Washington on September 11, 2001, perhaps carried the potential for a grand, unifying response. In any event the opportunity was seized for relatively narrow, combative policy choices. Had the impasse in the electoral system in the 2000 presidential election proceeded from breakdown to full governmental stoppage and economic collapse, the kinds of radical reform of our political system that have not gotten off the pages of books and speeches might have

come into play. But that didn't happen. Malaise unaccompanied by either
breakdown or a compelling reform agenda does not a tranformative crisis
make.

· · ·

What useful models of reform leadership for the future do we have then?
Model building is speculative; real life is partly accidental. The Rooseveltians
came together, in part, because Roosevelt was the peculiar individual he
was: no intellectual or theorist himself, but instinctively drawn to the project
of harnessing such people to his struggle to manage successive crises. Without *him* managing the political end of the equation, finessing and co-opting
opposition in Congress and in the country, those ambitious thinkers' and
operators' impact would have been small. Without *them* his innovative impulses in action would have been vague. Events, and a high tide of reform
prompted by them, brought them together.

What the Rooseveltians wrought was, in all events, our first modern
national experience (the eighteenth-century drama of the founding of our
nation was of a different order) of organized, large-scale collaboration between thinkers and doers; theoreticians and politicians. Events motivated
and informed them. That, and the nature of their ideas, connected them
to people and politics in the trenches and at the grassroots level. The leaders
among them were at least as practical as they were radical, or idealistic.
Nothing they achieved was possible without the discipline and sacrifice that
accompanies broadscale coalition building and compromise. They understood ideas and politics as instruments for democratic transaction and interaction; not as movement zeal. They were communal beyond their own
intellectual circle; they were political, dealing people in. They made mistakes, were flawed; in various ways they failed. But in various ways, still
resonating, they succeeded.

NOTES

Manuscript Source Collections

Dean G. Acheson Papers, Manuscripts and Archives, Yale University, New Haven, Conn.

Francis Biddle Papers, Franklin D. Roosevelt Library, Hyde Park, N.Y.

Thomas G. Corcoran Papers, Manuscripts Division, Library of Congress, Washington, D.C.

Thomas G. Corcoran Wiretap Transcripts, Harry S. Truman Library, Independence, Mo.

Ernest Cuneo Papers, Franklin D. Roosevelt Library, Hyde Park, N.Y.

William O. Douglas Papers, Manuscripts Division, Library of Congress, Washington, D.C.

James V. Forrestal Papers, Seeley G. Mudd Manuscript Library, Princeton University, Princeton, N.J.

Abe Fortas Papers, Manuscripts and Archives, Yale University, New Haven, Conn.

Jerome Frank Papers, Manuscripts and Archives, Yale University, New Haven, Conn.

Harold L. Ickes Papers, Manuscripts Division, Library of Congress, Washington, D.C.

Eliot Janeway Oral History, Columbia Oral History Collection, Columbia University, New York, N.Y.

Eliot Janeway File, Federal Bureau of Investigation, Washington, D.C.

Eliot Janeway Papers, Lyndon B. Johnson Library, Austin, Tex.

Lyndon B. Johnson Papers, Lyndon B. Johnson Library, Austin, Tex.

Henry R. Luce Papers, Time, Inc. Archives, New York, N.Y.

Walter P. Reuther Papers, Archives of Labor and Urban Affairs, Wayne State University, Detroit, Mich.

Franklin and Eleanor Roosevelt Papers, Franklin D. Roosevelt Library, Hyde Park, N.Y.

James Rowe Jr. Papers, Franklin D. Roosevelt Library, Hyde Park, N.Y.

Russian Center for the Preservation and Study of Documents of Recent History, Moscow, Russia

Harry S. Truman Papers, Harry S. Truman Library, Independence, Mo.

Rexford G. Tugwell Papers, Franklin D. Roosevelt Library, Hyde Park, N.Y.

Henry A. Wallace Diaries, Columbia Oral History Collection, Columbia University, New York, N.Y.

Abbreviations

COHC	Columbia Oral History Collection
EHJOH	Elizabeth (Hall) Janeway Oral History, COHC
EJOH	Eliot Janeway Oral History, COHC
FDRL	Franklin D. Roosevelt Library
HSTL	Harry S. Truman Library
LBJL	Lyndon B. Johnson Library
LOC	Library of Congress

Preface

1. According to Herbert Stein, chairman of the Council of Economic Advisers under Presidents Nixon and Ford, the statement "We are all Keynesians now," often attributed to Nixon, was actually made by conservative economist Milton Friedman in 1965. Nixon's exact words in 1971 and 1972 appear to have been "Now I am a Keynesian." See "Nixon Reportedly Says He Is Now a Keyensian," *New York Times*, January 7, 1971, p. 19; Herbert Stein, "Doctor, Am I Really a Keynesian?" *Wall Street Journal*, April 13, 1981, p. 18.

For Reagan and Gingrich, see Henry Mitchell, "The President Makes His Centennial Rounds," *Washington Post*, January 29, 1982, p. D1; Bernard Weinraub, "The Reagan Legacy," *New York Times*, June 22, 1986, section 6, p. 13; "The 104th Congress: The Republican Leader; Excerpts from Gingrich's Speech on Party's Agenda for the 104th Congress," *New York Times*, January 5, 1995, p. A23.

2. David Halberstam, *The Powers That Be* (New York: Random House, 1979), p. 6.

1. Government by Brains Trust

1. Geoffrey C. Ward, *A First-Class Temperament: The Emergence of Franklin Roosevelt* (New York: Harper and Row, 1989), p. xiii. See Gary J. Aichele, *Oliver Wendell Holmes, Jr.: Soldier, Scholar, Judge* (Boston: Hall, 1989), for speculation that the aged Holmes might have been referring back to Theodore Roosevelt.

"The brains department" was *New York Times* Albany correspondent James Kieran's first published tagline for Governor Roosevelt's inner circle of advisers, on September 6, 1932. R. G. Tugwell, *The Brains Trust* (New York: Viking, 1968), pp. 3–5; Raymond Moley, with Elliott A. Rosen, *The First New Deal* (New York: Harcourt Brace, 1966), p. 17.

Joseph P. Lash, *Dealers and Dreamers: A New Look at the New Deal* (New York: Doubleday, 1988), pp. 283–284, citing Stanley High in 1936.

2. Daniel T. Rodgers, *Atlantic Crossings: Social Politics in a Progressive Age* (Cambridge: Harvard University Press, 1998), p. 412; Bernard Sternsher, *Rexford Tugwell and the New Deal* (New Brunswick, N.J.: Rutgers University Press, 1964), p. 5.

3. Moley, *The First New Deal*, pp. 15–17; Sternsher, *Rexford Tugwell and the New Deal*, pp. 39–41; Arthur M. Schlesinger Jr., *The Age of Roosevelt: The Crisis of the Old Order* (Boston: Houghton Mifflin, 1957), pp. 190–198, 398–400.

4. Thomas G. Corcoran, "Rendezvous with Destiny," unpublished memoir, draft for "Law of Unintended Consequences" chapter, pp. 9–10, Corcoran Papers, Box 589, LOC; henceforth Corcoran, memoir, Corcoran Papers.

For a slightly different version of this incident, see Arthur M. Schlesinger Jr., *The Age of Roosevelt: The Politics of Upheaval* (Boston: Houghton Mifflin, 1960), p. 280.

5. Alan Brinkley, *The End of Reform: New Deal Liberalism in Recession and War* (New York: Knopf, 1995), p. 7.

6. Thomas G. Corcoran to Eliot Janeway, September 13, 1945, FBI Transcripts of Wiretaps on Thomas G. Corcoran, President's Secretary File, HSTL; henceforth Corcoran Wiretap Transcripts.

7. Monica Lynne Niznik, "Thomas G. Corcoran: The Public Service of Franklin Roosevelt's 'Tommy the Cork,'" Ph.D. diss., Department of History, Notre Dame, April 1981, p. 103; William O. Douglas, *Go East, Young Man* (New York: Random House, 1974), pp. 286–287; Townsend Hoopes and Douglas Brinkley, *Driven Patriot: The Life and Times of James Forrestal* (New York: Knopf, 1992), pp. 115, 117.

8. David Halberstam, *The Powers That Be*, pp. 159–160; Joseph Alsop and Robert Kintner, *Men Around the President* (New York: Doubleday, 1939), pp. 5–11; Robert E. Herzstein, *Henry R. Luce: A Political Portrait of the Man Who Created the American Century* (New York: Scribner's, 1994), p. xvi; biographical account of Ernest Cuneo's career in finder's aid to Cuneo Papers, FDRL.

9. See chapter 3, page 41, this volume, and note 35, for negative assessments of the New Deal by scholars such as Theodore Lowi and Michael J. Sandel.

10. Walter Isaacson and Evan Thomas, *The Wise Men: Six Friends and the World They Made* (New York: Simon and Schuster, 1986), p. 19.

At the Versailles Peace Conference of 1919 Keynes and the young Jean Monnet both worked in vain for initiatives for American investment in European recovery—models of their work that came to fruition only after World War II. Margaret MacMillan, *Paris 1919: Six Months That Changed the World* (New York: Random House, 2001), p. 183.

11. Theodore J. Lowi, *The End of Liberalism: The Second Republic of the United States*, 2d ed. (New York: Norton, 1979), p. xiii.

12. See Michael Janeway, *Republic of Denial: Press, Politics, and Public Life* (New Haven: Yale University Press, 1999), pp. 29–42, for an analysis of these themes.

13. Lister Hill to Thomas G. Corcoran, December 15, 1945, Corcoran Wiretap Transcripts; Alvah Johnston, "White House Tommy," *Saturday Evening Post*, July 31, 1937, p. 7; William Lasser, *Benjamin V. Cohen: Architect of the New Deal* (New Haven: Yale University Press, 2002), p. 51.

14. Eliot Janeway, *The Struggle for Survival: A Chronicle of Economic Mobilization in World War II* (New Haven: Yale University Press, 1951), p. 231.

15. Arthur M. Schlesinger Jr., *The Age of Roosevelt: The Coming of the New Deal* (Boston: Houghton Mifflin, 1958), p. 523.

16. Francis Biddle to Thomas G. Corcoran, September 16, 1945, Corcoran Wiretap Transcripts.

17. Douglas, *Go East, Young Man*, p. 457; Eliot Janeway, May 22 and May 25, 1941 diary entries, Eliot Janeway Papers, LOC.

18. See chapter 4, this volume; and James F. Simon, *Independent Journey: The Life of William O. Douglas* (New York: Harper and Row, 1980), pp. 257–275.

2. Tommy Corcoran and the New Dealers' Gospel

1. Katie Louchheim, ed., *The Making of the New Deal: The Insiders Speak* (Cambridge: Harvard University Press, 1983), Frank Watson entry, p. 106.

2. Ibid., Gerhard A. Gesell entry, p. 139, Frank Watson entry, p. 108.

3. The song, known variously as "Unreconstructed Rebel" or "Good Old Rebel," has a complicated history. It began as a satirical poem by an aristocratic former Confederate officer, Innes Randolph. Curtis Carroll Davis, "Elegant Old Rebel: Innes Randolph of Virginia and Baltimore," *Virginia Cavalcade* (Summer 1958) 42(8): 1; Reid Mitchell, "Good Old Rebel," www.rockzilla.net, May 2003; Edwin Anderson Alderman and Joel Chandler Harris, eds., *Library of Southern Literature* (New Orleans: Martin and Hoyt, 1910), p. 349.

Elizabeth (Hall) Janeway, oral history interview no. 2, July 21, 1986, pp. 18–19, EHJOH.

4. Thomas G. Corcoran to Lyndon Johnson, December 20, 1945; Benjamin Sonnenberg to Corcoran, October 11, 1945, Corcoran Wiretap Transcripts.

5. Lash, *Dealers and Dreamers*, p. 282, 353; William O. Douglas, *The Court Years* (New York, Vintage, 1981), p. 260; Alvah Johnston, "White House Tommy," *Saturday Evening Post*, July 31, 1937, p. 6; Alvah Johnston, "The Saga of Tommy the Cork" (Part 3), *Saturday Evening Post*, October 27, 1945, p. 44.

6. Douglas, *The Court Years*, p. 260; Eliot Janeway to William O. Douglas, July 25, 1945, Douglas Papers, Box 342.

7. Louchheim, *The Making of the New Deal*, Thomas Corcoran entry, pp. 24–25.

8. Lash, *Dealers and Dreamers*, p. 62; Jordan Schwarz, *The New Dealers: Power Politics in the Age of Roosevelt* (New York: Knopf, 1993), p. 140; Peter H. Irons, *The New Deal Lawyers* (Princeton: Princeton University Press, 1982), pp. 123–124; Laura Kalman, *Abe Fortas* (New Haven: Yale University Press, 1990), p. 23.

9. Alsop and Kintner, *Men Around the President*, pp. 53–72; Schwarz, *The New Dealers*, pp. 138–156; Brinkley, *The End of Reform*, pp. 49–55; Schlesinger, *The Politics of Upheaval*, pp. 225–228; Lash, *Dealers and Dreamers*, pp. 52–70 ff.

10. For Corcoran citing Holmes, see Thomas G. Corcoran, interview for unpublished memoir, May 30, 1979 (supplemental), p. 16, Corcoran Papers, Book File folders, Box 587.

For Rayburn and Wheeler on Corcoran and Cohen, see D. B. Hardeman and Donald C. Bacon, *Rayburn* (Austin: Texas Monthly Press, 1987), pp. 152, 170–171.

11. Schwarz, *The New Dealers*, pp. 146–147; Lash, *Dealers and Dreamers*, p. 171.

12. Lash, *Dealers and Dreamers*, p. 230; Niznik, "Thomas G. Corcoran," pp. 131–133, 147–149; Schlesinger, *The Politics of Upheaval*, p. 227–230.

13. For LeHand as Roosevelt's "other wife," see Doris Kearns Goodwin, *No Ordinary Time: Franklin and Eleanor Roosevelt, The Home Front in World War II* (New York: Simon and Schuster, 1994), pp. 115–119.

For Corcoran's account, see Lash, *Dealers and Dreamers*, pp. 230–231.

14. Louchheim, *The Making of the New Deal*, Joseph L. Rauh Jr. entry, p. 110.

For Corcoran and the Coast Guard, see Alsop and Kintner, *Men Around the President*, pp. 60–61; Niznik,"Thomas G. Corcoran," p. 58; Lasser, *Benjamin V. Cohen*, p. 194.

For Corcoran and Rayburn, see Hardeman and Bacon, *Rayburn*, pp. 212–213.

15. Schwarz, *The New Dealers*, pp. 138, 150–151; Lash, *Dealers and Dreamers*, pp. 287, 290; Louchheim, *The Making of the New Deal*, Joseph L. Rauh Jr. entry, pp. 111–112.

16. Cohen wrote his friend Jane Harris in 1935, while drafting the Public Utilities Holding Act, "Tom and I will be branded as dangerous radicals again, although we are in fact the only real conservatives in Washington." See Lasser, *Benjamin V. Cohen*, p. 119.

See also Louchheim, *The Making of the New Deal*, Joseph L. Rauh Jr. entry, p. 113; Lasser, *Benjamin V. Cohen*, p. 79; Anthony Badger, *The New Deal: The Depression Years, 1933–1940* (New York: Hill and Wang, 1989), p. 99.

17. Lash, *Dealers and Dreamers*, p. 193.

18. Ibid., pp. 131–136, 334–350; Schwarz, *The New Dealers*, pp. 148–151; Niznik, "Thomas G. Corcoran," pp. 73 f., pp. 222–223, 346–348; Kenneth S. Davis, *FDR: Into the Storm, 1937–1940* (New York: Random House, 1993), pp. 201, 255–256.

19. Schwarz, *The New Dealers*, p. xiv.

20. Thomas G. Corcoran to Benjamin V. Cohen, January 10, 1946, Corcoran Wiretap Transcripts.

21. Thomas G. Corcoran to Eliot Janeway, September 13, 1945; Corcoran to John Carter Vincent, June 28, 1945, Corcoran Wiretap Transcripts.

The subject of Corcoran's "one of those guys" remark was an attorney for Truman's friend and backer Edwin W. Pauley.

22. Thomas G. Corcoran, memoir, "Preface," p. 14, Corcoran Papers.

23. Douglas, *Go East, Young Man*, pp. 282, 286; Schwarz, *The New Dealers*, pp. 98–100, 297–342; Rexford Guy Tugwell, *The Stricken Land: The Story of Puerto Rico* (New York: Doubleday, 1947), p. 64 ff.

24. Nelson Lichtenstein, *The Most Dangerous Man in Detroit: Walter Reuther and the Fate of American Labor* (New York: Basic, 1995), chapter 8, especially pp. 166, 173–174, 479, note 35; Janeway, *The Struggle for Survival*, p. 231.

25. Thomas G. Corcoran, memoir, "Tangling the Threads" chapter, p. D1, Corcoran Papers.

26. Eliot Janeway, oral history interview no. 3, May 16, 1986, p. 16–17, EJOH.

For portraits of Douglas as an "operator," see Louchheim, *The Making of the New Deal*, Milton Katz entry, pp. 126–127; Gerhard Gesell entry, pp. 136–137; Milton V. Freeman entry, pp. 142–143.

27. Lash, *Dealers and Dreamers*, p. 6; Martin Weil, "Benjamin Cohen, Architect of New Deal, Dies," *Washington Post*, August 16, 1983, p. 1; Benjamin V. Cohen to Thomas G. Corcoran, July 5, 1945, Corcoran Wiretap Transcripts.

28. Douglas, *The Court Years*, pp. 275–276; James MacGregor Burns, *Roosevelt: The Lion and the Fox* (New York: Harcourt, Brace, 1956), p. 423.

29. Eliot Janeway to Henry R. Luce, June 12, 1946, Janeway Memoranda File, Time, Inc. Archives.

30. Thomas G. Corcoran, memoir, "The Truman Years" chapter, pp. 6–7, Corcoran Papers.

31. Lash, *Dealers and Dreamers*, pp. 273–274, 355–362; Schwarz, *The New Dealers*,

pp. 151–153; Max Lowenthal, "Thomas G. Corcoran's Relation to Wm. O. Douglas" (1948), pp. 4–5, Lowenthal Papers, University of Minnesota Archives.

32. James Rowe Jr. to Missy LeHand, January 14, 1941; Rowe to Franklin D. Roosevelt, June 25, 1941; Rowe to Roosevelt, October 2, 1941; all in Rowe Papers, Box 10.

Frank Freidel, *Franklin D. Roosevelt: A Rendezvous with Destiny* (Boston: Little, Brown, 1990), p. 347; Lash, *Dealers and Dreamers*, pp. 399–400.

33. Schwarz, *The New Dealers*, p. 154; Kenneth S. Davis, *FDR: The War President, 1940–1943* (New York: Random House, 2000), p. 330.

34. Eliot Janeway, oral history interview no. 1, April 2, 1986, p. 32, EJOH; James Rowe Jr. to Franklin D. Roosevelt, June 25, 1941, Rowe Papers, Box 10; Rowe to Francis Biddle, October 15, 1942; Rowe to Biddle, January 16, 1943; Rowe to Biddle, February 6, 1943; Rowe to Biddle, February 10, 1943; all in Rowe Papers, Box 33; Rowe to Biddle, April 29, 1942; Rowe to Biddle, June 19, 1942; both in Biddle Papers, Box 2; Eliot Janeway, oral history interview no. 1, April 2, 1986, p. 32.

Francis Biddle, *In Brief Authority* (New York: Doubleday, 1962), pp. 254–255.

35. Thomas G. Corcoran to John Carter Vincent, June 28, 1945, Corcoran Wiretap Transcripts.

The case in question, involving a radio station in New York City, is described in jaundiced fashion, minus the Roosevelts' sons' connection, in Alvah Johnston, "The Saga of Tommy the Cork" (Part 1), *Saturday Evening Post*, October 13, 1945, pp. 10–11. For a fragment of Corcoran's version, see the transcript of interview with Corcoran dated May 30, 1979, pp. 27–30, Book File folder, Corcoran Papers, Box 592.

36. Thomas G. Corcoran to Eliot Janeway, December 4, 1945, Corcoran Wiretap Transcripts.

A man with a lyrical ear, Corcoran here alludes to Robert Browning: "Grow old along with me / The best is yet to be / The last of life, for which the first was made."

37. James Rowe Jr. to Blaine Hallock, November 16, 1953; Thomas G. Corcoran to William O. Douglas, December 1, 1953; Douglas to Corcoran, December 3, 1953; Mildred Douglas to Corcoran, 1953; all in Corcoran Papers, Box 125; Abe Fortas to Rebecca Judge, December 20, 1977; Judge to Fortas, July 27, 1979; both in Fortas Papers, Box 106.

Robert Dallek, *Lone Star Rising: Lyndon Johnson and His Times, 1908–1960* (New York: Oxford, 1991), pp. 251, 283, 339–342, 411; Robert Dallek, *Flawed Giant: Lyndon Johnson and His Times, 1961–1973* (New York: Oxford, 1998), pp. 233, 611; Douglas Frantz and David McKean, *Friends in High Places: The Rise and Fall of Clark Clifford* (Boston: Little, Brown, 1995), pp. 3–9, 196–197; Kalman, *Abe Fortas*, pp. 200–209; Simon, *Independent Journey*, pp. 286–287.

38. Elizabeth Janeway, oral history interview no. 2, July 21, 1986, p. 11, EHJOH; Douglas, *The Court Years*, p. 337; Simon, *Independent Journey*, p. 331–332; Eliot Janeway, oral history interview no. 1, April 2, 1986, p. 92, EJOH.

39. Roger K. Newman, *Hugo Black: A Biography* (New York: Pantheon, 1994), p. 386; Kalman, *Abe Fortas*, pp. 114, 186; Lash, *Dealers and Dreamers*, pp. 445–457.

In *Wild Bill: The Legend and Life of William O. Douglas* (New York: Random House, 2003), citing Lash, Bruce Allen Murphy claims Corcoran was publicly unfaithful to Peggy before and after they married (pp. 198, 594). This is unsupported by Lash.

But David McKean's forthcoming biography, *Tommy the Cork* (Royalton, Vt.: Steer-forth, 2004), reports that Corcoran fell into a brief affair in Latin America in 1942 that produced an illegitimate child.

40. Dallek, *Lone Star Rising*, 234–235; 247–251; James Reston Jr., *The Lonestar: The Life of John Connally* (New York: Harper and Row, 1989), pp. 56–58.

41. For Johnson, Connally, Fortas, and Forrestal see Dallek, *Lone Star Rising*, pp. 189–191; Reston, *The Lonestar*, pp. 104, 297–299; Kalman, *Abe Fortas*, pp. 195–196; Hoopes and Brinkley, *Driven Patriot*, pp. 80–81, 216–224.

For Corcoran on Fortas, see Ernest Cuneo to Thomas G. Corcoran, January 19, 1946, Corcoran Wiretap Transcripts.

For Black on Douglas, see Newman, *Hugo Black*, pp. 476–477.

For Corcoran and Douglas, see Mildred Douglas to Corcoran, 1953, Corcoran Papers, Box 125; Corcoran to Blaine Hallock, May 6, 1953, Douglas Papers, Box 242; Simon, *Independent Journey*, pp. 239, 285–287, 319; Murphy, *Wild Bill*, pp. 292–295.

In a set of interview notes for his unpublished memoir, "Rendezvous with Destiny," Corcoran says of Mildred Douglas, "I made a hell of a deal for her." Summary of Conversation, October 30, (1979?), p. 3, Book Files, Corcoran Papers, Box 589. See also chapter 4, p. 65, this volume, and note 69.

42. Louchheim, *The Making of the New Deal*, James Rowe Jr. entry, p. 287.

43. Thomas G. Corcoran to Eliot Janeway, September 13, 1945, Corcoran Wiretap Transcripts; Wolfgang Saxon, "Thomas G. Corcoran, Aide to Roosevelt, Dies," *New York Times*, December 7, 1981, p. D18.

44. For Corcoran, see Schwarz, *The New Dealers*, pp. 155–156; Lash, *Dealers and Dreamers*, pp. 447–448, 461–462.

For Johnson, see "The Multimillionaire," *Time*, August 21, 1964, pp. 15–16; Keith Wheeler and William Lambert, "How LBJ's Family Amassed Its Fortune," *Life*, August 21, 1964, pp. 62–72; "The Story of the Johnson Family Fortune," *U.S. News and World Report*, May 4, 1964, pp. 38–45; Dallek, *Lone Star Rising*, pp. 247–252, 409–415.

For Fortas, see Kalman, *Abe Fortas*, pp. 366–376; "Ex-Justice Abe Fortas Dies at Seventy-one; Shaped Historic Rulings on Rights," *New York Times*, April 7, 1983, p. 1.

For Douglas, see Simon, *Independent Journey*, pp. 391–400, 409–410; Murphy, *Wild Bill*, pp. 430–438, 441; "William O. Douglas Is Dead at Eighty-one; Served Thirty-six Years on Supreme Court," *New York Times*, January 20, 1980, p. 1.

45. For Roosevelt's "Farmer" rhetoric see, for example, Ward, *A First-Class Temperament*, pp. 264, 279; Frank Freidel, *Franklin D. Roosevelt: The Triumph* (Boston: Little, Brown, 1956), p. 97. Schlesinger, *The Politics of Upheaval*, p. 424.

46. Thomas G. Corcoran to Harold L. Ickes, September 13, 1946, Corcoran Wiretap Transcripts.

47. Federal civilian employment more or less doubled between Roosevelt's assumption of the presidency in 1933 and the start of preparation for war in 1940, whether the measure is for Washington, D.C. alone (from 70,261 to 139,770) or in total (from 603,587 to 1,042,420). The big jumps came during World War II—the numbers peaked at 284,665 in Washington in 1943 and 3.8 million nationally in 1945—and dropped sharply after the war, before resuming their climb in the 1950s. Federal employment in Washington stood at 325,900 in 2000, or 41,235 more

than the World War II peak. Total federal employment was 2.7 million. But these figures (counted slightly differently than in the 1930s and forties) mask the effects of "outsourcing" various government functions to the private sector. *Statistical Abstract of the USA* (Washington, D.C.: U.S. Census Bureau, 2000), pp. 355–357; *Historical Statistics, from Colonial Times to 1970,* part 2, (Washington, D.C.: U.S. Census Bureau, 1975); *The Fact Book: Federal Civilian Workforce Statistics* (Washington, D.C.: U.S. Office of Personnel Management, 2001), p. 8.

The proliferation of structure is more apparent in such measures as the number of subsecretaries of each cabinet department (typically one, two, or three at the start of World War II, compared to dozens today), size of the Office of the President, and size of congressional staffs.

Lowi, *The End of Liberalism,* p. 273.

48. For Rowe and Clifford, see Frantz and McKean, *Friends in High Places,* pp. 70–74; Alonzo L. Hamby, *Man of the People: A Life of Harry S. Truman* (New York: Oxford, 1995), pp. 430–431.

Thomas G. Corcoran to Lyndon B. Johnson, February 3, 1965, Corcoran Papers, Box 66.

For discussion of the New Deal's influence on Johnson's "War on Poverty," see chapter 11, this volume, and notes. The most nuanced discussion of competing influences is in Nicholas Lemann, *The Promised Land: The Great Black Migration and How It Changed America* (New York: Knopf, 1991), chapter 3, "Washington," pp. 111–221.

Ira Katznelson offers a concise review of scholarly discussions of the Great Society, and his own perspective, in "Was the Great Society a Missed Opportunity?" in Steve Fraser and Gary Gerstle, *The Rise and Fall of the New Deal Order* (Princeton: Princeton University Press, 1989), pp. 185–211.

3. Making the New Deal Revolution

1. Michael Straight, *After Long Silence* (New York: Norton, 1983), p. 200.

2. The "Governments can err" line was Raymond Moley's. Kenneth S. Davis, *The New Deal Years: 1933–1937* (New York: Random House, 1979), p. 637.

3. Eric Foner, *The Story of American Freedom* (New York: Norton, 1998), pp. 122–123; G. Edward White, *Justice Oliver Wendell Holmes: Law and the Inner Self* (New York: Oxford, 1993), pp. 324–328.

4. There are narrow and broad definitions of legal realism. I follow here the "generous" one laid out by William Fisher III, Morton J. Horowitz, and Thomas A. Reed in their introduction to their anthology *American Legal Realism* (New York: Oxford University Press, 1993), p. xiii.

Jerome Frank cited in Laura Kalman, *The Strange Career of Legal Liberalism* (New Haven: Yale University Press, 1996), p. 17.

5. Irons, *The New Deal Lawyers,* p. 7; Douglas, *Go East, Young Man,* p. 160.

6. Kalman, *The Strange Career of Legal Liberalism,* p. 17; Bruce Ackerman, *We the People: Transformations* (Cambridge: Harvard University Press, 1998), p. 417; Franklin D. Roosevelt, *The Public Papers and Addresses of Franklin D. Roosevelt: 1937 Volume, The Constitution Prevails,* ed. Samuel Rosenman (New York: Macmillan, 1941), pp. 125, 132.

7. G. Edward White, "Recapturing New Deal Lawyers," in *Intervention and Detachment: Essays in Legal Jurisprudence* (New York: Oxford, 1994), p. 189.

8. Edward Purcell, employing "a Holmesian metaphor," calls the line "the first cannon shot in his fifty-year battle against legalistic formalism." Edward A. Purcell Jr., *The Crisis of Democratic Theory: Scientific Naturalism and the Problem of Value* (Lexington: University Press of Kentucky, 1973), p. 76; Oliver Wendell Holmes Jr., *The Common Law* (Boston: Little, Brown, 1945), p. 1.

9. Robert Skidelsky, *John Maynard Keynes: The Economist as Savior, 1920–1937* (New York: Allen Lane/Penguin, 1992), pp. 482, 492; Schlesinger, *The Politics of Upheaval*, pp. 404–406.

10. The authoritative text on the New Dealers' response to the "Roosevelt Recession" of 1937–1938 is Alan Brinkley's *The End of Reform*. For the "Corcoran crowd," see ibid., p. 91; see also ibid. pp. 7–8, 129–130; Schwarz, *The New Dealers*, pp. 134–135. For Nixon as a Keynesian, see preface, note 1.

11. Robert Jerome Glennon, *The Iconoclast as Reformer: Jerome Frank's Impact on Modern American Law* (Ithaca: Cornell University Press, 1985), pp. 18–31; Thurman Arnold, "Judge Jerome Frank," *University of Chicago Law Review* 24:633; Schwarz, *The New Dealers*, pp. 177–183; G. Edward White, "Cardozo, Learned Hand, and Frank," in *Judicial Tradition: Profiles of Leading American Judges* (New York: Oxford, 1976), p. 273–275; Irons, *The New Deal Lawyers*, p. 119–122.

12. Jerome Frank, *Law and the Modern Mind* (New York: Coward-McCann, 1930), pp. 252, 253, 259; Glennon, *The Iconoclast as Reformer*, pp. 21, 47–51; Irons, *The New Deal Lawyers*, p. 121.

13. Laura Kalman, *Legal Realism at Yale: 1927–1960* (Chapel Hill: University of North Carolina Press, 1986), pp. 16, 19.

14. Schwarz, *The New Dealers*, pp. 159–162; Simon, *Independent Journey*, pp. 116–119.

15. Douglas, *Go East, Young Man*, pp. 167–168, 171–172. In his oral history my father offers a variation on the oft-repeated line about Arnold: "Douglas used to say, the drunker Thurman is, the more unbeatable he is in the courtroom." Eliot Janeway, oral history interview no. 1, April 2, 1986, p. 81, EJOH.

Arnold, having spent so many hours in merry pranks with Douglas, was on hand in 1959, just past midway through his friend's years on the bench, to celebrate him as the most notable judicial hell-raiser in American history:

"Two score years and seven hours ago (give or take an hour) our guest of honor . . . took his seat on the Supreme Court of the United States . . .

"I was present and the scene is etched in the tablet of my memory. [I remember the] Crier of the Supreme Court . . . saying immediately after Justice Douglas took his seat, 'God save the United States and this honorable Court . . . '

"A lesser man would have modified his prayer to make the relief demanded seem more reasonable. He would have said, 'In the event that both objectives seem impossible of accommodation in light of our new appointment, God save the United States *or* this honorable Court,' thus giving Providence its choice.

"But the Crier did not waiver. . . . He decided to go for broke."

Arnold to David Ginsburg, April 24, 1959 (with text of speech), in Thurman Arnold, *Voltaire and the Cowboy: The Letters of Thurman Arnold* (Boulder: Colorado Associated University Press, 1977), pp. 427–428.

16. Thurman Arnold, *The Folklore of Capitalism* (New Haven: Yale University Press, 1937), pp. 31–32, 118, 146–148, 357.

Laura Kalman notes the realists' use of modern linguistic theory: "The realists who read Ogden and Richards's *The Meaning of Meaning* learned that despite words' apparently fixed meaning, they could be understood only through an examination of their ever-changing contest. 'Negligence' as applied by one judge to a certain set of facts did not have precisely the same meaning as 'negligence' applied by another judge to a different set of facts." Kalman, *Legal Realism at Yale*, p. 19.

17. Abe Fortas, "Thurman Arnold and the Theatre of Law," *Yale Law Journal* 79(6):988–989; Janeway, *The Struggle for Survival*, p. 187–188.

18. Douglas taught Cuneo while still on the Columbia University Law School faculty, before moving to Yale.

Ernest Cuneo, "The Near-Presidency of William O. Douglas," pp. 4, 10, unpublished manuscript in Cuneo Papers, Box 18.

19. Simon, *Independent Journey*, pp. 110–111, 128–136; Murphy, *Wild Bill*, pp. 77–85, 95–104, 132–135; "Transcript of Remarks of SEC Chairman William O. Douglas," *Wall Street Journal*, September 23, 1937, p. 11; Schwarz, *The New Dealers*, p. 169; William O. Douglas, *Democracy and Finance* (New Haven: Yale University Press, 1940), pp. 10–11.

20. Kalman, *Legal Realism at Yale*, p. 28; Eliot Janeway, "Bill Douglas, Fighter," *Nation*, January 11, 1941, p. 49.

21. William O. Douglas to Eliot Janeway, November 12, 1959, Douglas Papers, Box 344; Douglas, *Go East, Young Man*, p. 290.

22. William O. Douglas to Ernest Cuneo, August 16, 1968, Cuneo Papers, Box 18.

23. Eliot Janeway, oral history interview no. 1, April 2, 1986, pp. 23–24, EJOH; Douglas, *Go East, Young Man*, p. 284.

24. Thurman Arnold, *Democracy and Free Enterprise* (Norman: University of Oklahoma Press, 1941), p. 37; Schwarz, *The New Dealers*, p. xi.

25. Michael K. Brown, *Race, Money, and the American Welfare State* (Ithaca: Cornell University Press, 1999), pp. 42–45, 61, 85–86; Paul E. Mertz, *New Deal Policy and Southern Rural Poverty* (Baton Rouge: Louisiana State University Press, 1978), pp. 47–51, 221–252.

For Roosevelt in 1938, see Mertz, *New Deal Policy and Southern Rural Poverty*, pp. 227 and 230.

James T. Patterson, *Congressional Conservatism and the New Deal: The Growth of the Conservative Coalition in Congress, 1933–1939* (Lexington: University of Kentucky, 1967), pp. 242–246.

26. Schwarz, *The New Dealers*, p. 247.

27. Lash, *Dealers and Dreamers*, pp. 139, 143, 388–389; Schwarz, *The New Dealers*, p. 182; Irons, *The New Deal Lawyers*, pp. 126–129; White, "Revisiting the New Deal Legal Generation," *Intervention and Detachment*, pp. 134–137, 190, 200, note 48.

28. Henry H. Adams, *Harry Hopkins: A Biography* (New York: Putnam, 1977), pp. 30–31; White, "Recapturing New Deal Lawyers," p. 190.

29. Kalman, *Abe Fortas*, pp. 8–9, 28, 43; White, "Revisiting the New Deal Legal Generation," p. 134, and "Recapturing New Deal Lawyers," 190.

30. Holmes told Corcoran, who read Adams's *The Education* and *Mont St. Michel and Chartres* to the justice in the 1920s, "You can't just sit outside and do nothing

but criticize. You've got to be down in the arena where you're working with the actual problems of government." Louchheim, *The Making of the New Deal*, Thomas Corcoran entry, p. 24.

White, "Revisiting the New Deal Legal Generation," pp. 136–137; Schlesinger, *The Crisis of the Old Order*, pp. 12–15; Ira Katznelson, "The Southern Origins of Our Time," unpublished MS, chapter 1, "Painting the New Deal, p. 28, quoted with permission of the author.

31. James A. Farley, *Jim Farley's Story: The Roosevelt Years* (New York: McGraw-Hill, 1948), p. 80.

32. White, "Cardozo, Learned Hand, and Frank," p. 273.

33. Purcell, *The Crisis of Democratic Theory*, p. 91; Louis Menand, *The Metaphysical Club: A Story of Ideas in America* (New York: Farrar, Straus and Giroux, 2001), p. 440.

34. The theologian was Francis Lucey, quoted in Kalman, *Legal Realism at Yale*, pp. 121, 267, note 101. See also Purcell, *The Crisis of Democratic Theory*, p. 92; Glennon, *The Iconoclast as Reformer*, pp. 57–59, 154–155; Thurman Arnold, "Free-Wheeling Among Ideas and Ideals," *Saturday Review*, June 22, 1945, p. 10; Arnold to Jerome Frank, June 18, 1945, in *Voltaire and the Cowboy*, p. 358; Frank to Arnold, June 25, 1945, Frank Papers, Box 46; Arnold, "Judge Jerome Frank," pp. 634–635.

35. Lowi, *The End of Liberalism*, pp. 62–63, 93, 313; Michael J. Sandel, *Democracy's Discontent: America in Search of a Public Philosophy* (Cambridge: Harvard University Press, 1996), pp. 43–44, 252, 262–266.

36. Oliver Wendell Holmes to Harold Laski, March 4, 1920, in Mark DeWolfe Howe, ed., *The Holmes-Laski Letters: The Correspondence of Mr. Justice Holmes and Harold J. Laski, 1916–1935* (Cambridge: Harvard University Press, 1953), p. 249; White, "Revisiting the New Deal Legal Generation," pp. 142–143.

37. Thomas G. Corcoran, memoir, "Credo," p. 25, Corcoran Papers.

4. The Fight for the Rooseveltian Succession

1. Edwin W. Pauley to Jonathan Daniels, forwarded to Daniels by Matthew J. Connelly, January 27, 1950, on the selection of Harry S. Truman for the 1944 Democratic vice presidential nomination, White House Confidential File, HSTL (hereafter Pauley Memorandum, HSTL), p. 7.

2. Simon, *Independent Journey*, pp. 17–26; Douglas, *Democracy and Finance*, pp. 10–11.

3. Douglas and Thomas E. Dewey became friends at Columbia Law School and considered opening a firm together. But Douglas claims he told Dewey the latter's ambitions for elective office made it a bad idea. Douglas, *Go East, Young Man*, pp. 150–153.

4. For Douglas and Richard Whitney, see Simon, *Independent Journey*, pp. 173–175, 184–188; Schwarz, *The New Dealers*, pp. 171–172; Douglas, *Go East, Young Man*, pp. 289–290; Louchheim, *The Making of the New Deal*, Milton V. Freeman entry, p. 143.

5. For the Roosevelt-Douglas relationship, see Simon, *Independent Journey*, pp. 220–221; Schwarz, *The New Dealers*, pp. 172–173; Douglas, *Go East, Young Man*, pp. 317–318, 330–342. Douglas's recollection of mixing FDR's martinis is in the second volume of his memoirs, *The Court Years*, p. 276.

6. William O. Douglas to Franklin D. Roosevelt, June 10, 1942, Roosevelt to Douglas, September 5, 1942, Douglas Papers, Box 368.

See also Simon, *Independent Journey*, p. 261; Schwarz, *The New Dealers*, p. 175; Douglas, *The Court Years*, pp. 267–269.

7. In *Go East, Young Man* Douglas states that the childhood illness was polio. Bruce Allen Murphy mounts a fairly persuasive case that this statement—suggesting a striking parallel with Franklin Roosevelt's life story, compounded by them sharing a physician—was a fabrication. Douglas, *Go East, Young Man*, pp. 31–33; Murphy, *Wild Bill*, pp. 280–286.

A measure of Douglas's problems with dependency is that in his memoirs he mentions a number of people who worked for his political advancement but not, in that connection, the key three cited in accounts by the many other participants in those efforts, and by historians and biographers—Ickes, Corcoran, and my father. See Douglas, *The Court Years*, pp. 281–283.

For Douglas's illnesses, fears, and treatment and for Dr. George Draper, see also Murphy, *Wild Bill*, pp. 58–66; Simon, *Independent Journey*, pp. 24–25, 119–123.

8. Simon, *Independent Journey*, p. 123.

9. In August 1940, after the Democratic National Convention, Roosevelt told Harold Ickes, "I kept turning over in my mind all who might be available [including] you and Wallace and Bill Douglas," as well as Cordell Hull and others. "I consulted various party leaders. They told me that Bill Douglas would not do because he was not well enough known. They said that you could not be nominated but that they could nominate Wallace, although they would have trouble in doing so. This is exactly what happened." Harold L. Ickes, *The Secret Diary of Harold Ickes: Volume 3, The Lowering Clouds, 1939–1941* (New York: Simon and Schuster, 1954), p. 285–286.

As financial markets reformers who collaborated with Douglas in his work at the SEC, James Forrestal and his even more influential Wall Street ally Paul Shields pushed Douglas's name for the vice presidential nomination in 1940 with James Farley. Ernest Cuneo, "The Near-Presidency of William O. Douglas," pp. 4, 10, unpublished manuscript in Cuneo Papers, Box 18.

For Douglas in 1944 and 1948 see Murphy, *Wild Bill*, pp. 212–232, 252–263; Simon, *Independent Journey*, pp. 259–266, 270–273.

10. Simon, *Independent Journey*, pp. 260–266; Henry A. Wallace, January 30, 1943, diary, vol. 12, p. 2253, COHC; H. G. Nicholas, ed., *Washington Dispatches, 1941–45: Weekly Political Reports from the British Embassy* (Chicago: University of Chicago Press, 1981), p. 369.

11. For the network of alliances and socializing, see Simon, *Independent Journey*, pp. 264–269; Schwarz, *The New Dealers*, pp. 173–175; Newman, *Hugo Black*, p. 374; Dallek, *Lone Star Rising*, pp. 162–163; Robert A. Caro, *The Years of Lyndon Johnson: The Path to Power* (New York: Knopf, 1983), pp. 449–451; Kalman, *Abe Fortas*, p. 100; Hoopes and Brinkley, *Driven Patriot*, pp. 115–117.

James V. Forrestal to Eliot Janeway, October 21, 1944, Forrestal Papers, Box 60; Janeway, "Bill Douglas, Fighter," *Nation*, January 11, 1941, pp. 48–50.

12. Douglas, *The Court Years*, pp. 277, 334.

13. Elizabeth Janeway, oral history interview no. 2, July 21, 1986, p. 8, EHJOH; William O. Douglas to Elizabeth and Eliot Janeway, May 3, 1943; Douglas Pa-

pers, Box 342; Janeway to James V. Forrestal, October 8, 1943, Forrestal Papers, Box 58.

14. Henry A. Wallace, January 30, 1943, diary, vol. 12, p. 2253, COHC; Nicholas, *Washington Dispatches*, p. 369.

15. Douglas's closest friend among the regulars was Senator Francis Maloney of Connecticut; Schwarz, *The New Dealers*, p. 175.

For summaries of Wallace's problems by 1944, see Freidel, *Franklin D. Roosevelt*, pp. 529–533; *Time*, July 24, 1944, pp. 15–16 and July 31, 1944, pp. 12–13. For a subsequent, acid critique of Wallace from the anticommunist left, see Dwight Macdonald, "A Note on Wallese," in *Memoirs of a Revolutionist* (New York: Meridian, 1958), pp. 298–301.

16. Comparing Roosevelt to his successor, Douglas wrote, "In August 1945 [Truman] dropped our atomic bombs on Hiroshima and Nagasaki—civilian targets. By that act he introduced America to the world in a new image—a modern Genghis Khan bent on ruthless destruction." Douglas, *The Court Years*, p. 286.

For the justice's views on Roosevelt, China, and Vietnam see Douglas, *Go East, Young Man*, p. 402.

For Douglas's foreign policy thinking in the 1940s and fifties, see also Simon, *Independent Journey*; pp. 10, 267–268.

See also Murphy, *Wild Bill*, pp. 232, 608, note. Murphy adds that Douglas's Supreme Court appointments would have been superior to Truman's.

17. Simon, *Independent Journey*, pp. 267–268; Murphy, *Wild Bill*, pp. 232, 608, note.

18. For the background to Roosevelt's vice presidential calculations in 1944, see Freidel, *Franklin D. Roosevelt*, pp. 529–537; James MacGregor Burns, *Roosevelt: The Soldier of Freedom* (New York: Harcourt Brace Jovanovich, 1970), pp. 503–507; Robert H. Ferrell, *Choosing Truman: The Democratic Convention of 1944* (Columbia: University of Missouri Press, 1994), pp. 1–11; David Robertson, *Sly and Able: A Political Biography of James F. Byrnes* (New York: Norton, 1994), pp. 342–348, 352; James F. Byrnes, *All in One Lifetime* (New York: Harper, 1958), p. 225.

Roosevelt was especially cautious in giving the pawns on the board anything but equivocal signals, as James F. Byrnes and Henry Wallace found to their dismay. Douglas himself wrote in his memoirs, "I learned that FDR had preferred that I run with him" only after the convention; "he had never broached the matter to me." Douglas, *The Court Years*, p. 283. And when the party leaders persuaded Truman that, behind all the maneuvering, he was the president's choice, the senator is supposed to have exclaimed, "Why the hell didn't he tell me in the first place?" Ferrell, *Choosing Truman*, p. 61.

19. For the tensions on the Supreme Court, see Simon, *Independent Journey*, pp. 257–262; Schwarz, *The New Dealers*, p. 175.

20. Freidel, *Franklin D. Roosevelt*, p. 529; Ferrell, *Choosing Truman*, pp. 19–20.

21. Freidel, *Franklin D. Roosevelt*, pp. 531, 535.

22. Harold L. Ickes, July 9, 1944, unpublished diary MS, Ickes Papers, LOC; henceforth diary, Ickes Papers.

See also Robertson, *Sly and Able*, pp. 346–348, 351, and especially 360; *Time*, July 24, 1944, pp. 15–16; Abe Fortas to William O. Douglas, July 25, 1944, Douglas Papers, Box 537.

23. Henry A. Wallace, September 15, 1943, diary, vol. 15, p. 2722, COHC.

24. Pauley Memorandum, pp. 6–9, HSTL.

Some of the participants recalled that Mayor Edward Kelly of Chicago argued for Douglas. Freidel, *Franklin D. Roosevelt*, p. 533.

25. Grace Tully, *F.D.R., My Boss* (New York: Scribners, 1949), pp. 275–277; Murphy, *Wild Bill*, pp. 212–232, 605–608, note. Murphy draws in part on Ferrell, *Choosing Truman*, pp. 81–85.

But Murphy is too impressed with what has emerged as fresh evidence from sources associated with Harry Truman, as against what remains unknown about a matter that has intrigued political insiders and historians for so many decades. He charges (p. 608) that "this story of the names being switched was created initially by Tommy Corcoran and Ernie Cuneo," assisted in its dissemination by my father, as a convention ploy.

But why would Corcoran have been so sure about the letter and its order from the start, and have risked being repudiated by Roosevelt himself in so public an arena, if he didn't have a basis for his version? Murphy's account fails to consider how Corcoran knew so early about so closely held a handwritten letter, which did in fact exist, and never mentions the fact that Corcoran was extremely close to Grace Tully (who had been Missy LeHand's deputy as presidential secretary and succeeded her) and in a position to have learned from her what the original (or *an* original) note said. A stitch of this intriguing bit of history is still missing.

See also Freidel, *Franklin D. Roosevelt*, p. 534; Hamby, *Man of the People*, pp. 280–281; Robertson, *Sly and Able*, pp. 348–363, and see p. 595, note 357; Ferrell, *Choosing Truman*, pp. 81–85; Simon, *Independent Journey*, p. 264; Pauley Memorandum, pp. 12–13, HSTL.

26. Simon, *Independent Journey*, pp. 264–266; Robertson, *Sly and Able*, pp. 358–361; Pauley Memorandum, p. 13, HSTL.

27. Harold L. Ickes, June 10, 1944, July 16, 1944, July 23, 1944, diary, Ickes Papers.

Thomas G. Corcoran, memoir, "Truman Years" chapter, p. 6, Corcoran Papers. For on-the-scene speculation about Corcoran's role, see, for example, "Missourian Is Expected to Get Runner-Up Spot on Second Ballot," *Chicago Daily News*, July 20, 1944, p. 1.

See also Francis Maloney to William O. Douglas, July 10, 1944; Eliot Janeway to Douglas, July 11, 1944; Janeway to Douglas, August 4, 1944; Abe Fortas to Douglas, July 25, 1944; all in Douglas Papers, Box 537; Ernest Cuneo, "The Story of the Non-Election of a President in 1944," unpublished MS in Cuneo Papers, Box 18.

For Johnson's role, see Dallek, *Lone Star Rising*, p. 262; and Thomas G. Corcoran to Lyndon B. Johnson, January 5, 1964, Corcoran Papers, Box 66.

28. Francis Maloney to William O. Douglas, July 10, 1944, Douglas Papers, Box 537.

29. Eliot Janeway to William O. Douglas, July 11, 1944, Douglas Papers, Box 537.

30. William O. Douglas to Francis Maloney, July 14, 1944, Douglas Papers, Box 537.

31. Murphy, *Wild Bill*, p. 227.

32. Eliot Janeway, oral history interview no. 1, April 2, 1986, p. 64–65, EJOH.

33. Harold L. Ickes, July 23, 1944, diary, Ickes Papers.

34. Abe Fortas to William O. Douglas, July 25, 1944; Eliot Janeway to Douglas, August 4, 1944; both in Douglas Papers, Box 537; Robertson, *Sly and Able*, pp. 352–354; Ferrell, *Choosing Truman*, pp. 44–46.

35. "Kelly Offers Name of Lucas Amid Uproar," *Chicago Daily News*, July 21, 1944, p. 1; "Truman Winner Before Illinois Swings to Him," *Chicago Tribune*, July 22, 1944, p. 2.

36. Robert H. Ferrell's carefully researched *Choosing Truman: The Democratic Convention of 1944* stakes out a relatively benign view of Roosevelt in 1944. He finds the idea that FDR was setting up Byrnes as well as Wallace as straw men so he could slip other candidates through the middle "an intriguing explanation," but one that "credits the president with far more farsightedness and decisiveness than surely was the case." Yet some of Ferrell's own contributions to the record suggest that this is just what Roosevelt was doing—see, for example, Ferrell's account of Roosevelt's backhanded treatment of and private references to Wallace in the spring of 1944. Ibid., pp. 19–22. In any case, Ferrell's basic premise is that Truman's nomination was essentially inevitable after July 11 and that the effort on Douglas's behalf in particular was "marginal." Ibid. p. 105, note 56; p. 121, note 44.

In *Franklin D. Roosevelt: A Rendezvous with Destiny* the late Frank Freidel provides an alternative view of the "gusto and effectiveness" with which FDR played his cards in the 1944 "vice presidential poker game," even though this opened him "to charges that he had been a treacherous, aged tyrant lopping off the heads" of lesser players. Ibid., p. 531. David Robertson's research for *Sly and Able: A Biography of James F. Byrnes*, and Alonzo L. Hamby's for *Man of the People* also support the thesis that Roosevelt's design was sinuous.

37. Pauley Memorandum, pp. 14–16, HSTL.

38. Francis Maloney to William O. Douglas, July 27 1944, Douglas Papers, Box 537.

39. Eliot Janeway to William O. Douglas, August 4, 1944, Douglas Papers, Box 537.

40. Ibid.

41. Ibid.

42. "How the Bosses Did It," *Time*, July 31, 1944, p. 12; Eliot Janeway to William O. Douglas, August 4, 1944, Douglas Papers, Box 537; Janeway, oral history interview no. 1, April 2, 1986, pp. 65, EJOH. See also Murphy, *Wild Bill*, pp. 227–228.

43. Eliot Janeway to William O. Douglas, August 4, 1944, Douglas Papers, Box 537.

The proposition that FDR wanted a stalemate is supported by his endorsement of Mayor Kelly's "favorite son" tactic.

44. Pauley Memorandum, pp. 15–17, HSTL; Ferrell, *Choosing Truman*, pp. 85–88; Robertson, *Sly and Able*, pp. 357–363.

For Hopkins's remark, see Simon, *Independent Journey*, pp. 264.

45. Lash, *Dealers and Dreamers*, p. 281; Thomas G. Corcoran, unpublished memoir, "Truman Years" chapter, pp. 4–7, Corcoran Papers.

See also Eliot Janeway, "Birth of the Tickets," *Fortune*, September 1944, pp. 126–133.

46. Abe Fortas to William O. Douglas, July 25, 1944, Douglas Papers, Box 537.

47. Francis Maloney to William O. Douglas, July 27, 1944; Maloney to Douglas, August 17, 1944, Douglas Papers; Box 537.

48. Eliot Janeway to William Douglas, August 4, 1944; Janeway to Douglas, August 9, 1944; George Killion to Douglas, August 1, 1944; all in Douglas Papers, Box 537.

Defending the Roosevelt interests in Texas and their own congressional seats as well from heavy attack by state conservatives, neither Sam Rayburn nor Lyndon Johnson attended the convention, though Johnson had been given special administrative credentials for it. Corcoran claimed subsequently that, from Texas, Johnson worked for both Douglas and Rayburn as the vice presidential nominees. Dallek, *Lone Star Rising*, p. 262; Thomas G. Corcoran to Lyndon B. Johnson, January 5, 1964, Corcoran Papers, Box 66.

49. Freidel, *Franklin D. Roosevelt*, pp. 530–535.

50. Eliot Janeway to William O. Douglas, August 4, 1944, Douglas Papers, Box 537.

Freidel, *Franklin D. Roosevelt*, p. 535; Harold L. Ickes, October 7, 1944, diary, Ickes Papers; Douglas, *The Court Years*, p. 283.

51. I. F. Stone, "The Plot Against Wallace," *Nation*, July 1, 1944, pp. 7–8.

52. These friends sometimes exchanged quasi-psychiatric readings on each other. In the spring of 1945 my father wrote Douglas an account of James Forrestal's ambivalence about running for the Senate from New York, concluding wryly, "Do you think Freud more pertinent to our times than Marx?" Eliot Janeway to William O. Douglas, March 19, 1945, Douglas Papers, Box 342.

For Douglas on Forrestal, see Douglas, *Go East, Young Man*, pp. 287–289. See also James V. Forrestal, *The Forrestal Diaries*, ed. Walter Millis (New York: Viking, 1951), pp. 130, 134; Hoopes and Brinkley, *Driven Patriot*, pp. 115, 435–436, 440.

53. Janeway, "Birth of the Tickets."

54. Jerome Frank wrote to my mother that season that, according to his "hard-boiled" style, my father "won't admit that any man in public life has any disinterestedness—except Bill and (maybe) me." Jerome Frank to Elizabeth Janeway, June 14, 1944, Frank Papers, Box 57; Eliot Janeway to William O. Douglas, August 4, 1944, Douglas Papers, Box 537.

55. Schwarz, *The New Dealers*, pp. 167–174.

56. Henry A. Wallace, August 17, 1943, diary, vol. 15, p. 2624, COHC.

57. Eliot Janeway to William O. Douglas, August 4, 1944, Douglas Papers, Box 537; Janeway to Thomas G. Corcoran, July 26, 1945, Corcoran Wiretap Transcripts.

58. Thomas G. Corcoran to unidentified man, August 20, 1945, Corcoran Wiretap Transcripts.

59. Thomas G. Corcoran to Eliot Janeway, September 13, 1945, Corcoran Wiretap Transcripts.

60. William O. Douglas to Thomas G. Corcoran, February 15, 1946, Corcoran Wiretap Transcripts.

Simon, *Independent Journey*, pp. 268–269; Kalman, *Abe Fortas*, 116–121; Robert J. Donovan, *Conflict and Crisis: The Presidency of Harry S Truman, 1945–1948* (New York: Norton, 1977), pp. 178–184.

61. Thomas G. Corcoran to Lyndon B. Johnson, February 15, 1946; Ernest Cuneo to Corcoran, February 16, 1946; Corcoran Wiretap Transcripts.

For more on the plan whereby Douglas would have been given a political role well beyond the boundaries of the Interior Department, see Cuneo to Corcoran, February 17, 1946; Fred Vinson to Corcoran, February 21, 1946; Corcoran Wiretap Transcripts.

62. Ernest Cuneo to Thomas G. Corcoran, February 16, 1946; Cuneo to Corcoran, February 17, 1946, Corcoran Wiretap Transcripts.

Simon, *Independent Journey*, pp. 269–270.

Fred Vinson to Corcoran, February 21, 1946; Lyndon B. Johnson to Corcoran, February 21, 1946; James V. Forrestal to Corcoran, February 21, 1946; all in Corcoran Wiretap Transcripts.

63. Douglas, *The Court Years*, p. 288.

64. Thomas G. Corcoran to Harold Ickes, September 13, 1946, Corcoran Wiretap Transcripts.

65. Abe Fortas to William O. Douglas, August 18, 1947; Douglas to Fortas, August 23, 1947; Fortas Papers, Box 107.

Bert Andrews, "Douglas Civil-Liberties Speech Leads to Political Speculation," *New York Herald Tribune*, January 4, 1948, p. 28.

66. Truman's remark is quoted in Simon, *Independent Journey*, p. 272.

See also Douglas, *The Court Years*, p. 288; Simon, *Independent Journey*, pp. 266–275; Schwarz, *The New Dealers*, p. 175; Hamby, *Man of the People*, p. 449.

67. Eliot Janeway, oral history interview no. 1, April 2, 1986, p. 83; interview no. 7, January 9, 1987, pp. 2–3, EJOH; Murphy, *Wild Bill*, pp. 258–259. For Douglas's version of these calls, see Douglas, *The Court Years*, pp. 289–290, and Simon, *Independent Journey*, pp. 273–274.

68. Thomas Corcoran to William O. Douglas, July 20, 1948, Corcoran Papers, Box 125; Simon, *Independent Journey*, p. 274; Donovan, *Conflict and Crisis*, p. 405.

69. James Rowe Jr. to William O. Douglas, June 17, 1948, Douglas Papers, Box 537; Schwarz, *The New Dealers*, p. 176; Simon, *Independent Journey*, pp. 14, 358; Newman, *Hugo Black*, pp. 427, 435–436; Lucas A. Powe Jr., *The Warren Court and American Politics* (Cambridge: Harvard University Press, 2000), pp. 89, 98.

For Murphy quoting my father as his source for the alleged end of the Douglas-Corcoran relationship and the 1978 reunion, see Murphy, *Wild Bill*, pp. 298, 626, note; 503–504, 671, note. But for the continuity of the association in fact, see Corcoran to Douglas, April 27, 1954; Douglas to Corcoran, October 21, 1954; Corcoran to Douglas, May 29, 1956; Douglas to Board of Admissions, University Club, June 4, 1956; Douglas to Corcoran December 28, 1957; Douglas to Corcoran, June 26, 1958; all in Douglas Papers, Box 317; and Corcoran to Douglas, May 15, 1957; Corcoran to Mercedes Douglas, May 31, 1957 (that is the letter that remarks on their talk following Corcoran's operation); Corcoran Papers, Box 56.

For Douglas on Corcoran in his memoirs, see Douglas, *The Court Years*, p. 260.

For Corcoran on the Douglas divorce settlement and Douglas on the Court, see Corcoran, "Summary of our conversation this morning" (interviewer unknown), October 30, (1979?), pp. 3–4, Book Draft files, Corcoran Papers, Box 589.

70. Thomas G. Corcoran to Abe Fortas, August 31, 1945, Corcoran Wiretap Transcripts.

5. 1945—The New Dealers' Government-in-Exile

1. Woodrow Wilson, *The New Freedom: A Call for the Emancipation of the Generous Energies of a People*, ed. William Bayard Hale (New York: Doubleday, 1913), pp. 200–202; Kalman, *Abe Fortas*, p. 19.

2. Alpheus Thomas Mason, *Brandeis: A Free Man's Life* (New York: Viking, 1946), p. 585; Brinkley, *The End of Reform*, p. 114.

3. Rodgers, *Atlantic Crossings*, pp. 421, 436; Brinkley, *The End of Reform*, p. 44; Schwarz, *The New Dealers*, p. 152.

4. Hardeman and Bacon, *Sam Rayburn*, pp. 297–300; Thomas G. Corcoran to Eliot Janeway, December 4, 1945, Corcoran Wiretap Transcripts.

5. Robert E. Sherwood, *Roosevelt and Hopkins: An Intimate History* (New York: Harper, 1948), pp. 102–103; Freidel, *Franklin D. Roosevelt*, p. 285.

6. Kalman, *Abe Fortas*, pp. 125–126, 152; Thurman Arnold to J. R. Sullivan, June 26, 1945, in Arnold, *Voltaire and the Cowboy*, p. 358.

7. Frantz and McKean, *Friends in High Places*, pp. 96, 104–112, 121–122.

8. Fortas, "Thurman Arnold and the Theatre of Law," pp. 992, 996; Kalman, *Abe Fortas*, pp. 125–151, 153.

9. Thurman Arnold to Elizabeth Toll, March 17, 1952, in Arnold, *Voltaire and the Cowboy*, pp. 398–399.

10. Kalman, *Abe Fortas*, pp. 153, 166–177.

11. Ibid., pp. 161, 209–210, 216 ff., 293 ff.

12. Harold L. Ickes, February 24, 1946, diary, Ickes Papers; Kalman, *Abe Fortas*, p. 120.

13. For example, a 1966 note from Fortas to Johnson makes sport of Fortas's rival for Johnson's legal business, Edwin L. Weisl Sr. Kalman, *Abe Fortas*, p. 317.

14. Rowe began kicking Johnson in the shins for accommodating himself to conservative opinion in Texas as early as 1943; Dallek, *Lone Star Rising*, pp. 257, 368, 587.

See chapter 10, this volume, p. 177, and note 36, for Rowe's confrontation with Johnson about his treatment of staff.

15. William O. Douglas to Lyndon B. Johnson, August 21, 1961, Johnson to Douglas, September 8, 1961, Douglas Papers, Box 346; Douglas to Lyndon B. Johnson, August 12, 1967, in William O. Douglas, *The Douglas Letters: Selections from the Private Papers of Justice William O. Douglas*, ed. Melvin I. Urofsky (Bethesda: Adler and Adler, 1987), p. 250; Douglas, *The Court Years*, pp. 319–329; Simon, *Independent Journey*, p. 419.

16. Eliot Janeway to Lyndon B. Johnson, March 24, 1958; Johnson to Janeway, March 26, 1958; Johnson Papers, Selected Names, Box 20, LBJL; Hobart Taylor Jr. to Lyndon B. Johnson, October 29, 1965, enclosing Vartanig G. Vartan, "Monetary Shift Is Held Lagging," *New York Times*, October 23, 1965; Henry J. Fowler to Lyndon B. Johnson, August 27, 1965; Fowler to Johnson, January 25, 1966, Johnson Papers, WHCF Name File, Box 43.

Eliot Janeway, *The Economics of Crisis: War, Politics, and the Dollar* (New York: Weybright and Talley, 1968), pp. 280–286, 299–301; Clark Clifford, with Richard Holbrooke, *Counsel to the President: A Memoir* (New York: Random House, 1991), pp. 448–449.

17. Kalman, *Abe Fortas*, pp. 203–205.

18. Douglas, *The Court Years*, p. 337; Kalman, *Abe Fortas*, p. 293; Eliot Janeway, oral history interview no. 1, April 2, 1986, p. 92; EJOH.

19. Frantz and McKean, *Friends in High Places*, pp. 105–108.

20. Eliot Janeway, oral history interview no. 3, May 16, 1986, p. 44.

21. Ed Hart to Thomas G. Corcoran, July 10, 1945, Corcoran Wiretap Transcripts.

22. Lister Hill to Thomas G. Corcoran, July 12, 1945, Corcoran Wiretap Transcripts.

23. Thomas G. Corcoran to Edward F. Prichard Jr., Corcoran to Abe Fortas, August 20, 1945, Corcoran Wiretap Transcripts.

24. Stephen Schlesinger and Stephen Kinzer, *Bitter Fruit: The Untold Story of the*

American Coup in Guatemala (New York: Anchor-Doubleday, 1983), pp. 90–94, 102; Peter Grose, *Gentleman Spy: The Life of Allen Dulles* (Boston: Houghton Mifflin, 1994), pp. 371, 375.

25. "The Popping Cork," *Time*, May 30, 1960, pp. 72–74; "The Witness," *Newsweek*, May 30, 1960, p. 50.

26. Kai Bird and Max Holland, "The Tapping of 'Tommy the Cork,'" *Nation*, February 8, 1946, cover and pp. 142–144; Donovan, *Conflict and Crisis*, pp. 29–30, 183; Harvey Klehr and Ronald Radosh, *The Amerasia Spy Case: Prelude to McCarthyism* (Chapel Hill: University of North Carolina Press, 1996), pp. 111–112.

27. Hamby, *Man of the People*, pp. 256–257; Schwarz, *The New Dealers*, p. 316; Alvah Johnston, "The Saga of Tommy the Cork" (Part 2), *Saturday Evening Post*, October 20, 1945, p. 24 ff.; Niznik, "Thomas G. Corcoran," pp. 550–556; Janeway, *Struggle for Survival*, pp. 249–250.

28. Thomas G. Corcoran, memoir, "Credo," p. 18, Corcoran Papers; Niznik, "Thomas G. Corcoran," pp. 535–544, 556–559; Barbara Tuchman, *Stillwell and the American Experience in China, 1911–1945* (New York: Macmillan, 1971), pp. 220–221; Klehr and Radosh, *The Amerasia Spy Case*, pp. 114, 125; William P. Bundy, *A Tangled Web: The Making of Foreign Policy in the Nixon Presidency* (New York: Hill and Wang, 1998), pp. 45, 549, note 73, 550, note 85, 595, note 36.

29. Biddle, *In Brief Authority*, pp. 355–358; Harold L. Ickes, July 16, 1944 and July 23, 1944, diary, Ickes Papers; T. H. Watkins, *Righteous Pilgrim: The Life and Times of Harold Ickes, 1974–1952* (New York: Holt, 1990), p. 812.

30. Thomas G. Corcoran to Lister Hill, June 9, 1945; Hill to Corcoran, December 15, 1945; Corcoran Wiretap Transcripts.

31. Niznik, "Thomas G. Corcoran," p. 347; Tracey E. Danese, *Claude Pepper and Ed Ball: Politics, Purpose, and Power* (Gainesville: University Press of Florida, 2000), pp. 49–50; Schlesinger and Kinzer, *Bitter Fruit*, pp. 91–92; Thomas G. Corcoran to Lyndon B. Johnson, Nov. 30, 1961, Corcoran Papers, Box 66.

32. Klehr and Radosh, *The Amerasia Spy Case*, is the invaluable authority for Corcoran's and Service's interaction. See especially pp. 111–128, 215.

33. Robertson, *Sly and Able*, p. 443.

34. Lauchlin Currie to Thomas G. Corcoran, June 11, 1945, Corcoran Wiretap Transcripts.

35. Benjamin V. Cohen to Thomas G. Corcoran, June 14, 1945, Corcoran Wiretap Transcripts.

36. Klehr and Radosh, *The Amerasia Spy Case*, p. 122; Benjamin V. Cohen to Thomas G. Corcoran, July 4, 1945, Corcoran Wiretap Transcripts.

37. See, for example, Thomas G. Corcoran to Lister Hill, June 9, 1945; Lauchlin Currie to Corcoran, June 11, 1945; Ernest Cuneo to Corcoran, June 17, 1945; Irving Brant to Corcoran, June 19, 1945; Ed Hart to Corcoran, Corcoran to Charles Halleck, Corcoran to William Pawley, Joe (blank, probably J. Anthony Panuch) to Corcoran, July 10, 1945; Eliot Janeway to Corcoran, July 26, 1945; Corcoran to Edward F. Prichard Jr., August 20, 1945; all in Corcoran Wiretap Transcripts.

38. Schwarz, *The New Dealers*, p. 308.

39. Simon, *Independent Journey*, p. 274; Donovan, *Conflict and Crisis*, p. 405.

40. Drew Pearson to Thomas G. Corcoran, June 11, 1946, Corcoran Wiretap Transcripts.

41. Thomas G. Corcoran to Edward F. Prichard Jr., June 28, 1945, Corcoran Wiretap Transcripts.

42. Archbishop Francis Spellman to Thomas G. Corcoran, November 16, 1945; Corcoran to Abe Fortas (about a conversation with Attorney General Tom Clark), August 31, 1945; Bernard Baruch to Corcoran, September 24, 1946; Corcoran to J. Anthony Panuch, November 18, 1945; Corcoran Wiretap Transcripts.

43. Thomas G. Corcoran to Lister Hill, June 9, 1945, Corcoran Wiretap Transcripts.

44. Thomas G. Corcoran to Lister Hill, June 9, 1945, Corcoran Wiretap Transcripts.

45. Farley, *Jim Farley's Story*, pp. 80, 183, 238–239; Edward J. Flynn, *You're the Boss* (New York: Viking, 1947), pp. 150–151.

46. Burns, *Roosevelt: The Soldier of Freedom*, pp. 274–277, 510–513; Goodwin, *No Ordinary Time*, pp. 525, 526; Schwarz, *The New Dealers*, pp. 142–153; Brinkley, *The End of Reform*, pp. 145–146; Sam Rosenman, *Working with Roosevelt* (New York: Harper, 1952), pp. 463–470.

47. Lister Hill to Thomas G. Corcoran, July 12, 1945; Fred Vinson to Corcoran, February 21, 1946, Corcoran Wiretap Transcripts.

48. Fred Vinson to Thomas G. Corcoran (and Benjamin V. Cohen), February 21, 1946, Corcoran Wiretap Transcripts; Niznik, "Thomas G. Corcoran," pp. 250–251; Schlesinger, *The Politics of Upheaval*, pp. 595–596; Burns, *Roosevelt: The Lion and the Fox*, p. 436.

49. Thomas G. Corcoran to William Mahon (the transcript refers to him incorrectly as "William McMahon"), June 11, 1945; Corcoran to Ernest Cuneo, June 28, 1945; Eliot Janeway to Corcoran, Aug. 12, 1945, Corcoran Wiretap Transcripts.

50. Thomas G. Corcoran to Eliot Janeway, Dec. 4, 1945; James V. Forrestal to Corcoran, April 13, 1946; Corcoran Wiretap Transcripts; Hoopes and Brinkley, *Driven Patriot*, p. 240.

51. Ernest Cuneo to Thomas G. Corcoran, April 7, 1946, Corcoran Wiretap Transcripts.

52. Thomas G. Corcoran to George Killion, September 30, 1945, Corcoran Wiretap Transcripts.

53. Thomas G. Corcoran to Lister Hill, December 13, 1945; Corcoran to Ernest Cuneo, December 29, 1945; Corcoran Wiretap Transcripts.

54. C. P. Trussell, "Truman Calls on Public to Spur Congress to Act in Labor Crisis; Packers May Be Seized in Strike," *New York Times*, January 4, 1946, p. 1; Thomas G. Corcoran to Lister Hill, January 5, 1946, Corcoran Wiretap Transcripts.

55. Thomas G. Corcoran to Lister Hill, August 13, 1946; Corcoran to Worth Clark, August 13, 1946, Corcoran Wiretap Transcripts; "Ex-Senator La Follette Ends Life with a Gun in Washington," *New York Times*, February 25, 1953, p. 1; "'Young Bob' Followed Family's Political Steps," *Milwaukee Journal*, February 25, 1953, p. 12; Warren Unna, "Ex-Sen. La Follette, Crusader, Dies at Fifty-eight," *Washington Post*, February 25, 1953, p. 22.

56. Robert La Follette to Thomas G. Corcoran, August 14, 1946; William O. Douglas to Corcoran, August 18, 1946, Corcoran Wiretap Transcripts.

57. Thomas G. Corcoran to Worth Clark, August 14, 1946, Corcoran Wiretap Transcripts. Corcoran also held that President Truman and Democratic National Chairman Robert Hannegan contributed to the debacle by short-sightedly trying first to persuade La Follette to become a Democrat, and directing crossover ballot

efforts toward his defeat when he refused. Their reasoning, according to Corcoran, was that with the independently popular La Follette out of the picture an organization Democrat could be elected in November. Thomas G. Corcoran, memoir, "Truman Years" chapter, pp. 8–11, Corcoran Papers.

58. Drew Pearson to Thomas G. Corcoran, June 11, 1946; Corcoran Wiretap Transcripts.

59. Lash, *Dealers and Dreamers*, pp. 56–59 ff.; Brinkley, *The End of Reform*, pp. 50–55; Louchheim, *The Making of the New Deal*, Joseph L. Rauh Jr. entry, p. 63; Schwarz, *The New Dealers*, pp. 127–128, 140, 146, 154; Glennon, *Iconoclast as Reformer*, p. 103.

60. Simon, *Independent Journey*, pp. 217–219; Newman, *Hugo Black*, p. 322; Roger Newman, notes from interviews with Eliot Janeway, May 17, 1987, May 29, 1991, quoted with permission of the interviewer.

61. Lash, *Dealers and Dreamers*, pp. 448–450; Schwarz, *The New Dealers*, p. 154; Simon, *Independent Journey*, pp. 203–215; Newman, *Hugo Black*, p. 322; Niznik, "Thomas G. Corcoran," pp. 525–530; *Roosevelt and Frankfurter: Their Correspondence, 1928–1945*, ed. Max Freedman (Boston: Atlantic-Little, Brown, 1967), pp. 577–578; Davis, *FDR: The War President*, p. 330, Roger Newman, notes from interviews with Eliot Janeway, May 17, 1987 and May 29, 1991.

62. Alvah Johnston, "The Saga of Tommy the Cork" (Part 2), *Saturday Evening Post*, October 20, 1945, p. 24 ff.; Burns, *Roosevelt: The Soldier of Freedom*, pp. 38–39, 193; Louchheim, *The Making of the New Deal*, Joseph L. Rauh Jr. entry, pp. 63–64, 67, and Edward F. Prichard Jr. entry, pp. 69–62; Arthur M. Schlesinger Jr., *A Life in the Twentieth Century: Innocent Beginnings, 1917–1950* (Boston: Houghton Mifflin, 2000), p. 420; Simon, *Independent Journey*, p. 217; Thomas G. Corcoran to unidentified man, August 20, 1945, Corcoran Wiretap Transcripts.

63. Janeway, *The Struggle for Survival*, p. 140; Henry L. Stimson and McGeorge Bundy, *On Active Service in Peace and War* (New York: Harper, 1947), p. 334.

64. Goodwin, *No Ordinary Time*, pp. 86–88, 351; Sherwood, *Roosevelt and Hopkins*, p. 475; Douglas, *Go East, Young Man*, p. 337; Burns, *Roosevelt: Soldier of Freedom*, p. 194.

65. William O. Douglas to John Frank, November 18, 1958, in Douglas, *The Douglas Letters*, p. 93; Douglas, *Go East, Young Man*, pp. 331–332.

66. Louchheim, *The Making of the New Deal*, Edward F. Prichard Jr. entry, pp. 68–69, 73; Dean G. Acheson to Richard Goodwin, August 14, 1957, quoted in James Chace, *Acheson* (New York: Simon and Schuster, 1998), p. 74.

67. The Prichard-Frankfurter transcripts are archived with the Corcoran Wiretap Transcripts at HSTL. See also unsigned FBI Memorandum for the President and his Naval Aide Re: Possible Sources of Information in Drew Pearson's column of June 12, 1945, relating to the Hopkins-Stalin Conferences, August 17, 1945, in Corcoran Wiretap Transcripts.

68. Edward F. Prichard Jr. to Felix Frankfurter, June 2, 1945, Corcoran Wiretap Transcripts.

69. Thomas G. Corcoran to J. Anthony Panuch, November 18, 1945, Corcoran Wiretap Transcripts.

70. Thomas G. Corcoran to Edward F. Prichard Jr., June 28, 1945, Corcoran Wiretap Transcripts; Lash, *Dealers and Dreamers*, p. 447; Ernest Cuneo to Corcoran, March 23, 1946, Corcoran Wiretap Transcripts.
See also Edward F. Prichard Jr. to Felix Frankfurter, June 2, 1945; Corcoran Wiretap Transcripts.

71. Eliot Janeway to Henry R. Luce, April 24, 1946, Janeway Memoranda File, Time, Inc. Archives; Schlesinger, *A Life in the Twentieth Century*, p. 423.

72. Simon, *Independent Journey*, pp. 216–221; Louchheim, *The Making of the New Deal*, Edward F. Prichard Jr. entry, pp. 69–72; Drew Pearson to Thomas G. Corcoran, June 11, 1946, Corcoran Wiretap Transcripts.

73. Newman, *Hugo Black*, pp. 340–341; Milton R. Konvitz, "Will Nuremberg Serve Justice?" *Commentary*, January 1946, pp. 9–15; Douglas, *The Court Years*, pp. 28–29.

74. Black, according to his biographer, preferred his colleagues Douglas or Stanley Reed as chief justice. Newman, *Hugo Black*, pp. 321–322, 341–346; Douglas, *The Court Years*, pp. 28–31.

75. Drew Pearson to Thomas G. Corcoran, June 11, 1946, Corcoran Wiretap Transcripts.

76. Frankfurter, Ben Cohen, and James Rowe all had a hand in drafting this letter, for reasons ranging from manipulation in Frankfurter's case to a desire to protect Corcoran in Cohen's and Rowe's. Felix Frankfurter Memorandum for the President, January 8, 1941, in Freedman, *Roosevelt and Frankfurter*, pp. 577–578; James Rowe Jr. to Missy LeHand, January 14, 1941, Rowe Papers, Box 10; Niznik, "Thomas G. Corcoran," pp. 516–517.

77. Niznik, "Thomas G. Corcoran," pp. 520–535; Lash, *Dealers and Dreamers*, pp. 448–450; Schwarz, *The New Dealers*, pp. 153–155; Douglas, *Go East, Young Man*, p. 369; Hoopes and Brinkley, *Driven Patriot*, pp. 129–130.

78. Kalman, *Abe Fortas*, pp. 205–206; Frantz and McKean, *Friends in High Places*, p. 4; Douglas, *The Court Years*, pp. 187–188.

79. Thomas G. Corcoran to Lister Hill, June 9, 1945, Corcoran Wiretap Transcripts; Joseph Alsop with Adam Platt, *I've Seen the Best of It: Memoirs* (New York: Norton, 1992), p. 129.

80. Thoughtful critical treatments of the New Deal legacy include many sections of Schwarz, *The New Dealers*, but especially chapter 14 and the afterword, pp. 297–350; Brinkley, *The End of Reform*, pp. 265–271; and G. Edward White, "Recapturing New Deal Lawyers," in *Intervention and Detachment*, pp. 175–195.

81. Thomas G. Corcoran to William O. Douglas, August 1, 1948, enclosing unsigned, undated memorandum probably authored by Corcoran or his law partner James Rowe Jr., Corcoran Papers, Box 125.

6. Rise of an Insider

1. John Chamberlain, *A Life with the Printed Word* (Chicago: Regnery, 1982), pp. 42–43.

2. Eliot Janeway, oral history interview no. 1, April 2, 1986, pp. 4–7, 87–88, EJOH.

Tawney and Laski were on the London School of Economics faculties in those years. John Atkinson Hobson held no university position. Isaac Kramnick and Barry Sheerman, *Harold Laski: A Life on the Left* (New York and London: Allen Lane/Penguin, 1993), pp. 248, 320; Skidelsky, *Keynes: The Economist as Savior*, pp. 697. For a portrait of John Cornford, see Peter Stansky and William Abrahams, *Journey to the Frontier* (Boston: Atlantic-Little, Brown, 1966), pp. 188–200.

3. Eliot Janeway, oral history interview no. 1, April 2, 1986, p. 4, EJOH.

4. Chamberlain, *A Life with the Printed Word*, p. 43; Eliot Janeway, oral history interview no. 1, April 2, 1986, p. 12, 15–17, EJOH.

5. Eliot Janeway, "We Arm the Dictators," *Nation*, February 4, 1939; "The Price Boom," *Nation*, April 10, 1937; "How Industry Hides Its Profits," *Nation*, April 16, 1938, pp. 432–434.

6. Eliot Janeway, oral history interview no. 1, April 2, 1986, p. 19, EJOH.

For the "Roosevelt Recession" of 1937–1938 as a "capitalist strike," see Brinkley, *The End of Reform*, pp. 56–58.

7. Eliot Janeway to Jerome Frank, May 24, 1938, June 17, 1938, June 23, 1938; Frank to Janeway, September 12, 1938; Frank Papers, Box 30; Janeway, oral history interview no. 1, April 2, 1986, pp. 19–20, EJOH.

8. Jerome Frank to Eliot Janeway, July 12, 1938; Frank to Thomas G. Corcoran, December 7, 1938; Lauchlin Currie to Frank, December 15, 1938; Janeway to Frank, February 9, 1939; Janeway to Frank, February 14, 1939; Janeway to Frank, May 31, 1939; Janeway to Frank, June 22, 1939; Frank to Janeway, October 22, 1945; all in Frank Papers, Boxes 24, 30, 31, and 57.

Frank to Paul Appleby, September 8, 1939; Appleby to Frank, September 18, 1939; Frank Papers, Box 41.

Janeway to William O. Douglas, December 26, 1940, Douglas Papers, Box 343.

9. Jerome Frank to Eliot Janeway, August 26, 1939, Frank Papers, Box 30; Thomas G. Corcoran to Eliot Janeway, June 14, 1939; Corcoran Papers, Box 202; Jerome Frank to William O. Douglas, November 1, 1940, Douglas Papers, Box 329; Ickes, *Secret Diaries*, vol. 3, pp. 531, 533.

10. Eliot Janeway, oral history interview no. 1, April 2, 1986, pp. 20–21, EJOH.

11. Herzstein, *Henry R. Luce*, pp. 229, 263.

12. Henry R. Luce to Eliot Janeway, December 16, 1941; Janeway to Luce, November 19, 1943; all in Time, Inc. Archives, Janeway File.

On meetings between Luce and New Dealers, see Janeway to Luce, December 16, 1939, Time, Inc. Archives, Janeway File; Janeway to Jerome Frank, December 12, 1939; Janeway to Frank, February 16, 1940; Frank Papers, Boxes 30 and 31; Harold L. Ickes, April 10, 1943, diary, Ickes Papers.

13. Russell Davenport to Henry R. Luce, January 9, 1940, Time, Inc. Archives, Janeway File; Wendell Willkie to Luce, January 11, 1940; Eliot Janeway to Luce and Davenport, January 11, 1940; Time, Inc. Archives, Willkie File.

Janeway to Jerome Frank, April 13, 1940, Frank Papers, Box 31.

14. Undated memorandum (apparently 1942, "The registrant is Special Assistant to Henry R. Luce"), Time, Inc. Archives, Janeway File.

15. Rexford G. Tugwell, April 25, 1941, diary, Tugwell Papers, Box 32.

16. Hoopes and Brinkley, *Driven Patriot*, pp. 20, 53, 61, 62; Eliot Janeway to James V. Forrestal, September 12, 1940, and subsequent correspondence, Forrestal Papers, Boxes 53, 58, 60, 63, 74, 80.

17. Dallek, *Lone Star Rising*, pp. 161–162; Caro, *Path to Power*, pp. 449–451.

18. Janeway, *The Struggle for Survival*, pp. 220–229; Eliot Janeway, oral history interview no. 1, April 2, 1986, pp. 49–52, EJOH; Douglas, *Go East, Young Man*, p. 392; Lichtenstein, *The Most Dangerous Man in Detroit*, pp. 165, 171, 478, notes 25, 41, p. 497, note 49.

19. Newman, *Hugo Black*, pp. 307, 676, note 6; Eliot Janeway, oral history interview no. 1, April 2, 1986, p. 72, EJOH; "Independents Join to Back Roosevelt," *New York Times*, September 25, 1940, p. 1.

In National Committee of Independent Voters for Roosevelt and Wallace Papers, FDRL, see D. M. Spiegel to David Niles, October 18, 1940, David K. Niles File, Container 4; Janeway to Nelson Poynter and Tom Gerber, November 1, 1940, Speech Materials Files, Container 14; Janeway, oral history interview no. 1, April 2, 1986, p. 21–22, EJOH.

20. Allen Grover to Henry R. Luce, October 5, 1941, Time, Inc. Archives, Janeway File.

21. Ickes, *Secret Diaries*, vol. 3, pp. 531, 533.

Lewis Dabney to Thomas G. Corcoran, May 5, 1941; Corcoran to Dabney, May 23, 1941, Corcoran Papers, Box 66; Caro, *Path to Power*, pp. 683, 686; Dallek, *Lone Star Rising*, p. 216.

22. Tugwell, *The Stricken Land*, pp. 319, 326.

23. Kalman, *Abe Fortas*, pp. 100, 104, 109; Eliot Janeway, oral history interview no. 1, April 2, 1986, pp. 86, EJOH; Harold L. Ickes, April 10, 1943, diary, Ickes Papers.

24. Thomas G. Corcoran, memoir, "Truman Years" chapter, p. 21, Corcoran Papers; Bird and Holland, "The Tapping of 'Tommy the Cork,'" pp. 142–145.

Eliot Janeway to Corcoran, August 12, 1945; Janeway to Corcoran; August 23, 1945; Corcoran to Janeway, September 13, 1945; Corcoran to Janeway, December 4, 1945; all in Corcoran Wiretap Transcripts.

25. Alvin Wirtz to Eliot Janeway, January 4, 1946, Correspondence between Eliot Janeway and Alvin Wirtz, 1943–1946, Janeway Papers, LBJL.

My father's newspaper purchase explorations seem to have been premised on the idea of building a New Deal publishing group or chain. See Thomas G. Corcoran to Eliot Janeway, September 13, 1945, Corcoran Wiretap Transcripts; Janeway to William O. Douglas, August 3, 1945; Janeway to Palmer Hoyt, September 17, 1945 and March 30, 1946; all in Douglas Papers, Box 342; Abe Fortas to Douglas, August 6, 1945, Douglas Papers, Box 328.

For Forrestal, Luce, and Janeway see Hoopes and Brinkley, *Driven Patriot*, pp. 239–240. For Forrestal's speculations about running for office or becoming a publisher, see Corcoran to Janeway, September 13, 1945; Corcoran to Janeway, December 4, 1945, Corcoran Wiretap Transcripts; and Janeway to Douglas, March 19, 1945, Douglas Papers, Box 342.

26. Robert Skidelsky discusses Marxian rhetoric in "What's Left of Marx?" a review of Francis Wheen, *Karl Marx: A Life* (New York: Norton, 2000) in the *New York Review of Books*, November 16, 2000, p. 25.

Janeway, *The Economics of Crisis*, p. 24.

27. Elizabeth Janeway, oral history interview no. 1, June 14, 1986, pp. 41, 45, EHJOH.

28. Ibid., p. 29; "Columbia Students Press Anti-War Row," *New York Times*, May 28, 1935.

29. William Du Bois, "Old Maid and Married Sister," *New York Times Book Review*, October 17, 1943, p. 1; "Recent Fiction," *Time*, November 19, 1945, p. 106.

30. Time, Inc. (unsigned) to Eliot Janeway, July 17, 1944; Henry R. Luce to Janeway, August 9, 1945, Time, Inc. Archives, Janeway File.

31. My father, wrote the state's top political reporter, was "an aggressive personality who is well acquainted with the art of setting lures and traps in political maneuvering." Jack Zaiman, *Hartford Courant*, October 6, 1948.

Joseph I. Lieberman, *The Power Broker: A Biography of John M. Bailey* (Boston: Houghton, Mifflin, 1966), pp. 96–97; Eliot Janeway, oral history interview no. 1, April 2, 1986, pp. 75–77, EJOH.

32. *Bridgeport Post*, October 2, 1948; Eliot Janeway to Peter Maas, October 5, 1948, Both in Douglas Papers, Box 343. The late writer Peter Maas, son of friends of my parents, was my father's aide in the campaign.

See also Janeway, oral history interview no. 1, April 2, 1986, p. 79, EJOH.

33. Eliot Janeway, oral history interview no. 1, April 2, 1986, p. 41, EJOH.

Ralph G. Martin cites my father as the source for his crediting of a Clare Booth Luce–Lyndon Johnson liaison, *Henry and Clare: An Intimate Portrait of the Luces* (New York: Putnam, 1991), p. 389.

34. For a variation on the subject of FDR's treatment of Missy LeHand after she became ill, see Goodwin, *No Ordinary Time*, pp. 246, 336, 399–400, 536.

35. Elizabeth Janeway, oral history interview no. 2, July 21, 1986, p. 23, EHJOH; Eliot Janeway, oral history interview no. 1, April 2, 1986, p. 65, EJOH.

The 1941 occasion in my parents' story is recorded in a photo in the Roosevelt Library photographic archives dated August 31, 1941, Hyde Park File. See Figure 11, following p. 182.

36. Elizabeth Janeway, oral history interview no. 2, July 21, 1986, pp. 12–13, EHJOH.

37. For Corcoran's 1940 campaign role, see "Independents Join to Back Roosevelt," *New York Times*, September 25, 1940, p. 1; Niznik, "Thomas G. Corcoran," pp. 505–511; Eliot Janeway, oral history interview no. 1, April 2, 1986, p. 72, EJOH.

38. Davis, *FDR: Into the Storm*, pp. 616–617; Freidel, *Franklin D. Roosevelt*, pp. 353–354; Ferrell, *Choosing Truman*, pp. 16–17.

William O. Douglas to Ernest Cuneo, April 8, 1976, Cuneo Papers, Box 18; Douglas, *Go East, Young Man*, pp. 338–339.

39. Eliot Janeway, oral history interview no. 1, April 2, 1986, p. 72–73, EJOH.

40. Direction of the mutual deterrence whereby Henry Wallace's "Guru Letters" and the Willkie–Irita Van Doren liaison were suppressed came from the top. An early version of the Johnson and Nixon White House taping systems recorded FDR speaking to one of his aides on the subject in late August 1940: "*Now, now*, if they want to play dirty politics in the end, we've got our own people" who could assist in disseminating "this story about that *gal* that is spreading around the country." ("Awful nice gal," FDR added chivalrously.) Davis, *FDR: Into the Storm*, pp. 616–617; Freidel, *Franklin D. Roosevelt*, pp. 353–354.

A few weeks earlier Rexford Tugwell wrote in his diary: "Dinner with Eliot Janeway. Norman Thomas there. . . . Some interesting comments on Wendell Willkie's situation. His relationship with Irita Van Doren was amusingly told by Janeway who said that in Philadelphia when it was clear that Willkie would be nominated Mrs. Ogden Reid [wife of the publisher of the *New York Herald Tribune*] was observed supporting Irita to a washroom, she holding her head and moaning, 'Now I must give him up.'" Tugwell, July 25, 1940, diary, Tugwell Papers, Box 32.

For the La Guardia incident, see Thomas Kessner, *Fiorello H. La Guardia: The Making of Modern New York* (New York: McGraw-Hill, 1989), p. 481; "La Guardia Seizes a Detroit Heckler Who Asks if 'Boss Flynn' Controls Him," *New York Times*, October 22, 1940, p. 1; "Butch Is Tough, Heckler Learns," *New York Daily News*, October 22, 1940, p. 2.

41. Eliot Janeway, oral history interview no. 3, May 16, 1986, p. 10, EJOH.

42. Elizabeth Janeway, oral history interview no. 2, July 21, 1986, p. 21, EHJOH; Goodwin, *No Ordinary Time*, p. 17.

43. Eliot Janeway, oral history interview no. 1, April 2, 1986, pp. 73–74, EJOH. For Miriam Hopkins at the time see "A Lady of Courage," *New York Times*, June 20, 1943, p. 1, Sunday Arts section.

Willkie met with Henry Luce and my father several times. Russell Davenport to Luce, January 9, 1940, Time, Inc. Archives, Janeway File; and Janeway to Jerome Frank, April 13, 1940, Frank Papers, Box 31.

44. Author to William O. Douglas, April 1945, Douglas Papers, Box 342.

45. For John Hersey's version of Agee and Hobson at a vintage Time, Inc. staff party, see his introduction to James Agee and Walker Evans, *Let Us Now Praise Famous Men* (Boston: Houghton Mifflin, 1988), pp. vi–vii. This piece is also collected in John Hersey, *Life Sketches* (New York: Knopf, 1989), pp. 42–75.

With high irony, Agee also uses Roosevelt's "You are farmers" rhetoric in his text, p. 115.

46. Abe Burrows, *Honest Abe: Is There Really No Business Like Show Business?* (Boston: Atlantic Monthly Press/Little, Brown, 1980), pp. 26–32.

47. Eliot Janeway, oral history interview no. 4, June 27, 1986, pp. 5, 11, 31, EJOH.

48. Eliot Janeway to Lyndon Johnson, March 24, 1958; Johnson to Janeway, March 26, 1958; LBJ Archives Selected Names, Box 20, Eliot Janeway File, LBJL.

49. Eliot Janeway, oral history interview no. 8, April 2, 1988, p. 17, EJOH.

7. *Ends and Means*

1. Eliot Janeway to Thomas G. Corcoran, August 12, 1945, Corcoran Wiretap Transcripts.

2. Steve Neal, *Dark Horse: A Biography of Wendell Willkie* (New York: Doubleday, 1984), pp. 222–229; Eliot Janeway, oral history interview no. 4, June 27, 1986, pp. 4–6, EJOH.

3. Eliot Janeway, "Ideas of the Future," *Saturday Review of Literature*, August 21, 1948, p. 15.

4. Theodore H. White, *The Making of the President 1960* (New York: Atheneum, 1961), p. 45.

5. William O. Douglas to Jerome Frank, September 1, 1941, Frank Papers, Box 52.

See also Elizabeth Janeway to Jerome Frank, September 10, 1942, critiquing a long draft of Frank's second or third appeal to the president: "I would write three lines saying something like: 'When are you going to put Bill Douglas in? We all think he is the last hope of the New Deal. He is getting a mighty good press. The country needs a slugger.' Jerome, you have been writing too damn many briefs." Frank Papers, Box 57.

6. Janeway, *Struggle for Survival*, p. 361.

7. Eliot Janeway, "Roosevelt vs. Hitler: The U.S. Wages World Diplomatic War," *Life*, May 5, 1941, pp. 100–110; Rexford G. Tugwell, April 25, 1941, May 2, 1941, May 6, 1941, diary, Tugwell Papers, Box 32.

8. Eliot Janeway, "Roosevelt: The Master of Politics," *Life*, April 30, 1945, pp. 84–92.

9. Elizabeth Janeway, *The Question of Gregory* (New York: Doubleday, 1949), p. 245.

10. Drawing on New Deal securities industry regulation, Reuther also called on General Motors to open its books in order to demonstrate that it could well afford wage increases without price increases.

Eliot Janeway to Walter P. Reuther, February 20, 1946; Reuther to Janeway, July 15, 1946; Elizabeth Janeway to Reuther, January 13, 1947; Reuther to Elizabeth and Eliot Janeway, January 22, 1947; all in Reuther Papers, Box 101.

See also Lichtenstein, *The Most Dangerous Man in Detroit*, pp. 228–231, 237, 246–247, 497, note 49; Janeway to Harold Stassen, January 14, 1946; Janeway to Stassen, January 22, 1946, in Douglas Papers, Box 342; Janeway, oral history interview no. 1, April 2, 1986 , p. 88–91, EJOH.

11. Eliot Janeway to Walter P. Reuther, February 20, 1946, Reuther Papers, Box 101.

12. James Allen to Eliot Janeway, March 30, 1948, Janeway Papers, LOC.

13. Janeway, oral history interview no. 1, April 2, 1986, p. 35–36, EJOH; Janeway, *The Economics of Crisis*, p. 317; Hoopes and Brinkley, *Driven Patriot*, pp. 456, 464–465.

14. Thomas G. Corcoran, memoir, "Truman Years" chapter, p. 13, Corcoran Papers.

15. "'Young Bob' Followed Family's Political Steps," *Milwaukee Journal*, February 25, 1953, p. 12; Warren Unna, "Ex-Sen. La Follette, Crusader, Dies at Fifty-eight," *Washington Post*, February 25, 1953, p. 22; Schlesinger and Kinzer, *Bitter Fruit*, pp. 91–92; Grose, *Gentleman Spy*, p. 371.

16. "Margaret Corcoran, Twenty-eight, Dies," *Washington Post*, January 10, 1970, p. B8.

17. Janeway, *The Question of Gregory*, pp. 42–43.

18. Elizabeth Janeway, preface to *Leaving Home* (New York: Feminist Press, 1987), p. 3.

19. William O. Douglas to Elizabeth Janeway, May 16, 1959, Douglas Papers, Box 344; James V. Forrestal to Elizabeth Janeway, October 20, 1943, Box 58, Forrestal Papers; Lyndon B. Johnson to Eliot Janeway, February 8, 1946, Johnson Papers, Selected Names, Box 20, LBJL.

Johnson wrote my mother in 1949, "Lady Bird started reading [*The Question of Gregory*] immediately . . . sitting up nearly all night to finish it. . . . I remember so well that I read [*Daisy Kenyon*] in the same manner—without being able to put it down." Johnson to Elizabeth Janeway, September 6, 1949, Personal Papers of Michael C. and Eliot Janeway, LBJL, hereafter Janeway Papers.

20. Jerome Frank to Elizabeth Janeway, June 14, 1944, Frank Papers, Box 57; Elizabeth Janeway to Henry R. Luce, March, 1946, Time, Inc. Archives, Janeway File.

21. "Donald Cook, Ex-Chairman of SEC, Dies at Seventy-two," *New York Times*, December 17, 1981, D23.

8. *Forbidden Version*

1. "Carol Janeway's Tiles Have Fanciful Design," *Life*, July 23, 1945, pp. 13–14; "Renting Is Different in the Village . . ." *New York Post*, December 13, 1955, p. 3.

2. Cornell University registrar records.

3. Ronald Steel, *Walter Lippmann and the American Century* (Boston: Atlantic–Little, Brown, 1980), pp. 186–196.

A rare exception to my father's avoidance of Jewish-related subjects was an unusual memo to Henry Luce, after he ceased working full-time for Time, Inc. and began his consulting relationship with the publisher, cautioning Luce about *Time's* coverage of the Jews' postwar effort to create a homeland in the Middle East: "One rap *TIME* effectively beat was the once-prevalent impression that it was anti-semitic (remember [former foreign editor Laird] Goldsborough's famous [phrasing] 'Jew Litvinov'). I'm afraid that failure to call signals has caused a recurrence of this impression." Eliot Janeway to Henry R. Luce, July 9, 1946, Time, Inc. Archives, Janeway Memoranda File.

4. Some details in this account I learned only years later from research conducted by my cousin Joyce (Janeway) Mittenthal of Bingham Farms, Michigan, into the Jacobstein, Jankelvitz, and Siff family lines.

5. Lenora (Siff) Borker Kurzweil to Joyce Mittenthal, December 26, 1986, copy in author's possession.

6. Irving Howe, *World of Our Fathers* (New York: Simon and Schuster, 1976), pp. 252–253.

7. Joyce Mittenthal to author, December 15, 1996, in author's possession; Nancy Schoenburg and Stuart Schoenburg, *Lithuanian Jewish Communities* (New York: Garland, 1991), pp. 265–268, 271–277, 471.

8. Ibid., pp. 265–266, 271–274. Other spellings are Sakiai for Shaki, Siauliai for Shavli. Both were ravaged again and again in the nineteenth and twentieth centuries, especially by the retreating Russian army during World War I.

9. For Cornford at that time, see Abrahams and Stansky, *Journey to the Frontier*, pp. 188–200.

Vivid descriptions of Duranty as "the unofficial social host of Moscow" for visiting Westerners, and of their experiences of the early purge trials and other Soviet intrigues in his company, are found in S. J. Taylor, *Stalin's Apologist: Walter Duranty, The New York Times Man in Moscow* (New York: Oxford, 1990), pp. 146, 150–153, 174–176. See also Whitman Bassow, *The Moscow Correspondents: Reporting on Russia from the Revolution to Glasnost* (New York: Morrow, 1988), pp. 59–62, 70–72.

I have a vivid memory of such asides by my father. An approximation of them appears in Eliot Janeway, oral history interview no. 1, April 2, 1986, pp. 9, 87–88, EJOH.

10. Eliot Janeway master file no. 40–2712, Federal Bureau of Investigation, obtained through FOIA, in author's possession; hereafter Janeway master file, FBI.

11. Eliot Janeway, oral history interview no. 1, April 2, 1986, pp. 5–6. 11, EJOH; Skidelsky, *Keynes: The Economist as Savior*, p. 481.

12. J. Edgar Hoover to Marvin Watson, November 3, 1965, summarizing 1941 reports, in Janeway master file, FBI.

An unredacted version of the FBI's 1965 installment in the file is found in Marvin Watson to Lyndon B. Johnson, November 5, 1965, and J. Edgar Hoover to Marvin Watson, November 3, 1965, Johnson Papers, office files of Mildred Stegall, Box 280; hereafter J. Edgar Hoover to Marvin Watson, November 3, 1965, Johnson Papers. See chapter 11, this volume, p. 200, and note 56.

For Serge Dimanov's role, see Daniel Aaron, *Writers on the Left* (New York: Harcourt, Brace and World, 1961), pp. 135, 220.

13. J. Edgar Hoover to Marvin Watson, November 3, 1965, Johnson Papers. The strongly pro-Communist journalist Anna Louise Strong was editor of the *Moscow Daily News* at that time; Bassow, *The Moscow Correspondents*, p. 311.

14. J. Edgar Hoover to Marvin Watson, November 3, 1965, Johnson Papers; Eliot Janeway, oral history interview no. 1, April 2, 1986, pp. 10, EJOH.

15. "Bert Williams" to "Bill Rust," Autumn 1933, April 26, 1934, Russian Center for the Preservation and Study of Documents of Recent History.

16. Eliot Janeway, oral history interview no. 1, April 2, 1986, pp. 10, EJOH; memorandum on Eliot Janeway, December 19, 1961, Janeway master file, FBI.

17. J. Edgar Hoover to Marvin Watson, November 3, 1965, Johnson Papers; Janeway, oral history interview no. 1, April 2, 1986, pp. 13, EJOH; "Org. Commission CC, CPUSA" to Communist Party, Great Britain, April 26, 1934, Russian Storage and Research Center for Documents in Research History.

For the role of the American League Against War and Fascism as a Communist front in the 1930s, see Irving Howe and Lewis Coser, *The American Communist Party: A Critical History* (New York: Praeger, 1962), pp. 348–355; Earl Latham, *The Communist Controversy in Washington: From the New Deal to McCarthy* (Cambridge: Harvard University Press, 1966), pp. 66–71; Harvey Klehr, *The Heyday of American Communism: The Depression Decade* (New York: Basic, 1984), pp. 106–112.

18. Eliot Janeway, oral history interview no. 1, April 2, 1986, pp. 13, EJOH; Klehr, *The Heyday of American Communism*, p. 341; E. Lapin to "Comrade Sherman," Russian Center for the Preservation and Study of Documents of Recent History. This document was made available to me by Prof. Harvey Klehr and the publisher of much of his and his fellow scholars' work, the Yale University Press.

19. Chamberlain, *A Life with the Printed Word*, and Sam Tannenhaus, *Whitaker Chambers* (New York: Random House, 1997) are two of the many memoirs and biographies that provide insight into these writers and editors in relation to one another, and to Time, Inc. and other news organizations for which they worked. James R. Mellow, *Walker Evans* (New York: Basic, 1999) conveys the eclectic range of that milieu, from journalism to the arts to politics.

20. Eliot Janeway, oral history interview no. 1, April 2, 1986, p. 28; Roger J. Sandilands, *The Life and Political Economy of Lauchlin Currie* (Durham: Duke University Press, 1990), p. 96; John Earl Haynes and Harvey Klehr, *Venona: Decoding Soviet Espionage in America* (New Haven: Yale University Press, 1999), pp. 145–146.

21. Describing Currie, my father wrote Luce in a background memo preparatory to the dinner at which they were to meet, "The phrase, A passion for anonymity, was built around him. . . . Despairs because FDR is dogmatically his own expert, because this means he is swayed by most convenient policy of the moment. Endorses crack for which I demand credit: FDR never thinks about business until the market goes down 20 points, then fixes it up in two months, then forgets about it again." Eliot Janeway to Henry R. Luce, December 16, 1939, Time, Inc. Archives, Janeway File.

See also Janeway on Currie in the former's "Roosevelt vs. Hitler," *Life*, May 5, 1941, p. 100.

See also Janeway to Jerome Frank, November 1938; Janeway to Barrow Lyons,

February 14, 1939; Janeway to Frank, May 31, 1939; Janeway to Frank (telegram), June 22, 1939; all in Frank Papers, Boxes 30 and 31. For plans to bring the New Dealers together with Luce see Janeway to Frank, December 12, 1939; Janeway to Frank, February 23, 1940; Frank Papers, Box 31.

22. Klehr and Radosh, *The Amerasia Spy Case*, pp. 125–126. See also Lauchlin Currie to Thomas G. Corcoran, June 11, 1945, Corcoran Wiretap Transcripts.

Chambers first named Currie, along with Alger Hiss and others, in a meeting with Assistant Secretary of State Adolf Berle in September 1939. See Tannenhaus, *Whitaker Chambers*, pp. 161–162; Haynes and Klehr, *Venona*, pp. 90–92, 146–150; Allen Weinstein and Alexander Vassiliev, *The Haunted Wood* (New York: Random House, 1999), pp. 48, 143, 161, 163, 243, 358, note 27.

23. Sandilands, *The Life and Political Economy of Lauchlin Currie*, pp. 148–156; Haynes and Klehr, *Venona*, 146–150; Weinstein and Vassiliev, *The Haunted Wood*, pp. 159, 161, 163.

24. Robert Skidelsky, *John Maynard Keynes: Fighting for Freedom, 1937–1946* (New York: Viking, 2001), p. 240; Eliot Janeway to Jerome Frank, "Friday Morning" (apparently the first week of November 1938); Frank to Janeway, November 9, 1938, Eliot and Robert Janeway to Frank, December 2, 1938 (my father enlisted his brother Robert, then an engineer at Chrysler, in analysis of automotive and railroad industry trends); Janeway to Frank, December 20, 1938; all in Frank Papers, Box 30.

25. David Rees, *Harry Dexter White: A Study in Paradox* (New York: Coward, McCann and Geoghegan, 1973), pp. 83–84, 196–197, 202; Latham, *The Communist Controversy in Washington*, pp. 167–170; Haynes and Klehr, *Venona*, pp. 138–145; Weinstein and Vassiliev, *The Haunted Wood*, pp. 157–169, 265–267, 358, note 41.

26. Rees, *Harry Dexter White*, p. 317; Skidelsky, *John Maynard Keynes:*, p. 241–242; Sandilands, *The Life and Political Economy of Lauchlin Currie*, pp. 86–92.

27. Ibid.

Harold L. Ickes, April 10, 1943, diary, Ickes Papers; Eliot Janeway, oral history interview no. 1, April 2, 1986, p. 23, Herzstein, *Henry R. Luce*, p. 260.

28. My mother's character Kermit Bishop in her novel *Leaving Home*, reminiscent of my father when young, is a precociously important Treasury official on the eve of World War II—White's deputy, it would seem—in the thick of the intrigue of aiding the allies out of sight of the isolationists. Elizabeth Janeway, *Leaving Home* (New York: Doubleday, 1953), pp. 175–176.

For the Treasury's role and White's in aid to the allies, see Freidel, *Franklin D. Roosevelt*, p. 326; Rees, *Harry Dexter White*, pp. 73–75, 98–100. For Currie's role, see Sandilands, *The Life and Political Economy of Lauchlin Currie*, pp. 107–113; For Corcoran's role, see Lash, *Dealers and Dreamers*, pp. 461–462; and Thomas G. Corcoran, memoir, preface, p. 3, "Credo," p. 18, Corcoran Papers.

29. Rees, *Harry Dexter White*, pp. 83, 424–426; Walter Goodman, *The Committee* (New York: Farrar, Straus and Giroux, 1968), p. 252; Haynes and Klehr, *Venona*, pp. 139, 411, note 49.

30. Rees, *Harry Dexter White*, pp. 83, 424–426; Haynes and Klehr, *Venona*, pp. 138–145; Weinstein and Vassiliev, *The Haunted Wood*, pp. 157–169, 265–267, 358, note 41.

31. Sandilands, *The Life and Political Economy of Lauchlin Currie*, p. 149.

Walter Goodman wrote that Currie "seemed to suffer from a sneaking respect for the Communists around him, an emotion that the Communists managed to make use of." Goodman, *The Committee*, p. 252.

For Currie and KGB traffic, see Haynes and Klehr, *Venona*, pp. 146–147; Weinstein and Vassiliev, *The Haunted Wood*, p. 163.

32. Robert Dallek, *Franklin D. Roosevelt and American Foreign Policy, 1932–1945* (New York: Oxford, 1979), pp. 433–434; Louis Adamic, *Dinner at the White House* (New York: Harper, 1946), pp. 67–68; Skidelsky, *Keynes: Fighting for Freedom*, p. 242.

33. Eliot Janeway, oral history interview no. 1, April 2, 1986, p. 19, EJOH.

Far Eastern Survey, a publication of the Institute of Pacific Relations (IPR), published a series of reports by my father in 1938, all in-depth economic analyses of strategic commodities issues, critical of Japanese aggressive designs. See, for example, Eliot Janeway, "Japanese Purchases in the American Economy," *Far Eastern Survey*, June 4, 1938. pp. 121–128. The FBI took notice because of IPR's Communist associations (discussed by Klehr and Radosh, *The Amerasia Spy Case*, pp. 38–39, 151, 168–169). A. H. Belmont and F. J. Baumgardner, memorandum on Eliot Janeway, August 1, 1952, Janeway master file, FBI.

34. Rexford G. Tugwell, April 25, 1941, diary, Tugwell Papers, Box 32; B. E. Sackett to T. J. Donegan, May 23, 1941, in Janeway master file, FBI.

35. P. E. Foxworth, Memorandum for the Director, July 21, 1941; T. J. Donegan, Internal Security report on Eliot Janeway, July 22, 1941; both in Janeway master file, FBI.

36. A. H. Belmont to F. J. Baumgardner, August 1, 1952 summarizing Eliot Janeway investigations to date; and S. S. Alden to Mr. Ladd, February 16, 1942, citing Hoover memorandum dated July 23, 1941, both in Janeway master file, FBI.

For Cuneo's role see Janeway, oral history interview no. 1, April 2, 1986, p. 59–60, EJOH; Douglas, *Go East, Young Man*, p. 426.

Drew Pearson, *Diaries, 1949–1959*, ed. Tyler Abell (New York: Holt, Rinehart and Winston, 1974), also describes Cuneo's continuing influence; see note 46 to this chapter.

37. J. Edgar Hoover, handwritten note accompanying formal directive to continue the investigation, Hoover to T. J. Donegan, July 25, 1941; Hoover to Cyde Tolson, E. A. Tamm, P. E. Foxworth, July 23, 1941; Janeway master file, FBI.

38. P. E. Foxworth, "Memorandum for the Director," July 24, 1941, Janeway master file, FBI.

39. S. S. Alden to Mr. Ladd, February 16, 1942; J. Edgar Hoover to San Francisco Special Agent in Charge Vincent, October 2, 1945; J. Edgar Hoover to Harold Stassen, July 9, 1947, covering July 7, 1947, report on "Eliot Janeway, also known as Eliot Jacobson"; "Memorandum on Eliot Janeway, also known as Eliot Jacobsen, Jacolstein, Max Lehman," December 19, 1961, all in Janeway master file, FBI.

40. Eliot Janeway to Henry R. Luce, January 29, 1947, Time, Inc. Archives, Janeway Memoranda File.

41. Eliot Janeway to Henry R. Luce, January 29, 1947, Time, Inc. Archives, Janeway Memoranda File.

His sources were J. Anthony Panuch, a former aide to William O. Douglas and key State Department official who was at odds with undersecretary Dean Acheson over the handling of the Hiss case; and probably Cuneo and Corcoran too, for they all talked to each other about these disputes as they evolved. See Thomas G.

Corcoran to J. Anthony Panuch, November 18, 1945; Ernest Cuneo to Corcoran, March 23, 1946; Corcoran to Panuch, September 23, 1946; all in Corcoran Wiretap Transcripts. For Panuch's role, see "Mr. Secretary and the Hot Seat," *Newsweek*, March 20, 1950, pp. 21–22.

Hiss's boss in his first New Deal position, at the Agricultural Adjustment Administration, was Jerome Frank. Frank and others under his direction (including Lee Pressman) were fired in 1935 in a policy dispute; Hiss kept his job in circumstances that led Frank to question Hiss's character. As the Hiss-Chambers dispute came to trial in 1949, Hiss and his lawyers (and Hiss's sponsor from the start, Justice Felix Frankfurter) asked Frank to appear as a character witness for him.

In my father's version of the story, Frank called my parents in distress over what to do, and finally told Hiss's lawyers that the only testimony he could give would not help their client. Frank also refused to supply a written character reference. Janeway, oral history interview no. 1, April 2, 1986, pp. 37–38, oral history interview no. 6, October 31, 1986, p. 16–17, EJOH.

See also Glennon, *Iconoclast as Reformer*, p. 36; *The Reminiscences of Jerome Frank* (1960), pp. 186–189, COHL; Allen Weinstein, *Perjury: The Hiss-Chambers Case* (New York: Knopf, 1978), pp. 154–155, 168, 447.

For the issue of payments to White, see Haynes and Klehr, *Venona*, p. 141; Weinstein and Vassiliev, *The Haunted Wood*, p. 44.

For my father's, and Chambers's other Time, Inc. colleagues' view of him, see Eliot Janeway, oral history interview no. 1, April 2, 1986, p. 38–40; Tannenhaus, *Whitaker Chambers*, pp. 172–173, 208–209.

42. Eliot Janeway, oral history interview no. 1, April 2, 1986, pp. 44–45, oral history interview no. 6, October 31, 1986, p. 12–13, EJOH.

My father was in contact with Lee Pressman in part, yet again, through Jerome Frank. But the fact that Pressman and my father were both products of New York Jewish families who attended Cornell and became active in New York City Communist circles may have brought them together earlier. Janeway to Frank, October 30, 1938, Frank Papers, Box 30.

For accounts of Lee Pressman's career and Communist involvement see Schlesinger, *The Coming of the New Deal*, pp. 50–54; Howe and Coser, *American Communist Party*, pp. 374–375; Klehr, *The Heyday of American Communism*, pp. 229, 250–251; Lash, *Dealers and Dreamers*, pp. 218, 326; John J. Abt, with Michael Myerson, *Advocate and Activist* (Urbana and Chicago: University of Illinois Press, 1993), pp. 173–175.

For a fascinating impressionistic version, see Hope Hale Davis, *Great Day Coming* (South Royalton, Vt.: Steerforth, 1994), pp. 46, 98, 110, 138.

43. Haynes and Klehr, *Venona*, pp. 152–157; Weinstein and Vassiliev, *The Haunted Wood*, pp. 72–83; Straight, *After Long Silence*, p. 200.

44. William Phillips to Eliot Janeway, October 15, 1958; Janeway to Walter Jenkins, December 8, 1958; Jenkins to Janeway, December 15, 1958; all in Johnson Papers, U.S. Senate 1949–1961 Master File Index, Box 95.

45. Jerome Frank to Eliot Janeway, October 22, 1945, Frank Papers, Box 57; Felix Frankfurter to Edward F. Prichard Jr., September 15, 1945, Corcoran Wiretap Transcripts.

For the background on the Prichard tap, see chapter 5, this volume, pp. 84–85, and note 67.

46. For Cuneo's continuing influence, see J. Edgar Hoover to Ernest Cuneo, February 15, 1950; Hoover to Cuneo, January 29, 1951; Cuneo Papers, Box 26;

Eliot Janeway, oral history interview no. 1, April 2, 1986, p. 59–60, EJOH; Douglas, *Go East, Young Man*, p. 426; Pearson, *Diaries*, pp. 12, 17, 161.

47. "Edwin L. Weisl Sr., Key Democrat, Dies," *New York Times*, January 14, 1972. For Cohn and Weisl, and for Cohn's Democratic Party associations, see Nicholas von Hoffman, *Citizen Cohn* (New York: Doubleday, 1988), pp. 71, 239, 259, 281–282; "Roy Cohn, Aide to McCarthy and Fiery Lawyer, Dies at Fifty-nine," *New York Times*, August 3, 1986, p. 1.

9. Enter LBJ, Stage Center

1. Lyndon B. Johnson to Eliot Janeway, August 18, 1942, Janeway Papers, LBJL. The photo, accompanying a report on Johnson briefing the president on his tour of naval duty, emphasized LBJ's baggy eyes and big ears. "Fill-in from Australia," *Time*, July 27, 1942, p. 11.

2. Eliot Janeway to James V. Forrestal, May 21, 1946; Forrestal to Janeway, May 26, 1946; Forrestal Papers, Box 74.

3. Eliot Janeway to William O. Douglas, August 2, 1945, Douglas Papers, Box 342; Janeway to Lyndon B. Johnson, October 11, 1945, Johnson Papers, LBJL Selected Names File, Box 20.

4. Alvin Wirtz to Eliot Janeway, January 4, 1946, Janeway Papers, LBJL; Dallek, *Lone Star Rising*, pp. 277–278.

5. Dallek, *Lone Star Rising*, pp. 120–121, 145–146; Ickes, *Secret Diaries*, vol. 3, pp. 95, 186–187.

6. Dallek, *Lone Star Rising*, p. 146; Ickes, *Secret Diaries*, vol. 3, pp. 94–95, 104–105; Thomas G. Corcoran interview with author, May 1, 1964; Niznik, "Thomas G. Corcoran," pp. 104, 207–208.

7. Thomas G. Corcoran, interview with author, May 1, 1964; Dallek, *Lone Star Rising*, pp. 146, 160–162; Schwarz, *The New Dealers*, p. 270.

8. Unsigned, undated (1940) Memorandum to Franklin D. Roosevelt "re Lyndon Johnson—Texas situation," by James Rowe Jr. or Thomas G. Corcoran, Rowe Papers, Box 17, and in Corcoran Papers, Box 202; Ickes, *Secret Diaries*, vol. 3, p. 168; Dallek, *Lone Star Rising*, pp. 193–196.

9. James Rowe Jr. to Franklin D. Roosevelt, April 10, 1941; Rowe to Roosevelt, April 14, 1941; Rowe to Lyndon B. Johnson, June 5, 1941; all in Rowe Papers, Box 17; Eliot Janeway, diary, May 24, 1941, Janeway Papers, LOC; Dallek, *Lone Star Rising*, pp. 209, 214–215, 218–219.

10. Caro, *The Path to Power*, p. 449; Dallek, *Lone Star Rising*, p. 162. For the tenor of the early relationships see Lady Bird Johnson to Eliot Janeway, June 13, 1942, Janeway Papers, LBJL; Janeway to Lady Bird Johnson, August 10, 1942; John Connally to Janeway, August 26, 1942; Lyndon B. Johnson to Janeway, August 4, 1943; Johnson to Janeway, October 14, 1943; all in Johnson Papers, LBJ Archives/ Selected Names File, Box 20; and Janeway to Alvin Wirtz, August 24, 1945; Wirtz to Janeway, January 4, 1946; Janeway Papers, LBJL.

11. My father's fund-raising for Johnson is mentioned in Lewis Dabney to Thomas G. Corcoran, May 5, 1941; Corcoran to Dabney, May 23, 1941, Corcoran Papers, Box 66.

The "balance of payments" line is quoted in Caro, *The Path to Power*, pp. 683; see also p. 686; and Dallek, *Lone Star Rising*, p. 216.

Stanley Marcus to Eliot Janeway, July 22, 1942, Janeway Papers, LBJL.

12. Dallek, *Lone Star Rising*, pp. 256, 261; author interview with Donald C. Cook, February 2, 1964.

13. Schwarz, *The New Dealers*, pp. 280-281; Dallek, *Lone Star Rising*, pp. 198-199, 281.

14. James V. Forrestal to Carl Vinson, June 25, 1945; Forrestal to Donald C. Cook, July 2, 1945; Lyndon B. Johnson to Cook, July 2, 1945; all in Carl Vinson File, Janeway Papers, LBJL; author interview with Donald C. Cook, February 2, 1964.

15. "Texan Tells Grief of Young Guard," *New York Times*, April 13, 1945, p. 3.

16. James M. McPherson, *Battle Cry of Freedom: The Civil War Era* (New York: Oxford, 1988), pp. 290-292; Elbert B. Smith, *Francis Preston Blair* (New York: Free, 1980), pp. 262-263, 289-293; Marquis James, *The Raven: A Biography of Sam Houston* (Garden City: Blue Ribbon, 1929), p. 411.

17. Brinkley, *The End of Reform*, pp. 140-142; Brown, *Race, Money, and the American Welfare State*, p. 100.

18. V. O. Key, *Southern Politics in State and Nation* (New York: Knopf, 1950), p. 254; Seth Shepard McKay, *Texas and the Fair Deal, 1945-52* (San Antonio: Naylor, 1954), pp. 1-2, 13-14; Seth Shepard McKay, *W. Lee O'Daniel and Texas Politics* (Lubbock: Texas Technological College, 1944), pp. 402-403; George Fuerman, *The Reluctant Empire* (Garden City: Doubleday, 1957), p. 68; Michael Janeway, "Lyndon Johnson and the Rise of Conservatism in Texas," unpublished thesis, Department of History, Harvard University, March 1962, pp. 53-57; Leo Troy, *Union Sourcebook* (West Orange, N.J.: Industrial Relations Data Information Services, 1985), p. 7-4, table 7.2; *Historical Statistics of the United States* (Washington, D.C.: U.S. Department of Commerce, 1975), p. 178.

19. Key, *Southern Politics in State and Nation*, p 255; Alexander Heard, *A Two-Party South?* (Chapel Hill: University of North Carolina Press, 1952), pp. 152-155; McKay, *Texas and the Fair Deal*, p. 6.

20. For Johnson's congressional votes, see Dallek, *Lone Star Rising*, pp. 259-260, 289-290.

For Johnson's 1946 speech about farm prices, see the *Congressional Record*, 79th Congress, 2d session (July 2, 1946), p. 8188.

21. Dallek, *Lone Star Rising*, pp. 277, 287-288.

22. Robert Caro, *The Years of Lyndon Johnson: Master of the Senate* (New York: Knopf, 2002), pp. 723; see also pp. 760, 862.

23. Corcoran in fact represented a competing bidder for the pipelines. Dallek, *Lone Star Rising*, pp. 310, 652, note 105; Schwarz, *The New Dealers*, p. 281.

24. Thomas G. Corcoran to William O. Douglas, August 1, 1948, covering undated memo, Corcoran Papers, Box 125.

25. Author interview with Thomas G. Corcoran, May 1, 1964; Schwarz, *The New Dealers*, pp. 249-255.

26. Ickes, *Secret Diary*, vol. 3, pp. 106-107.

27. Dallek, *Lone Star Rising*, p. pp. 339, 341-342; Newman, *Hugo Black*, pp. 373-374; Thomas G. Corcoran to Lyndon B. Johnson, January 5, 1964, Corcoran Papers, Box 66.

28. Newman, *Hugo Black*, pp. 376.

29. Dallek, *Lone Star Rising*, pp. 346-348.

30. I heard this story from Johnson staffers Booth Mooney and Bill Brammer as a summer intern in Johnson's office in the late 1950s.

31. For Johnson in the 1950s, see Dallek, *Lone Star Rising*, chapters 12 and 13, and especially p. 464; Harry McPherson, *A Political Education* (Boston: Atlantic–Little, Brown, 1972), chapter 4 and especially pp. 110–114.

On Johnson overpowering his colleagues, see, for example, Robert Mann, *The Walls of Jericho: Lyndon Johnson, Hubert Humphrey, Richard Russell, and the Struggle for Civil Rights* (New York: Harcourt Brace, 1996), pp. 135, 140–141; Dallek, *Lone Star Rising*, pp. 474–475, 483.

32. Eliot Janeway, "Johnson of the Watchdog Committee," *New York Times Magazine*, June 17, 1951, pp. 13, 26–27; Lyndon B. Johnson to Eliot Janeway, June 16, 1951, Janeway Papers, LBJL.

33. Dallek, *Lone Star Rising*, p. 406.

34. Ibid., pp. 257, 368; Rowland Evans and Robert D. Novak, *Lyndon B. Johnson: The Exercise of Power* (New York: New American Library, 1966), p. 228.

35. For Johnson's civil rights posture in the 1940s, see Dallek, *Lone Star Rising*, pp. 276–277, 288–289.

For Senator Richard Russell's role in Johnson's rise, see Dallek, *Lone Star Rising*, pp. 390–391, 422–425, and Mann, *The Walls of Jericho*, pp. 107–112 ff.

For Johnson's maintenance of liberal ties, see Dallek, *Lone Star Rising*, p. 496; Simon, *Independent Journey*, p. 419; and Newman, *Hugo Black*, pp. 576–577.

36. Dallek, *Lone Star Rising*, pp. 496–497, 512–517; author interview with Dean G. Acheson, March 3, 1964.

37. Mann, *The Walls of Jericho*, p. 184.

38. Lemann, *The Promised Land*, pp. 136, 186.

39. Dallek, *Lone Star Rising*, pp. 517–528, 549–550; McPherson, *A Political Education*, pp. 144–149; Mann, *The Walls of Jericho*, pp. 199–224.

40. Fortas quoted in James Rowe Jr. to Lyndon B. Johnson, April 16, 1956, Fortas Papers, Box 114.

41. Dallek, *Lone Star Rising*, pp. 490, 493, 535–543, 552–555.

As the 1960 presidential season neared, my father worked as a bridge between Reuther and Johnson on legislation that, in Johnson's presidency, would become Medicare. Eliot Janeway to Walter P. Reuther, August 3, 1959, copy in Johnson Papers, LBJ Archives/Selected Names File, Box 21; Reuther to Janeway, January 18, 1960; Janeway to Reuther, February 4, 1960; Reuther to Janeway, February 5, 1960; Janeway to Reuther, March 14, 1960; Reuther to Janeway, April 15, 1960; Janeway to Reuther, June 7, 1960; all in Reuther Papers, Box 183.

42. "Commemorating the Twentieth Anniversary of Justice William O. Douglas' Appointment to the U.S. Supreme Court, April 17, 1959, Transcript of Remarks," Box 1759, Douglas Papers.

43. For the differences in these advisers' styles and roles, see Kalman, *Abe Fortas*, pp. 203–207; Frantz and McKean, *Friends in High Places*, pp. 137–138.

For Clifford and Fortas on Vietnam, see Frantz and McKean, *Friends in High Places*, pp. 239–252; Kalman, *Abe Fortas*, pp. 303–306.

44. Edwin L. Weisl Sr., oral history interview, May 13, 1969, pp. 4–7, 10–14, LBJL; Eliot Janeway, oral history interview no. 1, April 2, 1986, p. 105–106; oral history interview no. 2, April 23, 1986, p. 19, EJOH.

45. Thomas G. Corcoran to Lyndon B. Johnson, August 7, 1964, Corcoran

Papers, Box 66; Edwin L. Weisl Sr., oral history interview, May 13, 1969, pp. 10–15; LBJL; Evans and Novak, *Lyndon B. Johnson*, p. 190; Dallek, *Lone Star Rising*, p. 533.

46. Eliot Janeway to Lyndon B. Johnson, October 26, 1959; Johnson to Janeway, October 29, 1959; Johnson Papers, Johnson for President Files, 1959–1960, Senate Political Files, Box 113.

47. Lyndon B. Johnson to Eliot Janeway, April 11, 1959, Johnson Papers, U.S. Senate, 1949–61, Master File Index, Box 95.

"Despite his very pleasant and friendly personality," wrote Harold Ickes of FDR in his diary, "he is cold as ice inside," July 12, 1941, diary, Ickes Papers. "He was the coldest man I ever met," recalled Harry Truman, late in life. Thomas Fleming, "Eight Days with Harry Truman," *American Heritage*, July-August 1992, p. 56. "I was one of those who served his purposes," wrote Eleanor Roosevelt in her memoirs. Eleanor Roosevelt, *This I Remember* (New York: Harper, 1949), p. 349.

48. See Eliot Janeway to Walter Jenkins, June 8, 1959, enclosing a *New York Times* story about interest rates; Ruth Shrum to George E. Reedy, June 9, 1959. See also Lyndon B. Johnson to Reedy, undated, covering Janeway to Johnson, June 10, 1959; all in Johnson Papers, LBJA Selected Names File, Box 21.

49. Eliot Janeway to Walter Jenkins, April 8, 1958; Gerald W. Siegel to George E. Reedy, April 16, 1958; Reedy to Jenkins, April 17, 1958; all in Johnson Papers, LBJA Selected Names File, Box 21.

50. To my father's request that Johnson's office assist in setting up a meeting for him with Treasury Secretary Anderson, Johnson sent word, "I don't want to ask if he can see Anderson." Note attached to Eliot Janeway to Walter Jenkins, July 26, 1957. See also Janeway to Lyndon B. Johnson, January 24, 1958; Johnson to Janeway, January 28, 1958; all in Johnson Papers, LBJA Selected Names File, Box 21.

Johnson's senate and presidential aide Harry McPherson, a native of East Texas, on hearing the news by phone that Kennedy had been "shot in your state—in Dallas": "Insane city, insane wide-eyed bigoted Dallas bastards. Texans! 'In your state.' No, by God, I'm not one of them!" McPherson, *A Political Education*, p. 213.

51. Elizabeth Janeway to Lyndon B. Johnson, March 17, 1954; Johnson to Elizabeth Janeway, March 25, 1954; Johnson Papers, LBJA Selected Names File, Box 20.

10. 1960—Checkmate

1. Congressional Record, 85th Congress, 2d session, March 6, 1958, p. 3577. For other examples see William E. Leuchtenberg, *In the Shadow of FDR* (Ithaca: Cornell University Press, 1983), p. 132.

2. "For the 1960 Candidate, a Camp of Eggheads Is a Must," *Business Week*, June 18, 1960, pp. 170, 176.

3. McPherson, *A Political Education*, pp. 48–49.

4. Dallek, *Lone Star Rising*, pp. 537–538, 554.

5. McPherson, *A Political Education*, p. 162; 198–199.

6. Evans and Novak, *Lyndon B. Johnson*, 195–203.

7. Booth Mooney, a conservative Johnson staffer possessed at once of critical wit and constraint, would refer to Johnson's Capitol office as "that Turkish place."

Bill Brammer, *The Gay Place* (Boston: Houghton Mifflin, 1961), p. 17. (Brammer took his title came from a line of verse of Scott Fitzgerald's; this was before contemporary usage of *gay* became common.)

8. Dallek, *Lone Star Rising*, p. 545.

9. See also the authoritative account in Evans and Novak, *Lyndon B. Johnson*, pp. 253–267.

10. Ibid., pp. 250, 256.

11. Elizabeth Janeway to Eleanor Roosevelt, June 28, 1960; Roosevelt to Janeway, June 21, 1960; Eleanor Roosevelt General Correspondence 1957–1962, Box 3571, FDRL.

12. Evans and Novak, *Lyndon B. Johnson*, pp. 246, 259; William O. Douglas to Lyndon Johnson, May 21, 1959, Douglas, *Douglas Letters*, pp. 221–222; Simon, *Independent Journey*, p. 419; Thomas G. Corcoran, memoir, "The Boston-Austin Axis" chapter, pp. C7-C8, Corcoran Papers.

13. Thomas G. Corcoran, memoir, p. C10, Corcoran Papers.

14. Dallek, *Lone Star Rising*, p. 544; author interview with Dean G. Acheson, March 3, 1964; Evans and Novak, *Lyndon B. Johnson*, pp. 245–246; Thomas G. Corcoran, memoir, pp. C9–10, Corcoran Papers; Robert Dallek to author, January 30, 2003. The memoir's contextual references include key dates, places and presence of another discussant, James L. Landis, all of which point to its occurence in late 1959. See also note 37 to this chapter.

15. Eliot Janeway to Walter Jenkins, Summary of Telephone Conversation, April 3, 1960, May 16, 1960, Johnson Papers, U.S. Senate 1949–1961, Master File Index, Box 95.

16. Eliot Janeway to Walter Jenkins, Summary of Telephone Conversation, May 16, 1960, Johnson Papers, U.S. Senate 1949–1961, Master File Index, Box 95; Douglas, *The Court Years*, p. 314.

Two weeks later, Michigan Governor G. Mennen Williams accused my father of de facto blackmail on Johnson's behalf, in the form of word to Reuther that if Williams endorsed Kennedy, Johnson might not exert himself in support of Medicare, an urgent labor interest. Evans and Novak, *Lyndon B. Johnson*, p. 263.

17. Lyndon B. Johnson to Eliot Janeway, May 26, 1960, Johnson Papers, U.S. Senate 1949–1961, Master File Index, Box 95.

18. Transcript of Senator Johnson's News Conference on His Presidential Candidacy, *New York Times*, July 6, 1960, p. 18; Eliot and "Babs" Janeway to Lyndon B. Johnson, July 3, 1960, Johnson Papers, U.S. Senate 1949–1961 Master File Index, Box 95.

19. Evans and Novak, *Lyndon B. Johnson*, p. 274, Theodore H. White, *The Making of the President 1960* (New York: Atheneum, 1961), pp. 165–166.

20. Dallek, *Lone Star Rising*, pp. 572–573.

21. All the accounts of the Kennedy-Johnson interaction in Los Angeles, such as Dallek in *Lone Star Rising*, pp. 579–583, draw heavily on Philip Graham, "Notes on the 1960 Democratic Convention," July 19, 1960, printed as appendix B in Theodore H. White, *The Making of the President 1964* (New York: Atheneum, 1965), pp. 482–491.

Eliot Janeway, oral history interview no. 1, April 2, 1986, pp. 54–55; oral history interview no. 2, April 23, 1986, p. 15, EJOH; Thomas G. Corcoran, memoir, "Boston-Austin" chapter, pp. C13-A15, Corcoran Papers; Bobby Baker, with Larry L. King, *Wheeling and Dealing: Confessions of a Capitol Hill Operator* (New York: Norton, 1978) p. 126.

22. Thomas G. Corcoran, ibid.; Dallek, *Lone Star Rising*, pp. 576–579.

23. Lady Bird Johnson's notes on her conversation with Edwin L. Weisl Sr., July 14, 1960, Johnson Papers, 1960 VP Selection, Reference File.

In his oral history interview at the library, Weisl says of Johnson's decision to join the ticket not more than that "I felt very badly about it." Edwin L. Weisl Sr., oral history interview, May 13, 1969, p. 21, LBJL.

24. Graham memorandum in White, *The Making of the President 1964*, p. 487.

25. Eliot Janeway, oral history interview no. 1, April 2, 1986, p. 55, EJOH.

26. Graham, memorandum in White, *The Making of the President 1964*, p. 490.

27. William O. Douglas to Eliot Janeway, July 14, 1960, Douglas Papers, Box 344.

28. Thomas G. Corcoran to William O. Douglas, August 1, 1960, Douglas Papers, Box 317.

29. Abe Fortas to Lyndon B. Johnson, July 25, 1960, Fortas Papers, Box 156; Abe Fortas to William O. Douglas, July 25, 1960, Douglas Papers, Box 328.

30. Eliot Janeway to William O. Douglas, August 2, 1960, Douglas Papers, Box 344.

31. Kalman, *Abe Fortas*, pp. 209–210.

32. Eliot Janeway to William O. Douglas, May 11, 1960, Douglas Papers, Box 344. According to Bruce Allen Murphy, miserable over the failure of this shot at having a truly intimate friend in the White House and perhaps appointment as secretary of state, Douglas got royally drunk on a pack trip into the Cascade Mountains and commenced howling into the night, "They bought it! They bought the goddamned nomination!" Murphy claims to have interviewed witnesses to this scene, but the account sounds exaggerated. It is unlikely that the astute Douglas would have been surprised at his unscrupulous old friend Joe Kennedy's methods. Murphy, *Wild Bill*, p. 348–350.

Douglas writes in his memoirs that Kennedy "despised and mistrusted" Johnson, but there are various views on that score. Douglas's characterization there may reflect the sourness that crept into his view of Johnson after 1965. Douglas, *The Court Years*, p. 315.

33. See, for example, Evans and Novak, *Lyndon B. Johnson*, pp. 286–288.

34. Thomas G. Corcoran to Lyndon B. Johnson, November 5, 1960, Corcoran Papers, Box 66.

35. Dallek, *Lone Star Rising*, pp. 583, 587–587.

36. James Rowe Jr. to Lyndon B. Johnson, October 8, 1960. I am indebted to Harry McPherson for bringing this letter to my attention, and to James Rowe III for permission to quote from it. It has been sealed in Rowe's papers at the FDR Library; portions of it remain sealed for Mrs. Johnson's lifetime.

For Thomas Deegan, See John D. Morris, "Johnson Pledges Help to Kennedy," *New York Times*, July 14, 1960, p. 1.

37. Douglas, *The Court Years*, pp. 303, 314–315; Eliot Janeway, oral history interview no. 1, April 2, 1986, pp. 53–54, EJOH; Evans and Novak, *Lyndon B. Johnson*, p. 287.

Thomas Corcoran mentions Joseph Kennedy's financial offers to him personally, as well as for a Johnson-Kennedy ticket, in various drafts of his unpublished memoir. See, for example, "Boston-Austin Axis" chapter, pp. C7–9, Corcoran Papers, Box 586. For the "I'll make you rich, Tommy," quote, see draft for Boston-Austin" chapter, p. 16, Book Draft Materials, Corcoran Papers, Box 589.

A version of the Joe-Kennedy-to-LBJ financial deal is referred to as a rumor in Texas right-wing circles in Alfred Steinberg, *Sam Johnson's Boy: A Close-up of the President from Texas* (New York: Macmillan, 1968), p. 542. Steinberg was predisposed against Johnson. He claimed to have interviewed sources (including my father) who might have had a line on the tale, all since deceased, but he cites no source and does not pursue the matter.

In any event, such deals, if consummated, rarely find their way into recorded documents, short of criminal investigations. What is relevant is the baroque network of relationships, and range of possibility and probability.

Corcoran's account of the genesis and negotiation of the Kennedy-Johnson ticket in his unpublished memoir, on which he was working in the 1970s, states that his old friend Joseph Kennedy first approached him about a deal in 1959. Corcoran, unpublished memoir, "Boston-Austin" chapter, pp. C3-C4, Corcoran Papers. Corcoran is also emphatic about the timing in a letter to Lyndon Johnson much closer to the time of the events recalled (Corcoran to Johnson, October 9, 1965, Corcoran Papers, Box 66.) Robert Dallek argues persuasively in *Lone Star Rising* that Corcoran's recollections of the contacts had blurred and that they, in fact, began in October 1955. Dallek, *Lone Star Rising*, pp. 490–491, and p. 683, note 61, and p. 169 of this work. But Prof. Dallek agrees that Corcoran may have elided two sets of conversations, and that some of those he recalled did occur in 1959–1960. Robert Dallek to author, January 30, 2003.

As a broker of the 1960 Democratic ticket, Corcoran's terminology is intriguing, especially since he was a master at deal sweetening and hardly naive about Joe Kennedy's methodology: "I [was not] present when Lyndon sat down with the Kennedys to decide whether it would be worth his while to leave the Senate for the Vice Presidency." Corcoran, memoir, "Boston-Austin Axis" chapter, p. A15, Corcoran Papers.

See also Lyndon Johnson's curiously flirtatious letter to Joseph Kennedy in the south of France in the wake of the 1956 Democratic National Convention, and its even more curious placement at the start of Johnson's stately memoir, *The Vantage Point: Perspectives of the Presidency* (New York: Holt, Rinehart and Winston, 1971), p. 3. The implication—given the poison that Johnson and Robert Kennedy came to feel for each other by memoir-writing time—seems to be that the older men had arrangements to which "the boys" were never fully privy.

38. Dubious himself about naming his brother attorney general, the president-elect sent Clifford to try, in vain, to back Joseph Kennedy off his insistence on it. With "no rancor, no anger, no challenge," simply as a matter of fact, the senior Kennedy told Clifford, *"Bobby is going to be Attorney General."* Clifford recalled in his memoirs, "For a moment I had glimpsed the inner workings of that remarkable family, and, despite my admiration and affection for John F. Kennedy, I could not say I liked what I saw." Clifford, *Counsel to the President*, pp. 336–337; Frantz and McKean, *Friends in High Places*, pp. 161–162. See also chapter 11, note 35, this volume.

39. Evans and Novak, op. cit., p. 281.

40. Abe Fortas to William O. Douglas, July 25, 1960, Douglas Papers, Box 328.

41. Evans and Novak, *Lyndon B. Johnson*, pp. 314–318; Dallek, *Flawed Giant*, pp. 32–44.

42. Abe Fortas to William O. Douglas, February 27, 1962, Douglas Papers, Box 328.

43. Harry McPherson, oral history interview no. 1, tape no. 2, December 5, 1968, pp. 5–6, LBJL.

Johnson's vast majority leadership and committee outpost budgets were gone, Walter Jenkins wrote me when I asked to continue in Johnson's office as a summer staffer. Walter Jenkins to author, February 9, 1961, Johnson Papers, U.S. Senate 1949–1961, Master File Index, Box 95.

44. "Oklahoma's Kerr: Man of Confidence," *Time*, July 27, 1962, p. 10; "Oklahoma's Kerr: The Man Who Really Runs the Senate," *Newsweek*, August 6, 1962, pp. 15–17.

45. Dean G. Acheson to author, October 10, 1962, Dean G. Acheson Papers, Box 16.

11. President of All the People

1. James Rowe Jr. to Lyndon B. Johnson, October 8, 1960; sealed in Rowe Papers at FDRL, quoted with permission of James Rowe III. See chapter 9, note 36; Dallek, *Flawed Giant*, p. 44.

2. Dean G. Acheson to author, December 18, 1963, Acheson Papers, Box 16.

3. Harry McPherson has recorded several versions of this account of Johnson at St. Mark's Episcopal Church on November 24, 1963. I have used his oral history account closest to the occasion, supplemented by correspondence and a conversation in the present. The published accounts do not deal with the Secret Service agent's whispered message to Johnson, Johnson's physical response, or McPherson's inference after the fact that it was the president's first word of Oswald's killing.

Harry McPherson, oral history, interview no. 1, tape no. 2, December 5, 1968, pp. 18–20, LBJL; author interview with McPherson, December 1, 2002.

See also McPherson, *A Political Education*, pp. 214–215; William Manchester, *The Death of a President* (New York: Harper and Row, 1967), pp. 597–598.

4. See chapter 9, note 36, this volume. Only when the letter came to light in November 2002 did McPherson make full sense of the scene he witnessed in December 1963.

McPherson, oral history interview no. 1, tape no. 2, December 5, 1968, pp. 20–21, LBJL; McPherson to author (undated), November 2002, author interview with McPherson, December 1, 2002.

See also McPherson, *A Political Education*, pp. 215–216.

5. John M. Lee, "Economists Predict Brief Doubt," *New York Times*, November 25, 1963, p. 27.

6. Eliot Janeway, oral history interview no. 1, April 2, 1986, pp. 105, EJOH; Janeway, *The Economics of Crisis*, pp. 267–268; Edwin L. Weisl Sr., Oral History interview, May 13, 1969, p. 25, LBJL.

7. "Johnson Looms as Strongest Since FDR, Analyst Says," *Detroit Free Press*, December 3, 1963, p. 1; John M. Lee, "Economists Predict Brief Doubts," *New York Times*, November 25, 1963, pp. 27–40.

8. Elizabeth Janeway, "The First Lady: A Professional at Getting Things Done," *The Ladies' Home Journal*, April 1964, p. 64 ff.

9. Lyndon B. Johnson to Eliot Janeway, November 29, 1963; Walter Jenkins to Janeway, March 2, 1964; Janeway to Johnson, April 27, 1964; Johnson to Janeway, May 26, 1964; all in Johnson Papers, WHCF, Box 43.

10. Walter Jenkins to Eliot Janeway, March 2, 1964; Janeway to Lyndon B. Johnson, April 27, 1964; Johnson to Janeway, May 26, 1964; Johnson to Janeway, July 24, 1964; Bill D. Moyers to Janeway, November 5, 1964; Walter Heller to Johnson, December 8, 1964; all in Johnson Papers, WHCF Name File, Box 43. Johnson to Richard Russell, January 22, 1965, White House transcripts, in Michael Beschloss, ed., *Reaching for Glory: Lyndon Johnson's Secret White House Tapes: 1964–1965* (New York: Simon and Schuster, 2001), pp. 166–167; Edwin L. Weisl Sr., Oral History interview, May 13, 1969, pp. 26–27, LBJL; Janeway, *Economics of Crisis*, pp. 274–275.

11. Author interview with Thomas G. Corcoran, May 1, 1964.

12. Author interview with Aubrey Williams, March 17, 1964; author interview with Milo Perkins, April 15, 1964.

13. William O. Douglas to author, February 26, 1962, Douglas Papers, Box 344.

14. Douglas, *The Court Years*, pp. 306–310, 314; Evan Thomas, *Robert F. Kennedy: His Life* (New York: Simon and Schuster, 2000), p. 68, 109; Roger Newman, "William O. Douglas: How He Speaks to Us Today," Douglas Lecture at Whitman College, April 6, 1998, courtesy of the author; Powe, *The Warren Court and American Politics*, p. 209; Nan Burgess (Douglas's secretary) to Eliot Janeway, February 8, 1961, Douglas Papers, Box 344.

15. Author interview with Donald C. Cook, February 2, 1964.

16. The friends were Mary and William P. Bundy.
Kalman, *Abe Fortas*, p. 189.

17. Kalman, *Abe Fortas*, pp. 230–232, 242–245; Lyndon B. Johnson to Abe Fortas, November 4, 1965, Johnson to Richard B. Russell, January 22, 1965; Johnson to Mike Mansfield, July 30, 1965; all in Beschloss, *Reaching for Glory*, pp. 123–125, 166–167, 417.

18. Edwin L. Weisl Sr. to Lyndon B. Johnson, March 9, 1964, in Michael Beschloss, ed., *Taking Charge: The Johnson White House Tapes, 1963–1964* (New York: Simon and Schuster, 1997), pp. 274–276; Weisl, oral history interview, May 13, 1969, pp. 26–27, LBJL; Janeway, *Economics of Crisis*, p. 217; Evans and Novak, *Lyndon B. Johnson*, pp. 449–450; Dallek, *Flawed Giant*, p. 137; Jeff Shesol, *Mutual Contempt: Lyndon Johnson, Robert Kennedy, and the Feud that Defined a Decade* (New York: Norton, 1997), p. 339.

19. Eliot Janeway to Hubert Humphrey, August 9, 1960, Janeway Papers, LBJL; Evans and Novak, *Lyndon B. Johnson*, p. 449; Clark Clifford, oral history interview no. 2, July 2, 1969, p. 6, oral history interview no. 4, August 7, 1969, p. 6, LBJL; Thomas G. Corcoran, oral history interview, tape no. 3, September 9, 1969, p. 11, Corcoran Papers, Book Draft Materials, Box 588; Beschloss, *Taking Charge*, p. 471.

20. For McCarthy in 1964 see Evans and Novak, *Lyndon B. Johnson*, pp. 449, 460–461; Lewis Chester, Godfrey Hodgson, and Bruce Page, *An American Melodrama: The Presidential Campaign of 1968* (New York: Viking, 1969), p. 74; Jeremy Larner, *Nobody Knows: Reflections on the McCarthy Campaign of 1968* (New York: Macmillan, 1969), pp. 22–24.

21. Yet another angle: Corcoran states that in the weeks Johnson was "struggling desperately to get a Catholic" on the ticket with him he himself, along with Walter Jenkins (also a practicing Roman Catholic), was sent to McCarthy to encourage him. But, he claims, Robert Kennedy told Johnson point-blank that any Catholic other than himself (and especially McCarthy) would be anathema to the Kennedy camp. The Kennedy entourage had previously vetoed the name of another Catholic and Kennedy family member, brother-in-law Sargent Shriver. Dallek, *Flawed Giant*, pp. 137, 157–161; Thomas G. Corcoran, oral history interview, tape no. 3, September 9, 1969, p. 11; draft for "Boston-Austin Axis" chapter of memoir, pp. 26–27, Book Draft Materials, Corcoran Papers, Box 588.

22. Shades of daring, interpretation, and passage of time: Robert Dallek's biography (1998) has Johnson pronouncing the word "nigra," and Theodore White's version (1965) makes it "Negro." But Johnson's own version (1971) asserts that he threw the South's language back at the South: "Nigger."

Johnson, *The Vantage Point*, pp. 109–110; Dallek, *Flawed Giant*, p. 183; White, *The Making of the President 1964*, p. 432.

23. Dallek, *Flawed Giant*, pp. 219, 220.

24. Lyndon B. Johnson to Edwin L. Weisl Sr., in Beschloss, *Reaching for Glory*, pp. 119–122; White, *The Making of the President 1964*, p. 451; Pete Hamill, "When the Client Is a Candidate," *New York Times Magazine*, October 25, 1964.

25. Of subsequent, bitter lampoons of Johnson, Feiffer wrote, "Mine is the rage of a lover betrayed. I don't often trust public figures; Johnson seduced me. In the nine months following Kennedy's assassination, his actions were extraordinary. I thought he was the best president since FDR. . . . He was so good he was lousy to draw." Jules Feiffer, *Jules Feiffer's America: From Eisenhower to Reagan* (New York: Knopf, 1982), p. 79.

26. William Allen White, *The Autobiography of William Allen White* (New York: Macmillan, 1946), p. 648.

27. Thomas G. Corcoran to Lyndon B. Johnson, February 3, 1965, Corcoran Papers, Box 66.

28. Abe Fortas to Lyndon B. Johnson, August 22, 1960, Fortas Papers, Box 156. Fortas was noted among friends and colleagues for poor political judgment. In this letter he also pronounced that his "new and different approach [comes] from an angle that has nothing to do with the racial problem." But, as president, Johnson found as Roosevelt had that grand economic development and antipoverty programs could not be separated from racial politics. For Fortas's political judgment, see, for example, Kalman, *Abe Fortas*, pp. 2, 209, 304.

29. Dallek, *Flawed Giant*, p. 83; Lemann, *The Promised Land*, pp. 140–145.

30. Lemann, *The Promised Land*, pp. 133–134, 143–144.

31. Daniel Patrick Moynihan, *Maximum Feasible Misunderstanding: Community Action in the War on Poverty* (New York: Free, 1969), p. 168.

32. Robert Wood, "The Great Society in 1984: Relic or Reality?" in Marshall Kaplan and Peggy L. Cucity, eds., *The Great Society and Its Legacy: Twenty Years of U.S. Social Policy* (Durham: Duke University Press, 1986), p. 21; Henry J. Aaron, *Politics and the Professors: The Great Society in Perspective* (Washington, D.C.: Brookings Institution, 1978), p. 29.

33. Charles Murray, *Losing Ground: American Social Policy, 1950–1980* (New York: Basic, 1994), pp. 24–25; McPherson, *A Political Education*, p. 268; Lyndon B. Johnson to George E. Reedy, November 16, 1964; Johnson to Robert McNamara, January

NOTES TO PAGES 194–197

13, 1965, Johnson to McNamara, June 21, 1965; all in Beschloss, *Reaching for Glory*, pp. 143–144, 157–158, 364.

34. Moynihan, *Maximum Feasible Misunderstanding*, pp. 9; Lemann, *The Promised Land*, pp. 132–133.

35. There is perhaps a study to be made exploring the question whether the Kennedy brothers, and especially Robert as the one closest to his father, found in their relations with Lyndon Johnson an alternative channel for the son's classic need to confront a father who was in their case, truly all-powerful. The Kennedy brothers generally yielded to their father's will on fundamental issues; most notably, in the case of his insistence, over their resistance, that Robert Kennedy become his brother's attorney general in 1961, with protection of the family against J. Edgar Hoover a vital consideration. See also chapter 10, note 38, this volume. Thomas, *Robert F. Kennedy*, pp. 53, 75–76, 109–110; Clifford, *Counsel to the President*, pp. 336–337; Frantz and McKean, *Friends in High Places*, pp. 161–162.

Moynihan discusses the conceptual link to the Peace Corps, *Maximum Feasible Misunderstanding*, pp. 71–73.

See also Thomas, *Robert F. Kennedy*, pp. 51, 65; Steel, *In Love with Night*, 94–97, 194–195; Dallek, *Flawed Giant*, p. 75; Lemann, *The Promised Land*, pp. 135–136, 141–142; Shesol, *Mutual Contempt*, 235–237, 241.

36. Moynihan, *Maximum Feasible Misunderstanding*, pp. 82, 94–100, 141–142; Lemann, *The Promised Land*, pp. 145–149, 156–158; Shesol, *Mutual Contempt*, pp. 169–171.

37. Moynihan, *Maximum Feasible Misunderstanding*, pp. 142–146; Lemann, *The Promised Land*, pp. 166–167, 196.

38. Lemann, *The Promised Land*, p. 144.

39. Shesol, *Mutual Contempt*, p. 242.

40. Dallek, *Flawed Giant*, p. 232.

41. Dallek, *Flawed Giant*, pp. 232–233, 236; Douglas, *The Court Years*, pp. 318–319; Kalman, *Abe Fortas*, pp. 240–244.

42. Dean G. Acheson to author, October 6, 1966, Acheson Papers, Box 17.

In a letter a few weeks later, Acheson had second thoughts about his authorship of the remark, adding. "I have said far more brutal, and even ruder, things to him, but in the hot blood of battle, not just to give him a sly dig." Acheson to author, October 24, 1966, Acheson Papers, Box 17.

43. Senator McGovern told me this story off the record during an interview for a piece on Senate opposition to Johnson's Vietnam policies, "Washington Report," *Atlantic*, May 1968, pp. 4–14.

44. Bill Moyers and Richard Goodwin, then on the White House staff, each became concerned enough about Johnson's psychological state in 1965 to take their fears to psychiatrists. Goodwin wrote, "The diagnosis was the same: We were describing a textbook case of paranoid disintegration, the eruption of long-suppressed irrationalities. . . . The disintegration could continue, remain constant or recede, depending on the strength of Johnson's resistance." Richard Goodwin, *Remembering America* (Boston: Little, Brown, 1988), pp. 402–403.

Moyers recalled that others in contact with Johnson expressed parallel concerns. Dallek, *Flawed Giant*, pp. 281–284.

45. David Barrett's *Uncertain Warriors: Lyndon Johnson and His Vietnam Advisors* is the authoritative source for the evolution of the views of Fortas and Rowe.

See also Kalman, *Abe Fortas*, pp. 298, 304; author interview with Thomas G.

Corcoran, May 1, 1964; Corcoran to Lyndon B. Johnson, August 25, 1968; Corcoran Papers, Box 66; Thurman Arnold to Frank Serri, May 15, 1967; Arnold to Rexford G. Tugwell, August 22, 1967; in Arnold, *Voltaire and the Cowboy*, pp. 468-469, 472-475.

Elizabeth Janeway, oral history interview no. 2, July 21, 1986, p. 18, EHJOH; Lasser, *Benjamin V. Cohen*, p. 310; Douglas, *The Court Years*, pp. 329-330.

46. Douglas, *The Court Years*, pp. 319, 330, 337. This volume is notable for its coldness toward various people who had been close to Douglas, especially Corcoran and Johnson.

47. Barrett, *Uncertain Warriors*, pp. 33-34, 99-101, 139-140; Thurman Arnold to Rexford G. Tugwell, May 26, 1967; Arnold to Tugwell, August 22, 1967; Arnold to Frank Serri, May 15, 1967; in Arnold, *Voltaire and the Cowboy*, pp. 468-474.

48. Barrett, *Uncertain Warriors*, p. 140.

49. Eliot Janeway, oral history interview 1, April 2, 1986, pp. 82, 92-93, EJOH.

50. Barrett, *Uncertain Warriors*, pp 139-140; Clifford, *Counsel to the President*, p. 507.

51. Robert Dallek, *Flawed Giant*, 547, 569-573; Thomas G. Corcoran to Lyndon B. Johnson, August 25, 1968, Corcoran Papers, Box 66.

52. Winston Churchill, *Blood, Toil, Tears, and Sweat: The Speeches of Winston Churchill*, ed. David Cannadine (Boston: Houghton Mifflin, 1989), p. 256.

53. Janeway, *The Economics of Crisis*, pp. 3, 292-296.

54. Evans and Novak, *Lyndon B. Johnson*, pp. 562-565, Harrison Salisbury, *A Time for Change: A Reporter's Tale in Our Time* (New York: Harper, 1988), p. 171.

55. Eliot Janeway, oral history interview no. 2, April 23, 1986, pp. 18-19, EJOH; Eliot Janeway, *Prescriptions for Prosperity* (New York: Times, 1983), pp. 41-43; Henry H. Fowler to Lyndon B. Johnson, August 27, 1965; William Connell to Marvin Watson, January 5, 1967; both in Johnson Papers, WHCF Name File, Box 43; Rowland Evans and Robert D. Novak, "LBJ's Ex-Friend," *New York Herald Tribune*, March 8, 1966, p. 22.

56. Terrence Scanlon to John Macy, November 8, 1965, Box 284, Office Files of John Macy, LBJL; Marvin Watson to Lyndon B. Johnson, November 5, 1965, J. Edgar Hoover to Marvin Watson, November 3, 1965, Johnson Papers, Box 280.

In the bureau's spirit of keeping old flames alive, Hoover's letter to Watson notes that in 1950 my father's name was still to be found on the far-left-wing Institute for Pacific Relations' "List of Persons Qualified to Write on the Far East."

57. Author interview with Harry McPherson, August 1, 2001.

58. McPherson quoted in Barrett, *Uncertain Warriors*, p. 95; Clifford, *Counsel to the President*, p. 485.

59. Abigail McCarthy, *Private Faces/Public Places* (Garden City: Doubleday, 1972), p. 333.

60. Eliot Janeway, oral history interview no. 1, April 2, 1986, p. 103-104, EJOH.

61. Author interview with Donald C. Cook, February 2, 1964.

62. Barrett, *Uncertain Warriors*, pp. 56, 59-60; Lyndon B. Johnson to Richard Russell, March 6, 1965, in Beschloss, *Reaching for Glory*, p. 212; Doris Kearns (Goodwin), *Lyndon Johnson and the American Dream* (New York: Harper and Row, 1976), pp. 251.

63. Clifford, *Counsel to the President*, p. 518. Johnson told another member of his "Wise Men" council, George Ball, that the group had been "brainwashed." Barrett, *Uncertain Warriors*, p. 151.

64. Marjorie Williams, "Clark Clifford: The Rise of a Reputation," *Washington Post*, May 8, 1991, p. D9; Harry McPherson, oral history interview no. 4, tape no. 1, March 24, 1969, p.18, LBJL.

Thomas Finney had been assistant to Democratic Senator Mike Monroney of Oklahoma, a Johnson friend. A CIA veteran and skilled at political brokerage, Finney was the point-man in the Johnson-Stevenson "Stop Kennedy" collusion at the 1960 Democratic National Convention. See White, *Making of the President 1960*, p. 163; Chester, Hodgson, and Page, *An American Melodrama*, p. 411.

65. Clifford, *Counsel to the President*, pp. 502–505.

66. Thomas G. Corcoran to Lyndon B. Johnson, February 15, 1946, Corcoran Wiretap Transcripts.

67. Clifford, *Counsel to the President*, p. 558; Murphy, *Fortas*, p. 1.

68. For Johnson and Humphrey in 1968 see McPherson, *A Political Education*, p. 449; Theodore White, *The Making of the President 1968* (New York: Atheneum, 1969), pp. 271, 278–279.

69. Barrett, *Uncertain Warriors*, p. 153; Clifford, *Counsel to the President*, p. 606.

70. Author interview with Clark Clifford, October 22, 1975.

12. Last Act

1. Douglas, *The Court Years*, pp. 358–359; Simon, *Independent Journey*, p. 396; Frantz and McKean, *Friends in High Places*, pp. 270–272; Kalman, *Abe Fortas*, pp. 372–373.

2. William O. Douglas to Stanley Norman Young, November 11, 1969, in Douglas, *Douglas Letters*, p. 393; Eliot Janeway, oral history interview no. 1, April 2, 1986, p. 83, EJOH; Murphy, *Wild Bill*, p. 431–432.

3. Thomas F. Eagleton, letter to author, June 6, 2003.

4. Bob Woodward and Scott Armstrong, *The Brethren: Inside the Supreme Court* (New York: Simon and Schuster, 1979), pp. 79–85; Douglas, *The Court Years*, p. 260.

5. Eliot Janeway to William O. Douglas, September 13, 1972, Douglas Papers, Box 344; Thomas G. Corcoran, memoir, "Preface," p. 5, Corcoran Papers; Murphy, *Wild Bill*, 503–504, 671 note.

William O. Douglas to Eliot Janeway, February 3, 1978, Douglas Papers, Box 344.

6. James Rowe Jr. to author, February 9, 1983.

7. Fortas, "Thurman Arnold and the Theatre of the Law," pp. 991–995.

8. Elizabeth Wickenden to Abe Fortas, undated letter (early 1970s) in Fortas Papers, Box 125.

9. Lyndon B. Johnson, Remarks, Civil Rights Symposium, LBJ Library, December 12, 1972, pp. 1–2, in Fortas Papers, Box 114; Dallek, *Flawed Giant*, pp. 621–622.

10. Lyndon B. Johnson, Remarks, Civil Rights Symposium, LBJ Library, December 12, 1972, pp. 3–5, in Fortas Papers, Box 114.

11. For an example of the receiving end of such conversations, see Salisbury, *Time for Change*, p. 171.

12. "Wall St. Crumbles, Women Arise: The Janeways' Time Has Come," *People*, January 20, 1975, pp. 30–33; Chris Welles, "Eliot (Calamity) Janeway Worries About Our Economic Problems—And His Own," *Esquire*, November 21, 1978, pp. 59–71.

13. Eliot Janeway, oral history interview no. 8, April 22, 1988, p. 20, EJOH; "Jackson, Party Elders Break Bread," *Washington Post*, March 31, 1988, p. A11;

"LBJ," parts 1 and 2, written and produced by David Grubin, The American Experience, aired on Public Broadcasting System, January 1997.

14. Elizabeth Janeway, *Man's World, Woman's Place* (New York: Morrow, 1971), pp. 125–126.

15. Elizabeth Janeway, *Powers of the Weak* (New York: Knopf, 1980), pp. 84, 95, 102, 106.

16. Margaret Mead, review of *Man's World, Woman's Place, New York Times Book Review,* June 20, 1971, p. 7.

17. Justice Stewart had registered his pragmatic "I know it when I see it" criterion for obscenity in a 1964 opinion. Powe, *The Warren Court and American Politics,* p. 340.

Elizabeth Janeway to William O. Douglas, May 21 (undated but probably 1973, the year Jong's book was published), Douglas Papers, Box 344.

18. Nan Robertson, "Elizabeth Janeway: Writing for Her Life," *New York Times,* July 7, 1979, p. 42.

19. Elizabeth Janeway, *Powers of the Weak,* p. 111.

20. The authoritative source on the end of Clifford's career is Frantz and McKean, *Friends in High Places,* chapters 18–24.

21. Eliot Janeway, oral history interview no. 3, May 16, 1986, p. 5, 40–41, oral history interview no. 4, June 27, 1986, p. 13, 24, EJOH.

22. "Eliot Janeway, Economist and Author, Dies at Eighty, *New York Times,* February 9, 1993, p. C18.

Epilogue

1. Lowi, *The End of Liberalism,* p. xiii.

2. Ira Katznelson, "Was the Great Society a Missed Opportunity?" in Fraser and Gerstle, *Rise and Fall of the New Deal Order,* pp. 199–201.

3. Sidney Blumenthal, *The Rise of the Counter-Establishment: From Conservative Ideology to Political Power* (New York: Times, 1986), pp. 252–256; Brinkley, *The End of Reform,* pp. 157–160.

4. R. G. Ratcliffe, "Campaign '96: 3-Day 'Town Meeting' on Issues Starts Today," *Houston Chronicle,* January 18, 1996, p. A21; John E. Yang, "'Real People' Face Issues, Candidates in Experiment in Citizenship," *Washington Post,* January 21, 1996, p. A6.

5. Barrett, *Uncertain Warriors,* pp. 92–93, 157–158; Isaacson and Thomas, *The Wise Men,* p. 644.

6. Thurman Arnold to T. A. Larson, June 6, 1966, in Arnold, *Voltaire and the Cowboy,* p. 462; Arnold, *Democracy and Free Enterprise,* pp. 32–35; Brinkley, *The End of Reform,* pp. 120–122.

Jerome Frank to Eliot Janeway, July 12, 1938; Janeway to Frank, July 13, 1938; Frank Papers, Box 30.

7. Brinkley, *The End of Reform.,* pp. 122–131.

8. Katznelson, "Was the Great Society a Missed Opportunity?" in Fraser and Gerstle, *Rise and Fall of the New Deal Order,* pp. 188–205; Brinkley, *The End of Reform,* p. 103.

9. See chapter 11, p. 193, and notes 30 and 31.

10. Rodgers, *Atlantic Crossings,* pp. 412–413.

11. Ackerman, *We the People,* pp. 7–8. See also the author's *Republic of Denial,* pp. 175–177, with further reference to Ackerman, *We the People.,* pp. 70, 414.

ACKNOWLEDGMENTS

As I grew up with the stories told here, my daughter, Daisy Janeway Bowe, and my son, Samuel Janeway, grew up with an echo of them. From the time they were small children they had curiosity about my parents, their grandparents; intriguing, noisy (in the case of my father), but distant characters to them. What *did* make them tick? What was their world like? How should they feel when asked, as they still are now and again, if they "are any relation to ? . . ." They always wanted to know more about them, and also about my place in the story. They have given me distinctively helpful readings of pieces of this book along the way.

In 1960, as a junior at Harvard preparing to write an honors thesis the next year, my tutor was the nineteenth- and twentieth-century American historian Frank Freidel, later Charles Warren Professor of History at Harvard, who left five superb volumes of biography of Franklin D. Roosevelt among his contributions to the field. Frank Freidel was an inspired teacher in all settings. I was luckier than I knew in the two years that followed to be among those working with him in the intimate exchange of an undergraduate tutorial, and often one-on-one.

In two subsequent years, with Frank's support, I was accepted for graduate work in history at Harvard. Both times I chose alternative courses (first military service, then journalism). If I have found a way back to my road not taken then, with the help of a number of the scholars and colleagues cited below, it is in great part because of the interests instilled during my time as Frank's student as well as the encouragement and friendship he offered in the years that followed.

Looking forward and back, this book is dedicated therefore to Daisy and Sam, and to the memory of Frank Freidel.

. . .

Many friends, colleagues, scholars, and family members have helped me along the way, reading pieces or versions of a manuscript. The result has taken several turns in the ten years I have worked on it, at times because of their comments.

I owe special thanks to several teaching and research colleagues who read the manuscript through (a few, beyond the call of duty or friendship, more than once) and helped me to think, and think again, about its themes, strategy, and conclusions. They are Sidney Blumenthal, Alan Brinkley, Frances FitzGerald, Laura Kalman, Ira Katznelson, Nicholas Lemann, George Packer, Arthur M. Schlesinger Jr., and Daniel Yergin.

Friends and family members who have read early or later versions of the manuscript and urged me on, or through changes in direction, are Alice Arlen, Michael Arlen, Thomas F. Eagleton, Jules Feiffer, Penny Janeway, William Janeway, Ward Just, Harry McPherson, Daniel Okrent, Joel Snyder, and Richard Todd. To these I add Linda Healey, then an editor at Pantheon, who saw a way to think about this book early on and has given me bracing encouragement along the way. My thanks to them all.

I also thank these scholars who have helped with research questions and, in some cases, readings of chapters: Michael Beschloss, Jonathan Brent, Robert Dallek, Robert H. Ferrell, Harvey Klehr, Nelson Lichtenstein, Roger Newman, Andras Szanto, David Shreve, Carroll Stevens, Sam Tannenhaus, and John Fabian Witt. The late Jordan A. Schwarz, whose book *The New Dealers: Power Politics in the Age of Roosevelt* stands as one of the distinctive contributions to New Deal scholarship, was generous with ideas and help when I started down this road.

I am grateful to my friend from *Boston Globe* days, Steven Erlanger, in 1994 Moscow bureau chief for the *New York Times*, for his help in connecting me with an archivist in the former Soviet Union, Natalia I. Yegorova. And I thank James Hershberg, of the Woodrow Wilson Center's Cold War History Project, who put me in touch with Alexander O. Chubarian, director of the Institute of Universal History in Moscow. Ms. Yegorova and Dr. Chubarian assisted me greatly in the search for my father's trail as a young Communist abroad in the early 1930s.

All are exonerated from responsibility for what I have written.

. . .

I thank former Northwestern University president Arnold Weber, former Columbia provost Jonathan Cole, and former Columbia vice president of arts and sciences David Cohen for their support of my efforts at both universities to combine scholarly work with university administration through the last decade.

Thanks also to these dedicated, able library curators and archivists for their assistance: at the Library of Congress Daun van Ee; at the Lyndon B. Johnson Library Claudia Anderson, Tina Houston, and Harry Middleton; at the Harry S. Truman Library Dennis E. Bilger; at the Manuscripts and Archives office of the Yale University Library Nancy Lyon and William Massa; at the Seeley G. Mudd Manuscript Library at Princeton University Daniel Linke; at the Columbia University Oral History Collection Mary Marshall-Clark; at the Walter P. Reuther Library at Wayne State University Margaret Raucher; at the University of Minnesota Library and Archives Karen Klinkenborg; at the Time, Inc. Archives William Hooper and Pamela Wilson.

A succession of wonderful students at Columbia University's Graduate School of Journalism, and School of the Arts MFA Writing Program, have worked as research assistants for me; amazing me with their resourcefulness. They include James Beck, Anna Gorman, Jonathan Hull, Charles Loxton, Daniel Oppenheimer, and Jeremy Simon.

Peter Matson is a literary agent of taste and insight. He believed in the worth of this effort in the face of its defiance of easy categorization and, ably assisted by Saskia Cornes and James Rutman, taught me patience in finding an editor who would agree. That person is Peter Dimock of Columbia University Press, who has proved an incisive and inspirational critic and reader, and a fine editor. I thank him and his colleagues Anne Routon, Susan Pensak, and Liz Cosgrove.

Vivette Porges is everything a writer could wish for as a photo researcher.

Last, but first, Barbara Maltby, my wife, has endured ten years of my absorption in this work, mostly at the beautiful barn in the country she has more or less single-handedly turned into a home of beauty that welcomes the muse. She has offered love, support—and astute editing. My thanks to her cannot be adequately stated.

Lakeville, Connecticut
May 2003

INDEX